THE
AMERICAN
GOSPEL
OF
SUCCESS

THE American
Gospel of
SUCCESS

Individualism and *Beyond*

EDITED WITH AN INTRODUCTION BY

Moses Rischin

CHICAGO

Quadrangle Books

1965

Grateful acknowledgment is made to the following publishers for permission to reprint selections from copyrighted works:

American Journal of Economics and Sociology, for Fritz Redlich, "The Business Leader as a Daimonic Figure," copyright 1953 by the *American Journal of Economics and Sociology.*

Antioch Review, for Daniel Bell, "Crime as an American Way of Life," copyright 1953 by the Antioch Press; and Moses Rischin, "From Gompers to Hillman," copyright 1953 by the Antioch Press.

The Atlantic Monthly, for David Riesman, "Where Is the College Generation Headed?" copyright 1961 by The Atlantic Monthly Company.

The Bobbs-Merrill Company, Inc., for a selection from Bruce Barton, *The Man Nobody Knows,* copyright 1925 by The Bobbs-Merrill Company, Inc., renewed 1952 by Bruce Barton.

Chicago Review, for David Riesman, "The College Student in an Age of Organization," copyright 1958 by *Chicago Review.*

Daedalus and the American Academy of Arts and Sciences, for Jill Conway, "Jane Addams," copyright 1964 by the American Academy of Arts and Sciences.

Encounter, for David Riesman, "The Uncommitted Generation," copyright 1960 by *Encounter.*

Harper & Row, Inc., for selections from Joseph A. Schumpeter, *Capitalism, Socialism and Democracy,* copyright 1942, 1947 by Joseph A. Schumpeter, copyright 1950 by Harper & Brothers; Abraham Cahan, *The Rise of David Levinsky,* copyright 1917 by Harper & Brothers, renewed 1945 by Abraham Cahan; and John W. Gardner, *Self-Renewal,* copyright 1964 by John W. Gardner.

Harvard University Press, for selections from Francis X. Sutton, *et al., The American Business Creed,* copyright 1956 by the President and Fellows of Harvard College; Edward S. Mason, ed., *The Corporation in Modern Society,* copyright 1959 by the President and Fellows of Harvard College; Elting Morison, ed., *The Letters of Theodore Roosevelt,* copyright 1951 by the President and Fellows of Harvard College; Chester I. Barnard, *The Functions of the Executive,* copyright 1938 by the President and Fellows of Harvard College; Moses Rischin, *The Promised City,* copyright 1962 by the President and Fellows of Harvard College; and William Miller, "The Recruitment of the American Business Elite," *Quarterly Journal of Economics,* copyright 1950 by the President and Fellows of Harvard College.

Houghton Mifflin Company, for a selection from John Kenneth Galbraith, *The Affluent Society,* copyright 1958 by John Kenneth Galbraith.

Little, Brown and Company, for a selection from Clarence B. Randall, *A Creed for Free Enterprise,* copyright 1952 by Clarence B. Randall.

The Macmillan Company, for a selection from Michael Harrington, *The Other America,* copyright 1962 by Michael Harrington.

McGraw-Hill Book Company, for a selection from Vance Packard, *The Pyramid Climbers,* copyright 1962 by Vance Packard.

David McKay Company, Inc., for a selection from John Chase, ed., *Years of the Modern,* copyright 1949 by Longmans, Green and Company, Inc.

The New Republic, for Donald B. Meyer, "The Confidence Man," copyright 1955 by New Republic, Inc.; and Donald B. Meyer, "Billy Graham," copyright 1955 by New Republic, Inc.

The New York Times, for Eugene Burdick, "From Gold Rush to Sun Rush," copyright 1963 by The New York Times Company.

Oxford University Press, Inc., for a selection from Christopher Rand, *Cambridge, U.S.A.,* copyright 1964 by Christopher Rand.

Simon and Schuster, Inc., for selections from William H. Whyte, Jr., *The Organization Man,* copyright 1956 by William H. Whyte, Jr.

The University of Chicago Press, for selections from Boris Emmet and John E. Jeuck, *Catalogues & Counters,* copyright 1950 by the University of Chicago; and E. U. Essien-Udom, *Black Nationalism,* copyright 1962 by the University of Chicago.

The Viking Press, Inc., for a selection from Thorstein Veblen, *Absentee Ownership,* copyright 1923 by B. W. Heubsch, Inc.

John Wiley & Sons, Inc., for selections from Melville Dalton, *Men Who Manage,* copyright 1959 by John Wiley & Sons, Inc.

Yale Law Journal, for William Miller, "American Lawyers in Business and Politics," copyright 1951 by the Yale Law Journal Company, Inc.

For Gerald T. White

Preface

THIS BOOK is a pioneer effort to transcend the formal categories of sociology, literature, philosophy, religion, business management, economic theory, political science, social psychology, and history in treating a theme central to the understanding of the American national character. The purpose is to explore and define what may be called the "American Gospel of Success" by juxtaposing our inherited ideology with twentieth-century realities and the dilemmas of an economy shaped by the business mind. It is a fresh way of looking at change and continuity in American life in an era when the enormity of the leap from the past into the future threatens the American sense of balance in the present.

For the first time this book makes available in compact form, for the general reader and more especially for the student of American civilization, (1) the basic scriptures of the American Gospel of Success; (2) the strategic social facts that have raised doubts about the Gospel's validity; and (3) the most pertinent and contemporary commentary on the relation of the Gospel's tradition to a changing society and its ideals. (Although original editions have been cited as sources for the selections throughout, many are currently available in paperback form.) Hopefully, these selections will prompt disagreement and debate as well as assent; will suggest and, indeed, stir up new perspectives; and will contribute a noticeably absent historic dimension to a discussion that exercises and perplexes our society perhaps more than it has any generation of Americans.

M. R.

San Francisco, 1965

Acknowledgments

MY WIFE, Ruth, has contributed her special gifts as an editor to the making of this book. I wish to thank her especially for the deftness and wit with which she recast the Horatio Alger story and for her editing of the Mather and Barnum selections. Others deserving of my warmest appreciation are Donald B. Meyer of the University of California, Los Angeles, for inviting me to share his profound insights; William V. Shannon of the *New York Times,* for educating me in politics; Benjamin J. Klebaner of the City College of New York, for graciously allowing me to profit from his erudition in economics; Thomas N. Brown of the University of Massachusetts, for enlivening my understanding of the interplay of America's ethnics; David Riesman of Harvard University, for his generous encouragement; Roger Daniels of U.C.L.A., for his valuable suggestions; Donald Gallup of the Yale University Library, for providing me with a copy of Cotton Mather's *A Christian at His Calling*; Eugene Burdick, Peter Chew, William Miller, Fritz Redlich, and the trustees of the Brandeis estate for their generosity; the U.C.L.A. and Huntington Library staffs; Joyce Shober and Sheila Knights of the San Francisco State College Library, for their cooperation at all times; and Margaret Lorenz and Merilee Stucke for efficiently typing the manuscript. I am also grateful to those publishers who granted permission to use selections contained herein.

Contents

III / The Gospel Made Social

IV / The Outsiders

V / The Axioms of Exclusion

VI / The Dilemmas of Maturity

VII / The 1960's

VIII / The Gospel Revisited

THE
AMERICAN
GOSPEL
OF
SUCCESS

INTRODUCTION

—

The Heritage

IN ITS brief history the United States of America has had many inspiring meanings for peoples and nations around the globe. Liberty and freedom, democracy and equality, of course, come first to mind. Yet more powerful than any other has been the magnetism of individual success. Indeed, perhaps nowhere else in the world has a seemingly materialistic cult been so uninhibitedly transformed into a transcendent ideal, indeed into a veritable gospel that has been called a dream. Even Walt Whitman could write, in *Democratic Vistas,* "I perceive clearly that the extreme business energy, and this almost maniacal appetite for wealth prevalent in the United States are parts of amelioration and progress, indispensably needed to prepare the very results I demand. My theory includes riches, and the getting of riches." And Whitman, America's uncrowned laureate, but echoed Emerson, the nation's folk philosopher, and of course Franklin, the nation's founding grandfather—and all three bespoke the sentiments of the American. When William James labeled success "the American bitch-goddess," he was simply paying unwitting tribute to the American dream.

Ironically, "The American Cult of Success," a little-known and unpublished doctoral dissertation by A. Whitney Griswold, the late president of Yale University, was completed in the trough of the Great Depression. The author, apparently moved by tact or gallantry or both, made no great effort in 1933 or after to seek book publication. Yet today, over thirty years later, the American Gospel of Success continues to be without doubt America's most persistent claim to the fealty of everyman. Lure, promise, boast, and profound mandate, the Gospel of Success has been so overpowering and hypnotic that the historian Irvin Wyllie has argued that, social facts to the contrary notwithstanding, the belief in the agent of success, the self-made man, and the legendry of "rags to riches" is sufficient reality unto itself.

By focusing on the pursuit of success theme, investigators have slighted the intellectual and emotional dimensions of the individualist ethic as well as the operational complexities of a pluralist society, where the individualist ethic has been in considerable part transformed into a social ethic—and that also is being transformed. The most influential effort to define the social character of contemporary Americans, David Riesman's *The Lonely Crowd,* inevitably singled out the individualist or Protestant ethic for its keystone. Yet this deservedly acclaimed book inadvertently fails to explore and give weight to the religious ethos which served as the ethic's historic point of departure. Nor does it focus on the social and economic—no less than the demographic and psychological—forces that transformed America and Americans in the late nineteenth and early twentieth centuries.

The scholarly no less than the popular mind has associated the Protestant ethic in America almost exclusively with Ben Franklin as the prototype of American economic man. Yet a Puritan divine rather than an enlightenment philosopher set the terms of American individualism and adumbrated the American Gospel of Success with a completeness that eluded the skeptical Franklin. When Cotton Mather noted in 1710, in his *Essays to Do Good* (read by Franklin), that "obscure mechanics and husbandmen have risen to estates of which they had not the most distant expectations," he linked a Calvinistic doctrine of Two Callings with Poor Richard's "Way to Wealth" and thus anticipated the nineteenth-century democratic rags-to-riches saga that was to become central to the modern American dream.

Throughout most of the nineteenth century, the success ideology was trumpeted in hyper-individualistic terms and with an innocence and simplicity that did little to prepare Americans for the world of industry and organization which they soon faced. To Mather's "obscure mechanics and husbandmen," the merchant was added, but the ideology said nothing of industry or organization. Horatio Alger and Andrew Carnegie brought to all their writings the democratic mercantile glow of Jacksonian America, even as Emerson and McGuffey of an earlier generation embraced a romantic individualism. Appropriately, America's first successful ambassador of the Gospel of Success was a Yankee peddler. On December 29, 1858, three thousand Englishmen paid fifty to seventy-five cents each and packed St. James Hall in London to hear Phineas T. Barnum lecture on "The Art of Money-Getting," a lecture America's greatest showman was to deliver almost a hundred times, including riotous appearances to the tune of "Yankee Doodle" at Cambridge and Oxford.

That self-made man who, in an industrial age, preached the Gospel of Success with a candor unique in the world of business, in effect wrote of himself—a product of a fast-disappearing past. Andrew Carnegie's ideal businessman was not an engineer, financier, or promoter but a "merchant" or "maker." "I wish to make something tangible and sell it," he wrote. By Carnegie's standards, a salaried administrator was not a businessman. "Strictly speaking . . . a man, to be in business, must be at least part owner of the enterprise which he manages and to which he gives his attention, and chiefly dependent for his revenues not upon salary but upon its profits. . . . The businessman pure and simple plunges into and tosses upon the waves of human affairs without a life-preserver in the shape of a salary; he risks all." Carnegie even suspected the corporate form of business and favored the partnership.

The Alger story no less than the Carnegie story was unreal: it was obsolete, even in the writing. But where Carnegie had been hard-headed, Alger was the complete romantic. His heroes succeeded not because of occupational strategy but because of luck. Proper in manner, speech, and appearance, the Alger hero was a good samaritan without vices, strong of heart and keen of head in the face of relentless provocation. Although fatherless, he came of a good family that had suffered serious reverses, and he was driven to redeem name, fortune, and honor through a great triumph of character.

The death in 1899 of Horatio Alger and the organization in the following year of the United States Steel Corporation signaled the end of an age. The idea of individual success, the triumph of character over circumstance, lived on as a profound American commitment. But neither the fact-ridden world of Carnegie nor the fiction of Alger provided models for an open society bent on organization.

The Modern Big Business Style

In the second half of the twentieth century, America has become inseparably wedded to the terms of success and to the style of the giant corporations. The Horatio Alger Award, ceremoniously presented to business leaders who have risen from "rags to riches," is but a ritual for American nostalgia. Our vaunted business civilization is more than ever a Big Business civilization where top corporation executives, who exercise a broad, if not easily definable, social power, bear little resemblance to the ruggedly individualistic founding fathers. As Carl Kaysen has written:

Business influence on taste ranges from the direct effects through the design of material goods to the indirect and more subtle effects of the style of language and thought purveyed through the mass media—the school of style at which all of us are in attendance every day. Further, these same business leaders are dominant social models in our society; their achievements and their values are to a large extent the type of the excellent, especially for those strata of society from which leaders in most endeavors are drawn. This . . . is the familiar proposition that we are a business society, and that the giant corporation is the "characteristic," if not the statistically typical, institution of our society, and, in turn, the social role of high executives is that appropriate to leading men in the leading institutions.[1]

The American government itself is often referred to in terms which

1. Carl Kaysen, "The Corporation: How Much Power? What Scope?" in Edward S. Mason, ed., *The Corporation in Modern Society*, Cambridge, 1959, p. 101.

imply that it too is an extension of Big Business. The performance of the President of the United States is often judged in big corporation terms. That top executive of the largest and most public of corporations is said to conduct his office in a manner befitting either the chairman of the board or the active head of the organization. Indeed, big labor, big agriculture, big small business, big education, the big foundations, and big government have all become parts of the constellation of bigness of which Big Business has been the prototype and homogenizing agent.

The desirability of great corporate units is no longer questioned. The severest and most erudite critics of Big Business have accepted bigness as a good rather than an evil, as a blessing rather than a curse. Adolph A. Berle has noted, "Save that the community through the State will intervene to prevent monopoly, there is no apparent desire, and not much reason, to try to break up great economic organizations. When they do not perform satisfactorily, the most obvious remedy at present is not to change the system but to change the managers." [2]

Tomorrow's top managers will come from today's college men who, despite a taste for independent entrepreneurship, are realistically preparing to enter the great bureaucracies while philosophically accepting the spirited caveats of William H. Whyte's *The Organization Man*. Recent studies at ten representative colleges and universities reveal that although half of the undergraduates preferred to be independent entrepreneurs, three-quarters realistically expected to become salaried professionals. The present generation of college students seems to be taking the passing of the old individualism in its stride, despite the fact that the organization career runs counter to the nation's cultural heritage. "Fewer men were left in impersonal relations to markets where their personal eccentricities did not count, and where individual cleverness might win immediate cash rewards. More men had to try to please their organizational associates by some degree of conformity. Businessmen were voluntarily surrendering individual freedom in order to get ahead in a bureaucratic society." [3]

The professional manager contrasts sharply with the personally wealthy owner-manager entrepreneur. "Corporation executives as individuals . . . are men seeking careers in a structure offering rewards of power and position rather than profit or great wealth." [4] The rank order of business executives is not primarily a reflection of money success, as J. Kenneth Galbraith has so vividly reminded us.

The income of a businessman is no longer a measure of his achievement; it has become a datum of secondary interest. Business prestige . . . is over-

2. Adolph A. Berle, Jr., *Power Without Property*, New York, 1959, p. 87.
3. Thomas C. Cochran, *The American Business System*, Cambridge, 1957, p. 194.
4. Berle, *Power Without Property*, p. 68.

whelmingly associated with the size of the concern which the individual heads. Indeed, American business has evolved a system of precedence hardly less rigorous than that of Victorian England and based almost exclusively on corporate assets. . . . In the business peerage the ducal honors belong to the heads of General Motors, Standard Oil of New Jersey, DuPont, and the United States Steel Corporation. The earls, baronets, knights, and squires fall in behind in reasonably strict accordance with the assets of their respective firms. In our time the man who is merely rich is of little consequence. Homage is, to be sure, paid to the "small but successful" businessman. But the very form of the phrase shows that he has had to surmount the handicap of being small to earn his place in the sun.

And the implications of corporate size for managerial power are vast.

With size goes the ultimate responsibility for the decisions affecting the largest number of employees, over prices that affect the largest number of customers, over investment policies which work the greatest change in the income, livelihood, or landscape of the community.[5]

Big Corporation Success Patterns, 1900-1952

The executives of today's major corporations are predominantly a product of the "managerial revolution," inaugurated toward the close of the nineteenth century when the "great moguls" who had carved out industrial empires in mining, manufacturing, and the railroads began to yield their power to the ascendant finance of capitalists and their professional business executives. The trend toward industrial consolidation began with the railroads in the 1870's and was perhaps climaxed and best symbolized around 1900 with the organization of the United States Steel Corporation, in which J. P. Morgan, the chief architect of modern Big Business organization, superseded Andrew Carnegie, the classic American entrepreneur.

The managerial revolution developed further during the twentieth century, when professional managers acquired practical control of the big corporations by gaining power over surplus funds. The corporation thus became less dependent on the bank. By the early 1930's professional managers directed eighty-eight of the two hundred largest corporations, with 58 per cent of the assets of the two hundred.[6] By 1948 only one in twenty of the chief corporation officials studied by Mabel Newcomer owned as much as 5 per cent of their corporation's stock. And, according to Miss Newcomer, 75 per cent of the officials had reached the top by way of the promotion ladder, compared with 67 per cent in 1923 and about 40 per cent in 1899. Further re-

5. J. K. Galbraith, *American Capitalism: The Concept of Countervailing Power*, revised ed., Boston, 1958, p. 25.
6. Adolph A. Berle, Jr., and Gardner C. Means, *The Modern Corporation and Private Property*, New York, 1932, p. 96.

search by Miss Newcomer and other students of corporation management bears out the point that the ascendancy of the professional
manager in leading corporations is an accomplished fact, and that
founders who still head their corporations are a vanishing breed.
Similarly, the older management occupations of entrepreneur, capitalist,
banker, broker, and lawyer are less frequently seen among the top
executives of Big Business, and the proportions of engineers, scientists,
accountants, and, particularly, salaried administrators has risen sharply.[7]
A study of 159 Big Business executives in 1950 also revealed that only
four of them began as self-employed and that "only one of these four
was able to boost his company to national significance and remain
president—the other three men shortly sought employment with established concerns." [8]

Unlike the vividly publicized industrial and financial tycoons of
an earlier day, the managerial elite is made up of men whose names
are virtually unknown to the American public. The corporations they
direct and the brand names of their products have become household
words, but the men, through their tradition of privacy and the effect
of group control, have tended to remain relatively obscure. Indeed,
the ability to perform his duties behind the scenes of public life
is often an important index of executive ability. Crawford H. Greenewalt, one of the major figures in American business today, has remarked: "The more able the man, the less he stands out, the greater
his relative anonymity outside his own immediate circle." [9] The "style"
in which power is gained and exerted within the business bureaucracy,
and success achieved, is linked to the dominant social traditions of
American life that Big Business continues to represent.

The Social Origins of Successful Executives

During the late nineteenth and early twentieth century, the leaders
of American society—whether in business, government, education,
or the professions—were drawn, with only rare exceptions, from
Anglo-Saxon Protestant lineage. But this natural result of superior
numbers and talent became progressively and arbitrarily restrictive
in the pluralistic urban America that took form during these decades.
Believing themselves to be the major representatives of traditional
order, authority, and Americanism, older families felt that the successive waves of immigrants were a threat to these values. They saw
themselves becoming an isolated minority, particularly in those big
cities where they were surrounded by hosts of strangers and faced
radical new problems. Their response was to create a social and cultural

7. Mabel Newcomer, *The Big Business Executive,* New York, 1955, p. 90.
8. "More Facts About Presidents," *Corporate Director,* November 1950.
9. Crawford H. Greenewalt, *The Uncommon Man,* New York, 1959, p. 66.

network of schools, clubs, and careers that would not only preserve their identity but also guard and extend the scope of their power and prestige in American life. The result was an increasingly ethnic acceptance scale that subsumed individual characteristics beneath a group image. At the top were those Americans of British and colonial origins. Shading downward along the scale were the groups from northern and western Europe, and southern and eastern Europe; at the bottom were the racial minorities—the Orientals and Negroes. The progressively lesser breeds were expected to defer to those with Anglo-Saxon ancestry or its equivalent, to keep their distance, and to order their ambitions accordingly.

The era of highly ethnocentric and racist thinking paralleled the era of Big Business growth and bureaucraticization. The great corporations, from the managerial level down through the ranks, reflected the graduated scale of ethnic preferences as well as the more general and natural division, during this period of vast immigration, between a native white collar class and immigrant workers. Once it became clear that political control of the big cities would inevitably pass into the hands of the immigrant groups, Big Business came to be regarded as a new preserve of the older Americans, where their status and influence could continue to flourish. During the first decades of the twentieth century, the large corporations became the chief defenders of social and economic privilege, doggedly fighting every effort at public regulation, confident that they still represented in the new modern world the individualistic Protestant ethic on which traditional authority and Americanism were based.

The representatives of the Big Business bureaucracies were expected to share this heritage, which meant that from the outset they were likely to come from a relatively select group. The research of William Miller and others has established quite clearly that, contrary to popular legends of "rags to riches," the nation's business leaders have seldom been poor—uneducated farm boys or erstwhile greenhorns. "More likely, poor immigrants and poor farm boys who become business leaders have always been more conspicuous in American history books than in the American business elite." The career of an Andrew Carnegie, however much it served as a symbol of American opportunities, was a rarity in the annals of Big Business success. Of the 190 top business leaders of the first decade of the twentieth century, Miller found that poor immigrants and farm boys made up at most 3 per cent. The average big businessman of the period was not only American-born but likely to be of colonial ancestry and from British and New England stock. His church—Episcopal, Presbyterian, or Congregational —usually placed him among the more prosperous and influential segments of the society. Furthermore, he tended to be city-bred rather than country-bred, to be considerably above average in education, and to come from a family with a close interest in business affairs and with a relatively high social standing. In a similar study of lawyers associated with great corporations, Miller found that even those who started at or near the bottom still "shared the national, the religious, the old family . . . heritage" that provided the "bottom requisite" for attaining influence and wealth.

In the first four decades of the twentieth century, the business hierarchy, led by giant corporations, sanctioned and formalized the popular tendencies toward socio-religious and ethnic segregation in American society that, given the considerable differences among the major groups, had a certain superficial validity. These tendencies were strengthened by a series of economic crises and by an intensified passion for social order and homogeneity in an increasingly chaotic and heterogeneous culture. Big Business, parochial, defensive, and unwieldy, a prisoner of its size and torpor, zealously adhered to the rhetoric of free competition while ignoring criticism from without and restricting non-conformity and flexibility within its ranks.

The Closed Organization

The social patterns established within Big Business bureaucracies at the turn of the century helped to close off key areas of the economy and to keep them virtually impenetrable to even the most gifted outsiders. For one without the background, etiquette, and personal appearance to "fit in," and without sponsors to smooth his way, a career in one of the major corporations would be more like scaling a high wall than climbing a ladder.

Indeed, the principles of management organization accorded with those of ethnic exclusion and stratification. In the words of a leading executive of General Motors, Donaldson Brown, the object of Big Business management was to decentralize the decision-making and administrative process through the creation of a large complex of departments and staffs in order "to combine the economical advantages of modern business with as little sacrifice as possible of that intimate control and development of managerial ability that is the character of the well-managed small business." Under these circumstances of "intimate control and development," there was little need for any formalized code that discriminated in favor of white Anglo-Saxon Protestants or those who, in appearance and behavior, could readily pass as such. Judgments were made almost automatically in their favor, and executive recruitment and development could be left, for the most part, to proceed within the established social pattern.

However informal were the codes of selection and exclusion, the fact remains that during the first four decades of the twentieth century the new cleavages in American social life became most sharply defined and unbridgeable in the bureaucracies of the great corporations.

Chester I. Barnard, former president of both the New Jersey Bell Telephone Company and the Rockefeller Foundation, has provided, in public lectures and books, an unusually candid account of the rationale that tacitly but powerfully operated to restrict opportunities in the typical American corporation to those who were socially and ethnically "acceptable." More recently Francis X. Sutton, in *The American Business Creed* (1956), has commented on the actual nature of executive advancement:

In government, preferment through the favor of others is recognized and labeled as "politics," but the fact that a junior executive in business is completely dependent on the good will of a few of his superiors for promotion is not recognized in the ideology.

The "politics" of advancement in the corporation would, of course, depend on its particular traditions, the nature of its operation, the social attitudes of its chief executives, and other factors. But the various axioms of exclusion and preferment to be found in Barnard's writings would seem to be representative of the personnel philosophy that has guided American Big Business. In developing his rationale for the desirability—and perhaps the inevitability—of a socially homogeneous managerial elite, Barnard took countenance of the general politics of human relations that were found in a nation composed of highly visible and deeply self-conscious ethnic groups. In *Organization and Management* (1948) he wrote:

Where in a general society a low status is assigned, e.g., on race, nationality, sex, age, education, ownership of property, or family, it is difficult in general to acquire high status in formal organizations in that society.

Barnard's experience in the public utilities field, as well as his reflections upon the imperatives of the large business organization, produced the more specific principles that were believed to underlie the relation between one's executive ability and advancement and his social and ethnic background. Barnard distinguished between the formal structure and the "informal society" of the corporation. The latter, he believed, determined the actual nature of most organizations, to the extent that " 'learning the ropes' . . . is chiefly learning who's who, what's what, and why's why of its informal society." [10] Since the chief function of the informal society is "an expansion of the means of communication with reduction in the necessity for formal decisions, the minimizing of undesirable influences," Barnard found that "the essential property" of this informal organization is the "compatibility of personnel," [11] a concept which he discussed in terms of a deeper value which he called "communion."

10. Chester I. Barnard, *Functions of the Executive,* Cambridge, 1938, p. 121.
11. *Ibid.,* p. 227.

The condition of communion . . . is related to social compatibility, but is essentially different. It is the feeling of personal comfort in social relations that is sometimes called solidarity, social integration. . . . It is the opportunity for comradeship, for mutual support in personal attitudes.

The consequences and components of this condition of communion were noted as follows:

Perhaps often and certainly occasionally men cannot be promoted or selected or even must be relieved because they cannot function, because they "do not fit" where there is no question of formal competence. This question of "fitness" involves such matters as education, experience, age, sex, personal distinctions, prestige, race, nationality, faith, politics, sectional antecedents . . . manners, speech, personal appearance." [12]

A Test Case: The Jewish Style

The experiences of all outsiders in a period of rising expectations in the early twentieth century provide ample and edifying commentary on the shriveling of the American ideal of equality of opportunity— not to speak of equality itself. In an era when shared social origins were becoming critical to economic success in an organized society, social and cultural differences were acquiring unprecedented variety. Into the mainstream of an American economy in revolution entered for the first time en masse a series of groups whose race, religion, nationality, sex, or previous way of life were presumably only incidental to their talents as individuals. Yet these special attributes were to stifle their talents.

Perhaps best documented and most vivid was the experience of the Jews, close to the major business community and yet standing at arm's length. Heirs of a business style associated with a unique historic identity—indeed, a mystique—they provided a counterpoint to Big Business. Highly visible and representing an earlier stage of American business success and culture, they were to become extremely vulnerable to the ideological strains and social tensions of an America as yet unable to reconcile its traditional individualist ethic with the imperatives of organization in a democratic and pluralistic society.

In the years when the managerial criteria of the great corporations were being established, the pattern of Jewish preference for small business and the independent professions was also being traced out, a pattern running counter to the Big Business style. The habits of frugality, industry, and circumspection, together with the drive for education, enabled second-generation Jews to rise remarkably swiftly into the ranks of the American middle class. Even in the early years of the twentieth century, the East European Jew's reputation for intellectual prowess and business acumen had become widespread. To

12. *Ibid.,* p. 204.

one writer of the period, Edmund J. James, the accomplishments of Jewish immigrants and their sons in so short a time seemed to justify the prevailing Darwinian understanding of the social universe. In his foreword to *The Immigrant Jew in America* (1906), James concluded that "the exhibit of the modern Jew is, in a word, an illustration of the 'survival of the fittest,' for the immunity thus hardly gained has been transmitted from generation to generation." The genius of Judaism and Americanism seemed equally well joined to the editor of *McClure's Magazine;* in the issue of March, 1913, he promised that a series by Abraham Cahan (subsequently the basis for his novel, *The Rise of David Levinsky*) would show "by concrete example, the minute workings of that wonderful machine, the Jewish brain. The articles will make clear why it is that Jews . . . and . . . in the next hundreds of years the Semitic influence is likely to be almost preponderating in the United States."

In the ensuing years, however, this admiration for the gifts and energies that had arrived with the successive waves of Jewish immigrants was to turn into hostility and even panic whenever public confidence in America's economic ability to absorb its immigrant population was checked, and whenever the social adjustments of a new pluralistic society were brought close to home. The first such period came in the difficult years immediately before and after World War I, as masses of Jews were emerging from their city ghettos into the American world. As highly visible and active representatives of the modern, problematic America that had replaced the traditional society, the Jews—both German and Russian—came to be sharply identified with the economic instability and social agitation of the period by virtue of their roles in finance, small business, and the growing labor movement. The favorable image of the Jew split into those of the Wall Street conspirator, the aggressive social climber, and the dangerous radical. Opportunities for Jews in the American world began to narrow sharply, and schools and neighborhoods, business firms and professions began to exclude them. As John Higham has pointed out, the patterns of social discrimination had been developing since the 1880's; thereafter, the new kinds of exclusion that the Jews faced were mainly economic. In general, from 1920 forward, the channels of economic opportunity and social mobility that remained open to Jews in America lay in restricted areas of the culture. Big Business especially excluded them unashamedly.

The corporate bureaucracies, constituted along hierarchical lines, were particularly well suited for implementing theories of racial and religious stratification. Between 1900 and 1940 the social climate both in and out of the Big Business community encouraged personnel practices to which these organizations were structurally disposed. Conversely, the likelihood of being tripped up along the way inhibited even the most daring or fully assimilated Jews from entering Big Business management, except in those few corporations founded by Jews.

As a result, throughout these years few Jews were employed in the great corporations. Even those who were admitted sensed themselves to be outsiders, reminded in various ways that they did not quite fit and ever uncertain whether their careers would be determined by the merits of their work or by the fact that they were Jews. Furthermore, with their intense group self-consciousness, American Jews retained potent reminders and memories of their history within the ghettos of the Old World and had little desire to isolate themselves in an individual ghetto within the alien society of the corporation.

Those Jews who looked to positions of preferment, leadership, and prestige, who aspired to places in the major American world, generally had to prove themselves to be Jews unlike their kind, had to camouflage their identity or exchange it for one honored at a higher rate of social exchange. In any case they zealously conformed to the prevailing Anglo-Saxon Protestant social expectations and shed the visible marks of their background with a completeness and finesse not given to their less ambitious and less artful co-religionists. Some of these Anglicized Jews accepted Christianity in a secularized, pragmatic American form as the highest development of Judaism. Virtually all of them married Anglo-Saxon women, acquired proper social affiliations, and often appropriated euphonious and even distinguished Anglo-Saxon names.

Those Jews best equipped to meet the demands of society, however, often refused to do so. New York's German-Jewish banking elite, for example, which included such figures as Jacob H. Schiff of Kuhn, Loeb and Company, the only non-Yankee of the big six responsible for American finance capitalism, remained committed to the identity and historical consciousness of the Jew. As a result, according to Barry Supple, the historian of this group, the German-Jewish financiers formed "a society within a society . . . forced into being by prejudice" but "buttressed by participation in a specialized culture."

The "Germ Plasm": The Organization Man and the Individualist

Generally the code of exclusion which operated within Big Business was a tacit one. But occasionally its assumptions were made explicit and supplied with "evidence." This was particularly the case in the 1920's, the period of most extreme ethnocentricism in American history and one in which the American psyche fluctuated radically between an individualist ethic and the commitment to organization. Among the many racist and anti-immigration tracts published in the course of that decade, there appeared a book entitled *The Jews in America,* which contributed a new argument to the deeply entrenched anti-

Semitic position: *Jews and Big Business were fundamentally incompatible.* Originally published in the illustrated *World's Work,* the book edition carried on its lurid jacket the query, "With their un-American creed, will they ever be absorbed into the American commonwealth?" The author was Burton J. Hendrick, a reconstructed muckraker who had earlier gained fame for his exposure of the insurance companies, but who had since turned his considerable journalistic talents to the praise of Big Business. His book on the Jews may be fairly regarded as a companion to his study of *The Age of Big Business* (1919) which appeared in the popular "Chronicles of America" series published by the Yale University Press. This hymn to corporate enterprise as the art, the religion, and the poetry of American experience closed appropriately with a tribute to a new American folk hero whose career had become the symbol of American opportunity and whose achievements were offered as ideals for the new American industry that united organization and technology to produce high wages and low prices.

We began this review of American business with Cornelius Vanderbilt as the typical figure. It is a happy augury that it closes with Henry Ford in the foreground. Vanderbilt, valuable as were many of his achievements, represented that spirit of egotism that was rampant for the larger part of the fifty years following the war. He was always seeking his own advantage and he never regarded the public interest as anything worth a moment's consideration. With Ford, however, the spirit of service has been the predominating motive. . . . His money is not the product of speculation; Ford is a stranger to Wall Street and has built his business independent of the great banking interest. . . . Instead of taking advantage of great public demand to increase his prices, Ford has continually lowered them. Though his idealism may have led him into an occasional absurdity, as a businessman he may be taken as the full flower of American manufacturing genius. . . . Possibly America, as a consequence of universal war, is advancing to a higher state of industrial organization; but an economic system is not entirely evil that produces such an industry as that which has made the automobile the servant of millions of Americans.[13]

By 1922 Hendrick no longer could believe that the American economic system might have evil aspects. His view now was that "machinery was the Messiah." Ironically, it was the latest "absurdity" of his hero, Henry Ford, that Hendrick ostensibly set out to refute in *The Jews in America,* while at the same time he wished to endorse the immigration law of 1921 which was, as he said, "to restrict the entrance of Jews from eastern Europe." [14] Claiming that *The Jews in America* was to be read as a brief against the anti-Semitism promulgated in Ford's *Dearborn Independent,* Hendrick denounced Ford's

13. Burton J. Hendrick, *The Age of Big Business,* New Haven, 1919, pp. 186-187.
14. Burton J. Hendrick, *The Jews in America,* Garden City, 1923, p. 2.

accusation, based on the fraudulent Protocols of the Elders of Zion, "that the Jew is organized in a mighty secret plot having ramifications in all parts of the world for the undermining of Christian civilization." Hendrick called this merely "the most grotesque manifestation of that hysteria which is part of the psychosis which we owe to the World War." Further, he insisted that Ford's obsession was preposterous for no other reason than that Jews had no capacity for organization whatsoever. Indeed, their chief characteristic was their disabling individualism, and "the actual wonder," in Hendrick's words, "is not that the Jew has accomplished so much in the United States, but that he has really accomplished so little." [15]

Hendrick went on to show in detail that Jews played a remarkably insignificant role in the American economy, not because their numbers were small but because their "germ plasm" did not provide them with the qualities needed in a highly organized society. "The individualistic trading instinct of the Jew . . . is inherent in the very germ plasm of the race." The popular belief in the superiority of the Jewish mind was simply without basis: "The Jewish mind lacks two qualities—the creative faculty and the ability to organize and to cooperate," and Hendrick saw these qualities as distinguishing American business and industry in an era when individualism had become outdated. Even banking, contrary to popular belief, counted few important Jews, and Hendrick attributed the success of Kuhn, Loeb and Company to "perhaps the greatest financial genius of his time—a non-Jew, indeed so typical a Yankee as Edward H. Harriman." [16] Despite a certain weakening in his logic, Hendrick went to great lengths to demonstrate that the Jews who were actually a "menace" were not the few Sephardic and German Jews—whose achievements were "solid," if also a product of "the individualistic instinct"—but rather the East European immigrants who voted for Morris Hillquit and other radicals, who joined the dangerous unions, who read Abraham Cahan's socialist newspaper, *The Forward,* and who provided audiences for such anarchists as Emma Goldman and Alexander Berkman. The "scientific" basis of Hendrick's indictment was his finding that the Polish Jew differed in genetic origin from the Sephardic and German Jew.

The Jews in America proved to be a choice item for personnel managers in search of sanctions for discriminatory practices. The strange dialectic that led Hendrick to select Henry Ford, the last of the great rugged individualists, as a prototype of the organization man, and to use Ford's charge of a Jewish world conspiracy as an opportunity to demonstrate the wisdom of immigration laws barring Jews because of their non-conformity, is only one instance of the ideological

15. *Ibid.,* p. 69.
16. *Ibid.,* p. 77.

schizophrenia of an era driven to sidestep—indeed, to escape—the social dilemmas of a complex industrial society by taking refuge in "scientific" formulas.

Styles of Success: Catholic and Jewish

The social climate of the first half of the twentieth century contributed inevitably to a high degree of socio-religious segregation within the Big Business community, no less than in the larger society. Two detailed studies document success patterns for Catholics and Jews. Mabel Newcomer's study of 1,400 presidents and board chairmen of great corporations, comprising three generations of big industry executives from 1900 to 1950, revealed that those who were Catholics and Jews generally shared the same modest beginnings—but exhibited quite different styles of success. Forty per cent of the Jews organized their own businesses, against only 7 per cent of the Catholics; not a single Jew was chosen for a top post in another company, while nineteen of the Catholics were. Jews were bunched in merchandising, entertainment, and mass communications; only a few were in heavy industry or public utilities, and none were railway executives. The Catholics, who were mainly Irish, were most heavily represented in railroads and public utilities, a phenomenon largely explicable in terms of the important role that Irish laborers played in the construction of the railroads and later in municipal politics. In general Miss Newcomer found that the contrasting patterns of executive ascent for the thirty-three Jews and seventy Catholics, as well as the zones of the economy in which they clustered, reflected the influence of their social and cultural background, their occupational style, and the time and circumstance of the migration of their families to the United States.[17]

The more comprehensive data in Suzanne I. Keller's study confirm these findings of the Big Business executive pattern and provide a more detailed breakdown along religious lines. Miss Keller's analysis of 342 Big Business executives (in financial institutions as well as in industry, railroads, and utilities during 1950) emphasized the decidedly independent and entrepreneurial experience of the Jews who reached top executive posts. Forty-four per cent were self-made as compared to 7 per cent of the Catholics and 3 per cent of the Protestants. Thirty-three per cent of the Jews led family-made businesses as compared to 7 per cent of the Catholics and 9 per cent of the Protestants. Furthermore, only 22 per cent of the Jews rose through the corporate bureaucracy as compared to 70 per cent of the Catholic and Protestant executives. Differences in the routes and zones of success were also reflected in the age differences of top executives. Sixty-eight

17. Newcomer, *The Big Business Executive*, pp. 46-48.

per cent of the Catholics, 59 per cent of the Protestants, but only 44 per cent of the Jews were more than fifty years old when they reached the top.

Clearly then, the most successful Jews were still making places for themselves largely outside the sectors of the economy controlled by Big Business as late as 1950. They had pioneered new industries where the rewards and techniques of ascent closely resembled the pattern of an earlier American era of entrepreneurial innovation. Fourteen of the nineteen Jews in top executive positions in Miss Keller's study were bunched in the fields of merchandising, entertainment, and mass communications which were still in the pioneering stage that characterized manufacturing and mining in the late nineteenth century.[18]

Organization, Success and the New Technology

Since about 1940 the American people have been living in a new technological age that has already produced almost revolutionary social and intellectual consequences. One such result has been that ethnic, religious, and even sex—if not race—barriers and differences have lost much of their strength and distinctness. The explicit Protestant ethnocentrism that was accepted by millions of Americans has fallen for the most part into limbo. American society has not, of course, become entirely homogenized, but its members have become far more alike than at any time in over a century. The more odious minority group stereotypes, if persisting in benign guise, have accordingly given way before egalitarian attitudes, and many young people have found the way open to careers that were closed or only barely accessible to their parents for reasons of race, religion, sex, or ethnic origin.

The personnel policies of the great corporations set bounds to social mobility within the managerial structure, but many studies suggest increasing social mobility in the last generation and the declining importance of social and economic status, even, it is argued, at the top executive level. W. Lloyd Warner, who studied some 8,300 major business executives in great and middle-sized corporations, concluded that whereas in 1928, 32 per cent of the leaders of the largest corporations were sons of executives, in 1952 only 20 per cent were sons of executives. This leading sociologist then contrasted this trend with the pattern for the smallest corporations, where in 1928, 25 per cent of the managers were sons of executives as compared to 29 per cent in 1952. Mabel Newcomer concluded somewhat more cautiously that merit is more likely to prevail today than it did in the past because

18. Suzanne I. Keller, *Social Origins and Career Lines of Three Generations of American Business Leaders,* unpublished doctoral dissertation, Columbia University, 1954.

executive office in top corporations is less likely to be acquired by inheritance or purchase. Furthermore, a majority of the 1950 top executives, unlike earlier generations, reported no religious affiliation whatsoever, although the high prestige of the Anglo-American tradition persisted: Episcopalians were ten times more numerous among Miss Newcomer's 1950 big business executives than in the population as a whole.[19] Miss Keller's finding that in 1950, 50 per cent of the top big corporation executives were of colonial descent as compared to 70 per cent in 1900, and that 24 per cent of the big corporation executives of 1950 were first- and second-generation Americans as compared with 19 per cent in 1900, suggests a broadening of the ethnic as well as the social base. The business historian Thomas C. Cochran also reminds us that the styles set by today's managerial elite and their careers are more "democratically oriented" than was true of an earlier day, but also less tolerant of eccentricity.

Those closer to the business community, however, appear convinced that top executives in the giant corporations are being recruited with greater frequency than in the past from the relatively privileged groups, confirming the earlier prognosis of F. W. Taussig and C. S. Joslyn.[20] Indeed, the American Institute of Management insisted that it was not surprising that the six states of Massachusetts, Connecticut, New York, Pennsylvania, Ohio, and Illinois produced 55 per cent of the 204 top corporation presidents in 1950, "since the interests and habits of youth, plus the personal contacts formed in early years, carry over into manhood." [21] The editors of *Fortune* noted that whereas 14.9 per cent of the fathers of all of the nine hundred top executives in 1950 were themselves executives or founders of companies, 25.9 per cent of those under fifty came from this kind of business background and concluded that "new members of the Nine Hundred are tending to come increasingly from economically comfortable families." [22] But clearly the very debate is a sign of new health.

The need for increased individual freedom within the organization, as Harold Leavitt and Thomas L. Whisler have urged, is also apparently gaining the serious attention that it deserves.

Perhaps the biggest step managers need to take is an internal, psychological one. In view of the fact that information technology will challenge many long-established practices and doctrines, we will need to rethink some of the attitudes and values which we have taken for granted. In particular, we may have to reappraise our traditional notions about the worth of the individual as opposed to the organization, and about the mobility rights

19. Newcomer, *The Big Business Executive*, pp. 46, 150.
20. F. W. Taussig and C. S. Joslyn, *American Business Leaders—A Study in Social Origins and Social Stratifications*, New York, 1932.
21. "Facts About Presidents," *Corporate Director*, June 1950.
22. "The Nine Hundred," *Fortune*, November 1952, pp. 235-236.

of young men on the make. This kind of inquiry may be painfully difficult but will be increasingly necessary.[23]

Since the end of World War II, the narrowing of the gap between the methods and values of the intellectual and professional classes and those of the business community, the wide public sanction enjoyed by an American pluralism, and the development of the welfare state all reflect a new ideological consensus. Increasing similarities in background, education, and experience have developed social attitudes and social graces that have come to be shared and valued by all groups.

A reassessment of the nation's success patterns is apparently under way which may redound both to individual and social fulfillment and make room for the last of the outsiders. Frederic Harbison and Samuel Hill have pointed out that the second industrial revolution demands entirely new criteria for selecting personnel.

One needs to know how to detect the differences rather than the similarities between people. Objective discrimination and differential treatment are the vital skills required for selection and effective utilization of high-talent manpower. But it is far more difficult for a manager to deal with people differently than to treat them uniformly, because to many people differential treatment means unfair discrimination.[24]

In the final decades of the nineteenth century, the American Gospel of Success lost touch with its roots. When individualism became rugged and Darwinism social, the Gospel ran afoul of its own core assumptions by denying not only life in heaven but life on earth as well. As Donald Meyer has written:

In Franklin's case, drilling oneself for success had held the promise of an eventual freedom really to do what one's talents might suggest, whatever they were. In Social Darwinism no one was free to "be himself," only to be what survived.

The task of the second half of the twentieth century, given the American Gospel of Success, may require a reconsideration of the meaning and implications of the original Gospel, both for the individual and for society.

23. Harold Leavitt and Thomas L. Whisler, "Management in the 1980's," *Harvard Business Review*, XXXVI, November 1958, p. 48.

24. Frederic Harbison and Samuel Hill, *Manpower and Innovation in American Industry*, Princeton, 1957, pp. 65-66.

I

The Roots of
the Gospel

The Gospel of Success followed logically from the Protestant ethic which instructed men to lay up wealth for the greater glory of God. God did "sprinkle holy water on economic success," but success was not an end in itself. The Gospel never forgot the whole man. "A Christian, at his Two Callings *is a man in a Boat Rowing for Heaven. . . . If he mind but one of his Callings, be it which it will, he pulls the* oar, *but on one side of the Boat, and will make but a poor dispatch to the Shoar of Eternal Blessedness."*

Cotton Mather

A Christian at His Calling

The mind of orthodox Puritanism, which viewed business as a calling and a vital part of religion, is no better represented than in the utterances of Cotton Mather (1663-1728). The piety of individual prosperity found its most eloquent spokesman in the boy wonder of the New England clergy, even as Calvinism was on the decline. This selection is the most succinct statement of the Puritan business ethic. [*Cotton Mather*, A Christian at His Calling; Two Brief Discourses, one Directing a Christian in his General Calling; Another Directing Him in his Personal, *Boston, 1701, pp. 36 ff. Original on deposit in Yale University Library.*]

Genesis: xlvii:3
What is your Occupation?

. . . There are *Two Callings* to be minded by *All Christians*. Every Christian hath a GENERAL CALLING; which is, to Serve the Lord Jesus Christ, and Save his own Soul, in the Services of *Religion*, that are incumbent on all the Children of men. God hath *called* us, to *Believe* on His *Son,* and *Repent* of our *Sin,* and observe the Sacred Means of our *Communion* with Himself and bear our *Testimony* to His *Truths* and *Wayes* in the World: And every man in the world, should herein conform to the Calls of that God, who *hath called us with this Holy Calling.* But then, every Christian hath also a PERSONAL CALLING; or a certain *Particular Employment,* by which his *Usefulness,* in his Neighborhood, is distinguished. God hath made man a *Sociable* Creature. *We* expect Benefits from *Humane Society.* It is but equal, that *Humane Society* should Receive Benefits from *Us.* We are Beneficial to *Humane Society* by the Works of that Special OCCUPATION, in which we are to be employ'd, according to the Order of God.

A Christian at his *Two Callings,* is a man in a Boat, Rowing for Heaven; the *House* which our Heavenly Father hath intended for us. If he mind but one of his *Callings,* be it which it will, he pulls the *Oar,* but on *one side* of the Boat, and will make but a poor dispatch to the Shoar of Eternal Blessedness.

It is not only necessary, that a Christian should follow his *General Calling;* it is of necessity, that he follow his *Personal Calling* too. The CASE therefore now before us, is,

WHAT IS THAT GOOD ACCOUNT, THAT A CHRISTIAN SHOULD BE ABLE TO GIVE OF HIS OCCUPATION? Or, *How should a Christian be Occupied in the Business of his* PERSONAL CALLING, *that he may give a Good Account of it?* We will thus proceed in our Discourse upon it.

I. A Christian should be able to give this Account, *that he hath an Occupation.* Every Christian ordinarily should have a *Calling.* That is to say, There should be some *Special Business,* and some *Settled Business,* wherein a Christian should for the most part spend the most of his Time; and this, that so he may Glorify God, by doing of *Good* for *others,* and getting of *Good* for *himself.* . . . 'Tis not *Honest,* nor *Christian,* that a *Christian* should have no *Business* to do. There is a variety of *Callings* in the World; even as there are various *Objects,* about which the *Callings* of men are conversant, and various *Designs* unto which the *Callings* of men are Intended. Some *Callings,* are more immediately, to Serve the *Souls* of our Neighbours; and some their *Safety,* & some their *Defence;* and some their Bodies; and some their *Estates;* and some their *Delights.* But it is not lawful for a Christian ordinarily to Live without some *Calling* or another, until Infirmities have unhappily disabled him. Indeed a man cannot live without the *Help of other men.* But how can a man Reasonably look for the *Help of other men,* if he be not in some *Calling* Helpful to *other men?* . . . To be without a *Calling,* as 'tis against the *Fourth Commandment,* so 'tis against the Eighth Commandment; which bids men seek for themselves a comfortable Subsistence: How? But in the way of some good Occupation. And as a man is *Impious* towards God, if he be without a *Calling,* so he is *Unrighteous* towards his *Family,* towards his *Neighbourhood,* toward the *Commonwealth,* if he follow no *Calling* among them. . . . Yea, a *Calling* is not only our *Duty,* but also our *Safety.* Men will ordinarily fall into horrible *Snares,* and infinite *Sins,* if they have not a *Calling,* to be their *preservative.* . . . Tho' it were part of the Curse brought in by *Sin, In the Sweat of thy Face thou shalt eat Bread,* the *Curse* is become a *Blessing,* and our *Sweat* has a tendency to keep us from abundance of *Sin.* Ordinarily no man does *Nothing:* If men have *nothing* to do, they'l soon do *Too much;* do what they *ought not.* The Temptations of the *Devil,* are best Resisted by those that are least at *Liesure* [sic] to Receive them. An *Occupation* is an *Ordinance* of God for our safeguard against the *Temptations* of the Devil. A Bird on the *Wing* is not so soon catch'd by the *Hellish Fowler*. A man is upon the *Wing,* when he is at the *Work,* which God hath set him to do. . . .

II. But upon that Enquiry, *What is your Occupation?* a Christian should be able to give this further Account, *That he hath an Allowable Occupation, yea an Agreeable Occupation; and that he Entered into it with a suitable Disposition.* . . . If our *Calling* be that whereby God will be *Offended,* it cannot be a *Calling* wherein we shall be our selves *Befriended.* What can any man be the better for a *Calling* that will bring him under the *Wrath* of God? But the *Wrath* of God will cleave to all the *Gain* gotten by a *Calling* that shall be Forbidden by the *Word* of God. The man and his Posterity will Gain but little, by a *Calling* whereto God hath not *Called* him. For our *course of Life* then, we must consult the *Word* of God, if we would not fall into a *course of Sin,* when we go to chuse our Occupation. . . . Let this be taken for granted; except a *Calling* have a Tendency to the *Happiness* of Mankind, and except the *Spiritual,* or the *Temporal* Good of other men, be help'd forward by a *Calling,* a man may not meddle with it; the *Calling* is Naught, the Good God *calls* you to let it alone. . . .

Every *Calling,* whereby God will be Dishonored; every *Calling* whereby none but the Lusts of men are Nourished; every *Calling* whereby men are damnified in any of their true Interests; every such *Calling* is to be Rejected. . . . I say then, A Christian may not get his *Living* by a *Calling,* the Intention whereof is against *Sobriety,* or *Equity,* or *Piety.* No *Instrument* of *Sin* can be *Allowable.*

But this is not enough. A Christian should have it contrived, That his *Calling* be *Agreeable,* as well as *Allowable.* It is a wonderful Inconvenience for a man to have a *Calling* that won't *Agree* with him. See to it, O *Parents,* that when you chuse *Callings* for your *Children,* you wisely consult their *Capacities,* & their *Inclinations;* lest you Ruine them. And, Oh! cry mightily to God, by *Prayer,* yea with *Fasting* & *Prayer,* for His Direction when you are to resolve upon a matter of such considerable consequence. But, O *Children,* you also should be *Thoughtful* and *Prayerful,* when you are going to fix upon your *Callings;* and above all, propose deliberately *Right Ends* unto your selves in what you do; . . .

III. A Christian should be able to give a Good Account, not only, *What is his Occupation,* but also, *What he is in his Occupation.* It is not enough, That a Christian *have* an *Occupation;* but he must *mind* his *Occupation,* as it becomes a Christian. Well then, That a Christian may be able to give a *Good Account* of his *Occupation,* there are certain Vertues of Christianity with which he is to follow it. Particularly,

1. A Christian should follow his *Occupation* with INDUSTRY. . . . It seems a man *Slothful in Business,* is not a man *Serving the Lord.* By *Slothfulness* men bring upon themselves, What? but Poverty, but Misery, but all sorts of Confusion. . . . On the other Side, a man by

Diligence in his Business, What may he not come to? A *Diligent* man is very rarely an *Indigent* man. Would a man *Rise* by his Business? I say, then let him *Rise* to his Business. . . . I tell you, With *Diligence* a man may do marvellous things. *Young* man, *Work hard* while you are *Young:* You'll Reap the Effects of it, when you are *Old.* Yea, How can you ordinarily Enjoy any Rest at *Night,* if you have not been well at Work, in the *Day?* Let your *Business* Engross the *most* of Your Time. . . .

Come, come For shame, Away to your *Business:* Lay out your *Strength* in it, put forth your *Skill* for it; Avoid all impertinent *Avocations.* Laudable *Recreations* may be used now and then: But, I beseech you, Let those *Recreations* be used for *Sawce,* but not for *Meat.* If *Recreations* go to incroach too far upon your *Business,* give to them that put off. . . . It may be, there are some, that neglect their *Occupation,* and squander away one *Hour,* and perhaps, one *Day,* after another, Drinking, and Gaming, & Smoking, & Fooling, at those Drinking *Houses,* that are so Sinful as to Entertain them. Unto you, *O Miserables,* I must address a Language like that of our Saviour; *Thou wicked and slothful person,* Reform thy ways, or thou art not far from *Outer Darkness.* Is it nothing to thee, that by much *Slothfulness,* thy Money & Credit, and all is *Decaying,* and by the *Idleness of thy Hands,* thy *House* is coming to nothing? Is it nothing to thee, that thou art contracting the character of a *Vagabond,* and a *Prodigal?* . . . If the Lord Jesus Christ might find thee, in thy *Store House,* in thy *Shop,* or in thy *Ship,* or in thy *Field,* or where thy *Business* lies, who knows, what *Blessings* He might bestow upon thee? . . .

2. A Christian should follow his *Occupation* with DISCRETION. . . . It is a *Dishonour* to the profession of Religion, if there be no *Discretion* express'd in the Affairs of its Professors. Every man should with a praise worthy aemulation strive to get the praise once given to *Joseph, There is none so Discreet as thou art.*

More particularly: One *Memorandum* for you, is this: Let every man have the *Discretion* to be well instructed in, and well acquainted with, all the Mysteries of his *Occupation.* Be a master of your Trade; count it a Disgrace to be no *Workman.* And as *Discretion* would bid you, to have an *Insight* in your *Business* thus it also bids you have a *Foresight* in it. . . . Let every man therefore in his *Business,* observe the most proper *Time* for every thing; For, *There is a Time to every purpose:* The Wise man says, *There is a Time to Buy, and a time to Sell:* And, a *Wise man* will do what he can, *to Discern the time.* The same *Discretion* must show a *man,* how to proportion his *Business* unto his *Ability.* 'Tis an *Indiscreet* thing, for a man to overcharge himself in his *Business:* For a man to Distract his *Mind,* to confound his *Health,* to Lanch [sic] out beyond his *estate* in his *Business,* is a culpable *Indiscretion.* Be therewithal well advised by the Rules of *Discretion* with another *Caveat:* And that is, To suit your *Expenses* unto your *Revenues:* Take this Advice, O Christians; 'Tis a *Sin,* I say, 'Tis ordinarily a *Sin,* and it will at length be a *Shame,* for a man to *Spend* more than he *Gets,* or make his *Layings out* more than his *Comings in.* A frequent Inspection into the *State of your Business,* is therefore not among the least *Rules of Discretion.* It was among the Maxims of Wisdom given of old, *Be thou Diligent for to know the State of thy Flocks;* That is to say, Often Examine the Condition of thy *Business,* to see whether thou go forward or backward, and Learn how to Order thy Concerns accordingly. . . .

3. A Christian should follow his *Occupation* with HONESTY. . . . Truly, *Justice, Justice,* must be Exactly follow'd in that *Calling,* by which we go to get our *Living.* A Christian in all his *Business,* ought so *altogether Justly* to do everything that he should be able to say with him, Act. 23.1. *Men and Brethren, I have lived in all Good Conscience.* A Christian should imitate his Lord; Of Whom 'tis said, *He is Righteous in all His Wayes.* In your *Business,* you have Dealings with other Persons; but a certain Vein of *Honesty,* unspotted and Re-solved *Honesty,* should run through all your *Dealings.* You aim at the getting of *Silver* and *Gold,* by your *Occupation;* but you should always act by th[e] *Golden Rule.* . . . Shall I be more particular? I say then; Let a principle of *Honesty* in your *Occupation* cause you to speak the *Truth,* and nothing but the *Truth,* on all Occasions. . . . Well then; Don't conceal from any Customer, that which you ought in *Equity* or *Charity,* to acquaint him withal; and more especially, if your Customer do Rely upon your *Sincerity.* Don't exceed the *Truth,* either in Commendations or Disparagements of Commodities. Don't Assert any thing that is contrary to *Truth,* about the kind or the use, or the price of them. . . . In every *Bargain* that you make in your *Business,* let a principle of *Honesty* keep you from every *Fraudulent,* or *Oppressive* Action. . . . Wherefore, Take no Advan-tage, either from the *Necessity,* or from the *Unskilfulness,* of those with whom you are concerned: It is *Uncharitable,* it is *Disingenuous,* it is *Inhumane,* for one man to prey upon the *weakness* of another. And therefore also, Never, never make any *Bargain* with such, as you suspect have no just *Propriety,* in what you go to purchase from them. If you fear, that *Stollen* [sic] *Goods* are offered you, never touch those *Burning Coals,* nor incur that Brand, *When thou sawest a Thief, then thou contendest with him.* Are there also any *Manu-factures* that you are *to work up* for others? Let them all be *Well wrought.* Give every *Manufacture* its due *perfection.* Cheat no man with any thing, that shall be unserviceable to him. Do nothing *Slightly,* Do nothing *Basely,* Do nothing *Deceitfully.* But I have yet another thing to say: Let a principle of *Honesty,* cause you carefully to pay the *Debts,* which in your *Business* must fall upon

you. Run into *Debt,* as *Little* as you may, . . . But being in *Debt,* be as ready to *Get out of it,* as ever you were to *Get in to it.* Syrs, I must *Go to Law* with you; I'll bring you to the *Law;* All I mean is only to show you the *Law!* . . . Don't carelessly Run into *Debt,* and then as carelessly *Live* in it. Indeed *Business* cannot ordinarily be carried on, (especially, as the World now goes,) without something of *Debtor* and *Creditor.* Well, But let it be uneasy unto you, at any time to think, *I have so much of another mans Estate in my Hands, and I to his damage detain it from him.* Some, 'tis said, when they are fallen far into *Debt,* will use, I know not what *Counterfeits,* to cheat their *Creditors.* But unto those, I cannot use easier Terms than these; *Thou Thief; The Great God knows all thy counterfeit, and underhand practices; and thou shalt not prosper in them.* And, in fine; I have yet one thing more to say; Let a principle of *Honesty* cause you to keep your *Word,* in all your *Business.* You sometimes give your *Word;* let that *Word* then be as good as your *Bond.*

4. A Christian should follow his *Occupation* with CONTENTMENT. . . . [A] Christian should not be too ready to fall out with his *Calling.* It is the singular Favour of God, unto a man, That he can attend his *Occupation* with *Contentation* and *Satisfaction.* That one man has a Spirit formed & fitted for *One Occupation,* and another man for another, This is from the Operation of that God, who *forms the Spirit of man within him.* . . . Yea, But when a man comes to Dislike his *Occupation,* and every thing disturbs him, and vexes him in it; I am very much afraid, *That man is nigh unto mischief!* Wherefore, The thing to be first pressed upon you, is this. Count not your *Business* to be your *Burden* or your *Blemish.* Let not a *proud Heart* make you asham'd of that *Business* wherein you may be a *Blessing.* For my part, I can't see an honest man hard at Work in the way of his Occupation, be it never so mean, (and tho' perhaps driving of a *Wheel barrow*) but I find my Heart sensibly touch'd with Respect for such a man. 'Tis possible, You may see others in some greater and richer *Business;* and you may think, that you might be, your selves Greater and Richer, if you were in some other *Business.* Yea, But hath not the God of Heaven cast you into that Business, which now takes you up? . . . Is your *Business* here clogg'd with any *Difficulties* and *Inconveniences? Contentment* under those *Difficulties,* is no little part of your *Homage* to that God, who hath placed you where you are. Fall not into any fretful *Discontent;* but with *patience* make the conclusion of the Prophet; *Truly, This is a grief, & I must bear it! I must bear it!* . . . And hence, another thing to be press'd upon you, is This; Let all persons take heed of *too suddenly leaving* that *Business,* wherein God has fixed them. When a man is become unfit for his *Business,* or his *Business* becomes

unfit for him, unquestionably he may *Leave* it; And a man may be
otherwise Invited sometimes justly to *change* his *Business;* I make
no question of it. But many a man, meerly from *Covetousness* and
from *Discontent* throws up his *Business;* and how many, do you
think, *Repent* of their doing so? . . . I refer it unto your own particular Observations. For my own part, I have a special value for the
Neighbours who *Go down to the Sea in Ships, and do Business on
the Great Waters.* They are a sort of men, that lay the Publick under
as great obligation, as almost the men of any *Occupation* whatsoever.
And the *Genius* of many *Young men* leading them to the *Sea,* it
must not be discouraged. But yet, say, O my *Young men.* Very many
of you were in good *Business* ashore, and might have made a good
Subsistence on your *Business.* But the hope of getting more at *Sea,*
has *too far* Enchanted some of them: To *Sea* they have betaken
themselves: *Quarae,* Whether *Ten to one* have not been undone by
doing so! All I will say is This; Holy Mr. *Tindal* said, *I take God
to witness to my Conscience, I desire of God for my self, no more
of this world, than that without which I cannot keep His Laws.* If
some could have said so, it had been well for them!

5. A Christian should with PIETY follow his *Occupation.* . . . Oh,
let every Christian *Walk* with *God,* when he *Works* at his *Calling,*
and Act in his *Occupation* with an Eye to *God,* Act as under the
Eye of *God.* Syrs, 'Tis a wondrous thing that I am going to say! A
poor man, that minds the *Business* of his Calling, and weaves a
Threed of *Holines* into all his *Business,* may arrive to some of the
highest Glories in Heaven at the last. . . .

But now, these things call for your Attention.

First; Let not the *Business* of your *Personal Calling* swallow up
the *Business* of your GENERAL CALLING. Man, Be jealous lest the Fate
of *Corah's* Company be thy Fate; even to be *Swallowed up of the
Earth.* . . . Forget not, O *Mortal man,* That thou hast an *Immortal
Soul* to be provided for. Let not that care, *What shall I Eat or Drink,
and wherewithal shall I be Clothed?* make you forgetful of that care,
What shall I do to be Saved? It may be said to many a man, who is
drown'd in the Encumbrances of his Occupation; as Luk. 10.41,42.
*Thou art careful and troubled about many Things; But one thing is
Needful.* Thus, thou art careful to do the *Business,* that must be done
for the Relief of thy *Bodily Wants;* It is well: Do it, Do it. But, thy
Soul, thy *Soul,* the Salvation of thy *Soul,* an Acquaintance with *Christ,*
and an Union with *Christ,* the only Saviour of thy *Soul;* This is the
ONE THING that is *Needful.* Be not so *Foolish* and *Unwise,* as to
Neglect *That,* whatever thou doest! Oh, try and see if you don't
upon trial find, besides the vast *Blessings of Eternity,* the Fulfilment
of that word, Mat. 6.33. *Seek first the Kingdom of God, & all these
things shall be added unto you.*

Wherefore, Be your *Business* never so much, yet use PRAYER with *Meditation* on the Word of God, *Every day,* both by *your selves,* and with your *Families,* & this both *Morning* and *Evening.* Rob not the Almighty God, of this *Daily Sacrifice,* whatever pressure of *Business* may ly [sic] upon you. And be assured, all your *Business* will go on the better, all the day, for your being thus faithful to God. But much more, let your *Business* give way to the LORDS-DAY. On the *Lords day,* lay aside all *Business,* but that of Conversing with God, in the Exercises of Devotion. . . . This I would urge; Let there be no *Buying* and *Selling* on the *Lords day:* Don't *profane* the *Lords Day,* with so much as any Thoughts about your *Secular Business.* Let all but the Exercises of Devotion be *Shut out* of your Souls; let 'em lodge without until our *Sabbath* be over. Syrs, I am verily persuaded, That if you would make the Experiment, you would ordinarily find that you prosper *all the week* in your *Occupation* according to your *Strictness* in keeping the *First Day of the Week.*

Secondly, Let OBEDIENCE to GOD, be the *Spring,* and the *Strain* of all your *Business.* . . .

Thirdly, When you follow your *Business,* have your DEPENDENCE on God, for the succeeding of it.

Fourthly, Intermix with all your *Business,* DEVOTIONARY THOUGHTS, and EJACULATORY PRAYERS innumerable. How many Thousands of *Heavenly Thoughts,* may you have in the midst of all your *Business?* You may *Spiritualize* the most *Earthly Business* in the World, by a Chemistry that shall fetch *Heavenly Thoughts out* of it. These *Thoughts* you may Turn into *Prayers,* even while you are at your *Business.* And you may *Dart* up your *Prayers* to the *Heavens,* notwithstanding what you are doing on *Earth.* Here, Here would be a *Walk in the Spirit* indeed! What *Life* and *Peace,* would it bring to be so *Spiritually-minded!* Why do you find so many *Occupations* mentioned in the *Scriptures?* 'Tis partly, That so you may think on the *Scriptures,* in the midst of your *Occupations.* The Bible directs the *Merchant* unto this desire, *May I be a Wise Merchant, and find the Pearl of Great Price!* The *Husbandman* is directed unto this desire, *May the Fallow Ground of my Heart be ploughed up!* The *Mariner* unto this; *May I have the Anchor of my Hope cast within the Vail!* The *Carpenter* unto this; *May I be built up in my most Holy Faith!* The *Goldsmith* to this; *May I be Enriched with the true Gold tried in the Fire.* The *Tailor* to this; *May my Soul be furnished with the Garments of Salvation!* And who are they, that should come to Desire, *May my Feet be Shod with the Preparation of the Gospel of Peace!* . . . *May you all follow your good Occupations and may Goodness and Mercy follow you all, in your Occupations.*

II

The Gospel
Made Secular

Individualistic economic—indeed, character—virtues became guide-
lines for success and Americanism. Whether expressed in rules,
aphorisms, verses, lectures, or fables; whether enunciated by
Franklin, Emerson, McGuffey, Barnum, Carnegie, or Alger, they
were implicitly rooted in Protestant traditions. But the Gospel of
Success, by losing its theological explicitness, was also shedding
its religious texture and resilience and becoming secular.

Benjamin Franklin
The Way to Wealth

*The life and writings of Benjamin Franklin (1706-1790), more than
those of any other American, have come to represent the quintessential
Yankee virtues. Himself a success, he spent a good part of his remarkable career extolling the maxims of individual prosperity. His* Autobiography *became the first and most famous American success story,
dedicated to recording his own rise "from the poverty and obscurity
in which I was born and bred, to a state of affluence and some degree
of reputation in the world." This selection is perhaps the best known
of Franklin's many comments on character cultivation.* [*Jared Sparks,
ed.,* The Works of Benjamin Franklin; containing several political
and historical tracts not included in any former edition, and many
letters: official and private not hitherto published; with notes and a
life of the author, *Boston, 1856, II, 92-103.*]

As clearly shown in the preface
of an old Pennsylvania Almanac,
entitled, *Poor Richard Improved.*
(1757)

COURTEOUS READER,

I have heard, that nothing gives an author so great pleasure as to
find his works respectfully quoted by others. Judge, then, how much I
must have been gratified by an incident I am going to relate to you.
I stopped my horse lately, where a great number of people were
collected at an auction of merchants' goods. The hour of the sale
not being come, they were conversing on the badness of the times;
and one of the company called to a plain, clean, old man, with
white locks, "Pray, Father Abraham, what think you of the times?

Will not these heavy taxes quite ruin the country? How shall we ever be able to pay them? What would you advise us to do?" Father Abraham stood up, and replied, "If you would have my advice, I will give it you in short; for *A word to the wise is enough,* as Poor Richard says." They joined in desiring him to speak his mind, and gathering round him, he proceeded as follows.

"Friends," said he, "the taxes are indeed very heavy, and if those laid on by the government were the only ones we had to pay, we might more easily discharge them; but we have many others, and much more grievous to some of us. We are taxed twice as much by our idleness, three times as much by our pride, and four times as much by our folly; and from these taxes the commissioners cannot ease or deliver us, by allowing an abatement. However, let us hearken to good advice, and something may be done for us; *God helps them that help themselves,* as Poor Richard says.

"I. It would be thought a hard government, that should tax its people one-tenth part of their time, to be employed in its service; but idleness taxes many of us much more; sloth, by bringing on diseases, absolutely shortens life. *Sloth, like rust, consumes faster than labor wears; while the used key is always bright,* as Poor Richard says. *But dost thou love life, then do not squander time, for that is the stuff life is made of,* as Poor Richard says. How much more than is necessary do we spend in sleep, forgetting, that *The sleeping fox catches no poultry,* and that *There will be sleeping enough in the grave,* as Poor Richard says.

"*If time be of all things the most precious, wasting time must be,* as Poor Richard says, *the greatest prodigality;* since, as he elsewhere tells us, *Lost time is never found again; and what we call time enough, always proves little enough.* Let us then up and be doing, and doing to the purpose; so by diligence shall we do more with less perplexity. *Sloth makes all things difficult, but industry all easy;* and *He that riseth late must trot all day, and shall scarce overtake his business at night;* while *Laziness travels so slowly, that Poverty soon overtakes him. Drive thy business, let not that drive thee;* and *Early to bed, and early to rise, makes a man healthy, wealthy, and wise,* as Poor Richard says.

"So what signifies wishing and hoping for better times? We may make these times better, if we bestir ourselves. *Industry need not wish, and he that lives upon hopes will die fasting. There are no gains without pains; then help, hands, for I have no lands;* or, if I have, they are smartly taxed. *He that hath a trade hath an estate; and he that hath a calling, hath an office of profit and honor,* as Poor Richard says; *but then the trade must be* worked at, and the calling followed, or neither the estate nor the office will enable us to pay our taxes. If we are industrious, we shall never starve; for, *At the working man's house hunger looks in, but dares not enter.* Nor will the bailiff nor the constable enter, for *Industry pays debts, while despair increaseth them.* What though you have found no treasure, nor has any rich relation left you a legacy, *Diligence is the mother of good luck, and God gives all things to industry. Then plough deep while sluggards sleep, and you shall have corn to sell and to keep.* Work while it is called to-day, for you know not how much you may be hindered to-morrow. *One to-day is worth two to-morrows,* as Poor Richard says; and further, *Never leave that till to-morrow which you can do to-day.* If you were a servant, would you not be ashamed that a good master should catch you idle? Are you then your own master? Be ashamed to catch yourself your family, your country, and your king. . . .

"Methinks I hear some of you say, 'Must a man afford himself no leisure?' I will tell thee, my friend, what Poor Richard says, *Employ thy time well, if thou meanest to gain leisure; and, since thou art not sure of a minute, throw not away an hour.* Leisure is time for doing something useful; this leisure the diligent man will obtain, but the lazy man never; for *A life of leisure and a life of laziness are two things. Many, without labor, would live by their wits only, but they break for want of stock;* whereas industry gives comfort, and plenty, and respect. *Fly pleasures, and they will follow you. The diligent spinner has a large shift; and now I have a sheep and a cow, everybody bids me good morrow.*

"II. But with our industry we must likewise be steady, settled, and careful, and oversee our own affairs with our own eyes, and not trust too much to others; for, as Poor Richard says, . . . *Keep thy shop, and thy shop will keep thee;* and again, *If you would have your business done, go; if not, send.* And again,

> He that by the plough would thrive,
> Himself must either hold or drive.

And again, *The eye of a master will do more work than both his hands;* and again, *Want of care does us more damage than want of knowledge;* and again, *Not to oversee workmen, is to leave them your purse open.* Trusting too much to others' care is the ruin of many; for *In the affairs of this world men are saved, not by faith, but by the want of it;* but a man's own care is profitable; for, *If you would have a faithful servant, and one that you like, serve yourself. A little neglect may breed great mischief; for want of a nail the shoe was lost; for want of a shoe the horse was lost; and for want of a horse the rider was lost, being over-taken and slain by the enemy; all for want of a little care about a horse-shoe nail.*

"III. So much for industry, my friends, and attention to one's own business; but to these we must add frugality, if we would make our industry more certainly successful. A man may, if he knows not how to save as he gets, keep his nose all his life to the grindstone, and die not worth a groat at last.

> *Many estates are spent in the getting,*
> *Since women for tea forsook spinning and knitting,*
> *And men for punch forsook hewing and splitting. . . .*

"Away then with your expensive follies, and you will not then have so much cause to complain of hard times, heavy taxes, and chargeable families; for

> *Women and wine, game and deceit,*
> *Make the wealth small and the want great.*

And further, *What maintains one vice would bring up two children.* You may think, perhaps, that a little tea, or a little punch now and then, diet a little more costly, clothes a little finer, and a little entertainment now and then, can be no great matter; but remember, *Many a little makes a mickle.* Beware of little expenses; *A small leak will sink a great ship,* as Poor Richard says; and again, *Who dainties love, shall beggars prove;* and moreover, *Fools make feasts, and wise men eat them.*

"Here you are all got together at this sale of fineries and knickknacks. You call them *goods;* but, if you do not take care, they will prove *evils* to some of you. You expect they will be sold cheap, and perhaps they may for less than they cost; but, if you have no occasion for them, they must be dear to you. Remember what Poor Richard says; *Buy what thou hast no need of, and ere long thou shalt sell thy necessaries. . . .* He means, that perhaps the cheapness is apparent only, and not real; or the bargain, by straitening thee in thy business, may do thee more harm than good. For in another place he says, *Many have been ruined by buying good pennyworths.* Again, *It is foolish to lay out money in a purchase of repentance;* and yet this folly is practised every day at auctions, for want of minding the Almanac. Many a one, for the sake of finery on the back, have gone with a hungry belly and half-starved their families. *Silks and satins, scarlet and velvets, put out the kitchen fire,* as Poor Richard says.

"These are not the necessaries of life; they can scarcely be called the conveniences; and yet, only because they look pretty, how many want to have them! By these, and other extravagances, the genteel are reduced to poverty, and forced to borrow of those whom they formerly despised, but who, through industry and frugality, have maintained their standing; in which case it appears plainly, that *A ploughman on his legs is higher than a gentleman on his knees,* as Poor Richard says. . . . *If you would know the value of money, go and try to borrow some; for he that goes a borrowing goes a sorrowing,* as Poor Richard says; and indeed so does he that lends to such people, when he goes to get it in again. . . . And again, *Pride is as loud a beggar as Want, and a great deal more saucy.* When you have bought one fine thing, you must buy ten more, that your appearance may all be of a piece; but Poor Dick says, *It is easier to suppress the first desire, than to satisfy all that follow it.* And it is as true folly for the poor to ape the rich, as for the frog to swell in order to equal the ox.

> *Vessels large may venture more,*
> *But little boats should keep near shore.*

It is, however, a folly soon punished; for, as Poor Richard says, *Pride that dines on vanity, sups on contempt. Pride breakfasted with Plenty, dined with Poverty, and supped with Infamy.* And, after all, of what use is this pride of appearance, for which so much is risked, so much is suffered? It cannot promote health, nor ease pain; it makes no increase of merit in the person; it creates envy; it hastens misfortune.

"But what madness must it be to *run in debt* for these superfluities? We are offered by the terms of this sale, six months' credit; and that, perhaps, has induced some of us to attend it, because we cannot spare the ready money, and hope now to be fine without it. But, ah! think what you do when you run in debt; you give to another power over your liberty. If you cannot pay at the time, you will be ashamed to see your creditors; you will be in fear when you speak to him; you will make poor, pitiful, sneaking excuses, and, by degrees, come to lose your veracity, and sink into base, downright lying; for *The second vice is lying, the first is running in debt,* as Poor Richard says; . . . whereas a free-born Englishman ought not to be ashamed nor afraid to see or speak to any man living. But poverty often deprives a man of all spirit and virtue. *It is hard for an empty bag to stand upright.*

"What would you think of that prince, or of that government, who should issue an edict forbidding you to dress like a gentleman or gentlewoman, on pain of imprisonment or servitude? Would you not say that you were free, have a right to dress as you please, and that such an edict would be a breach of your privileges, and such a government tyrannical? And yet you are about to put yourself under such tyranny, when you run in debt for such dress! Your creditor has authority, at his pleasure, to deprive you of your liberty, by confining you in gaol till you shall be able to pay him. When you have got your bargain, you may, perhaps, think little of payment; but, as Poor Richard says, *Creditors have better memories than debtors; creditors are a superstitious sect, great observers of set days and times.* The day comes round before you are aware, and the demand is made before you are prepared to satisfy it; or, if you bear your debt in mind, the term, which at first seemed so long, will, as it lessens, appear extremely short. Time will seem to have added wings to his heels as well as his shoulders. . . . At present, perhaps, you may think yourselves in thriving circumstances, and that you can bear a little extravagance without injury; but

> For age and want save while you may;
> No morning sun lasts a whole day.

Gain may be temporary and uncertain, but ever, while you live, expense is constant and certain; and *It is easier to build two chimneys, than to keep one in fuel,* as Poor Richard says; so, *Rather go to bed supperless, than rise in debt.*

> Get what you can, and what you get hold;
> 'Tis the stone that will turn all your lead into gold.

And, when you have got the Philosophers' stone, sure you will no longer complain of bad times, or the difficulty of paying taxes.

"IV. This doctrine, my friends, is reason and wisdom; but after all, do not depend too much upon your own industry, and frugality, and prudence, though excellent things; for they may all be blasted, without the blessing of Heaven; and therefore, ask that blessing humbly, and be not uncharitable to those that at present seem to want it, but comfort and help them. Remember, Job suffered, and was afterwards prosperous.

"And now, to conclude, *Experience keeps a dear school, but fools will learn in no other,* as Poor Richard says, and scarce in that; for, it is true, *We may give advice, but we cannot give conduct.* However, remember this, *They that will not be counselled, cannot be helped;* and further, that, *If you will not hear Reason, she will surely rap your knuckles. . . ."*

Thus the old gentleman ended his harangue. The people heard it, and approved the doctrine; and immediately practised the contrary, just as if it had been a common sermon; for the auction opened, and they began to buy extravagantly. I found the good man had thoroughly studied my Almanacs, and digested all I had dropped on these topics during the course of twenty-five years. The frequent mention he made of me must have tired any one else; but my vanity was wonderfully delighted with it, though I was conscious that not a tenth part of the wisdom was my own, which he ascribed to me, but rather the gleanings that I had made of the sense of all ages and nations. However, I resolved to be the better for the echo of it; and though I had at first determined to buy stuff for a new coat, I went away resolved to wear my old one a little longer. Reader, if thou wilt do the same, thy profit will be as great as mine. I am, as ever, thine to serve thee,

RICHARD SAUNDERS.

"HE IS BY CONSTITUTION EXPENSIVE, AND NEEDS TO BE RICH"

—

Ralph Waldo Emerson
Wealth

Nineteenth-century America may have vulgarized the ideas and senti-ments of its most oft-quoted philosopher, but there is no doubt that the dean of American transcendentalism did not underestimate the virtues of material success. "Self-Reliance" and "Wealth" were more than twin slogans of success to Ralph Waldo Emerson (1803-1882), but they were that too. [*Ralph Waldo Emerson,* The Complete Works of Ralph Waldo Emerson, *Boston, 1904, VI, 85 ff.*]

◉

As soon as a stranger is introduced into any company, one of the first questions which all wish to have answered, is, How does that man get his living? And with reason. He is no whole man until he knows how to earn a blameless livelihood. Society is barbarous until every industrious man can get his living without dishonest customs.

Every man is a consumer, and ought to be a producer. He fails to make his place good in the world unless he not only pays his debt but also adds something to the common wealth. Nor can he do justice to his genius without making some larger demand on the world than a bare subsistence. He is by constitution expensive, and needs to be rich.

Wealth has its source in applications of the mind to nature, from the rudest strokes of spade and axe up to the last secrets of art. Intimate ties subsist between thought and all production; because a better order is equivalent to vast amounts of brute labor. The forces and the re-sistances are nature's, but the mind acts in bringing things from where they abound to where they are wanted; in wise combining; in directing the practice of the useful arts, and in the creation of finer values by fine art, by eloquence, by song, or the reproductions of memory. Wealth is in applications of mind to nature; and the art of getting rich consists not in industry, much less in saving, but in a better order, in timeliness, in being at the right spot. One man has stronger arms or longer legs; another sees by the course of streams and growth of markets where land will be wanted, makes a clearing to the river, goes to sleep and wakes up rich. Steam is no stronger now than it was a hundred years ago; but is put to better use. A clever fellow was acquainted with the expansive force of steam; he also saw the wealth of wheat and grass rotting in Michigan. Then he cunningly screws on the steam-pipe to the wheat-crop. Puff now, O Steam! The steam puffs and expands as before, but this time it is dragging all Michigan at its back to hungry New York and hungry England. . . .

The strong race is strong on these terms. The Saxons are the merchants of the world; now, for a thousand years, the leading race, and by nothing more than their quality of personal independence, and in its special modification, pecuniary independence. No reliance for bread and games on the government; no clanship, no patriarchal style of living by the revenues of a chief, no marrying-on, no system of client-ship suits them; but every man must pay his scot. The English are prosperous and peaceable, with their habit of considering that every man must take care of himself and has himself to thank if he does not maintain and improve his position in society.

The subject of economy mixes itself with morals, inasmuch as it is a peremptory point of virtue that a man's independence be secured. Poverty demoralizes. A man in debt is so far a slave, and Wall Street thinks it easy for a *millionaire* to be a man of his word, a man of honor, but that in failing circumstances no man can be relied on to keep his integrity. And when one observes in the hotels and palaces of our Atlantic capitals the habit of expense, the riot of the senses, the absence of bonds, clanship, fellow-feeling of any kind—he feels that when a man or a woman is driven to the wall, the chances of integrity are frightfully diminished; as if virtue were coming to be a luxury which few could afford, or, as Burke said, "at a market almost too high for humanity." He may fix his inventory of necessities and of enjoyments on what scale he pleases, but if he wishes the power and privilege of thought, the chalking out his own career and having society on his own terms, he must bring his wants within his proper power to satisfy. . . .

Success consists in close appliance to the laws of the world, and since those laws are intellectual and moral, an intellectual and moral obedience. Political Economy is as good a book wherein to read the life of man and the ascendancy of laws over all private and hostile influences, as any Bible which has come down to us. . . .

Wealth brings with it its own checks and balances. The basis of political economy is non-interference. The only safe rule is found in the self-adjusting meter of demand and supply. Do not legislate. Meddle, and you snap the sinews with your sumptuary laws. Give no bounties, make equal laws, secure life and property, and you need not give alms. Open the doors of opportunity to talent and virtue and they will do themselves justice, and property will not be in bad hands. In a free and just commonwealth, property rushes from the idle and imbecile to the industrious, brave, and persevering.

The laws of nature play through trade, as a toy-battery exhibits the effects of electricity. The level of the sea is not more surely kept than is the equilibrium of value in society by the demand and supply; and artifice or legislation punishes itself by reactions, gluts, and bankruptcies. The sublime laws play indifferently through atoms and galaxies. Whoever knows what happens in the getting and spending of a loaf and a pint of beer, that no wishing will change the rigorous limits of pints and penny loaves; that for all that is consumed so much less remains in the basket and pot, but what is gone out of these is not wasted, but well spent, if it nourish his body and enable him to finish his task—knows all of political economy that the budgets of empires can teach him. The interest of petty economy is this symbolization of the great economy; the way in which a house and a private man's methods tally with the solar system and the laws of give and take, throughout nature; and however wary we are of the falsehoods and petty tricks which we suicidally play off on each other, every man has a certain satisfaction whenever his dealing touches on the inevitable facts; when he sees that things themselves dictate the price, as they always tend to do, and, in large manufactures, are seen to do. Your paper is not fine or coarse enough—is too heavy, or too thin. The manufacturer says he will furnish you with just that thickness or thinness you want: the pattern is quite indifferent to him; here is his schedule—any variety of paper, as cheaper or dearer, with the prices annexed. A pound of paper costs so much, and you may have it made up in any pattern you fancy. . . .

There are few measures of economy which will bear to be named without disgust; for the subject is tender and we may easily have too much of it, and therein resembles the hideous animalcules of which our bodies are built up—which, offensive in the particular, yet compose valuable and effective masses. Our nature and genius force us to respect ends, whilst we use means. We must use the means, and yet, in our most accurate using somehow screen and cloak them, as we can only give them any beauty by a reflection of the glory of the end. That is the good head, which serves the end and commands the means. The rabble are corrupted by their means; the means are too strong for them, and they desert their end.

1. The first of these measures is that each man's expense must proceed from his character. As long as your genius buys, the investment is safe, though you spend like a monarch. Nature arms each man with

some faculty which enables him to do easily some feat impossible to any other, and thus makes him necessary to society. This native determination guides his labor and his spending. He wants an equipment of means and tools proper to his talent. And to save on this point were to neutralize the special strength and helpfulness of each mind. Do your work, respecting the excellence of the work, and not its acceptableness. This is so much economy that, rightly read, it is the sum of economy. Profligacy consists not in spending years of time or chests of money—but in spending them off the line of your career. The crime which bankrupts men and states is job-work—declining from your main design, to serve a turn here or there. Nothing is beneath you, if it is in the direction of your life; nothing is great or desirable if it is off from that. I think we are entitled here to draw a straight line and say that society can never prosper but must always be bankrupt, until every man does that which he was created to do. . . .

2. Spend after your genius, *and by system*. Nature goes by rule, not by sallies and saltations. There must be system in the economies. Saving and unexpensiveness will not keep the most pathetic family from ruin, nor will bigger incomes make free spending safe. The secret of success lies never in the amount of money, but in the relation of income to outgo; as, after expense has been fixed at a certain point, then new and steady rills of income, though never so small, being added, wealth begins. But in ordinary, as means increase, spending increases faster, so that large incomes, in England and elsewhere, are found not to help matters—the eating quality of debt does not relax its voracity. . . .

5. Now these things are so in nature. All things ascend, and the royal rule of economy is that it should ascend also, or, whatever we do must always have a higher aim. Thus it is a maxim that money is another kind of blood, *Pecunia alter sanguis:* or, the estate of a man is only a larger kind of body, and admits of regimen analogous to his bodily circulations. So there is no maxim of the merchant which does not admit of an extended sense, e.g., "Best use of money is to pay debts"; "Every business by itself"; "Best time is present time"; "The right investment is in tools of your trade"; and the like. The counting-room maxims liberally expounded are laws of the universe. The merchant's economy is a coarse symbol of the soul's economy. It is to spend for power and not for pleasure. It is to invest income; that is to say, to take up particulars into generals; days into integral eras—literary, emotive, practical—of its life, and still to ascend in its investment. The merchant has but one rule, *absorb and invest;* he is to be capitalist; the scraps and filings must be gathered back into the crucible; the gas and smoke must be burned, and earnings must not go to increase expense, but to capital again. Well, the man must be capitalist. Will he spend his income, or will he invest? His body and every organ is under the same law. His body is a jar in which the liquor of life is stored. Will

he spend for pleasure? The way to ruin is short and facile. Will he not spend but hoard for power? It passes through the sacred fermentations, by that law of nature whereby everything climbs to higher platforms, and bodily vigor becomes mental and moral vigor. The bread he eats is first strength and animal spirits; it becomes, in higher laboratories, imagery and thought; and in still higher results, courage and endurance. This is the right compound interest; this is capital doubled, quadrupled, centupled; man raised to his highest power.

The true thrift is always to spend on the higher plane; to invest and invest, with keener avarice, that he may spend in spiritual creation and not in augmenting animal existence. Nor is the man enriched, in repeating the old experiments of animal sensation; nor unless through new powers and ascending pleasures he knows himself by the actual experience of higher good to be already on the way to the highest.

The McGuffey Reader
Try, Try Again

Almost every schoolboy learned his lessons at McGuffey's knee. Whether eclectic or otherwise, the Readers *of William Holmes McGuffey (1800-1873), the Ohio schoolmaster, were virtual compendia of familiar quotations. More important, they were guidebooks to character, enterprise, and success which left a powerful impress on the American mind, as this selection makes clear.* [McGuffey's Newly Revised Eclectic Second Reader, *Cincinnati, 1853, pp. 29-30.*]

Once or twice though you should fail,
    Try, Try Again;
If you would, at last, prevail,
    Try, Try Again;
If we strive, 'tis no disgrace,
Though we may not win the race;
What should you do in that case?
    Try, Try Again.
If you find your task is hard,
    Try, Try Again;
Time will bring you your reward,
    Try, Try Again;
All that other folks can do,
Why, with patience, should not you:
Only keep this rule in view;
    Try, Try Again.

P. T. Barnum

The Art of Money-Getting

The cult of success found its most gifted impresario in Phineas T. Barnum (1810-1891); The Life of P. T. Barnum, Written by Himself (1854) sold nearly half a million copies. The "Rules for Success" that appeared in his autobiography were incorporated in good part into Barnum's lecture, "The Art of Money-Getting," which he delivered over a hundred times. This is the lecture that Horace Greeley thought "worth a hundred-dollar greenback to a beginner in life." After Barnum's death it was said that more newspaper space was devoted to his career than to that of any other American not a President of the United States. [P. T. Barnum, The Art of Money-Getting, *or* Hints and Helps How to Make a Fortune, *New York, 1882, passim.]*

In the United States, where we have more land than people, it is not at all difficult for persons in good health to make money. In this comparatively new field there are so many avenues of success open, so many vocations which are not crowded, that any person of either sex who is willing, at least for the time being, to engage in any respectable occupation that offers, may find lucrative employment.

Those who really desire to attain an independence, have only to set their minds upon it, and adopt the proper means, as they do in regard to any other object which they wish to accomplish, and the thing is easily done. But however easy it may be found to make money, I have no doubt many of my hearers will agree it is the most difficult thing in the world to keep it. The road to wealth is, as Dr. Franklin truly says, "as plain as the road to mill." It consists in expending less than we earn; that seems to be a very simple problem. Mr. Micawber, one of those happy creations of the genial Dickens, puts the case in a strong light when he says that to have an income of twenty pounds, per annum, and spend twenty pounds and sixpence, is to be the most miserable of men; whereas, to have an income of only twenty pounds, and spend but nineteen pounds and sixpence, is to be the happiest of mortals. Many of my hearers may say, "We understand this; this is economy, and we know economy is wealth; we know we can't eat our cake and keep it also." Yet I beg to say that perhaps more cases of failure arise from mistakes on this point than almost any other. The fact is, many people think they understand economy when they really do not.

True economy is misapprehended, and people go through life without properly comprehending what that principle is. Some say, "I have an income of so much, and here is my neighbor who has the same; yet every year he gets something ahead and I fall short. Why is it? I know all about economy." He thinks he does, but he does not. There are many who think that economy consists in saving cheese-parings and candle ends, in cutting off two pence from the laundress' bill and doing all sorts of little, mean, dirty things. Economy is not meanness. The misfortune is also that this class of persons let their economy apply in only one direction. They fancy they are so wonderfully economical in saving a half-penny where they ought to spend two pence, that they think they can afford to squander in other directions. A few years ago, before kerosene oil was discovered or thought of, one might stop over night at almost any farmer's house in the agricultural districts and get a very good supper, but after supper he might attempt to read in the sitting room, and would find it impossible with the inefficient light of one candle. The hostess, seeing his dilemma, would say: "It is rather difficult to read here evenings; the proverb says 'You must have a ship at sea in order to be able to burn two candles at once'; we never have an extra candle except on extra occasions." These extra occasions occur, perhaps, twice a year. In this way the good woman saves five, six, or ten dollars in that time; but the information which might be derived from having the extra light would, of course, far outweigh a ton of candles.

But the trouble does not end here. Feeling that she is so economical in tallow candles, she thinks she can afford to go frequently to the village and spend twenty or thirty dollars for ribbons and furbelows, many of which are not necessary. This false economy may frequently be seen in men of business, and in those instances it often runs to writing paper. You find good business men who save all the old envelopes and scraps, and would not tear a new sheet of paper, if they could avoid it, for the world. This is all very well; they may in this way save five or ten dollars a year, but being so economical (only in note paper), they think they can afford to waste time; to have expensive parties, and to drive their carriages. This is an illustration of Dr. Franklin's "saving at the spigot and wasting at the bung-hole"; "penny wise and pound foolish." "Punch" in speaking of this "one-idea" class of people says "they are like the man who bought a penny herring for his family's dinner and then hired a coach and four to take it home." I never knew a man to succeed by practising this kind of economy.

True economy consists in always making the income exceed the out-go. Wear the old clothes a little longer if necessary; dispense with the new pair of gloves; mend the old dress; live on plainer food if need be; so that under all circumstances, unless some unforeseen accident occurs, there will be a margin in favor of the income. A penny here, and a dollar there, placed at interest, goes on accumulating, and in this way the desired result is attained. It requires some training, perhaps, to accomplish this economy, but when once used to it, you will find there is more satisfaction in rational saving, than in irrational spend-ing. Here is a recipe which I recommend; I have found it to work an excellent cure for extravagance and especially for mistaken economy: When you find that you have no surplus at the end of the year, and yet have a good income, I advise you to take a few sheets of paper and form them into a book and mark down every item of expenditure. Post it every day or week in two columns, one headed "necessaries" or even "comforts," and the other headed "luxuries," and you will find that the latter column will be double, treble, and frequently ten times greater than the former. The real comforts of life cost but a small portion of what most of us can earn. Dr. Franklin says, "It is the eyes of others and not our own eyes which ruin us. If all the world were blind except myself I should not care for fine clothes or furniture." It is the fear of what Mrs. Grundy may say that keeps the noses of many worthy families to the grindstone. In America many persons like to repeat "We are all free and equal," but it is a great mistake in more senses than one.

That we are born "free and equal" is a glorious truth in one sense, yet we are not all born equally rich, and we never shall be. One may say, "There is a man who has an income of fifty thousand dollars per annum, while I have but one thousand dollars; I knew that fellow when he was poor like myself; now he is rich and thinks he is better than I am; I will show him that I am as good as he is; I will go and buy a horse and buggy—no, I cannot do that but I will go and hire one and ride this afternoon on the same road that he does, and thus prove to him that I am as good as he is."

My friend, you need not take that trouble, you can easily prove that you are as good as he is; you have only to behave as well as he does, but you cannot make anybody believe that you are as rich as he is. Besides, if you put on these "airs," and waste your time and spend your money, your poor wife will be obliged to scrub her fingers off at home, and buy her tea two ounces at a time, and everything else in proportion, in order that you may keep up "appearances," and after all, deceive nobody. On the other hand, Mrs. Smith may say that her next-door neighbor married Johnson for his money, and "everybody says so." She has a nice one-thousand-dollar camel's hair shawl, and she will make Smith get her an imitation one and she will sit in a pew right next to her neighbor in church, in order to prove that she is her equal.

My good woman, you will not get ahead in the world, if your vanity and envy thus take the lead. In this country, where we believe the majority ought to rule, we ignore that principle in regard to fashion, and let a handful of people, calling themselves the aristocracy, run up a false standard of perfection, and in endeavoring to rise to that standard, we constantly keep ourselves poor; all the time digging away for the sake of outside appearance. How much wiser to be a "law unto ourselves" and say, "We will regulate our out-go by our income, and lay up something for a rainy day." People ought to be as sensible on the subject of money-getting as on any other subject. Like causes produce like effects. You cannot accumulate a fortune by taking the road that leads to poverty. It needs no prophet to tell us that those who live fully up to their means, without any thought of a reverse in this life, can never attain a pecuniary independence.

Men and women accustomed to gratify every whim and caprice, will find it hard, at first, to cut down their various unnecessary expenses, and will feel it a great self denial to live in a smaller house than they have been accustomed to, with less expensive furniture, less company, less costly clothing, fewer servants, a less number of balls, parties, theatre-goings, carriage-ridings, pleasure excursions, cigar-smokings, liquor-drinkings, and other extravagances; but, after all, if they will try the plan of laying by a "nest-egg," or in other words, a small sum of money, at interest or judiciously invested in land, they will be surprised at the pleasure to be derived from constantly adding to their little "pile," as well as from all the economical habits which are engendered by this course.

The old suit of clothes, and the old bonnet and dress, will answer for another season; the Croton or spring water will taste better than champagne; a cold bath and a brisk walk will prove more exhilarating than a ride in the finest coach; a social chat, an evening's reading in the family circle, or an hour's play of "hunt the slipper" and "blind man's buff," will be far more pleasant than a fifty- or a five-hundred-dollar party, when the reflection on the difference in cost is indulged in by those who begin to know the pleasures of saving. Thousands of men are kept poor, and tens of thousands are made so after they have acquired quite sufficient to support them well through life, in consequence of laying their plans of living on too broad a platform. Some families expend twenty thousand dollars per annum, and some much more, and would scarcely know how to live on less, while others secure more solid enjoyment frequently on a twentieth part of that amount. Prosperity is a more severe ordeal than adversity, especially sudden prosperity. "Easy come, easy go," is and old and true proverb. A spirit of pride and vanity, when permitted to have full sway, is the undying cankerworm which gnaws the very vitals of a man's worldly possessions, let them be small or great, hundreds or millions. Many persons, as they begin to prosper, immediately expand their ideas and commence expending for luxuries, until in a short time their expenses swallow up their income, and they become ruined in their ridiculous attempts to keep up appearances, and make a "sensation."

I know a gentleman of fortune who says, that when he first began to prosper, his wife would have a new and elegant sofa. "That sofa," he says, "cost me thirty thousand dollars!" When the sofa reached the house, it was found necessary to get chairs to match; then side-boards, carpets, and tables "to correspond" with them, and so on through the entire stock of furniture; when at last it was found that the house itself was quite too small and old-fashioned for the furniture, and a new one was built to correspond with the new purchases; "thus," added my friend, "summing up an outlay of thirty thousand dollars caused by that single sofa, and saddling on me, in the shape of servants, equippage, and the necessary expenses attendant upon keeping up a fine 'establishment,' a yearly outlay of eleven thousand dollars, and a tight pinch at that; whereas, ten years ago, we lived with much more real comfort, because with much less care, on as many hundreds. The truth is," he continued, "that sofa would have brought me to inevitable bankruptcy, had not a most unexampled tide of prosperity kept me above it, and had I not checked the natural desire to 'cut a dash.' "

The foundation of success in life is good health; that is the sub-stratum of fortune; it is also the basis of happiness. A person cannot accumulate a fortune very well when he is sick. He has no ambition; no incentive; no force. Of course, there are those who have bad health and cannot help it; you cannot expect that such persons can accumulate wealth; but there are a great many in poor health who need not be so.

If, then, sound health is the foundation of success and happiness in life, how important it is that we should study the laws of health, which is but another expression for the laws of nature! The closer we keep to the laws of nature, the nearer we are to good health, and yet how many persons there are who pay no attention to natural laws, but absolutely transgress them, even against their own natural inclination. We ought to know that the "sin of ignorance" is never winked at in regard to the violation of nature's laws; their infraction always brings the penalty. A child may thrust its finger into the flame without know-ing it will burn, and so suffers; repentance even will not stop the smart. Many of our ancestors knew very little about the principle of ventilation. They did not know much about oxygen, whatever other "gin" they might have been acquainted with; and consequently, they built their houses with little seven-by-nine-feet bedrooms, and these good old pious Puritans would lock themselves up in one of these cells, say their prayers, and go to bed. In the morning they would devoutly return thanks for the "preservation of their lives" during the night, and nobody had better reason to be thankful. Probably some big crack in the window, or in the door, let in a little fresh air, and thus saved them.

Many persons knowingly violate the laws of nature against their better impulses, for the sake of fashion. For instance, there is one thing that nothing living except a vile worm ever naturally loved, and that is tobacco; yet how many persons there are who deliberately train an unnatural appetite, and overcome this implanted aversion for tobacco, to such a degree that they get to love it. They have got hold of a poisonous, filthy weed, or rather that takes a firm hold of them. Here are married men who run about spitting tobacco juice on the carpet and floors, and sometimes even upon their wives besides. They do not kick their wives out of doors like drunken men, but their wives, I have no doubt, often wish they were outside of the house. Another perilous feature is that this artificial appetite, like jealousy, "grows by what it feeds on"; when you love that which is unnatural, a stronger appetite is created for the hurtful thing than the natural desire for what is harmless. There is an old proverb which says that "habit is second nature," but an artificial habit is stronger than nature. Take for instance an old tobacco-chewer; his love for the "quid" is stronger than his love for any particular kind of food. He can give up roast beef easier than give up the weed.

Young lads regret that they are not men; they would like to go to bed boys and wake up men; and to accomplish this they copy the bad habits of their seniors. Little Tommy and Johnny see their fathers or uncles smoke a pipe and they say, "If I could only do that I would be a man, too; Uncle John has gone out and left his pipe of tobacco, let us try it." They take a match and light it, and puff away. "We will learn to smoke; do you like it, Johnny?" That lad dolefully replies: "Not very much; it tastes bitter"; by and by he grows pale, but he persists, and he soon offers up a sacrifice on the altar of fashion; but the boys stick to it and persevere until at last they conquer their natural appetites and become the victims of acquired tastes.

I speak "by the book," for I have noticed its effects on myself, having gone so far as to smoke ten or fifteen cigars a day, although I have not used the weed during the last fourteen years, and never shall again. The more a man smokes, the more he craves smoking; the last cigar smoked, simply excites the desire for another, and so on incessantly.

Take the tobacco-chewer. In the morning when he gets up, he puts a quid in his mouth and keeps it there all day, never taking it out except to exchange it for a fresh one, or when he is going to eat; oh! yes, at intervals during the day and evening, many a chewer takes out a quid and holds it in his hand long enough to take a drink, and then pop! it goes back again. This simply proves that the appetite for rum is even stronger than that for tobacco. When the tobacco chewer goes to your country seat and you show him your grapery and fruit house and the beauties of your garden, when you offer him some fresh, ripe fruit, and say, "My friend, I have got here the most delicious apples and pears and peaches and apricots; I have imported them from Spain, France, and Italy,—just see those luscious grapes; there is nothing more delicious nor more healthy than ripe fruit, so help yourself; I want to see you delight yourself with these things," he will roll the dear quid under his tongue and answer, "No, I thank you, I have got tobacco in my mouth." His palate has become narcotized by the noxious weed, and he has lost, in a great measure, the delicate and enviable taste for fruits. This shows what expensive, useless, and injurious habits men will get into. I speak from experience. I have smoked until I trembled like an aspen leaf, the blood rushed to my head, and I had a palpitation of the heart which I thought was heart disease, till I was almost killed with fright. When I consulted my physician, he said, "Break off tobacco using." I was not only injuring my health and spending a great deal of money, but I was setting a bad example. I obeyed his counsel. No young man in the world ever looked so beautiful as he thought he did behind a fifteen-cent cigar or a meerschaum!

These remarks apply with ten-fold force to the use of intoxicating drinks. To make money, requires a clear brain. A man has got to see that two and two make four; he must lay all his plans with reflection and forethought, and closely examine all the details and the ins and outs of business. As no man can succeed in business unless he has a brain to enable him to lay his plans, and reason to guide him in their execution, so, no matter how bountifully a man may be blessed with intelligence, if the brain is muddled, and his judgment warped by intoxicating drinks, it is impossible for him to carry on business successfully. How many good opportunities have passed, never to return, while a man was sipping a "social glass" with his friend! How many foolish bargains have been made under the influence of the "nervine" which temporarily makes its victim think he is rich. How many important chances have been put off until to-morrow, and then forever, because the wine cup has thrown the system into a state of lassitude, neutralizing the energies so essential to success in business. Verily, "wine is a mocker." The use of intoxicating drinks as a beverage is as much an infatuation as is the smoking of opium by the Chinese, and the former is quite as destructive to the success of the business man as the latter. It is an unmitigated evil, utterly indefensible in the light of philosophy, religion, or good sense. It is the parent of nearly every other evil in our country.

DON'T MISTAKE YOUR VOCATION.—The safest plan, and the one most sure of success for the young man starting in life, is to select the vocation which is most congenial to his tastes. Parents and guardians are often quite too negligent in regard to this. It is very common for a father to say, for example: "I have five boys. I will make Billy a clergyman; John a lawyer; Tom a doctor, and Dick a farmer." He then goes into town and looks about to see what he will do with Sammy.

He returns home and say, "Sammy, I see watch-making is a nice, genteel business; I think I will make you a goldsmith." He does this regardless of Sam's natural inclinations, or genius.

We are all, no doubt, born for a wise purpose. There is as much diversity in our brains as in our countenances. Some are born natural mechanics, while some have great aversion to machinery. Let a dozen boys of ten years get together and you will soon observe two or three are "whittling" out some ingenious device; working with locks or complicated machinery. When they were but five years old, their father could find no toy to please them like a puzzle. They are natural mechanics; but the other eight or nine boys have different aptitudes. I belong to the latter class; I never had the slightest love for mechanism; on the contrary, I have a sort of abhorrence for complicated machinery. I never had ingenuity enough to whittle a cider tap so it would not leak. I never could make a pen that I could write with, or understand the principle of a steam engine. If a man was to take such a boy as I was and attempt to make a watchmaker of him, the boy might, after an apprenticeship of five or seven years, be able to take apart and put together a watch; but all through life he would be working uphill and seizing every excuse for leaving his work and idling away his time. Watch-making is repulsive to him. . . .

SELECT THE RIGHT LOCATION.—. . . When I was in London in 1858, I was passing down Holborn with an English friend and came to the "penny shows." They had immense cartoons outside, portraying the wonderful curiosities to be seen "all for a penny." Being a little in the "show line" myself, I said, "Let us go in here." We soon found ourselves in the presence of the illustrious showman, and he proved to be the sharpest man in that line I had ever met. He told us some extraordinary stories in reference to his bearded ladies, his albinos, and his armadillos, which we could hardly believe, but thought it "better to believe it than look after the proof." He finally begged to call our attention to some wax statuary, and showed us a lot of the dirtiest and filthiest wax figures imaginable. They looked as if they had not seen water since the Deluge.

"What is there so wonderful about your statuary?" I asked.

"I beg you not to speak so satirically," he replied. "Sir, these are not Madam Tussaud's wax figures, all covered with gilt and tinsel and imitation diamonds, and copies from engravings and photographs. Mine, sir, were taken from life. Whenever you look upon one of those figures, you may consider that you are looking upon the living individual."

Glancing casually at them, I saw one labelled "Henry VIII" and feeling a little curious upon seeing that it looked like Calvin Edson, the living skeleton, I said:

"Do you call that 'Henry the Eighth'?"

He replied, "Certainly, sir; it was taken from life at Hampton Court by special order of His Majesty, on such a day."

He would have given the hour of the day if I had insisted. I said, "Everybody knows that Henry VIII was a great, stout old king, and that figure is lean and lank. What do you say to that?"

"Why," he replied, "you would be lean and lank yourself, if you sat there as long as he has."

There was no resisting such arguments. I said to my English friend, "Let us go out; do not tell him who I am; I show the white feather; he beats me."

He followed us to the door, and seeing the rabble in the street he called out, "Ladies and gentlemen, I beg to draw your attention to the respectable character of my visitors," pointing to us as we walked away. I called upon him a couple of days afterward; told him who I was, and said:

"My friend, you are an excellent showman, but you have selected a bad location."

He replied, "That is true, sir; I feel that all my talents are thrown away; but what can I do?"

"You can go to America," I replied. "You can give full play to your faculties over there; you will find plenty of elbow room in America; I will engage you for two years; after that you will be able to go on your own account."

He accepted my offer and remained two years in my New York Museum. He then went to New Orleans and carried on a travelling show business during the summer. To-day he is worth sixty thousand dollars, simply because he selected the right vocation and also secured the proper location. The old proverb says, "Three removes are as bad as a fire," but when a man is in the fire, it matters but little how soon or how often he removes.

AVOID DEBT.—Young men starting in life should avoid running into debt. There is scarcely anything that drags a person down like debt. It is a slavish position to get in, yet we find many a young man hardly out of his "teens" running in debt. He meets a chum and says, "Look at this; I have got trusted for a new suit of clothes." He seems to look upon the clothes as so much given to him. Well, it frequently is so, but, if he succeeds in paying and then gets trusted again, he is adopting a habit which will keep him in poverty through life. Debt robs a man of his self-respect, and makes him almost despise himself. Grunting and groaning and working for what he has eaten up or worn out, and now when he is called upon to pay up, he has nothing to show for his money: this is properly termed "working for a dead horse." I do not speak of merchants buying and selling on credit, or of those who buy on credit in order to turn the purchase to a profit. The old Quaker said to his farmer son, "John, never get trusted; but if thee gets trusted for anything, let it be for manure, because that will help thee pay it back again."

Mr. Beecher advised young men to get in debt if they could to a small amount in the purchase of land in the country districts. "If a young man," he says, "will only get in debt for some land and then get married, these two things will keep him straight, or nothing will." This may be safe to a limited extent, but getting in debt for what you eat and drink and wear is to be avoided. Some families have a foolish habit of getting credit at the stores, and thus frequently purchase many things which might have been dispensed with.

It is all very well to say, "I have got trusted for sixty days, and if I don't have the money, the creditor will think nothing about it." There is no class of people in the world who have such good memories as creditors. When the sixty days run out, you will have to pay. If you do not pay, you will break your promise and probably resort to a falsehood. You may make some excuse or get in debt elsewhere to pay it, but that only involves you the deeper. . . .

Money is in some respects like fire—it is a very excellent servant but a terrible master. When you have it mastering you, when interest is constantly piling up against you, it will keep you down in the worst kind of slavery. But let money work for you, and you have the most devoted servant in the world. It is no "eye-servant." There is nothing animate or inanimate that will work so faithfully as money when placed at interest, well secured. It works night and day, and in wet or dry weather.

I was born in the blue-law State of Connecticut, where the old Puritans had laws so rigid that it was said they fined a man for kissing his wife on Sunday. Yet these rich old Puritans would have thousands of dollars at interest, and on Saturday night would be worth a certain amount; on Sunday they would go to church and perform all the duties of a Christian. On waking up on Monday morning, they would find themselves considerably richer than the Saturday night previous, simply because their money placed at interest had worked faithfully for them all Sunday, according to law!

Do not let it work against you; if you do, there is no chance for success in life so far as money is concerned. John Randolph, the eccentric Virginian, once exclaimed in Congress, "Mr. Speaker, I have discovered the philosopher's stone: pay as you go." This is indeed nearer to the philosopher's stone than any alchemist has ever yet arrived.

PERSEVERE.—When a man is in the right path, he must persevere. I speak of this because there are some persons who are "born tired"; naturally lazy and possessing no self-reliance and no perseverance. . . .

It is this go-aheaditiveness, this determination not to let the "horrors" or the "blues" take possession of you, so as to make you relax your energies in the struggle for independence, which you must cultivate.

How many have almost reached the goal of their ambition, but losing faith in themselves have relaxed their energies, and the golden prize has been lost forever. . . .

Take two generals; both understand military tactics, both educated at West Point, if you please, both equally gifted; yet one, having this principle of perseverance, and the other lacking it, the former will succeed in his profession, while the latter will fail. One may hear the cry, "The enemy are coming, and they have got cannon!"

"Got cannon?" says the hesitating general.

"Yes."

"Then halt every man."

He wants time to reflect; his hesitation is his ruin. The enemy passes unmolested, or overwhelms him. The general of pluck, perseverance, and self-reliance goes into battle with a will, and amid the clash of arms, the booming of cannon, and the shrieks of the wounded and dying, you will see this man persevering, going on, cursing and slashing his way through with unwavering determination, and if you are near enough, you will hear him shout, "I will fight it out on this line if it takes all summer."

WHATEVER YOU DO, DO WITH ALL YOUR MIGHT.—Work at it, if necessary, early and late, in season and out of season, not leaving a stone unturned, and never deferring for a single hour that which can be done just as well *now*. The old proverb is full of truth and meaning, "Whatever is worth doing at all, is worth doing well." Many a man acquires a fortune by doing his business thoroughly, while his neighbor remains poor for life because he only half does it. Ambition, energy, industry, perseverance, are indispensable requisites for success in business.

Fortune always favors the brave, and never helps a man who does not help himself. It won't do to spend your time like Mr. Micawber, in waiting for something to "turn up." To such men one of two things usually "turns up": the poor-house or the jail; for idleness breeds bad habits, and clothes a man in rags. The poor spendthrift vagabond said to a rich man:

"I have discovered there is money enough in the world for all of us, if it was equally divided; this must be done, and we shall all be happy together."

"But," was the response, "if everybody was like you, it would be spent in two months, and what would you do then?"

"Oh! divide again; keep dividing, of course!"

I was recently reading in a London paper an account of a like philosophic pauper who was kicked out of a cheap boardinghouse because he could not pay his bill, but he had a roll of papers sticking out of his coat pocket, which, upon examination, proved to be his plan for paying off the national debt of England without the aid of a penny. People have got to do as Cromwell said: "not only trust in Providence, but keep the powder dry." Do your part of the work, or you cannot succeed. Mahomet, one night, while encamping in the desert, overheard one of his fatigued followers remark: "I will loose my camel, and trust it to God." "No, no, not so," said the prophet, "tie thy camel, and trust it to God!" Do all you can for yourselves, and then trust in Providence, or luck, or whatever you please to call it, for the rest.

DEPEND UPON YOUR OWN PERSONAL EXERTIONS.—. . . I hold that every man should, like Cuvier, the French naturalist, thoroughly know his business. So proficient was he in the study of natural history, that you might bring to him the bone or even a section of a bone of an animal which he had never seen described, and reasoning from analogy, he would be able to draw a picture of the object from which the bone had been taken. On one occasion his students attempted to deceive him. They rolled one of their number in a cow skin and put him under the Professor's table as a new specimen. When the philosopher came into the room, some of the students asked him what animal it was. Suddenly the animal said, "I am the devil and I am going to eat you." It was but natural that Cuvier should desire to classify this creature, and examining it intently, he said,

"Divided hoof; graminivorous; it cannot be done!"

He knew that an animal with a split hoof must live upon grass and grain, or other kind of vegetation, and would not be inclined to eat flesh, dead or alive, so he considered himself perfectly safe. The possession of a perfect knowledge of your business is an absolute necessity in order to insure success.

Among the maxims of the elder Rothschild was one, an apparent paradox: "Be cautious and bold." This seems to be a contradiction in terms, but it is not, and there is great wisdom in the maxim. It is, in fact, a condensed statement of what I have already said. It is to say, "You must exercise your caution in laying your plans, but be bold in carrying them out." A man who is all caution, will never dare to take hold and be successful; and a man who is all boldness, is merely reckless, and must eventually fail. A man may go on "change" and make fifty or one hundred thousand dollars in speculating in stocks, at a single operation. But if he has simple boldness without caution, it is mere chance, and what he gains to-day he will lose to-morrow. You must have both the caution and the boldness, to insure success.

The Rothschilds have another maxim: "Never have anything to do with an unlucky man or place." That is to say, never have anything to do with a man or place which never succeeds, because, although a man may appear to be honest and intelligent, yet if he tries this or that thing and always fails, it is on account of some fault or infirmity that you may not be able to discover, but nevertheless which must exist.

There is no such thing in the world as luck. There never was a man who could go out in the morning and find a purse of gold in the street to-day, and another to-morrow, and so on, day after day. He may do so once in his life; but so far as mere luck is concerned, he is as liable to lose it as to find it. "Like causes produce like effects." If a man adopts the proper methods to be successful, "luck" will not prevent him. If he does not succeed, there are reasons for it, although perhaps he may not be able to see them.

USE THE BEST TOOLS.—Men in engaging employees should be careful to get the best. Understand, you cannot have too good tools to work with, and there is no tool you should be so particular about as living tools. If you get a good one, it is better to keep him, than keep changing. He learns something every day, and you are benefited by the experience he acquires. He is worth more to you this year than last, and he is the last man to part with, provided his habits are good and he continues faithful. If, as he gets more valuable, he demands an exorbitant increase of salary on the supposition that you can't do without him, let him go. Whenever I have such an employee, I always discharge him; first, to convince him that his place may be supplied, and second, because he is good for nothing if he thinks he is invaluable and cannot be spared. . . .

DON'T GET ABOVE YOUR BUSINESS.—Young men after they get through their business training, or apprenticeship, instead of pursuing their avocation and rising in their business, will often lie about doing nothing. They say, "I have learned my business, but I am not going to be a hireling; what is the object of learning my trade or profession, unless I establish myself?"

"Have you capital to start with?"

"No, but I am going to have it."

"How are you going to get it?"

"I will tell you confidentially; I have a wealthy old aunt, and she will die pretty soon; but if she does not, I expect to find some rich old man who will lend me a few thousands to give me a start. If I only get the money to start with, I will do well."

There is no greater mistake than when a young man believes he will succeed with borrowed money. Why? Because every man's experience coincides with that of Mr. Astor, who said it was more difficult for him to accumulate his first thousand dollars, than all the succeeding millions that made up his colossal fortune. Money is good for nothing unless you know the value of it by experience. Give a boy twenty thousand dollars and put him in business and the chances are that he will lose every dollar of it before he is a year older. Like buying a ticket in the lottery, and drawing a prize, it is "easy come, easy go." He does not know the value of it; nothing is worth anything, unless it costs effort. Without self-denial and economy, patience and perseverance, and commencing with capital which you have not earned, you are not sure to succeed in accumulating. Young men instead of "waiting for dead men's shoes" should be up and doing, for there is no class of persons who are so unaccommodating in regard to dying as these rich old people, and it is fortunate for the expectant heirs that it is so. Nine out of ten of the rich men of our country to-day, started out in life as poor boys, with determined wills, industry, perseverance, economy, and good habits. They went on gradually, made their own money and saved it; and this is the best way to acquire a fortune. Stephen Girard started life as a poor cabin boy; now he pays taxes on a million and a half dollars of income per year. John Jacob Astor was a poor farmer boy, and died worth twenty millions. Cornelius Vanderbilt began life rowing a boat from Staten Island to New York; now he presents our government with a steamship worth a million of dollars, and he is worth fifty millions.

"There is no royal road to learning," says the proverb, and I may say it is equally true there is no royal road to wealth. But I think there is a royal road to both. The road to learning is a royal one; the road that enables the student to expand his intellect and add every day to his stock of knowledge, until, in the pleasant process of intellectual growth, he is able to solve the most profound problems, to count the stars, to analyze every atom of the globe, and to measure the firmament—this is a regal highway, and it is the only road worth travelling.

So in regard to wealth. Go on in confidence, study the rules, and above all things, study human nature; for "the proper study of mankind is man," and you will find that while expanding the intellect and the muscles, your enlarged experience will enable you every day to accumulate more and more principal, which will increase itself by interest and otherwise, until you arrive at a state of independence. You will find, as a general thing, that the poor boys get rich and the rich boys get poor. For instance, a rich man at his decease, leaves a large estate to his family. His eldest sons, who have helped him earn his fortune, know by experience the value of money, and they take their inheritance and add to it. The separate portions of the young children are placed at interest, and the little fellows are patted on the head, and told a dozen times a day, "You are rich; you will never have to work, you can always have whatever you wish, for you were born with a golden spoon in your mouth." The young heir soon finds out what that means; he has the finest dresses and playthings; he is crammed with sugar candies and almost "killed with kindness," and he passes from school to school, petted and flattered. He becomes arrogant and self-conceited, abuses his teachers, and carries everything with a high hand. He knows nothing of the real value of money, having never earned any; but he knows all about the "golden spoon" business. At college, he invites his poor fellow-students to his room where he "wines and dines" them. He is cajoled and caressed, and called a glorious good fellow, because he is so lavish of his money. He gives his game suppers, drives his fast horses, invites his chums to fetes and parties, determined to have lots of "good times." He spends the night in frolics and debauchery, and leads off his companions with the familiar song, "We won't go home till morning." He gets them to join him in pulling down signs, taking gates from their hinges and throwing them into back yards and horse-ponds. If the police arrest them, he knocks them down, is taken to the lock-up, and joyfully foots the bills.

"Ah! my boys," he cries, "what is the use of being rich, if you can't enjoy yourself?"

He might more truly say, "if you can't make a fool of yourself"; but he is "fast," hates slow things, and don't [sic] "see it." Young men loaded down with other people's money are almost sure to lose all they inherit, and they acquire all sorts of bad habits which, in the majority of cases, ruin them in health, purse, and character. In this country, one generation follows another, and the poor of to-day are rich in the next generation, or the third. Their experience leads them on, and they become rich, and they leave vast riches to their young children. These children, having been reared in luxury, are inexperienced and get poor; and after long experience another generation comes on and gathers up riches again in turn. And thus "history repeats itself," and happy is he who by listening to the experience of others avoids the rocks and shoals on which so many have been wrecked.

LEARN SOMETHING USEFUL.—Every man should make his son or daughter learn some trade or profession, so that in these days of changing fortunes—of being rich to-day and poor to-morrow—they may have something tangible to fall back upon. This provision might save many persons from misery, who by some unexpected turn of fortune have lost all their means.

LET HOPE PREDOMINATE, BUT BE NOT TOO VISIONARY.—Many persons are always kept poor, because they are too visionary. Every project looks to them like certain success, and therefore they keep changing from one business to another, always in hot water, always "under the harrow." The plan of "counting the chickens before they are hatched" is an error of ancient date, but it does not seem to improve by age.

DO NOT SCATTER YOUR POWERS.—Engage in one kind of business only, and stick to it faithfully until you succeed, or until your experience shows that you should abandon it. A constant hammering on one nail will generally drive it home at last, so that it can be clinched. When a man's undivided attention is centered on one object, his mind will constantly be suggesting improvements of value, which would escape him if his brain was occupied by a dozen different subjects at once. Many a fortune has slipped through a man's fingers because he was engaging in too many occupations at a time. There is good sense in the old caution against having too many irons in the fire at once.

BE SYSTEMATIC.—Men should be systematic in their business. A person who does business by rule, having a time and place for everything, doing his work promptly, will accomplish twice as much and with half the trouble of him who does it carelessly and slipshod. By introducing system into all your transactions, doing one thing at a time, always meeting appointments with punctuality, you find leisure for pastime and recreation; whereas the man who only half does one thing, and then turns to something else and half does that, will have his business at loose ends, and will never know when his day's work is done, for it never will be done. Of course there is a limit to all these rules. We must try to preserve the happy medium, for there is such a thing as being too systematic. There are men and women, for instance, who put away things so carefully that they can never find them again. It is too much like the "red tape" formality at Washington, and Mr. Dickens' "Circumlocution Office"—all theory and no result.

When the Astor House was first started in New York City, it was undoubtedly the best hotel in the country. The proprietors had learned a good deal in Europe regarding hotels, and the landlords were proud of the rigid system which pervaded every department of their great establishment. When twelve o'clock at night had arrived and there were a number of guests around, one of the proprietors would say, "Touch that bell, John"; and in two minutes sixty servants with a water bucket in each hand, would present themselves in the hall. "This," said the landlord, addressing his guests, "is our fire bell; it will show you we are quite safe here; we do everything systematically." This was before the Croton water was introduced into the city. But they sometimes carried their system too far. On one occasion when the hotel was thronged with guests, one of the waiters was suddenly indisposed, and although there were fifty waiters in the hotel, the landlord thought he must have his full complement, or his "system" would be interfered with. Just before dinner time he rushed down stairs and said, "There must be another waiter, I am one waiter short, what can I do?" He happened to see "Boots" the Irishman. "Pat," said he, "wash your hands and face; take that white apron and come into the dining-room in five minutes." Presently Pat appeared as required, and the proprietor said: "Now, Pat, you must stand behind these two chairs and wait on the gentlemen who will occupy them; did you ever act as a waiter?"

"I know all about it sure, but I never did it."

Like the Irish pilot, on one occasion when the captain, thinking he was considerably out of his course, asked, "Are you certain you understand what you are doing?"

Pat replied, "Sure and I knows every rock in the channel."

That moment "bang" thumped the vessel against a rock.

"Ah! be jabers, and that is one of 'em," continued the pilot. But to return to the dining-room. "Pat," said the landlord, "here we do everything systematically. You must first give the gentlemen each a plate of soup, and when they finish that, ask them what they will have next."

Pat replied, "Ah! an' I understand parfectly the vartues of shystem."

Very soon in came the guests. The plates of soup were placed before them. One of Pat's two gentlemen ate his soup, the other did not care for it. He said, "Waiter, take this plate away and bring me some fish." Pat looked at the untasted plate of soup, and remembering the injunctions of the landlord in regard to "system," replied.

"Not till ye have ate yer supe!"

Of course that was carrying "system" entirely too far.

READ THE NEWSPAPERS.—Always take a trustworthy newspaper and thus keep thoroughly posted in regard to the transactions of the world. He who is without a newspaper is cut off from his species. . . .

BEWARE OF "OUTSIDE OPERATIONS."—We sometimes see men who have obtained fortunes, suddenly become poor. In many cases this arises from intemperance, and often from gaming and other bad habits. Frequently it occurs because a man has been engaged in "outside operations" of some sort. When he gets rich in his legitimate business, he is told of a grand speculation where he can make a score of thousands. He is constantly flattered by his friends, who tell him that he is born lucky, that everything he touches turns into gold. Now if he forgets that his economical habits, his rectitude of conduct, and a personal attention to a business which he understood, caused his success in life, he will listen to the siren voices. He says:

"I will put in twenty thousand dollars. I have been lucky, and my good luck will soon bring me back sixty thousand dollars."

A few days elapse and it is discovered he must put in ten thousand dollars more; soon after he is told it is all right, but certain matters not foreseen require an advance of twenty thousand dollars more, which will bring him a rich harvest; but before the time comes around to realize, the bubble bursts, he loses all he is possessed of, and then he learns what he ought to have known at the first, that however successful a man may be in his own business, if he turns from that and engages in a business which he don't [sic] understand he is like Samson when shorn of his locks—his strength has departed, and he becomes like other men.

If a man has plenty of money, he ought to invest something in everything that appears to promise success and that will probably benefit mankind; but let the sums thus invested be moderate in amount, and never let a man foolishly jeopardize a fortune that he has earned in a legitimate way, by investing it in things in which he has had no experience.

DON'T INDORSE WITHOUT SECURITY. . . .

ADVERTISE YOUR BUSINESS. . . .

BE POLITE AND KIND TO YOUR CUSTOMERS.—Politeness and civility are the best capital ever invested in business. Large stores, gilt signs, flaming advertisements, will all prove unavailing if you or your employees treat your patrons abruptly. The truth is, the more kind and liberal a man is, the more generous will be the patronage bestowed upon him. "Like begets like." The man who gives the greatest amount of goods of a corresponding quality for the least sum (still reserving to himself a profit) will generally succeed best in the long run. This brings us to the golden rule, "As ye would that men should do to you, do ye also to them"; and they will do better by you than if you always treated them as if you wanted to get the most you could out of them for the least return. Men who drive sharp bargains with their customers, acting as if they never expected to see them again, will not be mistaken. They never will see them again as customers. People don't like to pay and get kicked also.

One of the ushers in my Museum once told me he intended to whip a man who was in the lecture room as soon as he came out.

"What for?" I required.

"Because he said I was no gentleman," replied the usher.

"Never mind," I replied, "he pays for that, and you will not convince him you are a gentleman by whipping him. I cannot afford to lose a customer. If you whip him, he will never visit the Museum again, and he will induce friends to go with him to other places of amusement instead of this, and thus, you see, I should be a serious loser."

"But he insulted me," muttered the usher.

"Exactly," I replied, "and if he owned the Museum, and you had paid him for the privilege of visiting it, and he had then insulted you, there might be some reason in your resenting it, but in this instance he is the man who pays, while we receive, and you must, therefore, put up with his bad manners."

My usher laughingly remarked, that this was undoubtedly the true policy, but he added that he should not object to an increase of salary if he was expected to be abused in order to promote my interests.

BE CHARITABLE.—Of course men should be charitable, because it is

a duty and a pleasure. But even as a matter of policy, if you possess
no higher incentive, you will find that the liberal man will command
patronage, while the sordid, uncharitable miser will be avoided. . . .

The best kind of charity is to help those who are willing to help
themselves. Promiscuous almsgiving, without inquiring into the worthiness of the applicant, is bad in every sense. But to search out and quietly
assist those who are struggling for themselves, is the kind that "scat-
tereth and yet increaseth." But don't fall into the idea that some persons
practise, of giving a prayer instead of a potatoe, and a benediction
instead of bread, to the hungry. It is easier to make Christians with full
stomachs than empty.

DON'T BLAB.—Some men have a foolish habit of telling their business secrets. If they make money they like to tell their neighbors how it
was done. Nothing is gained by this, and ofttimes much is lost. Say
nothing about your profits, your hopes, your expectations, your intentions. And this should apply to letters as well as to conversation.
Goethe made Mephistopheles say: "Never write a letter nor destroy
one." Business men must write letters, but they should be careful what
they put in them. If you are losing money, be specially cautious and not
tell of it, or you will lose your reputation.

PRESERVE YOUR INTEGRITY.—It is more precious than diamonds or
rubies. The old miser said to his sons: "Get money; get it honestly,
if you can, but get money." This advice was not only atrociously wicked,
but it was the very essence of stupidity. It was as much as to say, "If
you find it difficult to obtain money honestly, you can easily get it
dishonestly. Get it in that way." Poor fool, not to know that the most
difficult thing in life is to make money dishonestly; not to know that
our prisons are full of men who attempted to follow this advice; not
to understand that no man can be dishonest without soon being found
out, and that when his lack of principle is discovered, nearly every
avenue to success is closed against him forever. The public very properly
shun all whose integrity is doubted. No matter how polite and pleasant
and accommodating a man may be, none of us dare to deal with him
if we suspect "false weights and measures." Strict honesty not only lies
at the foundation of all success in life financially, but in every other
respect. Uncompromising integrity of character is invaluable. It secures to its possessor a peace and joy which cannot be attained without
it—which no amount of money, or houses and lands can purchase. A
man who is known to be strictly honest, may be ever so poor, but he has
the purses of all the community at his disposal;—for all know that if
he promises to return what he borrows, he will never disappoint
them. As a mere matter of selfishness, therefore, if a man had no higher
motive for being honest, all will find that the maxim of Dr. Franklin
can never fail to be true, that "honesty is the best policy."

To get rich, is not always equivalent to being successful. "There are many rich poor men," while there are many others, honest and devout men and women, who have never possessed so much money as some rich persons squander in a week, but who are nevertheless really richer and happier than any man can ever be while he is a transgressor of the higher laws of his being.

The inordinate love of money, no doubt, may be and is "the root of all evil," but money itself, when properly used, is not only a "handy thing to have in the house," but affords the gratification of blessing our race by enabling its possessor to enlarge the scope of human happiness and human influence. The desire for wealth is nearly universal, and none can say it is not laudable, provided the possessor of it accepts its responsibilities, and uses it as a friend to humanity.

The history of money-getting, which is commerce, is a history of civilization, and wherever trade has flourished most, there, too, have art and science produced the noblest fruits. In fact, as a general thing, money-getters are the benefactors of our race. To them, in a great measure, are we indebted for our institutions of learning and of art, our academies, colleges, and churches. It is no argument against the desire for, or the possession of wealth, to say that there are sometimes misers who hoard money only for the sake of hoarding, and who have no higher aspiration than to grasp everything which comes within their reach. As we have sometimes hypocrites in religion, and demagogues in politics, so there are occasionally misers among money-getters. These, however, are only exceptions to the general rule. But when, in this country, we find such a nuisance and stumbling block as a miser, we remember with gratitude that in America we have no laws of primogeniture, and that in the due course of nature the time will come when the hoarded dust will be scattered for the benefit of mankind. To all men and women, therefore, do I conscientiously say, make money honestly, and not otherwise, for Shakespeare has truly said, "He that wants money, means, and content, is without three good friends."

—

Horatio Alger

Struggling Upward,
or Luke Larkin's Luck

Luck and Pluck, Bound to Rise, Brave and Bold, *and* Sink or Swim
*were representative of the 135 titles in the "rags-to-riches" saga that
Horatio Alger (1834-1899) contrived to keep pace with the insatiable
demand of some fifty million readers. In theme and style,* Struggling
Upward *(in this condensed version) neatly conveys the saga of every-
boy.* [*Horatio Alger,* Struggling Upward; or Luke Larkin's Luck, New
York, 1890, passim. *(Serialized in* Golden Argosy, 1886, "Way to Success Series.")]

One Saturday afternoon in January a lively and animated group of boys
were gathered on the western side of a large pond in the village of
Groveton. Prominent among them was a tall, pleasant-looking young
man of twenty-two, the teacher of the Center Grammar School, Frederic
Hooper, A.B., a recent graduate of Yale College. Evidently there was
something of importance on foot. What it was may be learned from
the words of the teacher.

"Now, boys," he said, holding in his hand a Waterbury watch, of
neat pattern, "I offer this watch as a prize to the boy who will skate
across the pond and back in the least time. You will all start together,
at a given signal, and make your way to the mark which I have placed
at the western end of the lake, skate around it, and return to this point.
Do you fully understand?"

"Yes, sir!" exclaimed the boys, unanimously.

Before proceeding, it may be well to refer more particularly to some of the boys who were to engage in the contest.

First, in his own estimation, came Randolph Duncan, son of Prince Duncan, president of the Groveton Bank, and a prominent town official. Prince Duncan was supposed to be a rich man, and lived in a style quite beyond that of his neighbors. Randolph was his only son, a boy of sixteen, and felt that in social position and blue blood he was without a peer in the village. He was a tall, athletic boy, and disposed to act the part of a boss among the Groveton boys.

Next came a boy similar in age and physical strength, but in other respects, very different. . . . This was Luke Larkin, the son of a carpenter's widow, living on narrow means, and so compelled to exercise the strictest economy. Luke . . . filled the position of janitor at the school which he attended, sweeping out twice a week and making the fires. He had a pleasant expression, and a bright, resolute look, a warm heart, and a clear intellect, and was probably, in spite of his poverty, the most popular boy in Groveton. In this respect he was the opposite of Randolph Duncan, whose assumption of superiority and desire to "boss" the other boys prevented him from having any real friends.

These two boys were looked upon as the chief contestants for the prize. . . .

"I think Luke will get the watch," said Fred Acken, a younger boy.

"I don't know about that," said Tom Harper. "Randolph skates just as well, and he has a pair of club skates. His father sent to New York for them last week. . . ."

"Of course that gives him the advantage," said Percy Hall. "Look at Luke's old-fashioned wooden skates!"

"It's a pity Luke hasn't a better pair," said Harry Wright. "I don't think the contest is a fair one. Luke ought to have an allowance of twenty rods to make up for the difference in skates."

"He wouldn't accept it," said Linton Tomkins, the son of a manufacturer in Groveton, who was an intimate friend of Luke, and preferred to associate with him, though Randolph had made advances toward intimacy, Linton being the only boy in the village whom he regarded as his social equal. "I offered him my club skates, but he said he would take the chances with his own."

Linton was the only boy who had a pair of skates equal to Randolph's. He, too, was a contestant, but being three years younger . . . , had no expectation of rivaling them. . . .

"Are you ready, boys?" asked Mr. Hooper.

Most of the boys responded promptly in the affirmative; but Luke, who had been tightening his straps, said quickly: "I am not ready, Mr. Hooper. My strap has broken!"

"Indeed, Luke, I'm sorry to hear it," said the teacher, approaching and examining the fracture. "As matters stand, you can't skate."

. . . "The prize is yours now," whispered Tom [to Randolph].

"It was before," answered Randolph, conceitedly.

Poor Luke looked disappointed. He knew that he had at least an even chance of winning, and he wanted the watch. Several of his friends of his own age had watches, and this seemed, in his circumstances, the only chance of securing one. . . .

"It's a pity you shouldn't skate, Luke," said Mr. Hooper, in a tone of sympathy. "You are one of the best skaters, and had an excellent chance of winning the prize. Is there any boy willing to lend Luke his skates?"

. . . "You may use my skates, Luke," said Linton Tomkins. "I think they will fit you."

"You are very kind, Linton," said Luke, "but that will keep you out of the race."

"I stand no chance of winning," said Linton, "and I will do my skating afterward."

"I don't think that's fair," said Randolph, with a frown. "Each boy ought to use his own skates."

"There is nothing unfair about it," said the teacher, "except that Luke is placed at a disadvantage in using a pair of skates he is unaccustomed to."

"You are very kind, Linny," said Luke, regarding his friend affectionately. "I won't soon forget it." . . .

*   *   *

Tom Harper [was] not wholly disinterested in [his] championship of Randolph. [He was a] very ordinary skater, and stood no chance of winning the match [himself].

"I suppose, Randolph," he said, "if you win the watch you will give it to me?"

"Why should I?" asked Rondolph, surveying Tom with a cold glance.

"You've got a nice silver watch yourself, you know."

"I might like to have two watches."

"You'll have the ten dollars your father promised you."

"What if I have? What claim have you on me?"

Tom drew near and whispered something in Randolph's ear.

"I'll see about it," said Randolph, nodding.

"Are you ready?" asked the teacher, once more.

"Aye, aye!" responded the boys.

The boys darted off like arrows from a bow. Luke made a late start, but before they were half across the pond he was even with Randolph, and both were leading. Randolph looked sidewise, and shut his mouth tight as he saw his hated rival on equal terms with him and threatening to pass him. It would be humiliating in the extreme, he thought, to be beaten by such a boy. But beaten he seemed likely to be, for Luke was soon a rod in advance and slowly gaining. . . .

A branch of a tree had been placed at the western end of the pond, and this was the mark around which the boys were to skate. Luke made the circuit first, Randolph being about half a dozen rods behind. After him came the rest of the boys in procession, with one exception. This exception was Tom Harper, who apparently gave up the contest when half-way across, and began skating about, here and there, apparently waiting for his companions to return.

"Tom Harper has given up his chance," said Linton to the teacher.

"So it seems," replied Mr. Hooper, "but he probably had no expectation of succeeding."

Indeed, it seemed strange that Tom should have given up so quickly. It soon appeared that it was not caprice, but that he had an object in view, and that a very discreditable one.

He waited till the boys were on their way back. By this time Luke was some eight rods in advance of his leading competitor. Then Tom began to be on the alert. As Luke came swinging on to victory he suddenly placed himself in his way. Luke's speed was so great that he could not check himself. He came into collision with Tom, and in an instant both were prostrate. Tom, however, got the worst of it. He was thrown violently backward, falling on the back of his head, and lay stunned and motionless on the ice. Luke fell over him, but was scarcely hurt at all. He was up again in an instant, and might have kept the lead, but instead he got down on his knees beside Tom and asked anxiously: "Are you much hurt, Tom?"

Tom didn't immediately answer, but lay breathing heavily, with his eyes still closed.

Meanwhile, Randolph, with a smile of triumph, swept on to his now assured victory. Most of the boys, however, stopped and gathered around Luke and Tom.

This accident had been watched with interest and surprise from the starting-point.

"Tom must be a good deal hurt," said Linton. "What could possibly have made him get in Luke's way?"

"I don't know," said the teacher, slowly; "it looks strange."

"It almost seemed as if he got in the way on purpose," Linton continued.

"He is a friend of Randolph Duncan, is he not?" asked the teacher, abruptly. . . .

A minute more, and Randolph swept into the presence of the teacher.

"I believe I have won?" he said, with a smile of gratification. . . .

"You have come in first," said the teacher coldly.

"Luke was considerably ahead when he ran into Tom," suggested Linton.

"That's not my lookout," said Randolph, shrugging his shoulders. "The point is that I have come in first."

"Tom Harper is a friend of yours, is he not?" asked the teacher.

"Oh, yes!" answered Randolph, indifferently.

"He seems to be a good deal hurt. It was very strange that he got in Luke's way."

"So it was," said Randolph, without betraying much interest. . . .

"What made you get in my way, Tom?" asked Luke, puzzled.

"I don't know," answered Tom, sullenly.

"Are you much hurt?"

"I think my skull must be fractured," moaned Tom.

"Oh, not so bad as that," said Luke, cheerfully. "I've fallen on my head myself, but I got over it."

"You didn't fall as hard as I did," groaned Tom.

"No, I presume not; but heads are hard, and I guess you'll be all right in a few days."

Tom had certainly been severely hurt. There was a swelling on the back of his head almost as large as a hen's egg.

"You've lost the watch, Luke," said Frank Acken. "Randolph has got in first."

"Yes, I supposed he would," answered Luke quietly.

"It is true," said the teacher, slowly. "Randolph has won the race."

Randolph's face lighted up with exultation.

"But it is also evident," continued Mr. Hooper, "that he would not have succeeded but for the unfortunate collision between Luke Larkin and Tom Harper."

Here some of Luke's friends brightened up.

"I don't know about that," said Randolph. "At any rate, I came in first."

"I watched the race closely," said the teacher, "and I have no doubt on the subject. Luke had so great a lead that he would surely have won the race."

"But he didn't," persisted Randolph, doggedly.

"He did not, as we all know. It is also clear that had he not stopped to ascertain the extent of Tom's injuries he still might have won."

"That's so!" said half a dozen boys.

"Therefore I cannot accept the result as indicating the superiority of the successful contestant."

"I think I am entitled to the prize," said Randolph.

"I concede that; but, under the circumstances, I suggest to you that it would be graceful and proper to waive your claim and try the race over again."

The boys applauded, with one or two exceptions.

"I won't consent to that, Mr. Hooper," said Randolph, frowning. "I've won the prize fairly, and I want it."

"I am quite willing Randolph should have it, sir," said Luke. "I think I should have won it if I had not stopped with Tom, but that doesn't affect the matter one way or the other. Randolph came in first, as he says, and I think he is entitled to the watch."

"Then," said Mr. Hooper, gravely, "there is nothing more to be said. Randolph, come forward and receive the prize. . . ."

"I am sorry you have lost the watch, Luke," said the teacher, after Randolph's departure. "You will have to be satisfied with deserving it."

"I am reconciled to the disappointment, sir," answered Luke. "I can get along for the present without a watch."

Nevertheless, Luke did feel disappointed. He had fully expected to have the watch to carry home and display to his mother. As it was, he was in no hurry to go home, but remained for two hours skating with the other boys. He used his friend Linton's skates, Linton having an engagement which prevented his remaining.

Luke returns "to the little cottage" which he called home to tell his mother, "a pleasant woman of middle age," that Randolph won the watch. Even here, Luke shows the good sense of realizing that Tom's "bunch on the head almost as large as a hen's egg" is the only reward he can expect for his foul play in Randolph's service. But like all long-suffering devoted mothers, Mrs. Larkin finds no sympathy in her heart for Tom, and the dialogue between mother and son ends with Luke, wholesome in spirit and in body, announcing: "However, mother, watch or no watch, I've got a good appetite. I shall be ready when supper is."

After supper and his completion of the evening chores, Luke obliges his mother and takes a dress which she has finished sewing to one of Mrs. Larkin's customers. This "commonplace errand" is to begin a new chapter in Luke's life.

Of course, Luke had no thought of this when he set out. To him it had been a marked day on account of the skating match, but this had turned out a disappointment. He accomplished his errand, which occupied a considerable time, and then set out on his return. It was half-past eight, but the moon had risen and diffused a mild radiance over the landscape. Luke thought he would shorten his homeward way by taking a path through the woods. It was not over a quarter of a mile, but would shorten the distance by as much more. The trees were not close together, so that it was light enough to see. Luke had nearly reached the edge of the wood, when he overtook a tall man, a stranger in the neighborhood, who carried in his hand a tin box. Turning, he eyed Luke sharply.

"Boy, what's your name?" he asked.

"Luke Larkin," our hero answered, in surprise.

"Where do you live?"

"In the village yonder."

"Will you do me a favor?"

"What is it, sir?"

"Take this tin box and carry it to your home. Keep it under lock and key till I call for it."

"Yes, sir, I can do that. But how shall I know you again?"

"Take a good look at me, that you may remember me."

"I think I shall know you again, but hadn't you better give me a name?"

"Well, perhaps so," answered the other, after a moment's thought. "You may call me Roland Reed. Will you remember?"

"Yes, sir."

"I am obliged to leave this neighborhood at once, and can't conveniently carry the box," explained the stranger. "Here's something for your trouble."

Luke was about to say that he required no money, when it occurred to him that he had no right to refuse, since money was so scarce at home. He took the tin box and thrust the bank-bill into his vest pocket. He wondered how much it was, but it was too dark to distinguish.

"Good night!" said Luke, as the stranger turned away.

"Good night!" answered his new acquaintance, abruptly.

If Luke could have foreseen the immediate consequences of this apparently simple act, and the position in which it would soon place him, he would certainly have refused to take charge of the box. And yet, in so doing it might have happened that he had made a mistake. The consequences of even our simple acts are oftentimes far-reaching and beyond the power of human wisdom to know.

Luke thought little of this as, with the box under his arm, he trudged homeward.

"What have you there, Luke?" asked Mrs. Larkin as Luke entered the little sitting-room with the tin box under his arm.

"I met a man on my way home, who asked me to keep it for him."

"Do you know the man?" asked his mother, in surprise.

"No," answered Luke.

"It seems very singular. What did he say?"

"He said that he was obliged to leave the neighborhood at once and could not conveniently carry the box."

"Do you think it contains anything of value?"

"Yes, mother. It is like the boxes rich men have to hold their stocks and bonds. I was at the bank one day, and saw a gentleman bring in one to deposit in the safe."

"I can't understand that at all, Luke. You say you did not know this man?"

"I never met him before."

"And, of course, he does not know you?"

"No, he asked my name."

"Yet he put what may be valuable property in your possession."

"I think," said Luke, shrewdly, "he had no one else to trust it to. Besides, a country boy wouldn't be very likely to make use of stocks and bonds."

"No, that is true. I suppose the tin box is locked?"

"Yes, mother. The owner—he says his name is Roland Reed—wants it put under lock and key."

"I can lock it up in my trunk, Luke."

"I think that will be a good idea."

"I hope he will pay you for your trouble when he takes away the tin box."

"He has already; I forgot to mention it," and Luke drew from his vest pocket the bank-note he had thrust in as soon as received. "Why, it's a ten-dollar bill!" he exclaimed. "I wonder whether he knew he was giving me as much?"

"I presume so, Luke," said his mother, brightening up. "You are in luck!"

"Take it, mother. You will find a use for it."

"But Luke, this money is yours."

"No, it is yours, for you are going to take care of the box."

*   *   *

"I have been thinking, Luke," said his mother, at the breakfast-table, "that I should like to have you buy a Waterbury watch out of this money. It will only cost three dollars and a half, and that is only one-third."

"Thank you, mother, but I can get along without the watch. I cared for it chiefly because it was to be a prize given to the best skater. All the boys know that I would have won but for the accident, and that satisfies me."

"I should like you to have a watch, Luke."

"There is another objection, mother. I don't want any one to know about the box or the money. If it were known that we had so much property in the house, some attempt might be made to rob us."

"That is true, Luke. But I hope it won't be long before you have a watch of your own."

When Luke was walking, after breakfast, he met Randolph Duncan, with a chain attached to the prize watch ostentatiously displayed on the outside of his vest. He smiled complacently, and rather triumphantly, when he met Luke. But Luke looked neither depressed nor angry.

"I hope your watch keeps good time, Randolph," he said.

"Yes; it hasn't varied a minute so far. I think it will keep as good time as my silver watch."

"You are fortunate to have two watches."

"My father has promised me a gold watch when I am eighteen,"
said Randolph, pompously.

"I don't know if I shall have any watch at all when I am eighteen."

"Oh well, you are a poor boy. It doesn't matter to you."

"I don't know about that, Randolph. Time is likely to be of as much
importance to a poor boy as to a rich boy."

"Oh, ah! yes, of course, but a poor boy isn't expected to wear a
watch."

Here the conversation ended. Luke walked on with an amused smile
on his face.

"I wonder how it would seem to be as complacent and self-satisfied
as Randolph?" he thought. "On the whole, I would rather be as I am."

*Luke's even temper and amazing capacity for tolerance immediately
are rewarded. Florence Grant, "considered by many the prettiest girl
in Groveton," invites him to her birthday party Thursday evening
next.*

*With only one good suit to wear, and that short in the sleeves and
legs, Luke momentarily is downhearted by his appearance. The evening
of the party arrives, and Luke not only compensates for appearance
by his goodness, but has been taught the quadrille by his friend Linton.
He distinguishes himself on the dance floor and arouses the ire of
Randolph, jealous of this janitor putting on false airs, as he puts it.*

*The birthday festivities end, but once more the action is pushed
forward. On the way home Luke again is confronted by the tall stranger
who calls himself Roland Reed and who asks only, "Is the tin box
safe?" Luke muses on these strange doings and for the first time
wonders "who can he be?" and "why should he have trusted a complete
stranger—and a boy?"*

*Thus, what begins as a Hans Brinker skating story, in its zest and
wholesomeness worthy of inspiring the boy scouts, soon becomes en-
crusted with Alger intrigue, the vehicle for making possible the author's
poor boy's chronicle.*

*The plot thickens. Miss Sprague, village gossip, visits Mrs. Larkin
and spies the tin box in an open trunk. Mrs. Larkin's haste to close
the trunk only provokes Melinda Sprague's suspicion that something
is cooking. Randolph, in his jealousy of Luke, urges his father, a
school board official, to replace Luke with another lad as janitor. Thus
Luke loses his $1 weekly income.*

*Soon after, the news breaks that the Groveton Bank has been robbed
and that the stolen $30-40,000 in U.S. bonds was contained in a tin
box. Miss Sprague immediately fulfills her duty and reports to Squire
Duncan that she saw a suspicious-looking tin box in Mrs. Larkin's
trunk. Squire Duncan and the bank directors issue a search warrant
for the Larkin cottage. Luke and his mother are confronted that evening,*

*the one hitch being that Luke does not have the key to open the box.
Nonetheless, caution wins out and Luke is arrested on a charge of
robbing the bank. Until the day of the trial he is put in custody of
Constable Perkins. Nonplussed by the charge against him, Luke like a
good boy chops wood voluntarily for the constable.*

*Ten o'clock the morning of the trial arrives. Melinda Sprague testi-
fies that she saw a tin box in Widow Larkin's trunk. Other witnesses
protest in Luke's behalf. Luke is called to the stand and tells again
his "straightforward story." "A wild tale," Squire Duncan remonstrates,
and all seems lost until . . .*

" . . . A tall, dark-complexioned stranger pushed his way into the
courtroom. He advanced quickly to the front.

"I heard my name called," he said. "There is no occasion to doubt
my existence. I am Roland Reed!"

The effect of Roland Reed's sudden appearance in the courtroom,
close upon the doubt expressed as to his existence, was electric. Every
head was turned, and every one present looked with eager curiosity
at the mysterious stranger. They saw a dark-complexioned, slender, but
wiry man, above the middle height, with a pair of keen black eyes
scanning, not without sarcastic amusement, the faces turned toward him.

Luke recognized him at once.

"Thank God!" he ejaculated, with a feeling of intense relief. "Now
my innocence will be made known."

Squire Duncan was quite taken aback. His face betrayed his surprise and disappointment.

"I don't know you," he said, after a pause.

"Perhaps not, Mr. Duncan," answered the stranger, in a significant
tone, "but I know you."

"Were you the man who gave this tin box to the defendant?"

"Wouldn't it be well, since this is a court, to swear me as a witness?" asked Roland Reed, quietly.

"Of course, of course," said the squire, rather annoyed to be reminded of his duty by this stranger.

This being done, Mr. Beane questioned the witness in the interest
of his client.

"Do you know anything about the tin box found in the possession
of Luke Larkin?" he asked.

"Yes, sir."

"Did you commit it to his charge for safe-keeping?"

"I did."

"Were you previously acquainted with Luke?"

"I was not."

"Was it not a rather singular proceeding to commit what is presumably of considerable value to an unknown boy?"

"It would generally be considered so, but I do many strange things. I had seen the boy by daylight, though he had never seen me, and I was sure I could trust him."

"Why, if you desired a place of safe-keeping for your box, did you not select the bank vaults?"

Roland Reed laughed, and glanced at the presiding justice.

"It might have been stolen," he said.

"Does the box contain documents of value?"

"The contents are valuable to me, at any rate.'

"Mr. Beane," said Squire Duncan, irritably, "I think you are treating the witness too indulgently. I believe this box to be the one taken from the bank."

"You heard the remark of the justice," said the lawyer. "Is this the box taken from the bank?"

"It is not," answered the witness, contemptuously, "and no one knows this better than Mr. Duncan."

The justice flushed angrily.

"You are impertinent, witness," he said. "It is all very well to claim this box as yours, but I shall require you to prove ownership."

"I am ready to do so," said Roland Reed, quietly. "Is that the box on the table?"

"It is."

"Has it been opened?"

"No; the key has disappeared from the bank."

"The key is in the hands of the owner, where it properly belongs. With the permission of the court, I will open the box."

"I object," said Squire Duncan, quickly.

"Permit me to say that your refusal is extraordinary," said Mr. Beane, pointedly. "You ask the witness to prove property, and then decline to allow him to do so."

Squire Duncan, who saw that he had been betrayed into a piece of folly, said sullenly: "I don't agree with you, Mr. Beane, but I withdraw my objection. The witness may come forward and open the box, if he can."

Roland Reed bowed slightly, advanced to the table, took a bunch of keys from his pocket, and inserting one of the smallest in the lock easily opened the box.

Those who were near enough, including the justice, craned their necks forward to look into the box.

The box contained papers, certificates of stock, apparently, and a couple of missing bank-books.

"The box missing from the vault contained government bonds, as I understand, Squire Duncan?" said the lawyer.

"Yes," answered the justice, reluctantly.

"Are there any government bonds in the box, Mr. Reed?"

"You can see for yourself, sir."

The manner of the witness toward the lawyer was courteous, though in the tone in which he addressed the court there had been a scarcely veiled contempt.

"I submit, then, that my young client has been guilty of no wrong. He accepted the custody of the box from the rightful owner, and this he had a clear right to do."

"How do you know that the witness is the rightful owner of the box?" demanded the justice, in a cross tone. "He may have stolen it from some other quarter."

"There is not a shadow of evidence of this," said the lawyer, in a tone of rebuke.

"I am not sure but that he ought to be held."

"You will hold me at your peril, Mr. Duncan," said the witness, in clear, resolute tones. "I have a clear comprehension of my rights, and I do not propose to have them infringed."

Squire Duncan bit his lips. He had only a smattering of law, but he knew that the witness was right, and that he had been betrayed by temper, into making a discreditable exhibition of himself.

"I demand that you treat me with proper respect," he said angrily.

"I am ready to do that," answered the witness, in a tone whose meaning more than one understood. It was not an apology calculated to soothe the ruffled pride of the justice.

"I call for the discharge of my young client, Squire Duncan," said the lawyer. "The case against him, as I hardly need say, has utterly failed."

"He is discharged," said the justice, unwillingly.

Instantly, Luke's friends surrounded him and began to shower congratulations upon him. Among them was Roland Reed.

"My young friend," he said, "I am sincerely sorry that by any act of mine I have brought anxiety and trouble upon you. But I can't understand how the fact that you had the box in your possession became known."

This was explained to him.

"I have a proposal to make to you and your mother," said Roland Reed, "and with your permission I will acompany you home."

"We shall be glad to have you, sir," said Mrs. Larkin, cordially.

Roland Reed proves himself to be the first of the benefactors responsible for Luke's rise in the world, as we shall see.

Luke, his mother, and Reed return to the Larkin cottage, where Reed makes the first of a series of proposals that begin the reversal of the Larkin fortune, but not without causing a series of typical Alger adventures. First, Reed proposes that Luke accompany him to New

*York City so that they may bring his eight-year-old daughter as a paid
boarder to the sweet home of the good widow Larkin.*

*Luke accompanies Reed on this mission. On the train, Luke tells
Reed that his mother has a $300 mortgage on her cottage, which re-
cently was purchased by Squire Duncan. Duncan offered to buy the
cottage outright, rather than just the mortgage, but Reed encourages
Luke in Luke's conviction that under no circumstances should he sell
to Duncan.*

*Before picking up his daughter, Reed outfits Luke with two new
suits and, in the tradition of virtue rewarded, buys him a silver watch,
"superior even to a Waterbury."*

*En route to Groveton, business talk continues. Conversation turns
to the robbery of the bonds. Luke informs Reed that a Mr. Armstrong
presently traveling in Europe owned the bonds and left them in the
bank at Squire Duncan's suggestion. They were not registered, as Reed
explains to Luke, thus enabling the thief to dispose of them without a
formal transfer from the owner. Reed muses on the situation and says,
"I think Prince Duncan knows more about how those bonds were
spirited away than is suspected." Thus, new interest is aroused over
Duncan's involvement.*

*Reed switches the conversation and offers Luke a job at thirty cents
an hour as bookkeeper for him, a job which Luke accepts with pleasure.*

*The scene then shifts to Squire Duncan opening his morning mail.
Duncan, dismayed at having received a letter from John Armstrong,
owner of the stolen bonds, anxiously searches for a way out of his guilt.
"Drops of perspiration gathered on the brow of Prince Duncan as he
read this letter. What would Mr. Armstrong say when he learned that
the box had mysteriously disappeared? . . . He would ask . . . why
Mr. Duncan had not informed him of the loss by cable, and no satisfactory explanation could be given."*

*Trouble is just beginning for the first citizen of Groveton, U.S.A.
The second letter in Squire Duncan's morning mail is from his Wall
Street broker informing him that his Erie stocks bought on margin have
dropped and that he will either have to pay more or sell out.*

"What am I to do?" Prince Duncan asked himself anxiously. "I
must send money to the brokers, or they will sell me out, and I shall
meet with a heavy loss."

After a little thought he wrote a letter enclosing a check, but dated
it two days ahead.

"They will think it a mistake," he thought, "and it will give me
time to turn around. Now for money to meet the check when it arrives."

Prince Duncan went up-stairs, and, locking the door of his chamber,
opened a large trunk in one corner of the room. From under a pile of

clothing he took out a tin box, and with hands that trembled with excitement he extracted therefrom a dozen government bonds. One was for ten thousand dollars, one for five, and the remainder were for one thousand dollars each.

"If they were only sold, and the money deposited in the bank to my credit," he thought. "I am almost sorry I started in this thing. The risk is very great, but—but I must have money."

At this moment some one tried the door.

Prince Duncan turned pale and the bonds nearly fell from his hands.

"Who's there?" he asked.

"It is I, papa," answered Randolph.

"Then you may go down-stairs again," answered his father angrily. "I don't want to be disturbed."

"Won't you open the door a minute? I just want to ask a question."

"No, I won't. Clear out!" exclaimed the bank president angrily.

"What a frightful temper father has!" thought the discomfited Randolph.

There was nothing for it but to go down-stairs, and he did so in a very discontented frame of mind.

"It seems to me that something is going contrary," said Duncan to himself. "It is clear that it won't do to keep these bonds here any longer. I must take them to New York to-morrow—and raise money on them."

On second thought, tomorrow he decided only to take the five-thousand-dollar bond, and five of the one thousand, fearing that too large a sale at one time might excite suspicion.

Carefully selecting the bonds referred to, he put them away in a capacious pocket, and locking the trunk, went down-stairs again.

"There is still time to take the eleven-o'clock train," he said, consulting his watch. "I must do it."

Seeking his wife, he informed her that he would take the next train for New York.

"Isn't this rather sudden?" she asked, in surprise.

"A little, perhaps, but I have a small matter of business to attend to. Besides, I think the trip will do me good. I am not feeling quite as well as usual."

"I believe I will go, too," said Mrs. Duncan unexpectedly. "I want to make some purchases at Stewart's."

This suggestion was very far from agreeable to her husband.

"Really—I am—" he said, "I must disappoint you. My time will be wholly taken up by matters of business, and I can't go with you."

"You don't need to. I can take care of myself, and we can meet at the depot at four o'clock."

"Besides, I can't supply you with any money for shopping."

"I have enough. I might have liked a little more, but I can make it do."

"Perhaps it will look better if we go in company," thought Prince Duncan. "She needn't be in my way, for we can part at the station."

"Very well, Jane," he said quietly. "If you won't expect me to dance attendance upon you, I withdraw my objections."

The eleven-o'clock train for New York had among its passengers Mr. and Mrs. Duncan.

There was another passenger whom neither of them noticed—a small, insignificant-looking man—who occasionally directed a quick glance at the portly bank president.

Duncan takes the bonds to his New York broker, the office of Sharp & Ketchum, secures a loan on them, and thus hopes to avoid financial failure a while longer. Unknown to Duncan, however, the "small, insignificant-looking man on the train," Tony Denton, owner of the local saloon, observes Duncan on the train. He unfortunately notices the bonds fall from Duncan's pockets, and in his cagey way follows Duncan to the loan office, afterward tucking away for future reference this choice tidbit that Duncan has made a special trip to New York to cash some bonds.

Duncan returns from New York. Armstrong returns from Europe. The dreaded interview takes place. Duncan, trying to squirm through, again accuses Luke of having had something to do with the theft. The more Duncan protests, citing as evidence Luke's new clothes and silver watch purchased for him by Ronald Reed, the more suspicious Armstrong becomes of Duncan. The interview closes with Armstrong saying, "It may be too late to remedy your singular neglect, but I will now take the matter out of your hands."

Armstrong shows himself to be Benefactor Number Two, indispensable to an Alger hero. Luke meets Armstrong by accident, recapitulates the unpleasant story of the box, tells of Roland Reed's friendship, and arouses in Armstrong a desire to help him get ahead in the world.

"*A thoroughly good boy, and a smart boy, too!*" *said Armstrong to himself. "I must see if I can't give him a chance to rise. He seems absolutely reliable."*

This judgment was formed after Armstrong had a chance to state his philosophy in a nutshell to Luke:

"*When I was a boy of thirteen and fourteen I ran around in overalls and bare-footed. But I don't think it did me any harm," the old man added, musingly. "It kept me from squandering money on foolish pleasures, for*

I had none to spend; it made me industrious and self-reliant, and when I obtained employment it made me anxious to please my employer."

Luke, only a short time ago falsely accused of a bank theft, seems to be fulfilling the Alger formula.

"I have two influential friends, now," he said to himself—"Mr. Reed and Mr. Armstrong. On the whole, Luke Larkin, you are in luck, your prospects look decidedly bright, even if you have lost the janitorship."

Armstrong follows his judgment that Reed may be able to help him find the real embezzler and visits Reed in New York. Both confess to a suspicion that Duncan is responsible. Reed also adds, without going into particulars (these being cumbersome to Alger's technique), that at one time Duncan wronged him: "No one in Groveton—no one of his recent associates—knows the real nature of this man as I do."

Reed and Armstrong decide that the only way of proving embezzlement is to trace the numbers on the couponed bonds. Armstrong, unfortunately, has lost his own list, but he remembers that he had a reliable bookkeeper in his employ, who made the purchase for him, and who, if he could be tracked down, would have a duplicate in his possession. To complicate the narrative, Alger makes sure that the clerk in possession of the missing serial numbers on the bonds, one James Harding, has joined a sister living in the West. Thus, a messenger to the West must be found. Luke is appointed.

Our lucky hero sets out on the last of an extraordinary series of adventures that prove once and for all his worthiness of rising from low station to future security and position. These adventures smack of the usual saga of the greenhorn from the country sent on a mission to the wicked city. Luke has been amply provided with money, and is endowed with his own reliability and good sense—but alas, what he lacks is experience, and the warning against being "taken."

Luke's first adventure begins aboard the train for Chicago, his first stop in the search for James Harding. Here, Alger shows what can happen when city sharpy meets Main Street boy scout.

Some half dozen hours before reaching Chicago, a young man of twenty-five, or thereabouts, sauntered along the aisle, and sat down in the vacant seat beside Luke.

"Nice day," he said affably.

"Very nice," responded Luke.

"I suppose you are bound to Chicago?"

"Yes, I expect to stay there awhile."

"Going farther?"

"I can't tell yet."

"Going to school out there?"

"No."

"Perhaps you are traveling for some business firm, though you look pretty young for that."

"No, I'm not a drummer, if that's what you mean. Still, I have a commission from a New York business man."

"A commission—of what kind?" drawled the newcomer.

"It is of a confidential character," said Luke.

"Ha! close-mouthed," thought the young man. "Well, I'll get it out of him after awhile."

He didn't press the question, not wishing to arouse suspicion or mistrust.

"Just so," he replied. "You are right to keep it to yourself, though you wouldn't mind trusting me if you knew me better. Is this your first visit to Chicago?"

"Yes, sir."

"Suppose we exchange cards. This is mine."

He handed Luke a card, bearing this name:

J. MADISON COLEMAN

At the bottom of the card he wrote in pencil, "representing H. B. Claflin & Co."

"Of course you've heard of our firm," he said.

"Certainly."

"I don't have the firm name printed on my card, for Claflin won't allow it. You will notice that I am called for old President Madison. He was an old friend of my grandfather. In fact, grandfather held a prominent office under his administration—collector of the port of New York."

"I have no card with me," responded Luke. "But my name is Luke Larkin."

"Good name. Do you live in New York?"

"No; a few miles in the country."

"And whom do you represent?"

"Myself for the most part," answered Luke, with a smile.

"Good! No one has a better right to. I see there's something in you, Luke."

"You've found it out pretty quick," thought Luke.

"And I hope we will get better acquainted. If you're not permanently employed by this party, whose name you don't give, I will get you into the employ of Claflin & Co., if you would like it."

"Thank you," answered Luke, who thought it quite possible that he might like to obtain a position with so eminent a firm. "How long have you been with them?"

"Ten years—ever since I was of your age," promptly answered Mr. Coleman.

"Is promotion rapid?" Luke asked, with interest.

"Well, that depends on a man's capacity. I have been pushed right along. I went there as a boy, on four dollars a week; now I'm a traveling salesman—drummer as it is called—and I make about four thousand a year."

"That's a fine salary," said Luke, feeling that his new acquaintance must be possessed of extra ability to occupy so desirable a position.

"Yes, but I expect next year to get five thousand—Claflin knows I am worth it, and as he is a liberal man, I guess he will give it sooner than let me go."

"I suppose many do not get on so well, Mr. Coleman."

"I should say so! Now, there is a young fellow went there the same time that I did—his name is Frank Bolton. We were schoolfellows together, and just the same age, that is nearly—he was born in April, and I in May. Well, we began at the same time on the same salary. Now I get sixty dollars a week and he only twelve—and he is glad to get that, too."

"I suppose he hasn't much business capacity."

"That's where you've struck it, Luke. He knows about enough to be clerk in a country store—and I suppose he'll fetch up there some day. You know what that means—selling sugar, and tea, and dried apples to old ladies, and occasionally measuring off a yard of calico, or selling a spool of cotton. If I couldn't do better than that I'd hire out as a farm laborer."

Luke smiled at the enumeration of the duties of a country salesman. It was clear that Mr. Coleman, though he looked city-bred, must at some time in the past have lived in the country.

"Perhaps that is the way I should turn out," he said. "I might not rise any higher than your friend Mr. Bolton."

"Oh yes, you would. You're smart enough, I'll guarantee. You might not get on so fast as I have, for it isn't every young man of twenty-six that can command four thousand dollars a year, but you would rise to a handsome income, I am sure."

"I should be satisfied with two thousand a year at your age."

"I would be willing to guarantee you that," asserted Mr. Coleman, confidently. "By the way, where do you propose to put up in Chicago?"

"I have not decided yet."

"You'd better go with me to the Ottawa House."

"Is it a good house?"

"They'll feed you well there, and only charge two dollars a day."

"Is it centrally located?"

"It isn't as central as the Palmer, or Sherman, or Tremont, but it is convenient to everything."

I ought to say here that I have chosen to give a fictitious name to the hotel designated by Mr. Coleman.

"Come, what do you say?"

"I have no objection," answered Luke, after a slight pause for reflection.

Indeed, it was rather pleasant to him to think that he would have a companion on his first visit to Chicago who was well acquainted with the city, and could serve as his guide. Though he should not feel justified in imparting to Mr. Coleman his special business, he meant to see something of the city, and would find his new friend a pleasant companion.

"That's good," said Coleman, well pleased. "I shall be glad to have your company. I expected to meet a friend on the train, but something must have delayed him, and so I should have been left alone."

"I suppose a part of your time will be given to business?" suggested Luke.

"Yes, but I take things easy; when I work, I work. I can accomplish as much in a couple of hours as many would do in a whole day. You see, I understand my customers. When soft sawder is wanted, I am soft sawder. When I am dealing with a plain, businesslike man, I talk in a plain, businesslike way. I study my man, and generally I succeed in striking him for an order, even if times are hard, and he is already well stocked."

"He certainly knows how to talk," thought Luke. In fact, he was rather disposed to accept Mr. Coleman at his own valuation, though that was a very high one. . . .

As is to be expected, Coleman attempts to steal all of Luke's money. He and Luke share a hotel room, and thinking Luke asleep, Coleman steals down to the hotel clerk (after searching Luke's pockets) and requests the money, saying that he has been given permission from Luke. Naive in having trusted Coleman's judgment, Luke is endowed with sufficient luck to catch the would-be thief in time to save himself from his first maladventure.

Chicago nearly proves disastrous. However, Luke must pursue his quest of Harding. Just by coincidence, he learns from the hotel clerk, who directs him to the Ottawa House files, that Harding was registered at this very hotel in 1879. To complete this neat coincidence, Harding left behind his personal diary indicating that he now resides in Franklin, Minnesota. The clerk also is useful in describing Harding as an elderly man of fifty-five. Content with his Chicago expedition, Luke sums up his few days there as follows: "After all, I ought to be grateful to Mr. Coleman, notwithstanding his attempt to rob me. But for him I should never have come to the Ottawa House, and thus I should have lost an important clue."

The following day Luke takes the train for St. Paul, Minnesota, and

*registers at a hotel there. From the hotel clerk he learns that Harding
has decided to try his fortune in gold and that he and his sister have
moved to the Black Hills.*

*After a day's travel to a mining camp, he finds the former clerk,
James Harding, lying sick on a pallet in a cabin. In need of care
and food, Harding just happens to have the list of bond numbers in
the wallet inside his coat. Luke cares for Harding and copies the numbers, which he mails to Armstrong. Satisfied with the successful accomplishment of his mission, shortly thereafter he begins his return to
Groveton.*

Mr. Armstrong was sitting in his office one morning when the door
opened, and Luke entered, his face flushed with health, and his cheeks
browned by exposure.

"You see I've got back, Mr. Armstrong," he said, advancing with
a smile.

"Welcome home, Luke!" exclaimed the merchant heartily, grasping
our hero's hand cordially.

"I hope you are satisfied with me," said Luke.

"Satisfied! I ought to be. You have done yourself the greatest credit.
It is seldom a boy of your age exhibits such good judgment and
discretion."

"Thank you, sir," said Luke gratefully. "I was obliged to spend a
good deal of money," he added, "and I have arrived in New York with
only three dollars and seventy-five cents in my pocket."

"I have no fault to find with your expenses," said Mr. Armstrong
promptly. "Nor would I have complained if you had spent twice as
much. The main thing was to succeed, and you have succeeded."

"I am glad to hear you speak so," said Luke, relieved. "To me it
seemed a great deal of money. You gave me two hundred dollars, and
I have less than five dollars left. Here it is!" and Luke drew the sum
from his pocket and tendered it to the merchant.

"I can't take it," said Mr. Armstrong. "You don't owe me any
money. It is I who am owing you. Take this on account," and he drew
a roll of bills from his pocketbook and handed it to Luke. "Here are
a hundred dollars on account," he continued.

"This is too much, Mr. Armstrong," said Luke, quite overwhelmed
with the magnitude of the gift.

"Let me be the judge of that," said Mr. Armstrong kindly. "There
is only one thing, Luke, that I should have liked to have you do."

"What is that, sir?"

"I should like to have had you bring me a list of the numbers certified to by Mr. Harding."

Luke's answer was to draw from the inside pocket of his vest a paper signed by the old bookkeeper, containing a list of the numbers, regularly subscribed and certified to.

"Is that what you wished, sir?" he asked.

"You are a wonderful boy," said the merchant admiringly. "Was this your idea, or Mr. Harding's?"

"I believe I suggested it to him," said Luke modestly.

"That makes all clear sailing," said Mr. Armstrong. "Here are fifty dollars more. You deserve it for your thoughtfulness."

"You have given me enough already," said Luke, drawing back.

"My dear boy, it is evident that you still have something to learn in the way of business. When a rich old fellow offers you money which he can well afford, you had better take it."

"That removes all my objections," said Luke. "But I am afraid you will spoil me with your liberality, Mr. Armstrong."

"I will take the risk of it. But here is another of your friends."

The door had just opened, and Roland Reed entered. There was another cordial greeting, and Luke felt that it was pleasant, indeed, to have two such good friends.

"When are you going to Groveton, Luke?" asked Mr. Reed.

"I shall go this afternoon, if there is nothing more you wish me to do. I am anxious to see my mother."

"That is quite right, Luke. Your mother is your best friend, and deserves all the attention you can give her. I shall probably go to Groveton myself to-morrow."

After Luke had left the office, Mr. Reed remained to consult with the merchant as to what was the best thing to do. Both were satisfied that Prince Duncan, the president of the bank, was the real thief who had robbed the bank. There were two courses open—a criminal prosecution, or a private arrangement which should include the return of the stolen property. The latter course was determined upon, but should it prove ineffective, severer measures were to be resorted to.

The story is not quite over. It remains for Tony Denton to try and cash a second bond "extracted from the fears of Prince Duncan" before the virtuous men of business unseat the corrupt scion of wealth. In possession of the numbers of the stolen bonds, which have been circulated by Armstrong throughout the city, the brokers to whom Denton applies accuse him of being a thief. "I got them from Prince Duncan, president of the bank," protests the terrified Denton.

The game is up, and in the following manner the benevolent capitalist Armstrong wins his victory over corruption, assuring Luke of a promising future as well.

It was rather late in the day when Mr. Armstrong, accompanied by

Tony Denton, made their appearance at the house of Prince Duncan. When the banker's eyes rested on the strangely assorted pair, his heart sank within him. He had a suspicion of what it meant.

"We have called on you, Mr. Duncan, on a matter of importance," said Mr. Armstrong.

"Very well," answered Duncan faintly.

"It is useless to mince matters. I have evidence outside of this man's to show that it was you who robbed the bank of which you are president, and appropriated to your own use the bonds which it contained."

"This is a strange charge to bring against a man in my position. Where is your proof?" demanded Duncan, attempting to bluster.

"I have Mr. Denton's evidence that he obtained two thousand-dollar bonds from you."

"Very well, suppose I did sell him two such bonds?"

"They were among the bonds stolen."

"It is not true. They were bonds I have had for five years."

"Your denial is useless. The numbers betray you."

"You did not have the numbers of the bonds."

"So you think, but I have obtained them from an old bookkeeper of mine, now at the West. I sent a special messenger out to obtain the list from him. Would you like to know who the messenger was?"

"Who was it?"

"Luke Larkin."

"That boy!" exclaimed Duncan bitterly.

"Yes, that boy supplied me with the necessary proof. And now, I have a word to say; I can send you to prison, but for the sake of your family I would prefer to spare you. But the bonds must be given up."

"I haven't them all in my possession."

"Then you must pay me the market price of those you have used. The last one given to this man is safe."

"It will reduce me to poverty," said Prince Duncan in great agitation.

"Nevertheless, it must be done!" said Mr. Armstrong sternly. "Moreover, you must resign your position as president of the bank, and on that condition you will be allowed to go free, and I will not expose you."

Of course, Squire Duncan was compelled to accept these terms. He saved a small sum out of the wreck of his fortune, and with his family, removed to the West, where they were obliged to adopt a very different style of living. Randolph is now an office boy at a salary of four dollars a week, and is no longer able to swagger and boast as he has done hitherto. Mr. Tomkins, Linton's father, was elected president of the Groveton Bank in place of Mr. Duncan, much to the satisfaction of Luke.

Roland Reed, much to the surprise of Luke, revealed himself as a cousin of Mr. Larkin, who for twenty-five years had been lost sight of. He had changed his name, on account of some trouble into which he had been betrayed by Prince Duncan, and thus had not been recognized.

"You need be under no anxiety about Luke and his prospects," he said to Mrs. Larkin. "I shall make over to him ten thousand dollars at once, constituting myself his guardian, and will see that he is well started in business. My friend Mr. Armstrong proposes to take him into his office, if you do not object, at a liberal salary."

"I shall miss him very much," said Mrs. Larkin, "though I am thankful that he is to be so well provided for."

"He can come home every Saturday night and stay until Monday morning," said Mr. Reed, who, by the way, chose to retain his name in place of his old one. "Will that satisfy you?"

"It ought to, surely, and I am grateful to Providence for all the blessings which it has showered upon me and mine."

There was another change. Mr. Reed built a neat and commodious house in the pleasantest part of the village and there Mrs. Larkin removed with his little daughter, of whom she still had the charge. No one rejoiced more sincerely at Luke's good fortune than Linton, who throughout had been a true and faithful friend. He is at present visiting Europe with his mother, and has written an earnest letter, asking Luke to join him. But Luke feels that he cannot leave a good business position, and must postpone the pleasure of traveling till he is older.

Mr. J. Madison Coleman, the enterprising drummer, has got into trouble, and is at present an inmate of the State penitentiary at Joliet, Illinois. It is fortunate for the traveling public, so many of whom he has swindled, that he is for a time placed where he can do no more mischief.

So closes an eventful passage in the life of Luke Larkin. He has struggled upward from a boyhood of privation and self-denial into a youth and manhood of prosperity and honor. There has been some luck about it, I admit, but after all he is indebted for most of his good fortune to his own good qualities.

—

Andrew Carnegie
The Road to Business Success

The individualist business credo had no more exemplary and felicitous spokesman than Andrew Carnegie (1835-1919). His articulateness with the pen was so unusual among businessmen that it startled the Scottish immigrant lad himself. His succession of articles and lectures, incorporated into such books as Triumphant Democracy *(1886),* The Gospel of Wealth *(1900), and* The Empire of Business *(1902) from which this selection is drawn, expressed the ideology of the self-made man in its most lucid and popular form. [Andrew Carnegie, "The Road to Business Success," from an address to the students of the Curry Commercial College, Pittsburgh, June 23, 1885, in* The Empire of Business, New York, *1902, pp. 3-18.]*

It is well that young men should begin at the beginning and occupy the most subordinate positions. Many of the leading business men of Pittsburgh had a serious responsibility thrust upon them at the very threshold of their career. They were introduced to the broom, and spent the first hours of their business lives sweeping out the office. I notice we have janitors and janitresses now in offices, and our young men unfortunately miss that salutary branch of a business education. But if by chance the professional sweeper is absent any morning, the boy who has the genius of the future partner in him will not hesitate to try his hand at the broom. The other day a fond fashionable mother in Michigan asked a young man whether he had ever seen a young lady sweep in a room so grandly as her Priscilla. He said no, he never had, and the mother was gratified beyond measure, but then said he, after a pause, "What I should like to see her do is sweep out a room." It does not hurt the newest comer to sweep out the office if necessary. I was one of those sweepers myself, and who do you suppose were my fellow sweepers? David McCargo, now superintendent of the Alleghany Valley Railroad; Robert Pitcairn, Superintendent of the Pennsylvania Railroad, and Mr. Moreland, City Attorney. We all took turns, two each morning did the sweeping; and now I remember Davie was so proud of his clean white shirt bosom that he used to spread over it an old silk bandana handkerchief which he kept for the purpose, and we other boys thought he was putting on airs. So he was. None of us had a silk handkerchief.

Assuming that you have all obtained employment and are fairly started, my advice to you is "aim high." I would not give a fig for the young man who does not already see himself the partner or the head of an important firm. Do not rest content for a moment in your thoughts as head clerk, or foreman, or general manager in any concern, no matter how extensive. Say to yourself, "My place is at the top." *Be king in your dreams.* Make your vow that you will reach that position, with untarnished reputation, and make no other vow to distract your attention, except the very commendable one that when you are a member of the firm or before that, if you have been promoted two or three times, you will form another partnership with the loveliest of her sex —a partnership to which our new partnership act has no application. The liability there is never limited.

Let me indicate two or three conditions essential to success. Do not be afraid that I am going to moralize, or inflict a homily upon you. I speak upon the subject only from the view of a man of the world, desirous of aiding you to become successful business men. You all know that there is no genuine, praiseworthy success in life if you are not honest, truthful, fair-dealing. I assume you are and will remain all these, and also that you are determined to live pure, respectable lives, free from pernicious or equivocal associations with one sex or the other. There is no creditable future for you else. Otherwise your learning and your advantages not only go for naught, but serve to accentuate your failure and your disgrace. I hope you will not take it amiss if I warn you against three of the gravest dangers which will beset you in your upward path.

The first and most seductive, and the destroyer of most young men, is the drinking of liquor. I am no temperance lecturer in disguise, but a man who knows and tells you what observation has proved to him; and I say to you that you are more likely to fail in your career from acquiring the habit of drinking liquor than from any, or all, the other temptations likely to assail you. You may yield to almost any other temptation and reform—may brace up, and if not recover lost ground, at least remain in the race and secure and maintain a respectable position. But from the insane thirst for liquor escape is almost impossible.

I have known but few exceptions to this rule. First, then, you must not drink liquor to excess. Better if you do not touch it at all—much better; but if this be too hard a rule for you then take your stand firmly here:—Resolve never to touch it except at meals. A glass at dinner will not hinder your advance in life or lower your tone; but I implore you hold it inconsistent with the dignity and self-respect of gentlemen, with what is due from yourselves to yourselves, being the men you are, and especially the men you are determined to become, to drink a glass of liquor at a bar. Be far too much of the gentleman ever to enter a bar-room. You do not pursue your careers in safety unless you stand firmly upon this ground. Adhere to it and you have escaped danger from the deadliest of your foes.

The next greatest danger to a young business man in this community I believe to be that of speculation. When I was a telegraph operator here we had no Exchanges in the City, but the men or firms who speculated upon the Eastern Exchanges were necessarily known to the operators. They could be counted on the fingers of one hand. These men were not our citizens of first repute: they were regarded with suspicion. I have lived to see all of these speculators irreparably ruined men, bankrupt in money and bankrupt in character. There is scarcely an instance of a man who has made a fortune by speculation and kept it. Gamesters die poor, and there is certainly not an instance of a speculator who has lived a life creditable to himself, or advantageous to the community. The man who grasps the morning paper to see first how his speculative ventures upon the Exchanges are likely to result, unfits himself for the calm consideration and proper solution of business problems, with which he has to deal later in the day, and saps the sources of that persistent and concentrated energy upon which depend the permanent success, and often the very safety, of his main business.

The speculator and the business man tread diverging lines. The former depends upon the sudden turn of fortune's wheel; he is a millionaire to-day, a bankrupt to-morrow. But the man of business knows that only by years of patient, unremitting attention to affairs can he earn his reward, which is the result, not of chance, but of well-advised means for the attainment of ends. During all these years his is the cheering thought that by no possibility can he benefit himself without carrying prosperity to others. The speculator on the other hand had better never have lived so far as the good of others or the good of the community is concerned. Hundreds of young men were tempted in this city not long since to gamble in oil, and many were ruined, all were injured whether they lost or won. You may be, nay, you are certain to be similarly tempted; but when so tempted I hope you will remember this advice. Say to the tempter who asks you to risk your small savings, that if ever you decide to speculate you are determined to go to a regular and well-conducted house where they cheat fair. You can get fair play and about an equal chance upon the red and black in such a place; upon the Exchange you have neither. You might as well try your luck with the three-card monte man. There is another point involved in speculation. Nothing is more essential to young business men than untarnished credit, credit begotten of confidence in their prudence, principles, and stability of character. Well, believe me, nothing kills credit sooner in any Bank Board than the knowledge that either firms or men engage in speculation. It matters not a whit whether gains or losses be the temporary result of these operations. The moment a man is known to speculate, his credit is impaired, and soon thereafter it is gone. How can a man be credited whose resources may be swept away in one hour by a panic among gamesters? Who can tell how he stands among them? except that this is certain: he has given due notice that he may stand to lose all, so that those who credit him have themselves to blame. Resolve to be business men, but speculators never.

The third and last danger against which I shall warn you is one which has wrecked many a fair craft which started well and gave promise of a prosperous voyage. It is the perilous habit of indorsing— all the more dangerous, inasmuch as it assails one generally in the garb of friendship. It appeals to your generous instincts, and you say, "How can I refuse to lend my name only, to assist a friend?" It is because there is so much that is true and commendable in that view that the practice is so dangerous. Let me endeavor to put you upon safe honourable grounds in regard to it. I would say to you to make it a rule now, *never indorse*: but this is too much like never taste wine, or never smoke, or any other of the "nevers." They generally result in exceptions. You will as business men now and then probably become security for friends. Now, here is the line at which regard for the success of friends should cease and regard for your own honour begins.

If you owe anything, all your capital and all your effects are a solemn trust in your hands to be held inviolate for the security of those who have trusted you. Nothing can be done by you with honour which jeopardizes these first claims upon you. When a man in debt indorses for another, it is not his own credit or his own capital he risks, it is that of his own creditors. He violates a trust. Mark you then, never indorse until you have cash means not required for your own debts, and never indorse beyond those means.

Before you indorse at all, consider indorsements as gifts, and ask yourselves whether you wish to make the gift to your friend and whether the money is really yours to give and not a trust for your creditors.

You are not safe, gentlemen, unless you stand firmly upon this as the only ground which an honest business man can occupy.

I beseech you avoid liquor, speculation, and indorsement. Do not fail
in either, for liquor and speculation are the Scylla and Charybdis of
the young man's business sea, and indorsement his rock ahead.

Assuming you are safe in regard to these your gravest dangers, the
question now is how to rise from the subordinate position we have
imagined you in, through the successive grades to the position for which
you are, in my opinion, and, I trust in your own, evidently intended.
I can give you the secret. It lies mainly in this. Instead of the question,
"What must I do for my employer?" substitute "What can I do?"
Faithful and conscientious discharge of the duties assigned you is all
very well, but the verdict in such cases generally is that you perform
your present duties so well that you had better continue performing
them. Now, young gentlemen, this will not do. It will not do for the
coming partners. There must be something beyond this. We make
Clerks, Bookkeepers, Treasurers, Bank Tellers of this class, and there
they remain to the end of the chapter. The rising man must do something exceptional, and beyond the range of his special department.
HE MUST ATTRACT ATTENTION. A shipping clerk, he may do so by discovering in an invoice an error with which he has nothing to do, and
which has escaped the attention of the proper party. If a weighing
clerk, he may save for the firm by doubting the adjustment of the scales
and having them corrected, even if this be the province of the master
mechanic. If a messenger boy, even he can lay the seed of promotion
by going beyond the letter of his instructions in order to secure the
desired reply. There is no service so low and simple, neither any so
high, in which the young man of ability and willing disposition cannot readily and almost daily prove himself capable of greater trust
and usefulness, and, what is equally important, show his invincible determination to rise. . . .

One false axiom you will often hear, which I wish to guard you
against: "Obey orders if you break owners." Don't you do it. This is
no rule for you to follow. Always break orders to save owners. There
never was a great character who did not sometimes smash the routine
regulations and make new ones for himself. The rule is only suitable
for such as have no aspirations, and you have not forgotten that you are
destined to be owners and to make orders and break orders. Do not
hesitate to do it whenever you are sure the interests of your employer
will be thereby promoted and when you are so sure of the result that
you are willing to take the responsibility. You will never be a partner
unless you know the business of your department far better than the
owners possibly can. When called to account for your independent action, show him the result of your genius, and tell him that you knew
that it would be so; show him how mistaken the orders were. Boss
your boss just as soon as you can; try it on early. There is nothing
he will like so well if he is the right kind of boss; if he is not, he is

not the man for you to remain with—leave him whenever you can, even at a present sacrifice, and find one capable of discerning genius. Our young partners in the Carnegie firm have won their spurs by showing that we did not know half as well what was wanted as they did. Some of them have acted upon occasion with me as if they owned the firm and I was but some airy New Yorker presuming to advise upon what I knew very little about. Well, they are not interfered with much now. They were the true bosses—the very men we were looking for.

There is one sure mark of the coming partner, the future millionaire; his revenues always exceed his expenditures. He begins to save early, almost as soon as he begins to earn. No matter how little it may be possible to save, save that little. Invest it securely, not necessarily in bonds, but in anything which you have good reason to believe will be profitable, but no gambling with it, remember. A rare chance will soon present itself for investment. The little you have saved will prove the basis for an amount of credit utterly surprising to you. Capitalists trust the saving young man. For every hundred dollars you can produce as the result of hard-won savings, Midas, in search of a partner, will lend or credit a thousand; for every thousand, fifty thousand. It is not capital that your seniors require, it is the man who has proved that he has the business habits which create capital, and to create it in the best of all possible ways, as far as self-discipline is concerned, is, by adjusting his habits to his means. Gentlemen, it is the first hundred dollars saved which tells. Begin at once to lay up something. The bee predominates in the future millionaire.

Of course there are better, higher aims than saving. As an end, the acquisition of wealth is ignoble in the extreme; I assume that you save and long for wealth only as a means of enabling you the better to do some good in your day and generation. Make a note of this essential rule: Expenditure always within income.

* * *

And here is the prime condition of success, the great secret: concentrate your energy, thought, and capital exclusively upon the business in which you are engaged. Having begun in one line, resolve to fight it out on that line, to lead in it; adopt every improvement, have the best machinery, and know the most about it.

The concerns which fail are those which have scattered their capital, which means that they have scattered their brains also. They have investments in this, or that, or the other, here, there, and everywhere. "Don't put all your eggs in one basket" is all wrong. I tell you "put all your eggs in one basket, and then watch that basket." Look round you and take notice; men who do that do not often fail. It is easy to watch and carry the one basket. It is trying to carry too many baskets that breaks most eggs in this country. He who carries three baskets must put one on his head, which is apt to tumble and trip him up. One fault of the American business man is lack of concentration.

To summarize what I have said: Aim for the highest; never enter a bar-room; do not touch liquor, or if at all only at meals; never speculate; never indorse beyond your surplus cash fund; make the firm's interest yours; break orders always to save owners; concentrate; put all your eggs in one basket, and watch that basket; expenditure always within revenue; lastly, be not impatient, for, as Emerson says, "no one can cheat you out of ultimate success but yourselves."

I congratulate poor young men upon being born to that ancient and honourable degree which renders it necessary that they should devote themselves to hard work. A basketful of bonds is the heaviest basket a young man ever had to carry. He generally gets to staggering under it. We have in this city creditable instances of such young men, who have pressed to the front rank of our best and most useful citizens. These deserve great credit. But the vast majority of the sons of rich men are unable to resist the temptations to which wealth subjects them, and sink to unworthy lives. I would almost as soon leave a young man a curse, as burden him with the almighty dollar. It is not from this class you have rivalry to fear. The partner's sons will not trouble you much, but look out that some boys poorer, much poorer than yourselves, whose parents cannot afford to give them the advantages of a course in this institute, advantages which should give you a decided lead in the race—look out that such boys do not challenge you at the post and pass you at the grand stand. Look out for the boy who has to plunge into work direct from the common school and who begins by sweeping out the office. He is the probable dark horse that you had better watch.

III

The Gospel
Made Social

*The last decade of the nineteenth century and the early years of
the twentieth century were crisis times for American institutions
and culture. Massive organization was shaping and socializing a
new type of successful American. Those big corporation administrators who symbolized success and its achievement seemed
strangers to the Gospel folklore. Yet even as the individualist
ethic became less and less viable, the folklore seemed to gain in
intensity to compensate for the gap between myth and reality.*

David Riesman

The Saving Remnant:
An Examination of
Character Structure

If any single book crystallized the American characterological impasse in the mid-twentieth century, that book is The Lonely Crowd *(1950) by David Riesman (1909-   ). This selection succinctly summarizes Riesman's insights and researches into the historical and social forces that have shaped a new American ideology.* [*David Riesman, "The Saving Remnant: A Study in Character," in John W. Chase, ed.,* Years of the Modern: An American Appraisal, *New York, 1949, pp. 116-122, 130-133, 137-138.*]

My purpose here is to advance . . . understanding by tracing a shift I believe to have occurred in very recent times in [the] character structure of modern man: a shift from the predominance of a type I have called "inner-directed," whose source of guidance in life is an internalized authority, to a type I have called "other-directed," dependent on external authorities. We shall explore the relationship between these two types of character and the changing feelings in people as to their power to resist social pressures. For obviously, given the objectively identical social pressure, the individual's feeling and experience will depend upon his character, in which his previous life-experiences, especially those of mastery and submission, have been crystallized.

While our helplessness in the world is historically the condition of every advance in our mastery of it, the feeling of helplessness may today be so overpowering that regression, and not advance, ensues. But only when we have understood those forces that make for helplessness can we assay the probable outcome, and see what might be required for the new leap to security and freedom envisaged by Condorcet. One requirement is a type of character structure that can tolerate freedom, even thrive on it; I call persons of such type "autonomous," since they are capable of conscious self-direction. The very conditions that produce other-direction on the part of the majority today, who are heterono- mous—that is, who are guided by voices other than their own—may also produce a "saving remnant" who are increasingly autonomous, and who find strength in the face of their minority position in the modern world of power.

Throughout most of history, people have lived in the bosom of nature, and at her mercy. They have sought a kind of defensive power and command of nature through magic and animism, by which they attempted to personalize and to propitiate the environment. The Pueblo Indians of the American Southwest, for instance, still cope with fear of drought by preoccupation with word-perfect rituals of rain making —and by very practical communal organization of the available water supply. These tribes quiet their anxiety over the weather by substituting for it anxiety over the ritual, which remains in their control. In such a society, as in the feudal past, people live on a relatively unawakened level, with limited life-expectations and limited potentialities for choice. An over-all balance is struck between helplessness and power; institu- tions mediate this balance, and character structure builds upon it.

This balance altered radically in the West during the age that opens with the Renaissance and closes, to set an equally arbitrary date, with the virtual cutting off of immigration from Europe following World War I. During this period, men were forced to face a world of changed dimensions, changed social relations, and changed meanings. As a result, some felt increasingly helpless and alone: the Calvinist doctrines appealed to them because those doctrines stressed man's helplessness to secure grace, the "chosen" being predestined by a terrifying and inscrutable God. The practical Calvinist, however, did not merely wait for the day of judgment; he tried to force God's hand by a ritual. This ritual, unlike the Pueblo Indian's rain making, was symbolized by hard work in the worldly processes of production—even though the ultimate aim was other-worldly. The result for many was success in mundane pursuits—which was regarded as a sign of election. Thus both hard work and its practical fruits assuaged the feeling of helplessness in the new conditions of life and led to the attainment of a new balance between power and weakness.

This period was the age of the early physical and industrial frontiers —the frontiers of expanding industry and trade, as well as expanding geographical frontiers. This age also enlarged the frontiers of intel-

lectual and emotional discovery, excavating man's past and acquainting
him with other cultures. To pioneer on a frontier, whether an external
one—at the edge of a white settlement—or an internal one—at the edge
of the known in science, art, or industry—requires a somewhat new
type of character that is, to a degree, capable of self-piloting, a type
that can act when the guidance of custom breaks down or when a
choice must be made among several different sets of customs.

I call this type inner-directed, since the source of direction is internalized. By inner-direction, however, I do not mean genuine autonomy,
but rather obedience to an internal "gyroscope" which, installed in
childhood, continues to pilot the person as he struggles to master the
exigent demands of the frontier. This gyroscope is set going by the
parents, or rather by their idealized image (the Freudian superego);
or by heroes or great men of antiquity or revered elders taken as models.
Driven by these internal voices, the inner-directed person is often
ambitious—for fame, for goodness, for accomplishment in the world;
and this is as true of the bold men of the Renaissance as of the hard,
ascetic Puritans. By their own efforts at self-discipline and self-develop-
ment, these men often helped to "produce" their own characters; the
conquering of this internal frontier was accompanied and rewarded
by mastery over others and over nature.

In all I have said, I speak primarily of the middle classes, for it was
among them that inner-directed types arose; the lower classes moved
more slowly out of feudalism. In time, as the doctrine of predestination
became attenuated or forgotten, these middle classes developed an
ideology of liberalism and individualism that proclaimed for all men
the values of freedom and self-reliance compatible with characterological
inner-direction. The inner-directed person came to *feel* free and to *feel*
self-made: in his psychological innocence, he was not aware how many
of "his" choices had been made for him already by his parents and his
conditioning generally. He might have read the famous phrase of
Heraclitus—"Character is fate"—to mean that he, as an individual,
possessed his own fate, working in him through his own self-mastery;
while we today would read the same sentence to mean that our own
character is not truly ours, but is produced by our social environment,
our "fate" of living in a particular place and time—a new, more
sophisticated doctrine of predestination. Moreover, the inner-directed
person, living in a time of expanding frontiers, could in fact achieve
a small degree of the freedom that he felt. Many inner-directed persons
achieved a measure of psychic autonomy and independence as theocratic
controls declined in the eighteenth and nineteenth centuries.

This security of character was reinforced by the experience of a world
which itself appeared to be inner-directed. Adam Smith and other late
eighteenth-century thinkers saw society as operating "gyroscopically"
in a beneficent direction. In general the men who established the in-

dustrial revolution in England and America were as unaware of their countries' good luck as of the forces shaping their own characters. A world that seemed to be running on schedule was, of course, an illusion.

A number of great thinkers during this period did not, however, share the widespread optimism of the rising inner-directed middle class. Of these, Malthus is one of the most interesting. He insisted on the entirely temporary quality of any victory over nature, and, contrary to Condorcet, Godwin, and other progressive thinkers, warned that the natural bounty of the earth—now, so it seemed, thoroughly explored —stood in danger of being turned into parsimony by the "natural" growth of population. Yet even Malthus was, by modern standards, optimistic; for he saw the world not as a bad joke on man but as a meaningful obstacle race designed to develop man's capacities for rational self-restraint. In our terminology, though not of course in his, he advised people to become inner-directed as the sole means of keeping population in line with subsistence: that is, he advised them to plan ahead, to work hard, and to postpone marriage—thus accumulating wealth without accumulating children. Thus, in effect, he proposed a way out of nature's trap by characterological change.

We can see now, with the advantage of hindsight, that such a program never really had much chance of success. Inner-direction was never very widespread, but rather represented the ideal model toward which people strove. We have evidence that many people of that era tried desperately to conduct themselves in the approved inner-directed way, but were unable to conform. Thus, in Vermont of the eighteenth and nineteenth centuries many more people started diaries and account books—perfect symbols of inner-direction of which Malthus would have approved—than kept them up. Such people must have felt helpless in their efforts at self-mastery, particularly since they took as models those pre-eminent men, from George Washington to Andrew Carnegie, who then stood unshaken by disciples of Marx and Freud. Thus, in a very special sense, the feelings of potency were monopolized by those whose inner-direction was relatively stable and successful in the public mind, while a reservoir of hidden impotence existed. Yet for many of the unsuccessful, failure never seemed quite final, and so long as the future beckoned, or the belief in grace persisted, helplessness could be staved off. . . .

Let us examine several . . . factors that have robbed the middle-class individual of his defenses against the pressure of the group. We shall deal in somewhat more detail with changes in the nature of private property, of work, and of leisure, all of which at one time functioned as defenses.

In the feudal era, the individual was attached to property, largely land, by feudal and family ties. The breakdown of feudalism meant helplessness for many peasants, who were thrown off the land; but for the middle class the result was a gradual gain in consciousness of strength. A new type of relationship between persons and property developed: the person was no longer attached to property, but attached property to himself by his own energetic actions. Property, including land, became freely alienable; at the same time, it was felt to be an individual, not a family, possession. And property was satisfying, substantial—an extended part of the self. Inside the shell of his possessions, the inner-directed person could resist psychological invasion.

Today, however, property is not much of a defense. Taxes and other state activities, inflation and the panicky desire for liquid assets, have made it factually friable. Moreover, the fears of property-holders outrun the actual dangers. Thus, even powerful groups in America feel more frightened of Communism than its actual power warrants. Property no longer represents the old security for those who hold it, and the fear that it may vanish any day makes it as much a source of anxiety as of strength. The rich no longer dare flaunt wealth, but tread softly, guided by considerations of "public relations." Wealthy students often act as if ashamed of their wealth; I have sometimes been tempted to point out that the rich are a minority and have rights, too.

The change in the meaning of work is even plainer. For the inner-directed person, work seemed self-justifying: the only problem was to find the work to which one felt called. As we have seen, the age of expanding frontiers provided the individual with an inexhaustible list of tasks. Work, like property, moreover, was considered a mode of relating oneself to physical objects, and only indirectly to people. Indeed, the work-hungry inner-directed types of this period sometimes found that they were cut off from family and friends, and often from humanity in general, by their assiduity and diligence. And work, like property, was a defense against psychological invasion, a "do not disturb" sign guarding the industrious man of the middle class.

Today the meaning of work is a very different one, psychologically, though in many professions and industries the older modes still persist. To an increasing degree, the self is no longer defined by its productive accomplishments but by its role in a "Friendship" system. As the "isolate" or "rate-buster" is punished and excluded from the work force in the shop, so the lone wolf is weeded out of management; up-to-date personnel men use deep-probing psychological tests to eliminate applicants, whatever their other gifts, who lack the other-directed personality needed for the job.

To be sure, out of anxiety, a lingering asceticism, and a need for an impressive agenda, the professional and business men and women of the big cities continue to work hard, or more accurately, to spend long hours in the company of their fellow "antagonistic cooperators": "work" is seen as a network of personal relationships that must be constantly watched and oiled. Increasingly, both work and leisure call on the same sort of skills—sociability, sensitivity to others' feelings and wants, and the exercise of taste-preferences freed from direct considerations of economic advantage. Work in this case has a certain unreality for people, since it has almost floated free from any connection with technical crafts. The latter have been built into machines, or can be easily taught; but people must still go to the office and find ways of keeping, or at least looking, busy. Thus in many circles work and leisure are no longer clearly distinguished—as we can see by observing a luncheon or a game of golf among competitors.

The feeling of powerlessness of the other-directed character is, then, the result in part of the lack of genuine commitment to work. His life is not engaged in a direct struggle for mastery over himself and nature; he has no long-term goals since the goals must constantly be changed. At the same time, he is in competition with others for the very values they tell him are worth pursuing; in a circular process, one of these values is the approval of the competing group itself. Hence, he is apt to repress overt competitiveness both out of anxiety to be liked and out of fear of retaliation. In this situation, he is likely to lose interest in the work itself. With loss of interest, he may even find himself little more than a dilettante, not quite sure that he is really able to accomplish anything.

From this it follows that this type of other-directed person is not able to judge the work of others—for one thing, he is no longer sufficiently interested in work as such. He must constantly depend on specialists and experts whom he cannot evaluate with any assurance. That dependence is an inevitable and indeed a valuable fruit of the division of labor in modern society; but the inability even to dare to pass personal judgment is a defect rooted in the character of the other-directed person. . . .

I do not mean to imply that our society "produces" other-directed people because such people are in demand in an increasingly monopolistic, managerial economy. The relations between character and society are not that simple. Moreover, neither character nor society changes all at once. But it would take us too far afield to trace the many formative agencies in the still far-from-complete shift from inner-direction to other-direction in the middle classes.

Furthermore, I must guard against the implication that I think inner-direction is a way of life preferable to other-direction. Each type has its virtues and its vices: the inner-directed person tends to be rigid and intolerant of others; the other-directed person, in turn, is likely to be flexible and sensitive to others. Neither type is altogether comfortable in the world. But in different ways each finds the discomforts it needs psychologically in order, paradoxically, to feel comfortable. The inner-directed person finds the struggle to master himself and the environment quite appropriate; he feels comfortable climbing uphill. The other-directed person finds equally appropriate the malaise that he shares with many others. Engrossed in the activities that the culture provides, he can remain relatively unconscious of his anxiety and tonelessness. Moreover, the character type must always be judged in context. Many persons who are inner-directed and who, in an earlier age, would have gone through life in relative peace, today find themselves indignant at a big-city world in which they have not felt at home. Other-directed persons also may not feel at home, but home never had the same meaning for them. It would appear to the envious inner-directed observer, that the other-directed manage their lives better in a mass society. Conversely, the other-directed may envy the seeming firmness of the inner-directed, and look longingly back on the security of nineteenth-century society, while failing to see that firmness was often merely stubbornness and security merely ignorance.

===

George W. Perkins

The Modern Corporation

Cooperation rather than competition was the fundamental principle of life, and laissez-faire was outmoded—if not positively dangerous. This in brief summarizes the lecture delivered by George W. Perkins (1862-1920) at Columbia University in 1908 at the invitation of Nicholas Murray Butler. The candor of the former president of the New York Life Insurance Company and Morgan partner apparently shocked the university president, as yet unable to admit the corporate realities of Big Business. [George W. Perkins, The Modern Corporation, *New York, 1908.]*

In the modern corporation we are confronted with a fact and not a theory. Whatever may be the individual attitude towards it, the corporation is here. What caused it, what it is doing, and what is to become of it are live questions, vital to all the people.

A corporation, in a way, is but another name for organization. Broadly speaking, the first form of organization between human beings, of which we know, was the clan or tribe, in which the everyday conduct of the individuals was determined by the necessities of the group. This passed on into national organization, and then came the Church as a growing and vast organization. Latest of all has come the organizing of business.

But before all this, in the very beginning of things, the universe was organized—and all that man has done in society, in the Church, in business, and all that he ever can do in the centuries to come, can never bring to pass so complete a form of organization, so vast a trust, so centralized a form of control, as passes before our eyes in each twenty-four hours of our lives as we contemplate that all-including system of perfect organization called the Universe. It does not require a very vivid imagination to picture the waste, the destruction, the chaos that would follow if there were not perfect organization, perfect co-operation, perfect regulation, perfect control in the affairs of the universe. How could we live, for example, if there were constant competition between day and night, or a constant struggle for supremacy between the seasons? Does any one, for a moment, think that he would prefer such a condition to the co-operation that now exists through all the affairs of the universe?

Organization being the all-permeating principle of the universe, the presumption is, therefore, in favor of organization wherever we find it or wherever it can be used. The corporation of to-day is entitled to that presumption; its underlying cause is not the greed of man for wealth and power, but the working of natural causes—of evolution.

Business was originally done by individuals trading with one another; then by a firm of two or more individuals; then by a company; then by a corporation, and latterly by a giant corporation or what is commonly (though perhaps inaccurately) called a "trust." Each step was brought about by some great change that took place in the conditions under which the people of the world lived and worked; each step was, in fact, mainly determined by discoveries and inventions of the human mind.

With the ox-team and the hoe we had men trading as individuals with individuals; with the sailing vessel and the stage-coach we had trade carried on by firms; with the advent of the company we had the locomotive, the steamboat, the reaping machine, and the telegraph; with the birth of the larger corporation we had the express train, the Atlantic cable, the ocean liner, the local telephone, the seeder, the reaper, and the binder; with the giant corporation came the Twentieth Century Limited, the crossing of the ocean in five days, the long-distance telephone, wireless telegraphy, and a great extension of machinery into agricultural work.

In our forefathers' time it took about half as long to sail down the Hudson River from Albany to New York as it now takes to cross the Atlantic. The actual distance from Albany to New York is no less, nor is the distance from New York to London any less, now than then, but the inventions of man have so compressed both space and time that the financial and commercial markets of America and Europe are in constant exchange with one another every moment of the day. The business man in New York or Chicago can exchange several cable messages with London or Paris during the business hours of a day, and whenever an hour is clipped off the record of an ocean greyhound the people of the world are drawn so much nearer together. Because of the inventions of man, the great American desert of our boyhood geographies has, within a comparatively few years, largely become a vast fertile field, and, again, because of these inventions, coupled with organized business methods the product of this vast field is being marketed in remote parts of the globe.

The days when business was a local affair of individual with individual were the days when people were scattered, knowing little of each other and having no dealings with each other outside the radius of a few miles. Then steam and, later, electricity came into man's service; and then, by leaps and bounds, the possibilities of trade became extended to a radius of hundreds of miles, even of thousands of miles. Vast possibilities of international trade loomed up. The corporation sprang into active being as an inevitable result of this expansion of trade; for no one man, no firm, no small company, could provide the capital or the organization to cope with such opportunities. The only bridge that can span the ocean is the corporation. The real cause of the corporation was not so much the selfish aims of a few men as the imperative necessities of all men.

The first stage of corporationism was one of conflict—the old destructive competition carried forward under the new business forms. Trade could be carried further, much further than before; and so A invaded B's territory and B retaliated. The fighting became faster and more furious, and the war in commerce became a hand-to-hand conflict. The trenches were being filled with able, splendid men who fell in the colossal struggles. Cut rates and rebates became the order of the day. Many railroads and many houses which had been successful in legitimate lines of business went down in bankruptcy. Labor suffered and the public suffered. The cost of doing business steadily increased; for war costs money. It became imperative that something be done to end the havoc. Prosperity could come only with peace. Instinctively, in a way unconsciously, men began to get together—not so much for profit as for protection; and so, under conditions which, in the mechanical development of the world, came on as naturally as day follows night, the great corporation came into existence and is the live, burning issue of to-day.

Perhaps the most useful achievement of the great corporation has been the saving of waste in its particular line of business. By assembling the best brains, the best genius, the best energy in a given line of trade, and co-ordinating these in work for a common end, great results have been attained in the prevention of waste, the utilizing of by-products, the economizing in the manufacture of the products, the expense of selling, and through better and more uniform service.

This same grouping of men has raised the standard of their efficiency. Nothing develops man like contact with other men. A dozen men working apart and for separate ends do not develop the facility, the ideas, the general effectiveness that will become the qualities of a dozen men working together in one cause. In such work emulation plays a useful part; it does all the good and none of the harm that the old method of destructive competition did; the old competition was wholly self-seeking and often ruinous, while the new rivalry, within the limits of the same organization, is constructive and uplifting. Thus the great corporation has developed men of a higher order of business ability than ever appeared under the old conditions; and what a value this has for the coming generation! The opportunity, the inducement it provides to become all-around larger men than those of earlier generations could become!

We have heard many warnings that because of the great corporation we have been robbing the oncoming generation of its opportunities. Nothing is more absurd. The larger the corporation, the more certain is the office boy to ultimately reach a foremost place if he is made of the right stuff, if he keeps everlastingly at it, and if he is determined to become master of each position he occupies.

In the earlier days, the individual in business, as a rule, left his business to his children—the firm to its relations. Whether or not they were competent did not determine the succession. But the giant corporation cannot act in this way. Its management must have efficiency—above and beyond all else it must have the highest order of ability; and nothing has been more noticeable in the management of corporations in the last few years than that "influence," so called, as an element in selecting men for responsible posts, has been rapidly on the wane. Everything is giving way and must give way to the one supreme test of fitness.

And is it not possible that the accumulating of large fortunes in the future may be curtailed to a large extent through the very workings of these corporations? Are there not many advantages in having corporations in which there are a large number of positions carrying with them very handsome annual salaries, in place of firms with comparatively few partners—the annual profits of each one of whom were often so large that they amassed fortunes in a few years? A position carrying a salary so large as to represent the interest on a handsome fortune can be permanently filled only by a man of real ability, so that in case a man who is occupying such a position dies, it must, in turn, be filled with another man of the same order while the fortune might be, and most likely would be, passed on regardless of the heir's ability. Therefore, the more positions of responsibility, of trust and of honor, that carry large salaries, the more goals we have for young men whose equipment for life consists of integrity, health, ability, and energy.

Furthermore, the great corporation has been of benefit to the public in being able to standardize its wares, so that they have become more uniformly good. Wages are unquestionably higher and labor is more steadily employed; for, in a given line of trade, handled to a considerable extent by a corporation, there are practically no failures; while, under the old methods of bitter, relentless warfare, failures were frequent, and failure meant paralysis for labor as well as for capital.

The great corporation is unquestionably making general business conditions sounder. It is making business steadier; for one reason, because firms inevitably change and dissolve, while a corporation may go on indefinitely. It is making business steadier, for another and more potent reason—because it is able to survey the field much better than could a large number of firms and individuals and, therefore, vastly better able to measure the demand for its output and, if properly managed, to prevent the accumulation of large stocks of goods that are not needed—a condition which often arose under the old methods when many firms were in ruthless competition with one another in the same line of business, oftentimes producing serious financial difficulties for one and all.

Broadly and generally speaking, the corporation as we know it to-day, as we see it working and feel its results, is in a formative state. In many cases actual and desperately serious situations caused it to be put together hurriedly. In many cases serious mistakes have been made in the forms of organization, in the methods of management, and in the ends that have been sought. In some instances the necessity for corporations has grown faster than has the ability of men to manage them. Yes, mistakes have been many and serious. But the corporation is with us; it is a condition, not a theory, and there are but two courses open to us—to kill it or to keep it. If you would kill it you must kill the cause, or the thing will come back to plague you. The principal causes are steam and electricity.

Could anything be more dangerous to the public welfare than steam and electricity themselves? Then why not prohibit their use and, so far as possible, abolish them? Has anyone ever suggested this? No. Why? Because their benefits were too apparent, and so we have bent our energies towards regulating and controlling them—by using all that is good in them and carefully protecting ourselves from all that is injurious. If we are not willing to exterminate the cause of corporations we can never permanently exterminate the corporation itself. There is, then, but one thing left to do, viz., to regulate and control them; to treat them as we have treated steam and electricity; to use the best that is in them and to protect ourselves from the worst that is in them.

A large percentage of the mistakes of corporate management have occurred because managers have failed to realize that they were not in business as individuals, but were working for other people, their stockholders, whom they were in honor bound to honestly and faithfully serve; further, that they owed a duty to the general public and could, in the long run, best serve themselves and their stockholders by recognizing that duty and respecting it.

Then, too, many of our corporations, being of comparatively recent origin, have, at the outset, been managed by men who were previously in business, in some form or another, for themselves; and it has been very difficult for such men to change their point of view—to cease from looking at questions from the sole standpoint of personal gain and personal advantage, and to take the broader view of looking at them from the standpoint of the community of interest principle.

It is by no means clear that the danger-point in the development of corporations is found in the giant corporation. Indeed, it is more likely to be found in the corporation of lesser size; because the latter does not attract the eye of the public sufficiently to have its managers impressed with the fact that they are semi-private servants—responsible not only to their stockholders but to the public as well. It is easier and more natural for a giant corporation to adopt a policy of publicity with the public and of fair-dealing with its associates in the same trade, because such a course, from the broad, far-reaching view of the great corporation, becomes the wisest, most successful course. Then, again, the relation of the giant corporation to its labor is an entirely different relation from that of the small corporation or the firm to its labor; the officers and trustees of a giant corporation instinctively lose sight of the interest of any one individual because such interest at best is infinitesimal compared with the whole. This places the officers and trustees of the giant corporation in a position where they can look on all labor questions without bias and without any personal axe to grind —solely from the broadest possible standpoint of what is fair and right between the public's capital, which they represent, and the public's labor, which they employ. In short, they assume on all such matters the attitude of the real trustee, the impartial judge, the intelligent, well-posted, and fair arbitrator.

The great semi-public business corporations of the country, whether they be insurance, railroad, or industrial, have in our day become not only vast business enterprises but great trusteeships; and there would be far less attacking of corporations if this truth were more fully realized and respected. The larger the corporation becomes, the greater become its responsibilities to the entire community. Moreover, the larger the number of stockholders, the more it assumes the nature of an institution for savings.

It is not sufficient in corporate management to do the best one can from day to day. Corporate responsibility extends beyond to-day. It is the foresight, the planning ahead, the putting the house in order for the storms of the future, that are the true measure of the best and highest stewardship as well as of the highest order of managerial ability.

The corporations of the future must be those that are semi-public servants, serving the public, with ownership widespread among the public, and with labor so fairly and equitably treated that it will look upon its corporation as its friend and protector rather than as an ever-present enemy, above all believing in it so thoroughly that it will invest its savings in the corporation's securities and become working partners in the business. It would have been impossible, in the day of the ox-team, for people in every State of this Union to be partners in any one business; and yet to-day we have at least one giant corporation made up of partners resident not only in every one of our States, but in almost every country in the world, and reinforced by thousands of its own employees having become stockholders themselves.

During the past few months, when the campaign against corporations was most intense, when our country was in a turmoil of business perplexity and doubt, the people who, we are told, have so suffered because of the trusts and are so bitterly opposed to their existence, have been investing in these very securities to an unprecedented extent. To illustrate: During the past year the stockholders of the Great Northern Railway have increased in number from 2,800 to over 11,000. The stockholders of the Pennsylvania Railroad have increased from 40,000 to 57,000. The stockholders of the New York Central have increased from 10,000 to over 21,000. During the same period the number of the stockholders in the Steel Corporation is to-day about 98 shares per person. Can there, then, be any question that these great institutions have become semi-public, and when we contemplate the alternative of exterminating or of regulating them, must we not realize that they are owned not by a few individuals but by a vast number of people representing our thriftiest class? That these corporations have thus become not only vast business enterprises but great and growing institutions for savings surely imposes a new and more sacred reponsibility not only upon corporation managers but upon legislators as well.

If the managers of the giant corporations feel themselves to be semi-public servants, and desire to be so considered, they must of course welcome supervision by the public, exercised through its chosen representatives who compose the government. Those who ask the public to invest money in an enterprise are in honor bound to give the public, at stated intervals, evidence that the business in question is ably and honestly conducted; and they should be not only willing but glad that some authority, properly constituted by our government, should say to stockholders and the public from time to time that the management's reports and methods of business are correct. They should be willing to do this for their own relief of mind, since the responsibility of the management of a giant corporation is so great that the men in control should be glad to have it shared by proper public officials representing the people in a governmental capacity.

There is scarcely a corporation manager of today, who is alive to his responsibilities, to the future growth of this country, and to the enormous opportunities before us for foreign trade, who would not welcome this kind of supervision could he but feel that it would come from the National Government, acting through an intelligent and fair-minded official; but to be faced with the requirement to report to and be supervised and regulated by 40 or 50 governments, with varying ideas and laws, of course suggests difficulties that are almost insurmountable obstacles. For business purposes, at least in the larger business affairs of this country and from a practical standpoint, State lines have been obliterated. The telegraph, the express train, and the long-distance telephone have done their work. For business purposes in this country the United States Government is a corporation with 50 subsidiary companies, and the sooner this is realized the sooner we can get the right kind of supervision of semi-public business enterprises and, in this way, give the public the publicity and the protection to which it is entitled in the conduct of business by corporations. In no other way can the public be protected from evils in corporation management.

The criticism is often made that this would amount to bringing business into politics. That depends. We have at Washington a Supreme Court. Membership in that most honorable body is the goal of every aspiring lawyer. If, for distinguished service and ability, we honor lawyers by promoting them to decide our most difficult legal questions, why should we not honor our railroad men by promoting them to decide our most difficult railroad questions, our industrial men the industrial questions? For example: If we had at Washington a Railroad Board of Control, and that Board were composed of practical railroad men, would not membership in such a Board come gradually to be the goal of railroad men? And does any one, for a moment, think that if such a Board were composed of practical railroad men it would be especially partial to railroad interests? Certainly not. Once on such a Board a man could not fail to recognize the great responsibility and honor of the office and administer it for the best interests of the public and of the railroads at one and the same time. Thus the business man would merge into the public official, no longer controlled by the mere business view, and would act the part of a statesman, to the improvement of governmental administration and not to the lowering of its level.

This kind of expert, high-minded supervision would not be opposed by the business interests of the country. What they dread is unintelligent, inexperienced administration. National supervision, under a law requiring that those who supervise should be practical men thoroughly versed in their calling, would solve most of our difficult problems and be of the greatest posssible benefit and protection to one and all.

To such rational supervision may we not look forward as a result of the sober second thought of the people and our legislators—of their calming down from the bitter denunciation of corporations which has been the prevailing outcry for some years.

In spite of what apparently has been an almost persistent determination to misunderstand or ignore his real purpose, the fact is that President Roosevelt, from the time that he was Governor of New York down to his message to Congress last week, has repeatedly proclaimed his belief that modern industrial conditions are such that combination is not only necessary but inevitable; that corporations have come to stay, and that, if properly managed, they are the source of good and not evil.

The next period in corporation development should be a constructive one—constructive as to the relations of the corporation to its labor and to the public, and this can best be accomplished by the method of co-operation with supervision.

It is almost heresy to say that competition is no longer the life of trade, yet this has come to be the fact as applied to the old unreasoning and unreasonable competition, because of the conditions of our day. The spirit of co-operation is upon us. It must, of necessity, be the next great form of business development and progress. At this moment many people are looking askance upon the change, still believing in the old doctrine. They hold to it for several reasons: First, because they have inherited the belief. Second, because they think that competition means lower prices for commodities to the public. Third, because they think it provides the best incentive to make men work. This may have been the best known method at one time, but it is not and cannot be true in the mechanical, electrical age in which we live.

The highly developed competitive system gave ruinously low prices at one time and unwarrantedly high prices at another time. When the low prices prevailed labor was cruelly hurt; when the high prices prevailed the public paid the bills.

From every point of view the co-operative principle is to be preferred. It is more humane, more uplifting, and, with proper supervision, must provide a more orderly conduct of business—freer from failure and abuse, guaranteeing better wages and more steady employment to labor, with a more favorable average price to the consumer—one on which he can depend in calculating his living expenses or making his business plans.

So much for corporations. Now, may I detain you a moment longer while I say a word to the young men who are here today.

How hopeless would your condition be if the world were perfect— if there were nothing left for you to do to improve conditions—if those who had gone before had finished the job. Really, can you imagine a condition more discouraging, more hopeless to an oncoming generation? Happily, this is not your situation. Our corporations have made mistakes. Many of these have been pointed out. Things have been done wrongly. Many of these wrongs are now being corrected. But in those mistakes, in that mis-management, lies the opportunity of the man of today and of the young man of tomorrow. Your task will be to search out and eliminate the bad in all that has preceded you—retaining the good, preserving and adding to it for the benefit of yourselves and of those who follow you.

Let us, then, take the best that we find, cut out the worst that we find, improve, develop, make more useful and beneficial.

In this great country of ours there stands out pre-eminently the inventive genius, the masterful ability, the resourcefulness, the courage, the optimism of America's business men. At no period in the world's development have there been in any given country at any one time so many men of from 20 to 30 years of age, standing ready to embrace so many opportunities and to move on to such splendid achievements, as we have in our United States today. It cannot be possible that these young men will be pessimists—that they will miss the legion of opportunities that are theirs!

I wonder if many of you realize how fortunate in one respect alone you are as compared with the young men in many other countries. You are not obliged to spend a number of the most impressionable years of your lives in compulsory military service, learning to obey orders which have no relation to the realities of life and its actual successes. Those precious years in this country are given to you to observe, to learn, and to prepare for the practical work of the world. Your individuality is not hampered or circumscribed by your being moulded into a machine in your early manhood. You are free to make of yourself what you will. What would the young men of Europe give for their opportunities if some magic wand could give them one currency, one language, one government, one people, from London to Moscow!

Success does not come by chance. It is an opportunity that has been lassoed and organized. I doubt if a man ever met with success, worthy to be called success, who was not an optimist—who did not believe in something heart and soul, and who did not play fair. And remember that when you set about a task which you really want to accomplish, the work involved is not drudgery—it is the most invigorating sort of play.

Do not lose your red blood; whatever you are, wherever or however you are situated, keep your heart warm and your humanity at par. Push forward; be of good cheer. Believe in our people, in our methods, in our country, in your neighbor and in yourself; and remember, if you are going into business, that, after all is said and done—after your fortune is made, however great it may be—in the small hours of the night, in your heart of hearts, the thing you are really going to enjoy, take satisfaction in and be proud of—the thing that will carry you over the rough places—that will keep your heart strong and your brain clear, will be the thought of what you have done to help others—what you have left to a world that has offered so much to you.

"ACHIEVEMENTS COMPARABLE WITH THOSE OF THE ARTIST OR SCIENTIST, OF THE INVENTOR OR STATESMAN"

Louis D. Brandeis

Business—A Profession

Vast social change in the United States called for the cultivation of a new business mentality commensurate with the social responsibilities that imaginative individual businessmen were already assuming. Louis Brandeis (1856-1941) was among the earliest public figures to point out that in the new era business success would be judged by new and more sophisticated standards. [Louis D. Brandeis, an address delivered at Brown University Commencement Day, 1912, in Business—A Profession, *Boston, 1914, pp. 1-12.]*

Each commencement season we are told by the college reports the number of graduates who have selected the professions as their occupation and the number of those who will enter business. The time has come for abandoning such a classification. Business should be, and to some extent already is, one of the professions. The once meagre list of the learned professions is being constantly enlarged. Engineering in its many branches already takes rank beside law, medicine, and theology. Forestry and scientific agriculture are securing places of honor. The new professions of manufacturing, of merchandising, of transportation, and of finance must soon gain recognition. The establishment of business schools in our universities is a manifestation of the modern conception of business.

The peculiar characteristics of a profession as distinguished from other occupations, I take to be these:

First. A profession is an occupation for which the necessary preliminary training is intellectual in character, involving knowledge and to some extent learning, as distinguished from mere skill.

Second. It is an occupation which is pursued largely for others and not merely for one's self.

Third. It is an occupation in which the amount of financial return is not the accepted measure of success.

Is not each of these characteristics found today in business worthily pursued?

The field of knowledge requisite to the more successful conduct of business has been greatly widened by the application to industry not only of chemical, mechanical, and electrical science, but also the new science of management; by the increasing difficulties involved in adjusting the relations of labor to capital; by the necessary intertwining of social with industrial problems; by the ever extending scope of state and federal regulation of business. Indeed, mere size and territorial expansion have compelled the business man to enter upon new and broader fields of knowledge in order to match his achievements with his opportunities.

This new development is tending to make business an applied science. Through this development the relative value in business of the trading instinct and of mere shrewdness have, as compared with other faculties, largely diminished. The conception of trade itself has changed. The old idea of a good bargain was a transaction in which one man got the better of another. The new idea of a good contract is a transaction which is good for both parties to it.

Under these new conditions, success in business must mean something very different from mere money-making. In business the able man ordinarily earns a larger income than one less able. So does the able man in the recognized professions—in law, medicine, or engineering; and even in those professions more remote from money-making, like the ministry, teaching, or social work. The world's demand for efficiency is so great and the supply so small, that the price of efficiency is high in every field of human activity.

The recognized professions, however, definitely reject the size of the financial return as the measure of success. They select as their test, excellence of performance in the broadest sense—and include, among other things, advance in the particular occupation and service to the community. These are the basis of all worthy reputations in the recognized professions. In them a large income is the ordinary incident of success; but he who exaggerates the value of the incident is apt to fail of real success.

To the business of to-day a similar test must be applied. True, in business the earning of profit is something more than an incident of success. It is an essential condition of success; because the continued absence of profit itself spells failure. But while loss spells failure, large profits do not connote success. Success must be sought in business also in excellence of performance; and in business, excellence of performance manifests itself among other things, in the advancing of methods and processes; in the improvement of products; in more perfect organization, eliminating friction as well as waste; in bettering the condition of the workingmen, developing their faculties and promoting their happiness; and in the establishment of right relations with customers and with the community.

In the field of modern business, so rich in opportunity for the exercise of man's finest and most varied mental faculties and moral qualities, mere money-making cannot be regarded as the legitimate end. Neither can mere growth in bulk or power be admitted as a worthy ambition. Nor can a man nobly mindful of his serious responsibilities to society, view business as a game; since with the conduct of business human happiness or misery is inextricably interwoven.

Real success in business is to be found in achievements comparable rather with those of the artist or the scientist, of the inventor or the statesman. And the joys sought in the profession of business must be like their joys and not the mere vulgar satisfaction which is experienced in the acquisition of money, in the exercise of power, or in the frivolous pleasure of mere winning.

It was such real success, comparable with the scientist's, the inventor's, the statesman's, which marked the career of William H. McElwain of Boston, who died in 1908 at the age of forty-one. He had been in business on his own account but thirteen years. Starting without means, he left a fortune, all of which had been earned in the competitive business of shoe manufacturing, without the aid of either patent or trademark. That shows McElwain did not lack the money-making faculty. His company's sales grew from $75,957 in 1895 to $8,691,274 in 1908. He thus became one of the largest shoe manufacturers in the world. That shows he did not lack either ambition or organizing ability. The working capital required for this rapidly growing business was obtained by him without surrendering to outside investors or to bankers any share in the profits of business: all the stock in his company being owned either by himself or his active associates. That shows he did not lack financial skill.

But this money-making faculty, organizing ability, and financial skill were with him servants, not masters. He worked for nobler ends than mere accumulation or lust of power. In those thirteen years McElwain made so many advances in the methods and practices of the long-established and prosperous branch of industry in which he was engaged, that he may be said to have revolutionized shoe manufacturing. He found it a trade; he left it an applied science.

This is the kind of thing he did: In 1902 the irregularity in the employment of the shoe worker was brougth to his attention. He became greatly impressed with its economic waste, with the misery to the workers and the demoralization which attended it. Irregularity of employment is the worst and most extended of industrial evils. Even in fairly prosperous times the workingmen of America are subjected to enforced idleness and loss of earnings, on the average, probably ten to twenty per cent of their working time. The irregularity of employment was no greater in the McElwain factories than in other shoe factories. The condition was not so bad in shoe manufacturing as in many other branches of industry. But it was bad enough; for shoe manufacturing was a seasonal industry. Most manufacturers closed their factories twice a year. Some manufacturers had two additional slack periods.

This irregularity had been accepted by the trade—by manufacturers and workingmen alike—as inevitable. It had been bowed to as if it were a law of nature—a cross to be borne with resignation. But with McElwain an evil recognized was a condition to be remedied; and he set his great mind to solving the problem of irregularity of employment in his own factories; just as Wilbur Wright applied his mind to the aeroplane, as Bell, his mind to the telephone, and as Edison, his mind to the problems of electric light. Within a few years irregularity of employment had ceased in the McElwain factories; and before his death every one of his many thousand employees could find work three hundred and five days in the year.

Closely allied with the establishment of regularity of employment was the advance made by McElwain in introducing punctual delivery of goods manufactured by his company. Shoes are manufactured mainly upon orders; and the orders are taken on samples submitted. The samples are made nearly a year before the goods are sold to the consumer. Samples for the shoes which will be bought in the spring and summer of 1913 were made in the early summer of 1912. The solicitation of orders on these samples began in the late summer. The manufacture of the shoes commences in November; and the order is filled before July.

Dates of delivery are fixed, of course, when orders are taken; but the dates fixed had not been taken very seriously by the manufacturers; and the trade was greatly annoyed by irregularities in delivery. McElwain recognized the business waste and inconvenience attendant upon such unfulfilled promises. He insisted that an agreement to deliver on a certain day was as binding as an agreement to pay a note on a certain day.

He knew that to make punctual delivery possible, careful study and changes in the methods of manufacture and of distribution were necessary. He made the study; he introduced the radical changes found necessary; and he so perfected his organization that customers could rely absolutely upon delivery on the day fixed. Scientific management practically eliminated the recurring obstacles of the unexpected. To attain this result business invention of a high order was of course necessary—invention directed to the departments both of production and of distribution.

The career of the Filenes of Boston affords another example of success in professionalized business. In 1891 the Filenes occupied two tiny retail stores in Boston. The floor space of each was only twenty feet square. One was a glove stand, the other a women's specialty store. Twenty years later their sales were nearly $5,000,000 a year. In September, 1912, they moved into a new building with more than nine acres of floor space. But the significant thing about their success is not their growth in size or in profits. The trade offers many other examples of similar growth. The pre-eminence of the Filenes lies in the advance which has been made in the nature, the aims, and the ideals of retailing, due to their courage, initiative, persistence, and fine spirit. They have applied minds of a high order and a fine ethical sense to the prosaic and seemingly uninteresting business of selling women's garments. Instead of remaining petty tradesmen, they have become, in every sense of the word, great merchants.

The Filenes recognized that the function of retail distribution should be undertaken as a social service, equal in dignity and responsibility to the function of production; and that it should be studied with equal intensity in order that the service may be performed with high efficiency, with great economy, and with nothing more than a fair profit to the retailer. They recognized that to serve their own customers properly, the relations of the retailer to the producer must be fairly and scientifically adjusted; and, among other things, that it was the concern of the retailer to know whether the goods which he sold were manufactured under conditions which were fair to the workers —fair as to wages, hours of work, and sanitary conditions.

But the Filenes recognized particularly their obligations to their own employees. They found as the common and accepted conditions in large retail stores, that the employees had no voice as to the conditions or rules under which they were to work; that the employees had no appeal from policies prescribed by the management; and that in the main they were paid the lowest rate of wages possible under competitive conditions.

In order to insure a more just arrangement for those working in their establishment, the Filenes provided three devices:

First. A system of self-government for employees, administered by the store co-operative association. Working through this association, the employees have the right to appeal from and to veto policies laid down by the management. They may adjust the conditions under which employees are to work, and, in effect, prescribe conditions for themselves.

Second. A system of arbitration, through the operation of which individual employees can call for an adjustment of differences that may exist between themselves and the management as to the permanence of employment, wages, promotion, or conditions of work.

Third. A minimum wage scale, which provided that no woman or girl shall work in their store at a wage less than eight dollars a week, no matter what her age may be or what grade of position she may fill.

The Filenes have thus accepted and applied the principles of industrial democracy and of social justice. But they have done more— they have demonstrated that the introduction of industrial democracy and of social justice is at least consistent with marked financial success. They assert that the greater efficiency of their employees shows industrial democracy and social justice to be money-makers. The so-called "practical business man," the narrow money-maker without either vision or ideals, who hurled against the Filenes, as against McElwain, the silly charge of being "theorists," has been answered even on his own low plane of material success.

McElwain and the Filenes are of course exceptional men; but there are in America to-day many with like perception and like spirit. The paths broken by such pioneers will become the peopled highways. Their exceptional methods will become accepted methods. Then the term "big business" will lose its sinister meaning, and will take on a new significance. "Big business" will then mean business big not in bulk or power, but great in service and grand in manner. "Big business" will mean professionalized business, as distinguished from the occupation of petty trafficking or mere money-making. And as the profession of business develops, the great industrial and social problems expressed in the present social unrest will one by one find solution.

═══

William Miller

The Recruitment of the American Business Elite

There is no more impressive investigation of the social realities of the American business hierarchy in the years of critical transition at the turn of the century than the scholarly analyses of William Miller (1912-). Contrary to popular belief, poor immigrants and poor farm boys were little represented among the business elite who guided American corporate industry, as can been seen in the following selection. [William Miller, "The Recruitment of the American Business Elite," Quarterly Journal of Economics, LXIV, May 1950, pp. 329-337. (Reprinted in William Miller, ed., Men in Business, New York, 1962.)]

Almost twenty years ago, Professor F. W. Taussig and C. S. Joslyn published their book, *American Business Leaders: A Study in Social Origins and Social Stratification.* Although its appearance was without doubt a landmark in the study of the subject, it is the opinion of the present writer that it has won its reputation, at least in part, by default: there simply have been no other studies of comparable scope in the social origins of American business leaders. Of the few articles that have appeared, none has been addressed directly to Taussig and Joslyn's problem of determining the relative importance of heredity and environment in business success, and none has undertaken to test their conclusions.

My opinion that this book, while original and still useful, is limited in its achievement is supported by leading, if forgotten, reviews that appeared soon after its publication. That by Professor Morris Ginsberg in the *Economic Journal* speaks for many of the others. Professor Ginsberg said at the close of his review that "a study such as that made in the work before us, compelled as it is to confine itself to gross differences in the environment, and completely ignoring psychological and genetic analysis, cannot, it seems to me, hope to establish any reliable conclusions in a matter so intricate and complex as the share of genetic differences in social stratification."

The present paper, concerned with a generation of business leaders earlier than that studied by Taussig and Joslyn, but in objective rather more modest than their work, is one of a series aimed at extending our knowledge at least of the social characteristics of such men. In the first of these, I took issue with the description of the origins and upbringing of the "typical" American business leaders of the period since the Civil War that appears in those few American history books that have said anything at all about them. That description is virtually always of the "poor immigrant" or "poor farm" boy who, barely entering his teens, first found work in the meanest of jobs, and, "fired by a passionate will to succeed," rose from "obscure origins" and "from poverty to riches" mainly "by dint of unflagging industry and resourcefulness." In my analysis of 190 of the topmost American business leaders in the first decade of the twentieth century, however, poor immigrant and poor farm boys together are shown to have made up no more than three per cent of this group. The great majority was recruited from higher status families and among themselves shared still other social characteristics.[1]

In this paper the question to be discussed is: to what extent were these shared social characteristics found in large segments of the general population; to what extent were they found among the common run of people with whom business leaders by their own pronouncements on their origins have so often sought to identify themselves, yet over whom they have come to exercise great power?

---

1. In my earlier paper there is a full discussion of the method used in selecting these 190 business leaders and their companies. A list of the men and companies also appears there. Here it is sufficient to point out that each of these men was either president or chairman in the decade 1901-1910 of at least one of the largest American corporations in the following fields (the number in parentheses after each is the number of men selected from each field): manufacturing and mining (64), railroads (58), public utilities (31), and finance (commercial banking 19, and life insurance 9), or was a partner (9) in one of the five leading unincorporated investment banking houses. Except for these partners, all of these men were office holders; many of them never started a business of their own. On this account alone they may be described as America's first big business bureaucrats. That they were of great influence not only in their companies but in the business community generally is suggested by the following statistics on their business directorships. The 174 men about whom this information is available held approximately 2,720 directorships; a few held more than 100 each; the average was about 16.

II

In all classes of society and in all geographical, national, and religious groups in the United States in 1900 there must have been many adults who had not aspired to business eminence. If these could be separated from the rest of the people—and account be taken of them as a group apart—a population of aspirants would remain. This would be a better group than the whole population to compare with the business elite. For here it would be possible to point to the known failures as well as to the successes, and to identify more confidently and examine more closely than is now practicable the social conditions, attending disappointment and achievement.

Needless to say, this division of the population cannot be made. In lieu of it, however, one may point to certain social groups in the population which, whether aspiring to business eminence or not, failed altogether to be represented among the topmost business bureaucrats discussed here.

"It was too bad women didn't count in Guggenheim business affairs," writes Harvey O'Connor, the biographer of the Guggenheim family, "for many said that Gladys was the most capable of [Daniel Guggenheim's] children." Their failure to use female talent, of course, scarcely made the Guggenheims unique. Females made up almost 49 per cent of the total population of the United States in 1900 and 47.5 per cent of those 50 years of age—the average age that year of the 190 business leaders. But these figures only make them one of the largest of the absent groups.

About 12 per cent of the population of the United States in 1900 was non-white—Negro, Indian, Mexican, Oriental; of the 50-year-old males that year, such non-whites were 16.2 per cent. None, however, are found among these elite businessmen. Also unrepresented are southern and eastern Europeans and their descendants, but they were only a relatively small proportion of the whole population. Sizable numbers of men from European countries south and east of Germany had begun to settle in the United States by 1880; but by 1900 they and their adult offspring as yet accounted for only about two per cent of the adult white population. Another small fraction of the population, made up of white immigrants and their descendants, from South America, Asia, Africa, and the islands of the seas, also are missing from the business elite.

These unrepresented national and racial minorities, however small in some instances, are worth mentioning if only for the sake of completeness of presentation. But there is also a better reason. Though their absence from the group studied here may be due simply to the smallness of this group,[2] it may also point up other conditions governing elite recruitment, conditions suggested by the ascent of men from minorities actually represented in the group under view—notably the ascent of Jews.

Although in 1850 Jews accounted for only a small fraction of one per cent of the white population of the United States and although by 1900 their share had not yet risen much above one per cent, six of the business leaders studied here, or about three per cent of those whose religious heritage is known, were of Jewish descent—a better than average showing if it may be supposed that it would remain the same in a much larger sample.[3] None of these six Jews, however, was in a non-Jewish firm. All attained the high positions that make them eligible for this study not only in Jewish enterprises but in those started by their fathers or other relatives.

It is the operation of this factor in particular, this apparent tendency toward religious and national[4] and even family segregation within the business elite—shown as much by the failure of most firms to recruit for their executive hierarchies members of religious or national minorities, as by the practice of men in such minorities, when in power, of favoring their own people—which seems to be indicated most sharply by the history of the absent minorities. Among the latter there appears to have been no one as yet to affirm that their normal lower class goals could be transcended, no one to serve as a model for their sons' or their compatriots' aspirations, and, perhaps most important, no one to serve as the direct instrument of their ascent.

It is worth noting, too, that the envelopment by 1900 of many of the key areas of the economy by the extant business bureaucracies must have made the outlook all the more restricted for those seemingly excluded at once from these bureaucracies and from those key areas in which almost alone great business success could be won.

2. To have augmented this group appreciably, however, would have made it less representative of the topmost business leadership. If, for example, more men in my group had been taken from life insurance companies or from certain industrial lines, such men would have had to come from companies much smaller than those now used exclusively or from lower status jobs in the large firms. In either case, less highly influential men would have mingled with the national elite.

3. Only one of these Jews was an industrialist; the others were primarily private bankers and financiers.

4. It is interesting to note that five of these six Jews were also of German origin (the sixth was a Swiss). Including them, there are nineteen men of German origin among the business leaders studied here. Forty-seven per cent of these German-originated men (compared to only 14 per cent of the rest of these business leaders) attained their peak jobs in firms previously owned or managed by Germans. Excluding the German Jews, this figure becomes 21 per cent.

III

Published census information being what it is for the period of the lives of the men studied here, many distinctions less subtle than that between aspirants and nonaspirants to great business success also are impractical. In only a few categories, for example, can information on the 50-year-old white males in the population, as of 1900, be separated out from that on the population as a whole. In the following pages, where information on this age and sex group is unavailable, less exclusive comparisons are made between the business leaders and the population generally; and where census data are altogether lacking, other sources are used.

The twelfth census, 1900, does report the birthplaces of the population insofar as they may be identified as native or foreign, by sex, color, and age groups. These figures reveal a considerable disproportion between the foreign-born among all 50-year-old white males and the foreign-born in the business elite under view, those in the first group comprising 34.8 per cent, those in the second only 10 per cent. This census also reports on parents' birthplaces and shows that of all 50-year-old white males, 45.6 per cent had at least one foreign-born parent. Those of foreign-born or mixed parentage in the business elite make up only 19 per cent. It appears, therefore, that as many as four out of five among the business bureaucrats studied here, as against only slightly more than half of the 50-year-old white males generally, were native-born of native parents.

Predominantly of old American families, these business bureaucrats naturally were largely of British descent, 79 per cent of them tracing their origins to England, Scotland, the north of Ireland and other places in the British Empire, exclusive of the south of Ireland. Exactly how this proportion compares with that among the 50-year-old white males in 1900, or even with that in the population as a whole, is difficult to determine. Satisfactory estimates of the national origins of the Ameriman people are available only for 1790 and 1920. These are presented in Table I, together with the national origins of the business elite.

The proportion of persons of British (exclusive of south Irish) descent in the United States probably was never higher subsequent to 1790 than it was that year, while the proportions of those of south Irish and of German descent probably were never lower. Thus, the excess of the first group in the business elite in 1900, as compared to the proportion of this group in the population even in 1790, would appear to indicate a sizable over-representation in the elite of persons of British (exclusive of south Irish) ancestry. A comparison, on the other hand, of the estimates of persons of south Irish and of German origin in 1790 and 1920 with the relative size of such groups in the busines elite, seems to disclose a marked under-representation in the elite of persons of such ancestry.

TABLE 1

NATIONAL ORIGINS OF THE AMERICAN POPULATION
AND OF THE PATERNAL LINES OF THE BUSINESS ELITE

Country [1]	American Population 1790 [2] (Per Cent)	American Population 1920 [3] (Per Cent)	Business Elite Born about 1850 (Per Cent)
England and Wales	60.1		53
Scotland	8.1		7
North of Ireland	5.9	41.4 [4]	11
Canada	5 ⎬ 74.1	5.6 ⎬ 47.2	3 ⎬ 79
British Empire, other or unspecified	5	.2	5
South of Ireland	3.6	11.2	3
Germany	8.6	16.3	12
Other Countries	13.7	25.3	6
Percentage Total	100.0	100.0	100.0
Numerical Total	3,226,944	94,821,000	162

1. Last country before settlement of paternal family or businessman himself in colonies or the United States.

2. American Council of Learned Societies, "Report of the Committee on Linguistic and National Stocks in the Population of the United States," in *Annual Report of the American Historical Association, 1931* (3 volumes, Washington, D.C.: Government Printing Office, 1932), I, p. 124.

3. Thompson and Whelpton, *op. cit.*, p. 91. For explanation of why total cases in this column does not equal total population in 1920, see *ibid.*, p. 84.

4. This includes England and Wales, Scotland, and north of Ireland.

5. Numbers too small to count.

This seeming disproportion in the elite in favor of persons descended from the *national* majority appears to be somewhat reversed in the statistics on *religious* heritage. Here again only approximations are available. The twelfth census, 1900, does not report the religious composition of the 50-year-old white male group. The census of 1850, in turn, the one nearest the median year of birth of the business elite, reports only "church accommodations," that is, the seating capacity of the buildings used for worship—probably only a rough index of the actual size of the religious bodies in the United States that year. A comparison of these figures with those on the religious affiliations of the business elite discloses in the latter a somewhat above normal representation of Catholics and Jews (though the numbers involved are small) at the expense of the Protestant majority in general. The greatest differences between the elite and the population, however, as Table 2 shows, appear to be in the under-representation of the largely middle and lower class Protestant denominations, Methodist and Baptist, and the over-representation of Episcopalians and Presbyterians, denominations more often associated with higher status.

TABLE 2

THE RELIGIOUS HERITAGE OF THE AMERICAN POPULATION
AND THE BUSINESS ELITE

Denomination [1]	American Population, 1850 [2] (Per Cent)	Business Elite [3] (Per Cent)	
Episcopal	4.5 ⎱ 19.1	25 ⎱ 46	30 [4] ⎱ 55
Presbyterian	14.6 ⎰	21 ⎰	25 ⎰
Methodist	30.5 ⎱ 53.2	9 ⎱ 14	11 ⎱ 17
Baptist	22.7 ⎰	5 ⎰	6 ⎰
Unitarian	1.0	6	7
Other Protestant	22.0	8	11
Protestant, Unspecified	00.0	16	—
Total Protestant	95.3	90	90
Roman Catholic	4.6	7	7
Jewish	.1	3	3
Percentage Total	100.0	100	100
Numerical Total	14,270,139	174	174

1. In almost all instances this is the religion of the businessman himself, though most likely of his father too. In the few instances in which a shift is known to have occurred, the old religion only is counted.

2. Based on seating capacity of buildings used for worship. Actual total reported is about 61.5 per cent of the entire population, 1850. See J. D. B. DeBow, *Statistical View of the United States* (Washington: A. O. P. Nicholson, 1854), pp. 136-137.

3. All the businessmen about whom this information is known are included here, native-born as well as foreign-born. The distribution of religions among the latter is not sufficiently different from that for the whole group to affect the figures as shown in any significant way.

4. This column shows the distribution of the business leaders by religious denomination, on the assumption, safe enough it seems, that the "Protestant unspecified" group was distributed in the same proportions as the known specified Protestants.

IV

The immediate surroundings in which these great business bureaucrats were raised probably were as important in shaping their careers as
were their national and religious inheritances in opening such careers
to them.

Since these men not only were of old American families, but were
businessmen as well, they might be expected to have come not from the
farms but largely from the older commercial and industrial sections of
the country. And so they did, indeed even in greater proportions than
would normally be expected. Sixty-one per cent of the native-born among
them originated in New England and the Middle Atlantic states, which
area should, statistically speaking, have supplied only about 39 per cent.
These figures and the others for the population generally, in Table 3,
are based on reports of births in the seventh census, 1850.

TABLE 3

NATIVE-BORN LEADERS AND NATIVE-BORN FREE POPULATION
BY REGION OF BIRTHPLACE

Region [1]	Whites and Free Negroes Born in the United States, 1850 [2] (Per Cent)	Native-born Business Elite (Per Cent)
New England	11 ⎫	20 ⎫
Middle Atlantic	28 ⎬ 39	41 ⎬ 61
East North Central	25	25
South	31	10
West	5	4
Percentage Total	100	100
Numerical Total	548,837	169

1. These are census regions. Combined in "South" are South Atlantic, East
South Central, West South Central; in "West," West North Central, Mountain,
and Pacific states and territories.

2. DeBow, *op. cit.*, p. 111. Though free Negroes are combined with whites in
the census tabulation, there were not enough of them, even were their regional
distribution much different from that of the whites, to alter materially the distribution as shown.

Even more striking, in comparison to the distribution of the whole
population in 1850, is the proportion of the business elite born or
raised in the business atmosphere of American cities and larger towns.

Statistics on the occupations of the American population or any large segment of it in the nineteenth century are scanty, and those that are available, especially for the period before 1870, are notoriously unreliable. Still, none of the earlier ones suggest the need for any revision of the impression of an extraordinary concentration in the business elite of men with business family backgrounds, an impression given by the geographical origins of these men as compared with the geographic distribution of the population generally. Occupational statistics for 1870, in turn, are close enough to the period when the men in the business elite were being raised and launched on their business careers to afford relevant comparisons with the occupations of the fathers of these men. And the 1870 occupational data only strengthens the conclusions drawn from those on regional and city-size origins. Two summaries of 1870 occupational statistics are given in Table 5, together with the occupations of the fathers of the business elite. As shown there, well over half of these fathers were businessmen. Business and professional men together make up a remarkable 86 per cent.

TABLE 4

BUSINESS LEADERS BY SIZE OF BIRTHPLACE OR PLACE WHERE RAISED AND
THE AMERICAN POPULATION BY SIZE OF COMMUNITY

Size of Community	American Population, 1850 [1] (Per Cent)	Business Elite [2] (Per Cent)
City (over 8,000)	12.5 } 16.8	41 } 60
Town (2,500 to 8,000)	4.3	19
Rural (under 2,500)	83.2	40
Percentage Total	100.0	100
Numerical Total	23,191,876	170

1. Thompson and Whelpton, *op. cit.,* p. 20.

2. The size used here for each man's place of birth or upbringing is its size according to the census nearest the man's year of birth, not the census of 1850. Place of upbringing is used for all men who moved, before the age of seven, to places sufficiently larger or smaller than their birthplaces to alter their classification in the scale used in this table.

Of the 18 foreign-born business leaders, six who were brought to the United States before the age of seven and raised here are included in this tabulation. Of those excluded, only one was born in a rural place; most of the others were born in great cities.

TABLE 5

OCCUPATIONS OF AMERICAN MALES AND THE FATHERS OF THE BUSINESS ELITE

Occupation [1]	American Males, 1870		Fathers of the Business Elite (Per Cent)
	Taussig and Joslyn [2] (Per Cent)	C. Wright Mills [3] (Per Cent)	
Businessman	6.2	8.1	56 ⎱ 86
Professional	2.5	2.3	30 [6] ⎰
Farmer	32.0	28.2 ⎱ 58.7	12
Rural Worker	⎱ 56.7 [4]	61.4 ⎰ 30.5	0
Urban Worker	⎰	⎱ 30.9	2
Other	2.6	5	5
Percentage Totals	100.0	100.0	100
Numerical Totals	9,420,000	11,007,505	167

1. "Professional" includes independent as well as salaried men; most of those among the fathers of the businessmen were lawyers, engineers, or men engaged in politics, even if not always office holders. "Urban worker" includes wage as well as lower salaried occupations, manual as well as clerical and sales jobs.

2. From F. W. Taussig and C. S. Joslyn, op. cit., p. 273.

3. This distribution is adapted from White Collar: The American Middle Class (Oxford University Press, 1951) by Professor C. Wright Mills, who was generous enough to permit me to use his occupational data before the book's publication.

4. Taussig and Joslyn do not distinguish between rural and urban workers.

5. Only Taussig and Joslyn use this miscellaneous category.

6. In my earlier paper, where a comparison of the backgrounds of business and political leaders was made, this figure appeared as only 23 per cent, for the 7 per cent of these business leaders whose fathers were public officials were listed separately. Here it seemed sensible to include them with professionals.

These occupational statistics must make it clear that, as compared to the American population generally, few of the business leaders under discussion were born or raised in lower class families. The fact that, in a period when most American boys went to work very early in life, only 20 per cent of these business leaders had business jobs before they were sixteen, only strengthens this conclusion. It gains more strength still from statistics on education. In an age when the educational level of the American population generally certainly was no higher than elementary school graduate, only 22 per cent of these business leaders had terminated their formal schooling at that point. Thirty-seven per cent could point to a high school education or its equivalent. The remaining 41 per cent had gone to college, approximately three out of four of them graduating. How far this 41 per cent exceeded the proportion of college men in the population generally is indicated by the following statistics. In 1870, the census year nearest that in which most of these college-educated business leaders would have been in attendance, there were in the United States 2,067,144 white males between the ages of 15 and 20. That year there were 67,350 males in the colleges and universities of the country—a scant 3.3 per cent of the white males of college age.

V

If it be true, as leading American businessmen and leading American historians continue to assert, that, so to speak, anyone can become president of large business firms, it appears to be true also that at least in the early twentieth century most of the successful aspirants had certain social characteristics that distinguished them sharply from the common run of Americans of their time. Such distinguishing characteristics may have been less marked among American business leaders in the first half or three-quarters of the nineteenth century, though too little is known about that period to generalize with safety. In the bureaucratic twentieth century, however, many of these characteristics were so prevalent among the business leaders, and so rare among the rest of the population, that the presumption, at least, is strong that they constituted genuine advantages in the competition for business eminence.

———

William Miller

American Lawyers in Business and in Politics

Law, alone among the learned professions, has been linked to business on the one side and to politics on the other. Close identification with the marketplace, however, has tended to obscure the social milieu which conditioned the success of lawyers and politicians, no less than the more conventional business figures. Again, William Miller illuminates the human nexus that, at the turn of the century, inevitably contributed to the social exclusiveness of the corporate hierarchy, of which the lawyer was becoming an integral part. [William Miller, "American Lawyers in Business and in Politics: Their Social Backgrounds and Early Training," Yale Law Journal, LX, January 1951, pp. 66-76.]

I

It long ago became fashionable to describe business as an organized system of force and fraud. Nineteenth-century law did little to control this. Even in the so-called robber baron period in the latter part of the century much business "fraud" was likely to be defensible under the law then current and much business "force" to be beyond legal remedies as then applied. In the next era—which we may label bureaucratic [1]—, statute, decision, and administrative decree became increasingly hostile to business enterprise, but to a considerably larger extent

1. For justification of the use of this term, see Miller, *American Historians and the Business Elite*, 9 JOUR. ECON. HIST. 187-88 (1949).

big business managers tried to steer their enterprises, as they often explained, "well within the law." [2] This impelled them, on the one hand (the better to divert the popular anti-business feeling from making the law and its enforcement too strict) to develop increasingly systematic contacts with lawyers in public office; and, on the other, as the strictness of the law increased, to have growing recourse to private legal advice in the making of day to day business decisions. The demand for such advice, indeed, became so great that the best paid metropolitan lawyers almost without exception after 1900 made business counseling the focus of their work, at the expense of traditional advocacy; and many lawyers yielded to the blandishments of the corporations to become house counsel and even regular business executives themselves.[3]

These twin tendencies—the growing routinization of business politics and the growing representation of lawyers in business management— are largely twentieth-century developments. But in politics they can easily be traced back to the czardom of Speaker Thomas B. Reed in the House of Representatives, to the suzerainty of Nelson W. Aldrich over the Senate,[4] to the reign of Melville W. Fuller on the United States Supreme Court; and in business to the regimes of such solicitors as George F. Baer, an early "Morgan lawyer," or Adrian H. Joline, "the ablest practical master of reorganizations we have ever had," [5] who sometimes headed up the directorates of his salvaged firms, or Charles H. Tweed, son-in-law of William M. Evarts and erstwhile member of Southmayd and Choate, who became general counsel for the Huntington enterprises and partner in Speyer and Company, investment bankers.

2. For an intensive and costly effort in this direction as early as 1910 see PROCEEDINGS OF THE RAILROAD ATTORNEYS' CONFERENCE TO CONSIDER AND DISCUSS QUESTIONS ARISING UNDER THE MANN-ELKINS BILL (1910).

3. In 1920, Paul D. Cravath commented on the "striking phenomenon of the New York bar" that "advocacy has become almost a lost art." He thought this "a great pity, for with [its] decline our profession has suffered a real loss of glory and charm." This decline he attributed to "the materialism of our age" in which a young man must secure an income large enough to gain "those rewards of metropolitan life which only money will buy. He therefore becomes a lawyer of affairs. He seeks to become the adviser of great corporations and firms that deal with large financial transactions because it is for such services that the most liberal compensation is paid. . . ." 2 SWAINE, THE CRAVATH FIRM 265-66 (1948). See also Berle, *Modern Legal Profession*, 9 ENCYC. SOC. SC. 340-41 (1933); DOS PASSOS, THE AMERICAN LAWYER (1907); *Lawyers Looking at You*, 3 FORTUNE 61 (Jan. 1931).

On the development of the house counsel, see the study done for the Survey of the Legal Profession by Charles S. Maddock and published along with six case studies as CORPORATE LEGAL DEPARTMENTS, NO. 39, STUDIES IN BUSINESS POLICY, NAT. INDUST. CONF. BD. (1950).

4. Aldrich, of course, was not a lawyer himself, but a businessman; on his relations with lawyers in the inner circle of the Senate, see the very suggestive chapter IX in STEPHENSON, NELSON W. ALDRICH 132-37 (1930). See also HURST, THE GROWTH OF AMERICAN LAW 45 (1950).

5. DEWING, THE FINANCIAL POLICY OF CORPORATIONS 1084 (3rd rev. ed. 1934). See also, 1 STETSON *et al.*, SOME LEGAL PHASES OF CORPORATE FINANCING, REORGANIZATION, AND REGULATION 153 (1930).

Such men were in the van of a quiet revolution in business and politics and their reciprocal relations. This in itself may serve admirably as justification, if the prevailing blankness of present information were not enough, for writing of their social backgrounds and early training. For this subject, nevertheless, the particular selection of laywers examined here could perhaps easily be improved upon, so that a further word in explanation of this sample itself should be added.

This paper is actually the fourth in a series concerned primarily with leaders in American business and politics in the decade 1901-1910.[6] It is largely because of the historical circumstances outlined in the first two paragraphs above that lawyers enter the work at all. This conceivably could add to rather than diminish the strength of this sample of lawyers in business and politics, but it should be kept clear in either case that the only lawyers considered here are those who held high public or business office early in this century. It was on the basis of such office-holding in the first instance that the whole group of business and political leaders from which these lawyers are drawn was selected.[7] Hence these lawyers are of that class only, but perhaps representative of that class, which attained eminence not in the law alone (some in fact did not become eminent lawyers), but in politics or in business, between which the law itself might easily be conceived of as a natural bridge.[8]

6. The first of these is Miller, *supra* note 1; the second, Miller, *The Recruitment of the American Business Elite,* 64 Q. J. Econ. 242 (1950); the third, Miller, *The Business Elite in Business Bureaucracies*. All three essays are printed in the Harper Torchbook edition of *Men in Business* (1962).

7. There is a full discussion of the mode of selection of the over-all sample of business leaders and a full list, with company and position, of the 190 men in the sample, in Miller, *supra* note 1, at 189-96. Here it is sufficient to point out that each of these 190 men (and hence each of the lawyers in the present study taken from the business sample) was either president or chairman in the decade 1901-1910 of at least one of the largest American business corporations, or was a partner in one of the leading unincorporated investment banking houses. The over-all political sample of 188 men includes all the presidents, vice-presidents, cabinet members, and United States Supreme Court judges in office in this decade, these being 44 men; plus 67 United States Senators and 77 Representatives, selected from the whole group in each house largely on the basis of committee chairmanships in the 57th through the 61st Congresses. For more on this, see *id.* at 191 n. 22.

8. The following is the list of twenty-seven lawyers found among the business leaders:

Alexander, James W.	Fowler, Thomas P.	McCarter, Thomas N.
Baer, George F.	Gary, Elbert H.	McCurdy, Richard A.
Bancroft, William A.	Gaston, William A.	Peabody, Charles A.
Colt, Samuel P.	Green, Adolphus W.	Pierce, Winslow S.
Cortelyou, George B.	Herrin, William F.	Sheldon, Edward W.
Depew, Chauncy M.	Joline, Adrian H.	Shonts, Theodore P.
Elliott, Warren G.	Lincoln, Robert T.	Tweed, Charles H.
Finney, Frederick N.	Lovett, Robert S.	Walker, Roberts
Fish, Frederick P.	Mather, Robert	Wetmore, Charles W.

The following is the list of sixty-one lawyers from the political sample who were, as in the cases of Stephen B. Elkins, Charles W. F. Dick or Franklin MacVeagh, notably big businessmen themselves as well as being lawyers and politicians; or who

II

In the first of these earlier papers, given in part to a comparison of
the American business and political elites, I showed that the over-all
samples of 190 business leaders and 188 leaders in national politics had
some striking social characteristics in common.[9] Few in either group
were immigrants who had made good, and even of these almost none
was a *poor* immigrant. Three-fourths of these men were of colonial
American ancestry and more than half were of families that had settled
in America in the seventeenth century. Four out of five, moreover,
could point to British and more than half to English forebears.

Such homogeneity in origins, however, while auguring well for the
solidarity of these elites—especially as compared with the whole pop-

9. It would be impossible in the space available here to name in detail the sources
used for information about these men. Who's whos, encyclopedias, directories, individual and group biographies, newspaper and magazine files and the "morgues" of a
few newspapers and magazines all proved useful as did a rather voluminous correspondence with the families of many of these men, and with local historical societies,
libraries, and the companies of the business leaders.

---

were, as in the cases of Elihu Root, George W. Wickersham or Philander C. Knox,
outstanding and very close counsel to big business enterprises. Naturally not all of
the men listed here were as eminent as these named; a few, indeed, might be judged
marginal cases. Compared to the political lawyers in the list that follows this one,
however, these men appeared to me to have been those in politics with the closest
relations with big business in other than straight political capacities.

Allison, William B.	Hoar, George F.	Proctor, Redfield
Ballinger, Richard A.	Hopkins, Albert J.	Quarles, Joseph V.
Boutell, Henry S.	Hull, John A. T.	Reeves, Walter
Bradley, William O.	Kittredge, Alfred B.	Root, Elihu
Brown, Henry B.	Knox, Philander C.	Shaw, Leslie M.
Burnham, Henry E.	Knox, William S.	Sherman, James S.
Burton, Theodore E.	Lacey, John F.	Shiras, George, Jr.
Dillingham, William P.	Long, Chester I.	Simon, Joseph
Cannon, Joseph G.	Long, John D.	Skiles, William W.
Crawford, Coe I.	MacVeagh, Franklin	Smith, William A.
Dick, Charles W. F.	Mann, James R.	Spooner, John C.
Dickinson, Jacob M.	Mason, William E.	Steele, George W.
Elkins, Stephen B.	McKenna, Joseph	Stewart, William M.
Fairbanks, Charles W.	Metcalf, Victor H.	Straus, Oscar S.
Flint, Frank P.	Mondell, Frank W.	Sutherland, George
Foraker, Joseph B.	Nagel, Charles	Vreeland, Edward B.
Foss, George E.	Payne, Sereno E.	White, Edward D.
Fowler, Charles N.	Parker, Richard W.	Wickersham, George W.
Fuller, Melville W.	Peckham, Rufus W.	Wright, Luke E.
Hale, Eugene	Penrose, Boies	
Hitchcock, Frank H.	Platt, Orville H.	

Of the sixty-seven remaining lawyers from the political group, it is illuminating
to note, just about half were in the House as compared to only 28 percent from
the list just above. While 54 percent of the above list were in political jobs for
more than twenty years, this was true of as many as 68 percent of the politicians
to be listed next. Only 34 percent of the lawyers with big business connections were
appointed or elected to their peak political position from another political job. Most

ulation, from which they were widely divorced [10]—appears not to have
been sufficient to avert the development of broad differences between
them in religious heritage, early geographical and community environment, formal education, father's status, and similar categories. Such
differences, in turn, as well as some of the likenesses, seem to have been
carried over (the differences sometimes considerably enlarged) to the
lawyers recruited for the present study from each of these elite groups.

Where differences between the original over-all business and political
samples do occur, they are almost always such as to show the business
elite as the more favored. Thus it is not surprising to discover that
the lawyers found for this study in the business elite, as tables below
will show, were the most favorably born and bred of all. The lawyers
among the political elite, moreover, who had the closest direct relations
with big business—either as practicing lawyers as or big businessmen
themselves—were more highly favored in their origins and upbringing
than the rest of those in high political office.

10. A comparison of my findings about the business leaders and the whole population is the core of Miller, *The Recruitment of the American Business Elite,* 64 Q. J.
ECON. 242 (1950). All comparisons made in the present study between the lawyers
and the population are based on data about the latter in that essay.

---

of them came directly to the political top from law practice. Of the following list,
however, 51 percent rose to the top through the political hierarchy. These differences
in political experience would seem to go toward confirming the differences in business
and legal experiences imputed here to these two distinct groups of political lawyers.
It should be noted, too, that included in the following list are not only the political
hacks, party wheelhorses, reformers and googoos, who happened to be lawyers, but
also such political intellectuals as John Hay, Henry Cabot Lodge, Theodore Roosevelt,
Oliver Wendell Holmes, who, though rich themselves, found in business, as Hay
once put it, but "a dreary waste of heartless materialism." 1 THAYER, JOHN HAY 56
(1915).

Alexander, DeAlva S.	Fulton, Charles W.	McGuire, Bird S.
Beveridge, Albert J.	Garfield, James	McKinley, William
Bonaparte, Charles J.	Gillett, Frederick H.	Miller, James M.
Borah, William E.	Graff, Joseph V.	Moody, William H.
Brewer, David J.	Gray, Horace	Morgan, John T.
Brown, Norris	Grosvenor, Charles H.	Mudd, Sydney E.
Burke, Charles H.	Hamilton, Edward L.	Nelson, Knute
Burrows, Julius C.	Harlan, John M.	Overstreet, Jesse
Calderhead, William A.	Hawley, Joseph R.	Perkins, James B.
Carter, Thomas H.	Hay, John M.	Prince, George W.
Clapp, Moses E.	Hemenway, James A.	Pritchard, Jeter C.
Clark, Clarence D.	Henderson, David B.	Quay, Matthew S.
Cousins, Robert G.	Hepburn, William P.	Ray, George W.
Crumpacker, Edgar D.	Heyburn, Weldon B.	Roosevelt, Theodore
Cullom, Shelby M.	Holmes, Oliver W.	Smith, Samuel W.
Cummins, Albert B.	Jenkins, John J.	Stewart, James F.
Currier, Frank D.	Knapp, Charles L.	Taft, William H.
Curtis, Charles	LaFollette, Robert M.	Tawney, James A.
Davidson, James H.	Lawrence, George P.	Tayler, Robert W.
Day, William R.	Littlefield, Charles E.	Wanger, Irving P.
Dolliver, Jonathan P.	Lodge, Henry C.	Warnock, William R.
Foster, David J.	McComas, Louis E.	
Frye, William P.	McCumber, Porter J.	

III

Even where there is a considerable degree of similarity among all of these lawyers—as in the fact that no more than 6 per cent of any of the three groups were foreign born, or that no more than 12 per cent were first- or second-generation Americans, or that only between 12 and 18 per cent were of other than British origin [11] in the paternal line— more detailed analysis shows marked differences of importance. There were, for example, no men at all of foreign birth among the lawyers in the business sample; the latter, moreover, as Table I shows, were of Eastern birth appreciably more often than those in the other two groups. They were also considerably more likely to be of old family, even though among *all* of these lawyers the paternal lines generally were old enough to be unusual in the whole population.

From this it should perhaps follow that the lawyers in the business sample would also have been of English (not simply British) origin more frequently than the others. But that appears not to have been the case, those of Scottish descent among them (from Scotland and the North of Ireland), as Table III shows, being surprisingly numerous.

TABLE 1

AMERICAN BUSINESS AND POLITICAL LAWYERS BY REGION OF BIRTHPLACE

Birthplace *	Big Businessmen-Lawyers	Lawyers in Politics with big business connections	Lawyers in Politics with no big business connections	Total Lawyers
	(percent)	(percent)	(percent)	(percent)
East	70	54	39	50
West	23	30	43	34
South	7	11	12	11
	—	—	—	—
Total United States	100	95	94	95
Foreign	0	5	6	5
	—	—	—	—
Total cases (=100%)	27	61	67	155

* These are Census regions. Combined in "East" are New England and Middle Atlantic; in "West," East North Central, Mountain, and Pacific; in "South," South Atlantic, South Central, West South Central.

11. British here does not include South Irish.

TABLE 2

AMERICAN BUSINESS AND POLITICAL LAWYERS BY GENERATION OF
PATERNAL LINE IN AMERICA

Generation	Big Businessmen-Lawyers	Lawyers in Politics with big business connections	Lawyers in Politics with no big business connections	Total Lawyers
	(percent)	(percent)	(percent)	(percent)
First or Second	4	12	12	10
Third	0	13	10	10
Fourth or older	96	75	78	80
	—	—	—	—
Total cases (=100%) *	25	59	51	135

* Where "total cases" are fewer than in Table I, difference is due to lack of information for the missing number.

In religious heritage, again, all of these lawyers were rather uniformly Protestant, but again the sectarian differences are illuminating. As Table IV shows, more than half of the lawyers from the business sample were Episcopalian or Presbyterian, and this in a society in which both denominations together could claim scarcely one in five of the whole population. If Congregationalism be included with the elite sects, this disproportion becomes greater still. Obversely, while Methodists and Baptists, traditionally middle and lower class, accounted for more than half of the American population, in none of these groups of lawyers, as the table indicates, did they number more than 24 per cent.

IV

In 1920, Paul D. Cravath, long a luminary of the "financial bar" and by then its acknowledged dean, said in a talk at Harvard Law School that " 'family influence, social friendships and wealth count for little' " in helping a young lawyer to the pinnacle of a big business practice. "He emphasized," according to Robert T. Swaine, his one-

TABLE 3

AMERICAN BUSINESS AND POLITICAL LAWYERS BY
NATIONAL ORIGIN OF PATERNAL FAMILY

Family Origin *	Big Business-men Lawyers	Lawyers in Politics with big business connections	Lawyers in Politics with no big business connections	Total Lawyers
	(percent)	(percent)	(percent)	(percent)
England and Wales	59	70	45	58
Scotland and the North of Ireland	29	16	29	24
Other British Empire †	0	2	8	4
Total British Empire	88	88	82	86
South of Ireland	0	3	4	3
Germany	4	7	4	5
Other Countries	8	2	10	6
Total cases (=100%)	24	56	51	131

* Or country of lawyer's own origin if he was the first in his family to settle in America. In either case, *last country* before settlement in America.
† Excluding the South of Ireland.

time partner and historian of *The Cravath Firm,* the "large number of successful lawyers who had come to New York from small places and worked up from the bottom of the ladder without having any advantage of position or acquaintance.' " [12]

That Cravath might have gone on to name a galaxy of lawyers, not least among them himself and Swaine, who had risen as he said they had, no one will deny. Even most of *these* men, nevertheless, must have shared the national, the religious, the old family—the British, Protestant, Colonial—heritage that, in a society already on the way to becoming today's throbbing mosaic of complex patterns of segregation, would of itself have made them self-consciously of the elite and lent practicality to their professional aspirations.

Such a heritage, indeed, might be thought of—so almost universal was it among all the lawyers studied here—simply as the bottom requi-

12. 2 SWAINE, THE CRAVATH FIRM 265 (1948).

TABLE 4

AMERICAN BUSINESS AND POLITICAL LAWYERS BY RELIGIOUS HERITAGE

Denomination *	Big Businessmen-Lawyers	Lawyers in Politics with big business connections	Lawyers in Politics with no big business connections	Total Lawyers
	(percent)	(percent)	(percent)	(percent)
Episcopalian	28 ⎫	16 ⎫	7 ⎫	14 ⎫
Presbyterian	24 ⎬ 60	9 ⎬ 37	22 ⎬ 37	17 ⎬ 41
Congregationalist	8 ⎭	12 ⎭	8 ⎭	10 ⎭
Methodist	16 ⎫ 16	10 ⎫ 15	17 ⎫ 24	14 ⎫ 19
Baptist	0 ⎭	5 ⎭	7 ⎭	5 ⎭
Other Protestant	12	12	10	11
Protestant Unspecified	8	24	22	21
Total Protestant	96	88	93	92
Catholic	4	5	5	5
Jewish	0	3	0	1
Other or none	0	4	2	2
Total cases (=100%)	25	58	59	142

* In almost all instances this is the religion of the leader himself and most likely of his family as well. In a few instances where a shift in religion is known to have occurred, only the old religion is used.

site, as the floor from which, generally speaking, only young men so endowed might raise edifices among their professional peers. But if the material in the tables that follow is to be credited as reflecting reality more adequately than the animadversions of Cravath and Swaine, to reach their professional goals even such young men must, on the whole, have had other endorsements as well. This, as has been said, is especially reflected in the data on the lawyers from the sample of business leaders—on those, that is, most akin to the "financial bar" that Cravath singled out for notice. It is only slightly less true, however, of those lawyers in politics who were most closely associated with the financial community.

Take first this "coming from small places." Most of the lawyers in all three groups, but especially in both groups of politicians, did, of course, come from such places; how avoid it when in 1850, the census year nearest the date of birth of most of these men, the United States was so largely made up of farms, rural villages, and small towns? In that year 87.5 percent of the whole population resided in places with fewer than 8,000 persons. What is more striking, therefore, than the fact that such places supplied political lawyers in about the same proportion as their share of the whole population is that they supplied only 59 percent of the lawyers in the big business group. Forty-one percent of the latter, compared to but 12.5 percent of the nation in 1850, were from larger cities, 15 percent from the few metropolitan centers having populations in excess of 100,000.

To an unusual degree from urban centers, centers of wealth and power, of educational and professional opportunities, these lawyers were also largely from families in which such wealth and power were likely to be concentrated and the stimulus toward a professional career most direct. This again is most frequently true of the lawyers from the business sample.

That for most of these men, moreover, the opportunities for such professional development need not merely be inferred but can be documented, is shown by the statistics on their education. In an age when the overwhelming majority of their contemporaries in the American

TABLE 5

AMERICAN BUSINESS AND POLITICAL LAWYERS BY SIZE OF BIRTHPLACE

Size of Birthplace *	Big Business-men Lawyers	Lawyers in Politics with big business connections	Lawyers in Politics with no big business connections	Total Lawyers
	(percent)	(percent)	(percent)	(percent)
Under 8,000	59	84	89	82
8,000 to 100,000	26 ⎱ 41	11	5	11
Over 100,000	15 ⎰	5	6	7
	—	—	—	—
Total cases (=100%)	27	58	65	150

* Size of birthplace here is size of census nearest actual year of subject's birth and not census of 1850 except where that is nearest.

TABLE 6

AMERICAN BUSINESS AND POLITICAL LAWYERS
BY FATHER'S OCCUPATION

Occupation *	Big Business- men Lawyers	Lawyers in Politics with big business connections	Lawyers in Politics with no big business connections	Total Lawyers
	(percent)	(percent)	(percent)	(percent)
Businessman	32 ⎫	28 ⎫	31 ⎫	30 ⎫
Lawyer or Public	⎬ 60	⎬ 56	⎬ 41	⎬ 51
Official	28 ⎭	28 ⎭	10 ⎭	21 ⎭
Other Professional	24	10	17	32
Farmer	16	32	40	16
Worker	0	2	2	1
Total cases (=100%)	25	57	58	142

* Some fathers engaged in more than one occupation. The one used here was dominant in the period in which each man was raised. In only a few instances was this not clear, so a choice was made more or less arbitrarily by which business (including higher company positions as well as company ownership) took precedence over farming and professional, or public official over both. This conforms roughly to the ascending order of status used in classifying occupations today. "Public Official" includes professional politicians even if not office holders. "Other Professional" is made up of a scattering of engineers and clergymen, doctors, writers, etc.

population, or indeed only in the male part of it (females generally having far less education still), never progressed beyond grade school or its equivalent, almost 9 out of 10 of these lawyers in the business sample and an extraordinary proportion of those in the political group as well had gone to college.[13]

Business and professional men's sons, of course, often were poor boys; and poor boys sometimes went to college and became lawyers— even though a college education, in this era, was nowhere a prerequisite

13. In 1870, the census year nearest that in which most of these college-trained lawyers would have been in attendance, there were in the United States 2,067,144 white males between the ages of 15 and 20. That year there were 67,350 males in the colleges and universities of the country—a scant 3.3 percent of the males of college age. See Miller, *The Recruitment of the American Business Elite*, 64 Q. J. ECON. 242 (1950).

TABLE 7

AMERICAN BUSINESS AND POLITICAL LEADERS BY
HIGHEST EDUCATIONAL LEVEL ATTAINED

Education *	Big Business- men Lawyers	Lawyers in Politics with big business connections	Lawyers in Politics with no big business connections	Total Lawyers
	(percent)	(percent)	(percent)	(percent)
Grammar School	0	8	13	9
High School	11	22	25	21
College	89	70	62	70
	—	—	—	—
Total cases (=100%)	27	60	67	154

* I have reduced the many types of older schools to this modern terminology, including in "grammar school" institutions called by that name as well as district, public, common, and similar schools; in "high school," academies and others of similar rank. Counted among grammar-school boys are those who had little or no formal education as well as graduates; among high school boys, all who attended, whether graduates or not. A few who had private tutors well into their teens but did not attend college are counted with the high-school group. "College" includes all who attended.

for legal training or admission to the bar.[14] That most of the lawyers studied here, however, were scarcely poor boys; that college for them, indeed, was largely a way simply to enhance for professional purposes social endowments that were already theirs at birth, is suggested by the data in Table VIII.

Though sometime late in the nineteenth century, writes Professor Adolf A. Berle, "the responsible leadership in social development" moved, in America, "from the lawyer to the businessman," the "position of the lawyer had an even greater appeal than before. It remained one of the careers through which a man could attain influence and wealth even without having capital at the start." [15] This may remain a sound generalization still. But if one may generalize about lawyers from the evidence presented here on those who gained the greatest influence and wealth in politics and business as well as law, then it is clear that a considerable *social* capital at least helped smooth their way.

14. There is a good general discussion of legal education and admission to the bar in HURST, THE GROWTH OF AMERICAN LAW 256-285 (1950).
15. Berle *supra* note 3 at 341.

TABLE 8

AMERICAN BUSINESS AND POLITICAL LAWYERS BY
STATUS OF FAMILY

Status *	Big Business-men Lawyers	Lawyers in Politics with big business connections	Lawyers in Politics with no big business connections	Total Lawyers
	(percent)	(percent)	(percent)	(percent)
Upper	67	42	30	41
Middle	30	53	57	51
Lower	3	5	13	8
	—	—	—	—
Total cases (=100%)	27	60	63	150

* The problem of describing the class structure of the American population around the middle of the nineteenth century, when most of these lawyers were born and raised, is exceedingly complex. It is only less difficult to rank by class special groups in the population such as the fathers or families of these lawyers. This I undertook to do, however, on grounds and along lines fully described in Miller, *supra* note 1, at 204-06. On the class structure of the population in the period, see especially MARTIN, THE STANDARD OF LIVING IN 1860 (1942) and the citations there; and Tucker *The Distribution of Income Among Income Tax Payers in the United States,* 52 Q.J.ECON. 547 (1938).

—

W. Lloyd Warner

The Corporation Man

In the mid-twentieth century, W. Lloyd Warner (1898-   ), the so-cial anthropologist, argues, based on statistical comparison with the preceding generation, that "the top of the highly esteemed and power-ful hierarchy of corporate enterprise has become increasingly a pinnacle to which men of lowly origin can realistically aspire." If this is so, it would seem that a sharp break with the social tendencies of the late nineteenth and early twentieth centuries is being made in this genera-tion. [W. Lloyd Warner, "The Corporation Man," in Edward S. Mason, ed., The Corporation in Modern Society, *Cambridge, 1960, pp. 106-121.]*

◉

1. *Questions and Issues*

All Americans have been greatly interested in the roles of the managers of the great American corporations, and innumerable scientific inquiries have been made into the subject. Ever since this powerful elite first ap-peared, stormy debate has raged over its rightful place in our corporate structure and the country's economy and over the proper functions of such positions of prestige in our society. The emphasis of research investigation more often has been on the role rather than the personality of the manager, on the position within the structure of the economy or the society, rather than on the flesh-and-blood individuals. To under-stand fully what happens in corporate enterprise and the meaning of some of the behavior at managerial levels it is of course necessary to ask who the men themselves are; for what they are as men will greatly determine how they think, act, and feel as managers. Who they are as individuals crucially influences the decisions they make and how and when they will or will not make them. In brief, what a manager is as a person determines how he uses his position, whether he makes the most or the least of its power, the kind of power he uses, and, in the cases of some managers, the kinds of values and beliefs that are encouraged or discouraged in a corporation. To ask what kinds of men are managers raises a number of important questions of fact, theory, and public policy. Let us briefly state two of the more important ones. Broadly speaking, to understand managers as persons we must know the answers to two kinds of questions. What are they as social beings: what has been their social training and what set of social characteristics have they acquired? And what is the nature of the "inner men" that, as it were, lie beneath their managerial skins?

At the level of fact, we must first ask what are the economic and social backgrounds of these men. What did their fathers do for a living? Are they a birth elite, the sons of men of their own kind, or are they mobile men, who have fought their way up from lowly origins? If so, how did they do it? What were the social and economic means they used to climb to the top? And this learned, what do our findings signify? What issues does the evidence raise?

II. *What Kind of Men Are Managers?*

When we examine the occupational backgrounds of contemporary business leaders to learn who they are we can also discover how much mobility into the higher reaches of management actually exists, and we can use this knowledge to tell us something about the comparative flexibility and rigidity of our occupational and class hierarchies. Over half (52 per cent) of all the major executives of contemporary corporations are the sons of men who have been executives, major or minor, or owners of small or large enterprises. The other 48 per cent is constituted as follows: 15 per cent are sons of laborers, 8 per cent come from white-collar families, 14 per cent are sons of fathers in the professions, and another 9 per cent had fathers who were farmers (all other categories amounted to but 2 per cent). In the adult male population belonging to the different occupational categories in our country, the sons of business men are not found in the same high proportions. But, among the American executives with executive fathers, for every 100 that might be expected by their proportion in the general population, there are 473, or nearly five times more than would be expected by chance alone. Business and the professions (the latter with 350 for every 100 "expected") are the only two occupational categories among the fathers of business leaders that are overrepresented. Those fathers underrepresented are the white-collar men (80 instead of 100), the farmers (73), and the laborers (32), the last obviously well below their proportionate share.

These figures, important as they are, tell us nothing about what has been happening through the years to the status of the managerial group. Is this pinnacle today more or less accessible than it was a generation ago? Are we now more or less castelike than we were then? In 1928, when Taussig and Joslyn studied the executive leaders of great corporations, they found 967 executives who were the sons of executives, about twice as many as today's 473. There were then 433 sons of professional men, instead of 350. When we examined the numbers of executives who were the sons of fathers in occupations that are now underrepresented, there were only 24 sons of laborers (32 today), 32 instead of 33 sons of farmers, and only 71 sons of white-collar men, compared with 80 today. These figures seem to demonstrate that the status of the business leader in the great corporations for those at the lower social and economic levels is more open to free competition today than it was a generation ago. Moreover, these measurements indicate that it is a much less positive future for men born to families of high position. In brief, the top of the highly esteemed and powerful hierarchy of corporate enterprise has become increasingly a pinnacle to which men of lowly origins can realistically aspire. That the sons of the powerful and high-ranking are at a great advantage today cannot be denied; yet the evidence indicates that the skills, talents, and training of all levels of the society are increasingly being used to provide economic leadership.

Most of us would agree that this democratic tendency which through free competition brings up men from the bottom and thereby increases the likelihood of more men of ability occupying high position is unqualifiedly good and should continue to increase. However, second thoughts raise serious problems. Suppose that the present trend reached a point where the sons of business leaders were at a serious disadvantage numerically in the executive class. Many such men, losing the strong motivations of advancing and securing the family's interests and occupational traditions, might find it difficult to give their best to the job at hand. Moreover, it seems possible that social instability at the higher levels of our society, created by a shifting personnel, would create its own problems for the stability and well-being of the entire society. At issue is the problem of how we can best maintain the kind of leadership that a free society must have and the kinds of values that such men must possess if America is to compete successfully with the rest of the world and realize her own economic and cultural potentialities. The proper proportion of upward to downward movement at the highest occupational levels, in terms of the general well-being of the society, cannot be estimated. We know that today there is still not enough movement from the bottom and probably not enough down from the top. But we should not yield too easily to our Utopian fantasies that it would be impossible to have too much movement from the bottom to the top. Our Communist competitors with their hard-headed realism know better than this. On the other hand, we cannot sit complacently and feel that any movement at all up from the bottom is adequate.

The increase, in the last generation, in the amount of mobility from the bottom, and probably from the top down, as well as indications of more flexibility in our social and economic structure in general, raises the question of why this tendency has appeared. Are there discernible factors in operation, related to this increase in opportunity for those who aspire to corporate leadership? We shall briefly review the evidence for such factors, and then interpret their significance for our problem. Here and there we shall speculate on how these factors might help us to understand our society and to formulate public policies.

III. *What Do Higher Education and the Growth of Large Corporations Signify for Business Leadership?*

We have all become aware of the increasing importance of higher education to the society and to the individuals who compete for economic success. How much did higher education contribute to the careers of business leaders and what kind of an education did they get? Do certain kinds of institutions of higher learning, private or public, professional schools or colleges of the liberal arts, make or fail to make their contributions to the important task of training competent as well as wise business leadership? And, these questions answered, what are the meanings and significance of the answers, not only for corporate leadership but for a free society? Moreover, do the answers indicate educational policies that might, if encouraged, provide business and our country with better leadership?

During the generation that has passed since Taussig and Joslyn systematically studied business leaders, there has been an enormous increase in the proportion of executives of big business who attended college, far beyond the increase in college graduates in the general population. Today three fourths of the managers of large corporations have been to college. Of these, some graduated (57 per cent), some did not (19 per cent), and some, usually after receiving a bachelor's degree, advanced to higher degrees (19 per cent), frequently at the better universities. Only 7 per cent of the adult male population as a whole in 1950 were college graduates. Fifty-five per cent had less than a high-school education, in major contrast to the tiny 4 per cent of the business leaders who did not go beyond grammar school.

The relation of education to managerial achievement is most dramatically expressed in comparisons between the last and the present generations of big-business executives. Whereas today six out of ten corporate executives are college graduates, only three were in 1928. Fewer than one in twenty have had less than a high-school education today, but in

1928 approximately three out of ten quit at grammar school (27 per cent). During the intervening period, education has become the principal route for advancement to top positions. Given the facts that the sons of big-business leaders and those of men in the major professions are still disproportionately high among these "corporation men" and are also those most likely to go to college, there is still room for doubt that these figures do in fact represent increased opportunity and realized achievement for the sons of lower occupational levels. But further evidence demonstrates that advantages accrued at all levels. In 1928 only 8 per cent of the sons of unskilled or semiskilled workers graduated from college; today 34 per cent of the managers of corporations who came from this level received at least an A.B. degree, as did 34 per cent of the sons of skilled workers. Forty-eight per cent of those from white-collar origins graduated, as against 20 per cent in the previous generation. When these figures are compared with the 32 per cent for all business leaders who were college graduates in the previous generation, they indicate and probably measure the great importance of higher education as an influence in the increased movement of men from the lower occupational levels into the present top positions of the business elite. There can be little question but that higher education is positively related to the opening of the managerial status to those from below who are sufficiently talented and qualified. This means, of course, that college training is also positively related to an increase in free competition for the more powerful and prestige-bearing positions of authority in industry. Moreover, it implies, I believe, that membership requirements for both our corporate and social hierarchies throughout the country are more flexible and open today than a generation ago.

If highly qualified men are being drawn now more than ever before from all parts of the United States, rural as well as urban, and from all occupational levels, through the power of higher education to positions of leadership in the great corporations, what becomes of, and what must we say about, that curious contemporary epithet, "Organization Man," the corporation robot? It is true that ambitious men and their families move from position to position and, in the process, from community to community. It is also true that most of them center their dominant goals in occupational advancement. Yet if three fourths of these men are college-trained, and sizable proportions are from lowly origins, whence never before could they have attained such heights, it must mean that their capacity for satisfaction in and enjoyment of their roles as corporate men and citizens has greatly increased. They are not robots, slavishly following the iron demands of corporate enterprise, as they have been depicted. Moreover, for many of them positions of corporate leadership mean better and more productive service as citizens of their communities and their country. Since the careers of most, by their own voluntary choice, are not confined to one corporation but extend through several, they are not the organizational automata that the popular journals of the intelligentsia and other superficial analyses allege. The social significance of these men and their families, moving from community to community, must wait for a later section for full explanation. We must ask now what institutions educate them and what kind of an education they get when they go to college.

The colleges and universities attended by these men as undergraduates range through every variety of quality and kind, from the most obscure and scholastically poorest to the most highly esteemed, with the highest academic rank. It should be added that the corporation man is more likely to attend the latter than the former. The first four universities, graduating one fifth of all the managers, were, in the order named, Yale, Harvard, Princeton, and Cornell. The others most often chosen were both public and private, and in every region of the country, and included the Universities of Illinois, Michigan, Chicago, and Minnesota, in the Middle West; Berkeley and Stanford in the Far West; and the Universities of North Carolina and Texas in the South.

But here we must pause, for again such figures might mislead us. We must ask what kind of men went to the great universities? Who were the managers who graduated from the better colleges? Did such institutions contribute their share to the leavening process and train men from the wrong side of the tracks in the skills necessary for competition with those born on Upper Main Street? Or did they educate only the sons of the powerful few? All the managers who went to Yale as undergraduates were sons of business men or men in the higher professions; one half also had grandfathers in the business and professional elites. Three fourths of those who went to Harvard were sons of business elite; one half also had grandfathers in the business and professional elites. Among those attaining managerial rank, not one son of a laborer attended any of the large New England liberal arts colleges. It might be added that no manager who was a laborer's son was present at such places as Princeton, Northwestern, and Stanford, either. But where did these young men go?

The sons of workers were drawn to the larger state and city universities, as well as to some of the technical schools such as M.I.T. and Carnegie Tech. They were also spread through a complete spectrum of small and large denominational, state, and private universities. Although it seems probable that new scholarship programs and recent efforts of the more important colleges and universities to recruit the most able from a wide geographical and economic range are changing the composition of their student bodies, it must be said that the mobile men among today's business leaders were usually trained and prepared for their high and very responsible positions by those institutions least able financially and culturally to perform this important task. Unless more is done by the better-known universities to provide financial assistance, this situation seems likely to continue. However, the efforts of the great foundations, the smaller regional ones, and public and private donors to improve the quality and financing of such institutions obviously should increase not only the percentage of mobile men who use education for their advancement but—perhaps of even greater importance—the quality of the training, technical and cultural, which they receive.

It is at present fashionable for business men, when they strike a statesmanlike pose in their public pronouncements, to declare that what businesss needs and wants is young men broadly trained in the liberal arts. But despite these noble declarations, it does not take research to predict whether a personnel officer would pick the bright technical-college boy with solid training in business administration and procedure or the lad with a good record in philosophy, history, and literature acquired in a liberal arts college. The recruiters of future business leaders of great corporations spend less time waiting outside the doors of departments of philosophy than on the steps of business administration colleges. If the men who graduate from schools of business and other similar professional schools are to be trained properly in the fundamentals of higher learning, it will be necessary for these schools —as some are now doing—to require a foundation of training in the humanities and the behavioral sciences. When the leaders of the great corporations realize that their own self interest, and perhaps their very survival and that of their economy, is dependent upon a free society which functions properly, and when they know that they themselves and the quality of their own thinking as managers must be responsible for much of its well-being, it seems probable that an increasing number not only will add to their personal support of higher education but demand that their recruiting officers favor graduatess of those schools with a curriculum that embodies technical training well founded on the best of our cultural heritage. Men so trained and the corporations who employ them will have a clear advantage over their competitors.

Although higher education is a demonstrable factor in how and why men from lower levels now rise to the top and are able to compete more successfully than previously for managerial leadership, in itself it is not sufficient explanation for what is happening. It does not tell us why those born to the occupational elites of business and the professions are not now as well represented as previously at the executive level. These men also have gone to college in increasing proportions. College attendance by the sons of major executives who are now themselves executives rose from 52 per cent in 1928 to 74 per cent in 1952. The figures for the professions are, for the same dates, 47 and 73 per cent. Other factors need inspection to help us understand what has been happening.

Research findings demonstrate that during the last generation the huge billion-dollar corporations have increased enormously in size, in the number employed, and in the amount of business done. They are often attacked as undemocratic, and their effect on our equalitarian values is sometimes judged as bad. The truth or falsehood of these criticisms it is not our present purpose to argue. But the increase in the great corporations is directly related to the decrease in the proportion of present executives whose fathers were in the business elite. In the study of today's executives, the great corporations of all varieties were graded according to size, being placed in five categories according to their gross annual income. The proportion of executives who were sons of executives and that of those who were not were determined for each level, and the results demonstrated that the smaller the corporation, the larger the proportion of sons of business executives; the larger the corporation, the smaller the proportion of such men present. Step by step, as one moved from the smaller to the larger corporations, the proportion of sons of executives decreased. More specifically, whereas only 20 per cent of the executives of large corporations were sons of executives, the figure in the smallest corporation was 29 per cent.

In 1928 the story was quite different. Thirty-two per cent of the leaders of the great corporations were sons of executives (20 per cent are today), and only 25 per cent of those in the smallest corporations came from this occupational level (29 per cent now do). It appears that the increase in the number and importance of the giant corporations is directly related to the advance of men from the lower levels to top positions in management. When men from the bottom are able to prepare themselves for advancement, the most competent among all men are most likely to be selected. This means of course that under these conditions success on the basis of merit is possible to men from any level. The personnel officers of the great corporations now are more likely to select on the basis of ability, whereas in the smaller corporations (many of them family enterprises), it appears that the sons of executives and their friends have greater opportunity. In brief, social and economic status seems to carry less weight in the giant national and international American corporations. It must be remembered, however, that sizable proportions of both the sons of executives and those who are not are among the managers of all corporate categories.

The expansion of higher education explains a substantial part of the increase in upward and downward mobility among the business elite. But it does not tell the whole story. Other influences can be understood only by viewing the process in wider perspective. The following two sections are devoted to this task.

IV. *The Wives They Marry*

In too many inquiries into the kinds of men who are corporate managers, the structural influence of the American family on them as men and on their careers has not been sufficiently emphasized. The connection between family relationships and corporate enterprise is perhaps of more importance than any other single fact as an indicator of the well-being of a free and open society. At stake, I believe, are some of the fundamental values of this democracy and, in all probability, of its continuing economic and social progress. Despite the continuing importance of inheritance, elite positions, as we have seen, are increasingly open to free competition by properly prepared members of the society and not closed by family claims to all but a succession from fathers to sons.

But corporate executives not only have sons; they also frequently have wives! What kind of wives do they marry and who were their mothers? Since marriage is still the principal route of economic and and social mobility for women, the informal rules and values which govern the selection of mates by business leaders can and do have very important effects on the character of our society. If they and their fathers marry women only from their own economic class, such marriages tighten and close the status structure, emphasize aristocratic values in the training of the offspring, and thus contribute to a system of closed corporate and social rank; if they marry above or below themselves the class order is more likely to be open, and women and men from the lower ranks can compete for mates of higher status.

There can be no doubt that the managers of the great corporations more often marry women from their own class origins than from any other occupational group. This is true not only of men whose fathers were big-business executives but also of those who were the sons of laborers: over a third of the former (35 per cent) married daughters of big-business leaders, and some 42 per cent of the latter married daughters of laborers. Despite this tendency toward endogamy, a closer inspection demonstrates that while class values operate in the choice of mates, their marriages were nevertheless quite widely dispersed throughout all occupational categories. Thus the men who came from the laboring class more often married women of their own level of origin, but they also married daughters of big-business leaders (7 per cent) and daughters of professional men (9 per cent), and a still larger proportion married the daughters of farmers, small-business men, and white-collar workers. Managers who were the sons of big-business executives also married throughout the occupational hierarchy. The men whose fathers were in the white-collar class were less likely to marry into their own level than were those from any other category.

One of the principal relationships in the family, marriage seems (from these figures) to be relatively unconstrained by class barriers, for marriages among the top, bottom, and intermediate levels occur in sufficiently high proportion to demonstrate high flexibility in the family structure and rather high autonomy in the individual choice of a mate. These marriages also demonstrate the principle of women's mobility by marriage. Marriage assists the family in maintaining that more flexible system, which we have seen developing, where the sons of executives are less likely to inherit the father's position. The apparent decrease in endogamy and increase in marriages outside the occupational class may be related to the rise in the numbers of persons obtaining higher education. Since a higher proportion of children of all occupational groups goes to college, there now are more opportunities for men and women with diverse backgrounds to meet and become acquainted. When they go to college they leave the more rigid class controls of their local communities, where they are more likely to marry women of their own levels. The statistics for the correlation of level of education with in-laws' status between marriage partners provide substantial evidence for this hypothesis. For example, 21 out of every 100 executives who were the sons of white-collar workers and who graduated from college married daughters of the business elite, compared with 12 of every 100 with less than high-school education. Similar ratios between the amount of education and marriage into a higher occupational class prevail for all other occupations. However, education seems to operate in much the same way for the sons of business leaders; 37 out of every 100 college graduates of this group marry women of similar background, and only 23 who did not go beyond grade school marry at their own level. Higher education tends to increase the number of marriages to mates of higher levels and to decrease the likelihood of those born to the gold-lettered door marrying "beneath themselves."

v. Individual Autonomy and the Emergence of the Great Society

The whole meaning and significance of the social and psychological characteristics of the managers of great corporations and, for that matter, any understanding of the corporations themselves must be seen in larger perspective. The dynamics of change in America and the form they take are quite unlike most of what has been discussed in the literature of such disciplines as social anthropology, and not to be made clear by the usual explanations. I have called the type of change that is characteristic of America "emergent." The meaning and significance of emergence is of particular importance for our present purposes. During the several phases of development the emergent American society and others like it originate characteristics that more often come from within as part of the nature of the structure itself than as influences from the outside. Change is built into the very life of such a society; to be what it is the American society must always be in a constant state of becoming something else.

The efficient factors for change are integral parts of this emergent system. This means that the continuing available past, used and modified, comes forth into new ways as the future emerges. More concretely and specifically, the society moves in the direction of increasing heterogeneity, but to maintain cohesion in the expanding division of labor there is increasing need for coordination and unification. Along with increasing control over the natural and human environments, there has been an enormous increase in the power exercised by those at the top of the social, political, and economic hierarchies. There has also been an acceleration of social, economic, and scientific experimentation, as well as the development of a great national society.

The local communities remain, although they have been reduced in their scope, but increasingly the lives of their members are being woven into a great primary community which is national (not to say international) in its unity and breadth. Every day primary face-to-face interaction takes place among men from every part of the country as a regular and necessary part of their jobs. The society develops new political, social, and economic structures, which expand and relate the diversified life in the several regions into a unified whole. Meanwhile, new forms emerge and new characteristics must be domesticated and integrated into functioning and useful parts of our traditional way of life.

The very nature of corporate competition places many if not most executives at the most advanced positions of this frontier; here technological achievements and scientific experiment are incorporated into the activities of most corporations. Competitive advantage now demands that technology and science be a prime concern of the managers. Here they are not only corporate agents bent on competitive advantage but cultural mediators of the present as it moves from the past into the future. They are in the dilemma of holding to the structured past while making decisions that necessarily move them and their worlds into an unstructured and, as yet, imperfectly formed future. Not all men are emotionally and mentally capable, and not necessarily for lack of intelligence, to act adaptively and continuously for themselves and the corporations they lead in such ambiguous, conflict-filled situations. Yet many do with great success and brilliance. What kinds of men are they?

Perhaps the most outstanding characteristic of their personalties is what we shall call autonomy. An autonomous person (in Peaget's terms) is one who has internalized the group's rules and values sufficiently to act not slavishly as their creature but creatively as an individual. In an emergent society, those who lead must almost by necessity be autonomous; they must be free to make decisions in the poorly defined situations that are a natural part of an economy and a society that must be in continual change to realize its potentialities. The values controlling our family life also emphasize autonomy; for most individuals, the family nuclei in which they are born and the nuclei formed by marriage tend to be separate and free and not merged and under one control as they are in most societies. Families with such values are likely to train and produce individuals with personalities that are autonomous, capable of making decisions on their own, and to embody the spirit and values of competitive enterprise and democratic action.

A close inspection of the private worlds of the more successsful executives—no more than a thumbnail sketch can be given here—reveals more about these men. Perhaps their most dominant psychic characteristic is a feeling that they are on their own and capable of independent action. More deeply stated, their emotional identifications with their parents have been sufficiently loosened for them to be free and act in the present in terms of the immediate future. This does not mean hostility to either parent but, rather, freedom to make decisions on their own without reference to a past whose control might not be adaptive. They have left home not only in fact; they have left home also in spirit. Such men easily relate to their early superiors and later, as they move upward to higher command, just as easily disengage themselves from them as once again they relate to other authoritative figures in the organizations over which they assume direction. Moreover, their views of the immediate and distant worlds around them (as displayed in projective tests of their emotional and mental organization) are very instructive in terms of how they relate social reality to their psychic organization. They quickly structure what they see; events are not isolated and separate, but viewed as patterned and meaningful in terms of the decisions immediately present. Their personalities are such that they are capable of putting together the changing parts of their society and the flow of events within their economic life to form them into a world of meaning and significance for action. Such men can make decisions without being overcome by the anxiety of those who see too many alternatives of equal worth or equal ambiguity to permit action. Everyone knows that the staffs and other fact-finding agencies of great corporations pour a constant stream of information of the greatest variety across the desks of managers.

Even so, the unknown and the unverifiable are often the most important and crucial data for the decisions that must be made. It is in this world that the manager must create order out of a future that for others may seem chaotic. It is here he must act, frequently and well, if he is to succeed and his corporation prosper. The mental and emotional life of the manager, his total intelligence, here operates adaptively for him and his part of our emergent culture.

These and a number of other characteristics are important parts of the psychic make-up of most successful executives. Their personalities are products, and often adaptive ones, of our emergent society and of the autonomous families which train and rear these men. It has not been my intention to demonstrate a neat fit between society and individual or to say that the successful manager is self-contained and unlike the rest of society. Rather, I have tried to indicate what the private worlds of many successful executives look like to the investigator in order to show what their larger roles are in this emergent society and to say something about how such men have been produced.

Our society continues to grow and develop. Corporate men, academicians, churchmen, politicians, and those from other great organizations are all part of the necessary organizational expansion. In this sense all of us are "organizational men"; in this sense the managers of corporations and all of us are engaged in the highly important and perhaps fateful task of creating a new society, one perhaps which will be more democratic and more capable of developing and distributing its material and spiritual rewards to our people.

IV

The Outsiders

In an achieving business society, outsiders (selectively represented here) no less than insiders were driven to succeed. Each group, rejected by the establishment in an era of extreme transition, accommodated itself and its ambitions in ways sustained by its own cultural imperatives. In so doing each cast a brilliant light on the limitations and ironies of a Gospel of Success limited to the socially elect.

Region, religion, nationality, sex, and race defined the relations of individuals to the core society. The farmer, in no uncertain terms rejected by the land, rejected it even as the metropolitan "country gentleman" gilded the yeoman tradition. The Irish found in neglected urban politics an arena where liabilities in business were turned into assets. The Jews carved out new worlds of independent small business and industry, but their intense commitment to the labor movement suggested how corrosive was the prevailing success ideology to the needs of a democratic society. The Italians followed paths to success abandoned or bypassed by more respectable older Americans as well as earlier immigrants. Women, committed to the self-evident truth "that all men and women are created equal," demanded full integration even when the price was the whole woman. The Negro repeatedly looked to the Gospel, turned away from it, and both accepted and rejected it. Of all Americans, the Indian alone was immune to the individualist ethic.

"GOD MADE MAN IN HIS OWN IMAGE"

Edwin Markham

The Man with the Hoe

By the last decade of the nineteenth century, Thomas Jefferson's yeoman farmer, declining socially, depressed economically, isolated culturally, was no longer the representative American. That the famous poem The Man with the Hoe, *by Edwin Markham, could be seriously viewed as portraying the American farmer was a measure of the fall in esteem suffered by an American who once seemed far removed from the primordial peasant. [Edwin Markham,* The Man with the Hoe and Other Poems, *New York, 1902, pp. 15-18.]*

Written After Seeing Millet's World-Famous Painting

God made man in His own image,
In the image of God made He him.—*Genesis.*

Bowed by the weight of centuries he leans
Upon his hoe and gazes on the ground,
The emptiness of ages in his face,
And on his back the burden of the world.
Who made him dead to rapture and despair,
A thing that grieves not and that never hopes,
Stolid and stunned, a brother to the ox?
Who loosened and let down this brutal jaw?
Whose was the hand that slanted back this brow?
Whose breath blew out the light within this brain?

Is this the Thing the Lord God made and gave
To have dominion over sea and land;
To trace the stars and search the heavens for power;

To feel the passion of Eternity?
Is this the Dream He dreamed who shaped the suns
And marked their ways upon the ancient deep?
Down all the stretch of Hell to its last gulf
There is no shape more terrible than this—
More tongued with censure of the world's blind greed—
More filled with signs and portents for the soul—
More fraught with danger to the universe.

What gulfs between him and the seraphim!
Slave of the wheel of labor, what to him
Are Plato and the swing of Pleiades?
What the long reaches of the peaks of song,
The rift of dawn, the reddening of the rose?
Through this dread shape the suffering ages look;
Time's tragedy is in that aching stoop;
Through this dread shape humanity betrayed,
Plundered, profaned and disinherited,
Cries protest to the Judges of the World,
A protest that is also prophecy.

O masters, lords and rulers in all lands,
Is this the handiwork you give to God,
This monstrous thing distorted and soul-quenched?
How will you ever straighten up this shape;
Touch it again with immortality;
Give back the upward looking and the light;
Rebuild in it the music and the dream;
Make right the immemorial infamies,
Perfidious wrongs, immedicable woes?

O masters, lords and rulers in all lands,
How will the Future reckon with this Man?
How answer his brute question in that hour
When whirlwinds of rebellion shake the world?
How will it be with kingdoms and with kings—
With those who shaped him to the thing he is—
When this dumb Terror shall reply to God,
After the silence of the centuries?

===

Thorstein Veblen

The Independent Farmer

Despite Markham's elegy, "the Independent Farmer of the poets" lived on into the twentieth century and like other "pecuniary" Americans be- came fair game for the acid pen of Thorstein Veblen (1857-1929). This selection, if one disregards the point of view, is a masterful portrait of rural society—bypassed by corporate America and yet very close to the American mainstream. [*Thorstein Veblen,* Absentee Ownership and Business Enterprise in Recent Times, *New York, 1923, pp. 129-141.*]

The case of the American farmer is conspicuous; though it can scarcely be called singular, since in great part it is rather typical of the fortune which has overtaken the underlying populations throughout Christen- dom under the dominion of absentee ownership in its later developed phase. Much the same general run of conditions recurs elsewhere in those respects which engage the fearsome attention of these farmers. By and large, the farmer is so placed in the economic system that both as producer and as consumer he deals with business concerns which are in a position to make the terms of the traffic, which it is for him to take or leave. Therefore the margin of benefit that comes to him from his work is commonly at a minimum. He is commonly driven by cir- custances over which he has no control, the circumstances being made by the system of absentee ownership and its business enterprise. Yet he is, on the whole, an obstinately loyal supporter of the system of law and custom which so makes the conditions of life for him.

His unwavering loyalty to the system is in part a holdover from that obsolete past when he was the Independent Farmer of the poets; but in part it is also due to the still surviving persuasion that he is on the way, by hard work and shrewd management, to acquire a "competence"; such as will enable him some day to take his due place among the absentee owners of the land and so come in for an easy livelihood at the cost of the rest of the community; and in part it is also due to the persistent though fantastic opinion that his own present interest is bound up with the system of absentee ownership, in that he is himself an absentee owner by so much as he owns land and equipment which he works with hired help,—always presuming that he is such an owner, in effect or in prospect. It is true, the farmer-owners commonly are absentee owners to this extent. Farming is teamwork. As it is necessarily carried on by current methods in the great farming sections, farm work runs on such a scale that no individual owner can carry on by use of his own personal work alone, or by use of the man-power of his own household alone,—which makes him an absentee owner by so much. But it does not, in the common run, make him an absentee owner of such dimensions as are required in order to create an effectual collusive control of the market, or such as will enable him, singly or collectively, to determine what charges the traffic shall bear. It leaves him still effectually in a position to take or leave what is offered at the discretion of those massive absentee interests that move in the background of the market.

Always, of course, the farmer has with him the abiding comfort of his illusions, to the effect that he is in some occult sense the "Independent Farmer," and that he is somehow by way of achieving a competence of absentee ownership by hard work and sharp practice, some day; but in practical effect, as things habitually work out, he is rather to be called a quasi-absentee owner, or perhaps a pseudo-absentee owner, being too small a parcel of absentee ownership to count as such in the outcome. But it is presumably all for the best, or at least it is expedient for business-as-usual, that the farmer should continue to nurse his illusions and go about his work; that he should go on his way to complete that destiny to which it has pleased an all-seeing and merciful Providence to call him.

From colonial times and through the greater part of its history as a republic, America has been in the main an agricultural country. Farming has been the staple occupation and has employed the greater part of the population. And the soil has always been the chief of those natural resources which the American people have taken over and made into property. Through the greater part of its history the visible growth of the country has consisted in the extension of the cultivated area and the increasing farm output, farm equipment, and farm population. This progressive taking-over and settlement of the farming lands is the most impressive material achievement of the American people, as it is also the most serviceable work which they have accomplished hitherto. It still is, as it ever has been, the people's livelihood; and the rest of the industrial system has in the main, grown up, hitherto, as a subsidiary or auxiliary, adapted to and limited by the needs and the achieve-

ments of the country's husbandry. The incentives and methods engaged
in this taking-over of the soil, as well as the industrial and institutional
consequences that have followed, are accordingly matters of prime
consideration in any endeavor to understand or explain the national
character and the temperamental bent which underlies it.

The farm population—that farm population which counted substantially toward this national achievement—have been a ready, capable,
and resourceful body of workmen. And they have been driven by the
incentives already spoken of in an earlier passage as being characteristic
of the English-speaking colonial enterprise,—individual self-help and
cupidity. Except transiently and provisionally, and with doubtful effect,
this farm population has nowhere and at no time been actuated by a
spirit of community interest in dealing with any of their material concerns. Their community spirit, in material concerns, has been quite
notably scant and precarious, in spite of the fact that they have long
been exposed to material circumstances of a wide-sweeping uniformity,
such as should have engendered a spirit of community interest and
made for collective enterprise, and such as could have made any effectual collective enterprise greatly remunerative to all concerned. But they
still stand sturdily by the timeworn make-believe that they still are
individually self-sufficient masterless men, and through good report and
evil report they have remained Independent Farmers, as between themselves, which is all that is left of their independence,—Each for
himself, etc.

Of its kind, this is an admirable spirit, of course; and it has achieved
many admirable results, even though the results have not all been to
the gain of the farmers. Their self-help and cupidity have left them
at the mercy of any organisation that is capable of mass action and a
steady purpose. So they have, in the economic respect—and incidentally
in the civil and political respect—fallen under the dominion of those
massive business interests that move obscurely in the background of the
market and buy and sell and dispose of the farm products and the
farmers' votes and opinions very much on their own terms and at their
ease.

But all the while it remains true that they have brought an unexampled large and fertile body of soil to a very passable state of service, and their work continues to yield a comfortably large food supply
to an increasing population, at the same time that it yields a comfortable
run of free income to the country's kept classes. It is true, in the end
the farm population find themselves at work for the benefit of business-
as-usual, on a very modest livelihood. For farming is, perhaps necessarily, carried on in severalty and on a relatively small scale, even
though the required scale exceeds what is possible on a footing of strict
self-ownership of land and equipment by the cultivators; and there
is always the pervading spirit of self-help and cupidity, which unavoid-

ably defeats even that degree of collusive mass action that might otherwise be possible. Whereas the system of business interests in whose web
the farmers are caught is drawn on a large scale, its units are massive,
impersonal, imperturbable and, in effect, irresponsible, under the
established order of law and custom, and they are interlocked in an
unbreakable framework of common interests.

By and large, the case of America is as the case of the American
farm population, and for the like reasons. For the incentives and ideals,
the law and custom, and the knowledge and belief, on which the farm
population has gone about its work and has come to this pass, are the
same as have ruled the growth and shaped the outcome for the community at large. Nor does the situation in America differ materially
from the state of things elsewhere in the civilised countries, in so far
as these others share in the same material civilisation of Christendom.

In the American tradition, and in point of historical fact out of which
the tradition has arisen, the farmer has been something of a pioneer.
Loosely it can be said that the pioneering era is now closing, at least
provisionally and as regards farming. But while the pioneer-farmer
is dropping out of the work of husbandry, his pioneer soul goes march-
ing on. And it has been an essential trait of this American pioneering
spirit to seize upon so much of the country's natural resources as the
enterprising pioneer could lay hands on,—in the case of the pioneer-
farmer, so much of the land as he could get and hold possession of.
The land had, as it still has, a prospective use and therefore a prospective
value, a "speculative" value as it is called; and the farmer-pioneer was
concerned with seizing upon this prospective value and turning it into
net gain by way of absentee ownership, as much as the pioneer-farmer
was concerned with turning the fertile soil to present use in the creation
of a livelihood for himself and his household from day to day.

Habitually and with singular uniformity the American farmers have
aimed to acquire real estate at the same time that they have worked at
their trade as husbandmen. And real estate is a matter of absentee ownership, an asset whose value is based on the community's need of this
given parcel of land for use as a means of livelihood, and the value of
which is measured by the capitalised free income which the owner may
expect to come in for by holding it for as high a rental as the traffic
in this need will bear. So that the pioneering aim, in American farming, has been for the pioneer-farmers, each and several, to come in for
as much of a free income at the cost of the rest of the community as the
law would allow; which has habitually worked out in their occupying,
each and several, something more than they could well take care of.
They have habitually "carried" valuable real estate at the same time
that they have worked the soil of so much of their land as they could
take care of, in as effectual a manner as they could under these circumstances. They have been cultivators of the main chance as well as of the

fertile soil; with the result that, by consequence of this intense and un-
broken habituation, the farm population is today imbued with that
penny-wise spirit of self-help and cupidity that now leaves them and
their work and holdings at the disposal of those massive vested interests
that know the uses of collusive mass action, as already spoken of above.

But aside from this spiritual effect which this protracted habituation
to a somewhat picayune calculation of the main chance has had on the
farmers' frame of mind, and aside from their consequent unfitness
to meet the businesslike manoeuvres of the greater vested interests,
this manner of pioneering enterprise which the farmers have habitually
mixed into their farming has also had a more immediate bearing on the
country's husbandry, and, indeed, on the industrial system as a whole.
The common practice has been to "take up" more land than the farmer
could cultivate, with his available means, and to hold it at some cost.
Which has increased the equipment required for the cultivation of the
acres cultivated, and has also increased the urgency of the farmers'
need of credit by help of which to find the needed equipment and meet
the expenses incident to his holding his idle and semi-idle acres intact.
And farm credit has been notoriously usurious. All this has had the
effect of raising the cost of production of farm products; partly by
making the individual farm that much more unwieldy as an instrument
of production, partly by further enforcing the insufficiency and the
make-shift character for which American farm equipment is justly
famed, and partly also by increasing the distances over which the farm
supplies and the farm products have had to be moved.

This last point marks one of the more serious handicaps of American
farming, at the same time that it has contributed materially to enforce
that "extensive," "superficial," and exhausting character of American
farming which has arrested the attention of all foreign observers. In
American practice the "farm area" has always greatly exceeded the
"acreage under cultivation," even after all due allowance is made for
any unavoidable inclusion of waste and half-waste acreage within the
farm boundaries. Even yet, at the provisional close of the career of the
American pioneer-farmer, the actual proportion of unused and half-
used land included within and among the farms equalled the acreage
that was fully employed, even in that "extensive" fashion in which
American farming has habitually been carried on.

But there is no need of insisting on this high proportion of idle
acreage, which none will credit who has not a wide and intimate knowledge of the facts in the case. For more or less—for as much as all intelligent observers will be ready to credit—this American practice has
counted toward an excessively wide distribution of the cultivated areas,
excessively long distances of transport, over roads which have by consequence been excessively bad—necessarily and notoriously so—and
which have hindered communication to such a degree as in many in-

stances to confine the cultivation to such crops as can be handled with a minimum of farm buildings and will bear the crudest kind of carriage over long distances and with incalculable delays. This applies not only to the farm-country's highways, but to its railway facilities as well. The American practice has doubled the difficulty of transportation and retarded the introduction of the more practicable and more remunerative methods of farming; until makeshift and haphazard methods have in many places become so ingrained in the habits of the farm population that nothing but abounding distress and the slow passing of generations can correct it all. At the same time, as an incident by the way, this same excessive dispersion of the farming communities over long distances, helped out by bad roads, has been perhaps the chief factor in giving the retail business communities of the country towns their strangle-hold on the underlying farm population.

And it should surprise no one if a population which has been exposed to unremitting habituation of this kind has presently come to feel at home in it all; so that the bootless chicanery of their self-help is rated as a masterly fabric of axiomatic realities, and sharp practice has become a matter of conscience. In such a community it should hold true that "An honest man will bear watching," that the common good is a by-word, that "Everybody's business is nobody's business," that public office is a private job, where the peak of aphoristic wisdom is reached in that red-letter formula of democratic politics, "Subtraction, division, and silence." So it has become a democratic principle that public office should go by rotation, under the rule of equal opportunity, —equal opportunity to get something for nothing—but should go only to those who value the opportunity highly enough to make a desperate run for it. Here men "run" for office, not "stand" for it. Subtraction is the aim of this pioneer cupidity, not production; and salesmanship is its line of approach, not workmanship; and so, being in no way related quantitatively to a person's workmanlike powers or to his tangible performance, it has no "saturation point."

The spirit of the American farmers, typically has been that of the pioneer rather than the workman. They have been efficient workmen, but that is not the trait which marks them for its own and sets them off in contrast with the common run. Their passion for acquisition has driven them to work, hard and painfully, but they have never been slavishly attached to their work; their slavery has been not to an imperative bent of workmanship and human service, but to an indefinitely extensible cupidity which drives to work when other expedients fail; at least so they say. So they have been somewhat footloose in their attachment to the soil as well as somewhat hasty and shiftless in its cultivation. They have always, in the typical case, wanted something more than their proportionate share of the soil; not because they were driven by a felt need of doing more than their fair share of work or because they aimed to give the community more service than would be a fair equivalent of their own livelihood, but with a view to cornering something more than their proportion of the community's indispensable means of life and so getting a little something for nothing in allowing their holdings to be turned to account, for a good and valuable consideration.

The American farmers have been footloose, on the whole, more particularly that peculiarly American element among them who derive their traditions from a colonial pedigree. There has always been an easy shifting from country to town, and this steady drift into the towns of the great farming sections has in the main been a drift from work into business. And it has been the business of these country towns—what may be called their business-as-usual—to make the most of the necessities and the ignorance of their underlying farm population. The farmers have on the whole been ready to make such a shift whenever there has been an "opening"; that is to say, they have habitually been ready to turn their talents to more remunerative use in some other pursuit whenever the chance was offered, and indeed they have habitually been ready to make the shift out of husbandry into the traffic of the towns even at some risk whenever the prospect of a wider margin of net gain has opened before their eager eyes.

===

William V. Shannon

The Irish Style in Politics

*Perhaps no major immigrant group seemed as little suited for careers
in Big Business as the American Irish. To them politics offered careers
comparable if not equivalent to those which the business world seemed
to hold out for older Americans. A judicious, at times eloquent, explanation of the social role of the Irish in the American political economy is
contained in this selection by William V. Shannon (1927-   ), author
and* New York Times *editorial writer. [William V. Shannon,* The
American Irish, New York, *1963, pp. 60-67.]*

I

In the decades after the Civil War, the Irish developed their characteristic style in American politics. The Irishman as politician is the
member of the Irish community most familiar to other Americans. The
Irish brought to American politics two advantages other immigrants
did not have: a knowledge of the English language and an acquaintance
with the dominant Anglo-American culture. In addition to a common
language and a shared culture, they had gifts of organization and eloquence, a sense of cohesion, and the beginnings of a political tradition
in the nationalist agitation in Ireland. Their antagonism toward England
offended leaders of opinion along the eastern seaboard, but it did not
upset most Americans, since, in the nineteenth century, twisting the
lion's tail was the national sport.

The Irish made their big move into American politics at a time
when both the theory and practice of politics were at a peculiarly low
ebb. The nation's earliest political tradition originated in the seventeenth
and eighteenth centuries among the planters of Virginia and the Puritan

aristocrats and merchants of New England. This tradition held that politics is a serious affair worthy of the attention of the best class of men. The governing of mankind, in this view, is an enterprise too important for the natural leaders of society, the men of property and education, to leave to intermediaries and underlings. Washington, Jefferson, Madison, Jay, and the Adamses who organized the American Revolution, wrote the Constitution, and founded the national government shared this viewpoint. They were never guilty of the fatuous maxim "It's just politics."

The merchants and industrial entrepreneurs who came to the fore in the early nineteenth century produced a different theory of politics. What has become known as the Whig view of government contended that "that government is best which governs least." The primary task of politics was to make government a tidy, efficient housekeeper. The business community developed the comfortable and useful mythology that social conflict was unreal, that the interests of employers and workers, of farmers and city consumers, of businessmen and customers were actually identical. Since this was true, the two-party system was more a convenience than a necessity. If there were no social conflicts, then party warfare was devoid of meaning. Party affiliations could be regarded as matters of sentiment, as eccentric vestiges of the past rather than reflections of vital interests. By 1870 this view had become dominant in writings and discussions of politics among educated easterners. The "independent voter" who rejected both parties and chose the better man regardless of label was extolled as the best voter. In these years the business community not only attracted the best talents but also imposed upon politics its standards of efficiency and economical operation as ends in themselves rather than as means in attaining the larger public welfare. "Politics" became a naughty word associated with corrupt schemers and raids on the treasury. During the late Victorian age, the genteel tradition was as supreme in American politics as it was in literature.

This outlook was not without its critics. Edward Everett Hale, writing in 1889, argued that extreme laissez faire went counter to much of the nation's experience, pointing to the public ownership of schools and libraries, roads and canals, lighthouses and docks, and the post office. Hale noted that in the earlier years of our history when canals, railroads, and turnpikes had been built by private companies, these corporations had been chartered as public agents in much the same way as the English chartered companies had acted on behalf of the Crown in the development of India and the American colonies. The "friends of strong government," he concluded, "are acting on the lines of our best traditions." [1]

1. Arthur Mann, *Yankee Reformers in the Urban Age,* Cambridge, Belknap Press, 1954, pp. 14-15.

But Hale and other reformers were in the minority as the extreme individualist, antigovernment views of Herbert Spencer became the vogue. The chief exponent of the majority viewpoint was E. L. Godkin, long-time editor of the New York *Evening Post* and of the *Nation* magazine. Although monopolies, slums, child labor, periodic mass unemployment, and other evils ravaged society, Godkin and other writers on politics devoted most of their attention to the introduction of the civil service system and to thinking of ways to lure educated men into politics. Godkin wrote in "The Duty of Educated Men in a Democracy": "We should probably, in a college-graduate government, witness the disappearance from legislation of nearly all acts and resolutions which are passed for what is called 'politics'; that is, for the purpose of pleasing certain bodies of voters, without any reference to their value as contributions to the work of government." [2]

It is not astonishing that with this narrow, uncomprehending theory of politics in the ascendancy, the masses of immigrants crowding into the growing cities had to develop their own political institutions and their own political ethic. The immigrant laborer desperate for a job to feed his family, the immigrant family quarreling with the landlord, the widowed mother deprived of her income, the injured workman, the sweatshop employee, and the truant boy in trouble with the police needed someone or some agency more compassionate and helpful than routine "good government" no matter how purified by civil service reform or economically run by college graduates. Moreover, the immigrants perceived that when government at different levels did exercise positive power, it was usually on behalf of businessmen by granting land subsidies to railroad companies or using police to break strikes. Middle-class "mugwump" politics was unsound in theory, and when it was violated in practice it was always in behalf of a single interest in society. [3]

The Irish, the most numerous and advanced section of the immigrant community, took over the political party (usually the Democratic Party) at the local level and converted it into virtually a parallel system of government. The network of party clubhouses and the hierarchy of party committees with a citywide leader or "boss" at the apex constituted a "shadow government," a supplementary structure of power that performed some functions more vital than those of the nominal, legal government. The main objective of the party, of course, was to capture control of the city government, but even when the party was out of office, it could continue to function. It had revenue from the "tax" it levied upon saloons, houses of prostitution, gamblers, and contractors.

2. Edwin L. Godkin, *Problems of Modern Democracy*, New York, Scribner, 1896, pp. 200-201.
3. Richard Hofstadter, *The Age of Reform*, New York, Alfred A. Knopf, 1955; Vintage Edition, 1960, pp. 174-186.

Out of these funds, the party machine could provide the food and coal it gave to those who were destitute. It could finance the young lawyers who interceded in court for the delinquent, wrote letters home to the old country for the illiterate, and intervened at city hall for those bewildered by the regulations and intricacies of the government. It could pay for the torchlight parades, the children's picnics, and the one-day excursion trips up the river or to the beach which brought recreation and a touch of color to the lives of working-class families.

When the machine was in office, it could provide that most precious of all commodities: a job. Public construction work was one of the major sources of jobs and income. When reform administrations were in power, they cut back on construction to save money and reduce the tax rate. When the machine was in power, it expanded construction, building courthouses and schoolhouses, paving more streets, digging more subways, and erecting new bridges. The politicians at the top liked building programs because they could collect bribes from those who received the contract, make "a killing" on the sale of the land on the basis of their advance knowledge, profit by writing the insurance on the project, and sometimes organize a sand-and-gravel company and get cut into the actual construction as a subcontractor. This was "honest graft," sometimes known as "white graft" to distinguish it from the "dirty graft" collected via the police department from the underworld. The contractors liked this expansive attitude toward public -works projects because it increased their business, and so did the carpenters, plumbers, plasterers, and other skilled craftsmen. But, most of all, the newest and least skilled of the immigrants were enthusiastic because these projects enabled them to find work as laborers. Since, at the outset of their life in America, they were fitted only to do pick-and-shovel work, they were peculiarly dependent upon the machine and its free-and-easy spending of public money. No number of exposes by citizens' committees and good government groups of graft, payroll padding, and excessive spending on public projects shook their loyalty to the machine. If there were no "corrupt machine," they reasoned, there might not be any building projects, and if there were no projects to work on, how would they earn enough to live? Padded payrolls were better than no payrolls. Since the city usually needed the building or public improvement, it was not easy for critics to demonstrate to working-class voters what harm had been done.

II

The political machines the Irish built in most of the major cities of the North and Midwest developed out of the block and the neighborhood. Family friendships and neighborhood loyalties were the basis of power. The boyhood gangs with their emphasis on loyalty and cohesiveness provided the morale and the habits of mind that were easily transmuted, in adult years, into the rationale of the machine. The city-wide leaders, the ward and precinct captains, and the rank-and-file members of the party machines developed a set of political ethics and an attitude toward politics and power that were strikingly different from those of the native middle-class code. The Irish viewed municipal politics not as a conflict over how to obtain the best government at the lowest cost but as a struggle for power among competing groups.

The earliest leaders organized the Irish voters as a battering ram to break the power of a hostile majority. They put an end to elementary forms of discrimination such as the exclusive use of the King James Bible in the schools and the assignment of Protestant chaplains to Catholic inmates of hospitals, jails, and charitable institutions. Next, they fought for the appointment of Irish as schoolteachers and as policemen and firemen. Finally, they sought to take all political power into their own hands.

In the course of this struggle for power, the Irish community evolved an attitude of tolerant acceptance of political corruption. This was neither cynicism nor hypocrisy; rather it was close to a straightforward acceptance of graft as necessary and inevitable. Graft was part of the operating compromise between the formal rules of the political system and the facts of life as it was actually lived. Corruption was often viewed as a primitive mechanism for redistributing the wealth because, as people said, "at least it keeps the money in circulation." The Irish and their allies among other immigrants had the attitude typical of those who comprise a client group and not a ruling class. For a long period, they were people who had stature without status, power without responsibility. Only gradually did the social discipline grow to match the power, and only when that happened did the majority detach themselves from the values of the political machine.

For individual Irish, politics was an attractive career. Since newly naturalized voters were usually more willing to give their votes to another "son of the old country" than to a native-born candidate, politics was the only major profession in which it was an asset rather than a draw-back to be an immigrant. Politics, like baseball, prize-fighting, and the Church, was a career open to talents, a path of social mobility for the ambitious sons of impoverished families.

This Irish concept of politics as another profession—practical, profitable, and pursued every day in the year—diverged sharply from the ordinary civic code that draped politics in the mantle of "public service." According to the genteel tradition, the holding of office was an ephemeral activity; it might be thought of as an accident comparable to a call for jury service that might befall any citizen. For those who regarded the main business of America as business, service in a political office represented a sacrifice. In the Irish community, there was no talk of duty or sacrifice. Nor did those who gave their time to politics regard the holding of public office as an interlude or an accident. Politics was their career. Like every other profession, it was expected to reward its practitioners with money, prestige, and, if posssible, security. It was generally expected that a politician would make money out of his office, collaterally if not directly, and that if he lost he would be "taken care of" in a sinecure.*

Since Irish politicians were of working-class origin, they entered public office trailing long strings of needy relatives. Because the public payroll was the politician's only resource, he was expected to use it to succor his family and dependents. The result was the nepotism so frequently and so futilely condemned by civic reformers. This nepotism was usually controlled by some sense of official responsibilty. A halfwit or a drunkard would not be placed in a responsible job, but some other provision might be made for him. Indeed, some other provision had to be made for him. (What of his wife and children? If no one else would hire him, what politician would take the responsibility of sending "your own flesh-and-blood" to the relief rolls or the gutter?)

Nepotism had old-country roots. For generations, each immigrant who "went out to the States" had a fixed responsibility to send back money to pay for the subsequent passage of one of his brothers or sisters. In many families the oldest son came first, paid the fare of the next oldest who paid for the next, and so on. This recruitment practice was known as "sending for a greenhorn." The immigrant was also morally obligated to find jobs here for his relatives and for as many of his neighbors from the old country as he could. In this way, the kitchens of many a mansion and the police, fire, and streetcar departments of many a city were regularly staffed.

Conrad Arensberg, when he wrote his study *The Irish Countryman* in the 1930's, provided a graphic example of this process: "One little settlement called Cross, on the Loop Head peninsula which juts from Clare into the Atlantic at the Shannon's mouth, is said locally to be supported by the Shanghai police force. The first man to go is now Chief of Police in the International Settlement there, and many places in the Force have gone to men of Cross."

It is a short step from neighborliness to nepotism. However much such nepotism might be deplored, it could not be otherwise when men were bred from childhood to an urgent and overriding feeling of family duty and parochial loyalty.

* Shortly after World War II, the author was walking in Boston with a well-known local politician. The politician exchanged greetings with a passerby, an aged, poorly dressed woman. "When her husband was in the City Council with me," he remarked, "he was called 'Honest John.' But I never took it seriously. I figured he had an angle somewhere. But then he died and it was true. He didn't leave her a cent. Now what do you think of a dumbbell like that who wouldn't take a buck when he could get one and now his wife has to go out and work?"

Politics as a career not only required a minimum of education, preparation, and money; it also had the advantage over competing occupations that for the few who had the requisite talents it produced its rewards relatively quickly. In this respect, politics had the same appeal as professional athletics. It is significant how many politicians achieved power at an early age. James Curley was a congressman at thirty-six and mayor of Boston at thirty-nine; Joseph Tumulty of Jersey City became President Wilson's chief aide at thirty-three; Alfred E. Smith and James J. Walker were floor leaders in the New York legislature while still in their thirties. Charm, boldness, energy, a quick mind and a fluent tongue brought young politicos to the top; unlike careers in business and the professions, politics required neither long years of saving and scrimping nor any exact training.

The swiftness of success was probably important in shaping the psychology of many of these political leaders. Because of family necessity, a youth would become a part-time wage earner—a newsboy or bootblack or messenger—and thereby be forced into a premature maturity. He found himself drawn out of his own neighborhood, which up until then had seemed exciting and satisfying, and into the larger world. Back on his home block a dime had been a fortune, pot roast was a Sunday treat, and beer was his father's luxury after a ten- or twelve-hour shift. But in the brighter, faster-moving world in which he now entered, the youth encountered men who wore silk shirts, ate steak for lunch, and seemed to possess large sums of money. The ambitious adolescent went through several kinds of experience simultaneously. He became aware that, in material terms, there were ways of life better than that of his own family; he felt the first pangs of the adult desires for freedom, sex, and money; he felt the sharp twinges of class envy and personal hope. For many youths this accelerated coming of age in a materialistic society must have had permanently distorting effects. They could see that ordinary occupations—tending a machine or pounding a beat, pressing pants or making them, selling spools of thread or pecks of potatoes—were not going to bring quick success. For those with the right blend of imagination, audacity, and style, politics was the obvious answer.

A politician with this psychological background was obviously more vulnerable to the temptations to dishonesty in office than one who enjoyed a more secure and orderly transition through adolescence into adulthood. During the psychological crisis which shaped his personal sense of identity, certain material objects and a certain style of life obtained an excessive hold on his imagination. The keener his imagination and the better his mind, then the greater the potentiality for a certain kind of tragedy. The routine wardheeler may graft on a petty scale because the ethical code of his community condones it, but the abler and more ambitious politico grafts not only because it is permissible but also because he is subject to all the pressures and insecurities of the parvenu. Having entered politics to raise himself from the ranks of laborers and hodcarriers, he travels a long way vertically in a larger society which recognizes material success as its chief criterion. To move in the social circles and live in the manner which he desired took more money than the politician could possible acquire honestly. This was true even though he remained within the orbit of the rich and successful of his own kind. The races at Saratoga, the summer house at the seashore, daughter's grand piano—all these and other tangibles of success cost money. One does not have to join the Four Hundred to live beyond one's means. An Alfred E. Smith or Joseph Tumulty would have a code of rigid personal honesty or develop a set of social ideals to protect himself against the grafter's temptation, but the more typical politician could not avoid giving the wrong answer to the uneasy question: If it was not to travel with these people and live this way, then why did he ring doorbells, run for alderman, or go into politics in the first place?

Those who entered politics as a means of rapid personal advancement were acting from a motive that neither the theory of the founders of the nation nor the theory of the late nineteenth-century middle classes had taken into account or could accommodate. Moreover, Irish machine politics was carried on in an intellectual void. It was the intuitive response to practical necessities and unrelated to any comprehensive theory of politics and society. Until the emergence of Finley Peter Dunne's "Mr. Dooley" in the late 1890's and the realistic investigations of politics by Lincoln Steffens and other muckraking magazine writers early in this century, the code by which the Irish politicians and their mass of supporters lived and governed remained unarticulated and undefended. As a result, the larger society outside the Irish community looked upon the party bosses as grotesque; politics seemed a morality play in which, despite frequent scandals and exposures, vice always triumphed; and the gloomier observers despaired of democracy. But for the Irish, politics was a functioning system of power and not an exercise in moral judgment. While E. L. Godkin and Henry Adams despaired of the American experiment, the Irish took over City Hall.

George Washington Plunkitt
Honest Graft and Dishonest Graft

The intimate relationship between politics and business usually received moralistic rather than candid portrayals. But in William L. Riordon (1869-1909), political reporter for the old New York Post, *the subject found an authentic recorder, and in George Washington Plunkitt (1842-1924), a power in Tammany Hall under Croker and Murphy, a candid and uninhibited spokesman.* [William L. Riordon, Plunkitt of Tammany Hall, New York, 1905, pp. 3-8.]

Everybody is talkin' these days about Tammany men growin' rich on graft, but nobody thinks of drawin' the distinction between honest graft and dishonest graft. There's all the difference in the world between the two. Yes, many of our men have grown rich in politics. I have myself. I've made a big fortune out of the game, and I'm gettin' richer every day, but I've not gone in for dishonest graft—blackmailin' gamblers, saloon-keepers, disorderly people, etc.—and neither has any of the men who have made big fortunes in politics.

There's an honest graft, and I'm an example of how it works. I might sum up the whole thing by sayin': "I seen my opportunities and I took 'em."

Just let me explain by examples. My party's in power in the city, and it's goin' to undertake a lot of public improvements. Well, I'm tipped off, say, that they're going to lay out a new park at a certain place.

I see my opportunity and I take it. I go to that place and I buy up all the land I can in the neighborhood. Then the board of this or that makes its plan public, and there is a rush to get my land, which nobody cared particular for before.

Ain't it perfectly honest to charge a good price and make a profit on my investment and foresight? Of course, it is. Well, that's honest graft.

Or, supposin' it's a new bridge they're goin' to build. I get tipped off and I buy as much property as I can that has to be taken for approaches. I sell at my own price later on and drop some more money in the bank.

Wouldn't you? It's just like lookin' ahead in Wall Street or in the coffee or cotton market. It's honest graft, and I'm lookin' for it every day in the year. I will tell you frankly that I've got a good lot of it, too.

I'll tell you of one case. They were goin' to fix up a big park, no matter where. I got on to it, and went lookin' about for land in that neighborhood.

I could get nothin' at a bargain but a big piece of swamp, but I took it fast enough and held on to it. What turned out was what I counted on. They couldn't make the park complete without Plunkitt's swamp, and they had to pay a good price for it. Anything dishonest in that?

Up in the watershed I made some money, too. I bought up several bits of land there some years ago and made a pretty good guess that they would be bought up for water purposes later by the city.

Somehow, I always guessed about right, and shouldn't I enjoy the profit of my foresight? It was rather amusin' when the condemnation commissioners came along and found piece after piece of the land in the name of George Plunkitt of the Fifteenth Assembly District, New York City. They wondered how I knew just what to buy. The answer is—I seen my opportunity and I took it. I haven't confined myself to land; anything that pays is in my line.

For instance, the city is repavin' a street and has several hundred thousand old granite blocks to sell. I am on hand to buy, and I know just what they are worth.

How? Never mind that. I had a sort of monopoly of this business for a while, but once a newspaper tried to do me. It got some outside men to come over from Brooklyn and New Jersey to bid against me.

Was I done? Not much. I went to each of the men and said: "How many of these 250,000 stones do you want?" One said 20,000, and another wanted 15,000, and another wanted 10,000. I said: "All right let me bid for the lot, and I'll give each of you all you want for nothin'."

They agreed, of course. Then the auctioneer yelled: "How much am I bid for these 250,000 fine pavin' stones?"

"Two dollars and fifty cents," says I.

"Two dollars and fifty cents!" screamed the auctioneer. "Oh, that's a joke! Give me a real bid."

He found the bid was real enough. My rivals stood silent. I got the lot for $2.50 and gave them their share. That's how the attempt to do Plunkitt ended, and that's how all such attempts end.

I've told you how I got rich by honest graft. Now, let me tell you that most politicians who are accused of robbin' the city get rich the same way.

They didn't steal a dollar from the city treasury. They just seen their opportunities and took them. That is why, when a reform administration comes in and spends a half million dollars in tryin' to find the public robberies they talked about in the campaign, they don't find them.

The books are always all right. The money in the city treasury is all right. Everything is all right. All they can show is that the Tammany heads of departments looked after their friends, within the law, and gave them what opportunities they could to make honest graft. Now, let me tell you that's never goin' to hurt Tammany with the people. Every good man looks after his friends, and any man who doesn't isn't likely to be popular. If I have a good thing to hand out in private life, I give it to a friend. Why shouldn't I do the same in public life?

Another kind of honest graft. Tammany has raised a good many salaries. There was an awful howl by the reformers, but don't you know that Tammany gains ten votes for every one it lost by salary raisin'?

The Wall Street banker thinks it shameful to raise a department clerk's salary from $1500 to $1800 a year, but every man who draws a salary himself says: "That's all right. I wish it was me." And he feels very much like votin' the Tammany ticket on election day, just out of sympathy.

Tammany was beat in 1901 because the people were deceived into believin' that it worked dishonest graft. They didn't draw a distinction between dishonest and honest graft, but they saw that some Tammany men grew rich, and supposed they had been robbin' the city treasury or levyin' blackmail on disorderly houses, or workin' in with the gamblers and lawbreakers.

As a matter of policy, if nothing else, why should the Tammany leaders go into such dirty business, when there is so much honest graft lyin' around when they are in power? Did you ever consider that?

Now, in conclusion, I want to say that I don't own a dishonest dollar. If my worst enemy was given the job of writin' my epitaph when I'm gone, he couldn't do more than write:

"George W. Plunkitt. He Seen His Opportunities, and He Took 'Em."

"A POOR MAN IS A MAN THAT RAYFUSES TO CASH IN"

―――

Finley Peter Dunne
The Pursuit of Riches

Messrs. Hennessy and Dooley, conversational partners at the Archey Road saloon and creations of Chicago-born newspaper columnist and satirist Finley Peter Dunne (1867-1936), viewed success as an agonizing experience. From their vantage point the American business ideal seemed bloodless at best. [Finley Peter Dunne, Dissertations by Mr. Dooley, *New York, 1906, pp. 35-39.]*

◉

"Dear me, I wisht I had money," said Mr. Hennessy.

"So do I," said Mr. Dooley. "I need it."

"If I didn't," said Mr. Dooley, " 'twould be because I was poor or tired. But what d'ye want money f'r? Supposin' I lost me head an' handed over all me accumylated wealth? What wud ye do with that gr-reat fortune? Befure ye had spint half iv it ye'd be so sick ye'd come to me an' hand me back th' remainin' eighteen dollars.

"A man has more fun wishin' f'r th' things he hasn't got thin injyin' th' things he has got. Life, Hinnissy, is like a Pullman dinin'-car: a fine bill iv fare but nawthin' to eat. Ye go in fresh and hungry, tuck ye'er napkin in ye'er collar, an' square away at th' list iv groceries that th' black man hands ye. What'll ye have first? Ye think ye'd like to be famous, an' ye ordher a dish iv fame an' bid th' waither make a good an' hot. He's gone an age, an' whin he comes back ye'er appytite is departed. Ye taste th' ordher, an' says ye: 'Why, it's cold an' full iv broken glass.' 'That's th' way we always serve Fame on this car,' says th' coon. 'Don't ye think ye'd like money f'r th' second coorse? Misther Rockyfellar over there has had forty-two helpin's,' says he. 'It don't seem to agree with him,' says ye, 'but ye may bring me some,' ye says. Away he goes, an' stays till ye're bald an' ye'er teeth fall out

an' ye set dhrummin' on th' table an' lookin' out at th' scenery. By-
an'-by he comes back with ye'er ordher, but just' as he's goin' to hand
it to ye Rockyfellar grabs th' plate. 'What kind iv a car is this?' says ye.
'Don't I get annything to eat? Can't ye give me a little happiness?' 'I
wudden't ricommend th' happiness,' says th' waither. 'It's canned, an'
it kilt th' las' man that thried it.' 'Well, gracious,' says ye. 'I've got to
have something. Give me a little good health, an' I'll thry to make a
meal out iv that.' 'Sorry, sir,' says th' black man, 'but we're all out iv
good health. Besides,' he says, takin' ye gently by th' ar-rm, 'we're comin'
into th' deepo an' ye'll have to get out,' he says.

"An' there ye ar-re. Ye'll niver get money onless ye fix th' waither
and grab th' dishes away fr'm th' other passengers. An' ye won't do
that. So ye'll niver be rich. No poor man iver will be. Wan iv th'
sthrangest things about life is that th' poor, who need th' money th'
most, ar-re th' very wans that niver have it. A poor man is a poor
man, an' a rich man is a rich man. Ye're ayther born poor or rich. It
don't make anny diff'rence whether or not ye have money to begin with.
If ye're born to be rich ye'll be rich, an' if ye're born to be poor ye'll
be poor. Th' buttons on ye'er vest tell th' story. Rich man, poor man,
beggar man, rich man, or wurruds to that effect. I always find that I
have ayether two buttons or six.

"A poor man is a man that rayfuses to cash in. Ye don't get annything f'r nawthin', an' to gather in a millyon iv thim beautiful green
promises ye have to go down ivry day with something undher ye'er
ar-rm to th' great pawn-shop. Whin Hogan wants four dollars he
takes th' clock down to Mose's. Whin Rockyfellar wants tin millyon
he puts up his peace iv mind or his health or something akelly valy-
able. If Hogan wud hock his priceless habit iv sleepin' late in th'
mornin' he wud be able to tell th' time iv day whin he got up without
goin' to the corner dhrug-store.

"Look at McMullin. He's rowlin' in it. It bulges his pocket an'
inflates his convarsation. Whin he looks at me I always feel that he's
wondhrin' how much I'd bring at a forced sale. Well, McMullin an'
I had th' same start, about forty yards behind scratch an' Vanderbilt
to beat. They always put th' best man in anny race behind th' line.
Befure McMullin gets through he'll pass Vanderbilt, carry away th'
tape on his shoulders, an' run two or three times around th' thrack.
But me an' him started th' same way. Th' on'y diff'rence was that he
wud cash in an' I wudden't. Th' on'y thing I iver ixpicted to get money
on was me dhream iv avarice. I always had that. I cud dhream iv money
as hard as anny man ye iver see, an' can still. But I niver thought iv
wurrukin' f'r it. I've always looked at it as dishon'rable to wurruk
f'r money. I wurruk f'r exercise, an' I get what th' lawyers call an
honoraryium be dilutin' th' spirits. Th' on'y way I iver ixpict to make a
cint is to have it left to me be a rich relation, an' I'm th' pluthycrat iv
me fam'ly, or to stub me toe on a gambler's roll or stop a runaway

horse f'r Pierpont Morgan. An' th' horse mustn't be runnin' too fast. He must be jus' goin' to stop, on'y Morgan don't know it, havin' fainted. Whin he comes to he finds me at th' bridle, modesly waitin' f'r him to weep on me bosom. But as f'r scramblin' down-town arly in th' mornin' an' buyin' chattel morgedges, I niver thought iv it. I get up at siven o'clock. I wudden't get up at a quarther to siven f'r all th' money I dhream about.

"I have a lot iv things ar-round here I cud cash in if I cared f'r money. I have th' priceless gift iv laziness. It's made me what I am, an' that's th' very first thing ivry rich man cashes in. Th' millyionaires ye r-read about thryin' to give th' rest iv th' wurruld a good time be runnin' over thim in autymobills all started with a large stock iv indolence, which they cashed in. Now, whin they cud enjoy it they can't buy it back. Thin I have me good health. Ye can always get money on that. An' I have me frinds; I refuse to cash thim in. I don't know that I cud get much on thim, but if I wanted to be a millyionaire I'd tuck you an' Hogan an' Donahue undher me ar-rm an' carry ye down to Mose.

"McMullin did cash. He had no more laziness thin me, but he cashed it in befure he was twinty-wan. He cashed in his good health, a large stock iv fam'ly ties, th' affection iv his wife, th' comforts iv home, an' wan frind afther another. Wanst in a while, late in life, he'd thry to redeem a pledge, but he niver cud. They wasn't annything in the wurruld that McMullin wudden't change f'r th' money. He cashed in his vote, his pathreetism, his rellijon, his rilitives, and finally his hair. Ye heerd about him, didn't ye? He's lost ivry hair on his head. They ain't a spear iv vigitation left on him. He's as arid as th' desert iv Sahara. His head looks like an iceberg in th' moonlight. He was in here th' other day, bewailin' his fate. 'It's a gr-reat misfortune,' says he. 'What did ye get f'r it?' says I. 'That's th' throuble,' says he. 'Well, don't complain,' says I. 'Think what ye save in barber's bills,' I says, an' he wint away, lookin' much cheered up.

"No, Hinnissy, you and I, me frind, was not cut out be Provydence to be millyionaires. If ye had nawthin' but money ye'd have nawthin' but money. Ye can't ate it, sleep it, dhrink it, or carry it away with ye. Ye've got a lot iv things that McMullin hasn't got. Annybody that goes down to Mose's won't see ye'er peace iv mind hangin' in th' window as an unredeemed pledge. An', annyhow, if ye're really in search iv a fortune perhaps I cud help ye. Wud a dollar an' a half be anny use to ye?"

"Life is full iv disappointments," said Mr. Hennessy.

"It is," said Mr. Dooley, "if ye feel that way. It's thrue that a good manny have thried it, an' none have come back f'r post-gradjate coorse. But still it ain't so bad as a career f'r a young man. Ye niver get what ye ordher, but it's pretty good if ye'er appytite ain't keen an' ye care f'r th' scenery."

"A BIT OF ADVICE...: DO NOT TAKE A MOMENT'S REST"

===

Moses Rischin

Urban Economic Frontiers

The opportunities for achievement in trade, in small-scale new consumer industries, and in the independent professions proved magnetic to Jewish immigrants and their sons from Eastern Europe. But on urban economic frontiers there was no avoiding the sweatshop treadmill. The intense struggle to succeed in an arena of near-perfect competition exacted a heavy toll, even among people with an independent business tradition. [Moses Rischin, The Promised City: New York's Jews 1870-1914, *Cambridge, 1962, pp. 51-56, 74-75.]*

These people are dazzled by the brilliancy of the city, and believe that there is room for everyone in the Metropolis, where they suppose they can quickly earn a competence and follow all the laws, minor as well as important, that they have been led through so many generations to believe to be as vital as Life itself.—Report of the *United Hebrew Charities* (1893)

For East Europeans of the great Jewish migration New York was the promised city. There most of them were to find their first American employment and strike permanent roots. They had been preceded by a considerably smaller migration of Jews from Germany at mid-century which had engulfed the old Jewish families of the Knickerbocker mercantile community. A few of the German immigrants with connections on the continent became agents for the investment of German capital in American enterprise. Others became jobbers of Central European products and fashions, and wholesale trade invited their talents. Retailing, which had not counted a single Jewish firm in its front ranks, also attracted the thrifty and the industrious. German Jewish initiative and imagination led in the 1870's and 1880's to the growth of the modern department store out of the dry-goods bazaar, clothing store, and crockery shop. Altman's and Stern's came first, followed by the Strausses at Macy's, the brothers Ehrich, and the brothers Bloomingdale, creating a consumer's mecca that energized every aspect of the city's economy.

In 1890 Max Cohen of the *American Hebrew* systematically surveyed the role of Jews in New York enterprise. That investigator, aided by R. G. Dun, the leading credit-rating agency, sketched the business progress of Jews over the preceding thirty years. The most spectacular advance came in the wake of the Civil War. Between 1860 and 1870 Jewish firms worthy of commercial rating rose from 374 to 1714, as a multitude of the newly prosperous with capital to invest flocked to New York. After 1870 declining profits, tighter margins, and greater difficulty in acquiring capital curtailed the entrance of newcomers into the front ranks. In 1890 Jewish firms with a Dun rating stood at 2058, an increase of only 20 per cent over 1870. While in 1870 only about 10 per cent of the firms were capitalized at over $100,000, in 1890, 496 firms, nearly 25 per cent, reported a minimum capital of $125,000.

"Dry and fancy goods," which included the manufacture and sale of women's wear and materials, and household linens ranked as the top Jewish industry in 1890 as it had in 1870, with 125 firms capitalized at over $125,000 each. As clothiers turned to the manufacture of ready-to-wear clothing, men's wearing apparel and "gent's furnishings" rose to second place. Jews, in addition to being distributors of house furnishings, glass and paints, furniture, upholstery, and bedding, became prominent in the refection trades, including tobacco and smokers' articles, wines and liquor, and the meat business. But for long Jews were so rare among wholesale grocers that Park and Tilford even furnished Passover supplies. They were well represented in the sale and manufacture of jewelry, precious stones, optical goods, and in the hide and leather trade; more unusual was Samuel Adler's Marble and Granite Works, noted for turning out products "in the most artistic manner." Among the leading investment bankers were Kuhn Loeb & Company, Speyer, the Wormers, and the Seligmans. But more typical were the small private bankers, whose transactions lubricated the credit mechanism of the city. Although Jews had been associated with the Stock Exchange ever since it was organized around a buttonwood tree, they did not become numerous in Wall street until 1900. Booming land values also opened successful careers in real estate for many.

In scarcely a single generation, many German immigrants and their American sons had achieved a moderate prosperity. But before the turn of the century few Jews were to be counted among the city's multimillionaires; the exception, Henry Hart, a member of an older New York Jewish family and chief owner of the Third Avenue Elevated, was ranked thirty-second, far below such grand proprietors of wealth as John D. Rockefeller, the Astors, the Vanderbilts, and the many lesser magnates who chose to make their homes in the nation's greatest city. In 1892, of the 1103 New Yorkers in the *New York Tribune* list of 4047 American millionaires, approximately 60 were Jews.

The leading German Jewish merchants of New York, at the center of American foreign and domestic trade at the close of the nineteenth century, exuded optimism and proudly asserted the business virtues.

The causes of the remarkable progress made by the Jews in commerce are the simple homely virtues sung in rhythmic prose by Franklin and Smiles; patient toil; zealous application; intelligence infused into labor; frugal thrift and temperance in all things. They have had the self-denial to confine their wants to necessities until the means were provided for comforts; and to limit their desires to these until luxuries could be afforded. Realizing that the same social conditions which enabled others to amass wealth even with the most penurious beginnings to look back upon, held similar possibilities for themselves, they did not waste their energies in fruitless fretting at the conditions and fruitless efforts to change them, but devoted themselves to energetic endeavors to utilize them at their best.

These middle-class Central European Jews contrasted sharply with their coreligionists from Eastern Europe. The East Europeans landing in New York between 1870 and 1914 arrived with energies spent, nerves frayed, and purses emptied. Only a handful of them benefited from overseas ties, for they came from regions which had little direct trade with the United States. Wiadro of Kiev opened a tobacco factory in New York in 1892. The following year the Fain brothers brought their own textile machinery from Latvia and established the Fain Knitting Mills in Brooklyn. In 1903, A. Lubarsky came as an agent of the Wissotsky Tea Company, makers of "the only true Russian tea," packed in Moscow by "the world's greatest tea company." And several Jews employed their Russian connections in the fur trade. But these were the exceptions. The Russian government, although anxious to advance trade, forbade Jews to do so.

The East European Jews entered New York's social economy and attempted to make their place as had other immigrant groups before them. The new immigrants were not eager to leave for other parts of the country and efforts to disperse them met with limited success. Interior communities failed to cooperate and often returned newcomers to the city. So wretched were conditions in 1888 that 200 immigrants were shipped back to Europe in cattle steamers. Even the United Hebrew Charities, the Baron de Hirsch Fund, and the Jewish Agricultural and Industrial Aid Society showed unimpressive results. The more effective Industrial Removal Office, founded in 1901 specifically for the purpose of distributing immigrants, helped over 60,000 East European Jews to find a place outside of New York City in the following decade. Between 1906 and 1912 the Galveston Committee attempted to divert immigration away from the eastern seaboard to the trans-Mississippi South and West directly through the gulf ports. Zigismund Pestkof, newly of Dallas, wrote:

I may say that the south is a place where every emigrant will find the best chances, for his future; also Texas even it is a young state, but will raise some day, and will be the largest business state in the union. No matter who it is, a "balabos" [householder] or a tradesman, a young one or an old, a Socialist or a Zionist—for them is the best place only here in the south than in the ever crowded New York. This is my practice.

But only a small fraction of the Jewish immigrants were so aided and this new Texan, who signed himself, "yours for the freedom," proved exceptional. The absence of a wider Jewish fellowship, the abrupt break with the past, and the limited educational opportunities in the rural areas and small towns discouraged immigrants from leaving New York. New York was their lot, and their presence offered a challenge that long would affect the city's economic design.

The peddler's pack still provided the most direct introduction to American ways, the most promising school for the study of the country's speech, tastes, and economic needs, and the broadest field for the play of the aspiring tradesman's imagination. Potential peddlers were warned of the decrease in opportunities, but few failed to put this caution to the test of personal experience. The lure of commercial success, starting from the humble peddler's role, was magnetic. In the late 1880's, along the East Side from the Battery to Harlem, merchants in shoestrings, neckties, and sausages could be seen vending their wares. "Suspenders, collah buttons, 'lastic, matches, hankeches—please, lady, buy," went a familiar refrain. Compared with the alternative of seasonal sweatshop labor, peddling proved exhilarating. The rebuffs of housewives, the torments of young rowdies, and the harassment of the police intimidated the less venturesome and the more sensitive. But the number of peddlers at any one time barely suggested the multitudes who passed through this apprenticeship.

As the immigrant Jewish population swelled, the Lower East Side became the center of the pushcart trade. "Whole blocks of the East Side Jewry [were turned] into a bazaar with high-piled carts lining the curb," as few commodities failed to find a seller or buyer. "Bandannas and tin cups at two cents, peaches at a cent a quart, damaged eggs for

a song, hats for a quarter, and spectacles warranted to suit the eye . . .
for thirty-five cents." On Thursday night Hester Street, the chief market
center, resounded to the cries of bawling wives making their purchases
for the Sabbath. "Big carp, little carp, middle-sized carp, but everywhere carp." Here only the limitations of space contained the crowds
engaged in commerce, as the pinched economies of hundreds of trans-
planted *shtetls* competed amid plenty. "Every conceivable thing is for
sale, chiefly candles, dried fruit, and oilcloth; and the yolk or the white
of an egg, or a chicken leg or wing, or an ounce of tea, coffee or butter
is not an uncommon purchase." Peddlers, able to sell in small quantities—from a penny's worth up—accommodated a bargain-eager clientele
with limited storage space for perishable foods. Avid competition
among sellers, crippling to the peddlers, reduced living costs for many
an immigrant family from two to three dollars weekly.

The pushcart traffic, regularly increased by a host of seasonally unemployed garment workers, counted 25,000 peregrinating tradesmen in
1900. Predominantly Jews, augmented by Greeks and Italians who
dominated the fruit and vegetable trade, they spilled over into Little
Italy and on Saturdays intruded upon the Irish West Side to form the
Paddy's Market. Many an energetic pushcart peddler earned 15 to 20
dollars weekly and was able to advance to more settled types of commerce, leaving the itinerant trade to newcomers and to the less
successful.

The Lower East Side developed a fervent commercial life, infused
with a vitality that made it something more than a mass of tenements.
"Hurry and push, . . . the optimistic, whole-souled, almost religious
passion for business," permeated the community. In 1899, within the
Eighth Assembly District (coinciding essentially with the tenth ward)
2897 individuals were engaged in 182 different vocations and businesses. A total of 631 food mongers catered to the needs of the
inhabitants of this area. Most numerous were the 140 groceries which
often sold fruits, vegetables, bread, and rolls as well as the usual
provisions. Second in number were the 131 butcher shops which
proclaimed their wares in Hebrew characters. The other food vendors
included: 36 bakeries, 9 bread stands, 14 butter and egg stores, 24
candy stands, 62 candy stores, 1 cheese store, 20 cigar stores, 3
cigarette shops, 7 combination two-cent coffee shops, 10 delicatessens,
9 fish stores, 7 fruit stores, 21 fruit stands, 3 grocery stands, 7
herring stands, 2 meat markets, 16 milk stores, 2 matzo (unleavened
bread) stores, 10 sausage stores, 20 soda water stands, 5 tea shops,
14 tobacco shops, 11 vegetable stores, 13 wine shops, 15 grape wine
shops, and 10 confectioners. . . .

In 1905 the *New York Herald* published the results of a survey
of the occupational distribution of the Jews of the city. Although the
study failed to distinguish the variety of Jews, natives and immigrants,

Germans and Russians, employees and employers, it appeared to reflect a reasonably accurate, if incomplete, portrait of the Jews of New York. The survey disclosed the drift toward new occupations and the social and economic dynamism unleashed by exposure to new opportunities.

The cold statistics revealed economic mobility and fluidity. But few restraints bridled economic appetites "In the Great East Side Tread-mill," described by Jacob Riis, and the costs of success often proved high. The cunning and unscrupulousness that were often incidental to material rise, the anxiety that accompanied the blistering pace of frontier industries, and the fear of poverty and unemployment took a heavy toll on physical and psychological well-being. Yet men seemed without choice. A popular immigrant guidebook advised in all seriousness:

Hold fast, this is most necessary in America. Forget your past, your customs, and your ideals. Select a goal and pursue it with all your might. No matter what happens to you, hold on. You will experience a bad time but sooner or later you will achieve your goal. If you are neglectful, beware for the wheel of fortune turns quickly. You will lose your grip and be lost. A bit of advice for you: Do not take a moment's rest. Run, do, work and keep your own good in mind . . . A final virtue is needed in America—called cheek . . . Do not say, "I cannot; I do not know."

—

Moses Rischin

From Gompers to Hillman: Labor Goes Middle Class

The very intensity of the struggle for success in urban frontier indus-tries helped generate among Jewish immigrants visions and realities of group solidarity to counterpoint extreme individualism. For them and their typical leaders, Samuel Gompers and Sidney Hillman, the ideals of labor served as the social equivalent of the Irish practice of politics. [Moses Rischin, "From Gompers to Hillman: Labor Goes Middle Class," Antioch Review, XIII, Summer 1953, pp. 191-201.]

So much that has been socially significant in American life . . . has been reflected in the "coming of age" of American labor that it is appropriate at this nodal point in our national history to investigate the roots of this change. Samuel Gompers and Sidney Hillman may well qualify as foci for an examination of labor in modern America. Woven into the warp and woof of their careers, we shall find much that has contributed new dimensions to American life. The recent biography of Hillman by Matthew Josephson, an earlier sketch by George Soule, Rowland H. Harvey's biography of Gompers, and that worthy's own massive autobiography, provide us with a serviceable dossier.

The contrasts between Gompers and Hillman are between epochs as well as between men. It was Gompers' role to symbolize organized labor of the old school from the Haymarket riot of 1886 until shortly after the disastrous Great Steel Strike of 1919. Hillman's career is tied to the rise of the submerged forces of the "new immigration," the "poor whites," and the Negro, the great moral upsurge associated with the muckraker, the reformer, and the social worker, in the earlier years of the twentieth century, and the ultimate institutionalization of these elements during the Roosevelt Revolution.

A seeming triumph in Sam Gompers' career came with the assurance of the Clayton Anti-Trust Act in 1914 that "the labor of a human being is not a commodity or article of commerce." When Sidney Hillman was tendered the presidency of the Amalgamated Clothing Workers, the so-called "Magna Carta of Labor" had just been placed on the federal statute books. In 1914, Gompers at 64 was at his peak; Hillman, at 27, had just recently undergone his baptism of fire in the ranks of labor.

To twentieth-century reformers, "Gomperism" or trade unionism "pure and simple" has been anathema. Yet the *raison d'être* of Gompers' trade unionism, what Professor Selig Perlman has called "job and wage conscious" unionism, acquired much of its conviction as a reaction to the countless panaceas and blind alleys which exhausted labor's energies in the hungry 1870's. The titanic reshuffling of men, machinery, manufacturers, and geography of the late nineteenth and early twentieth century, almost organically defied reason, organization, or reform. Early immersion in the cosmopolitan potpourri of New York's East Side only reinforced Sam's predilection for a solid raft of trade unionism for his cigarmaking brethren and other craftsmen in a tumultuous sea of adventurous reformers and discontented revolutionists. German Forty-Eighters, Italian Carbonari, Irish Home Rulers, French communards, philosophical anarchists, feminists, co-operators, utopian socialists, and the Marxist remnant of the First International, presented a veritable Babel of tongues, ideologies, and temperaments. Emerging from such an ideological steambath, even a less pragmatic soul than the expert cigarmaker might well have acquired an eternal allergy to theory. What with Eight-Hour Day movements, Greenbackism, Single Taxism, Free Silverism in the wake of Populism, Sam Gompers was made virtually impervious to ideas. They were either foreign and impractical (especially those of the German-American socialists who contributed to his only defeat for the presidency of the American Federation of Labor and his "Sabbatical" of 1895), or just downright impractical, as with the Knights of Labor with their one big union district assemblies and producers' co-operatives.

In *Seventy Years of Life and Labor,* Gompers boasts (one can almost see Sam dictating this passage at his stentorian best) that he studied German with special diligence so that he might read Marx. One suspects that Sam, especially sensitive about his slim formal schooling, was trying to impress his readers. For Gompers was never a student by nature, much though he admired and even attempted

to hoard learning, much though he unabashedly makes claim to
elephantine feats of memory. Sam Gompers was too much the joiner,
the socializer, even the bon vivant and merry Andrew, to learn very
much from books or men who communed with them. If Sam was
a man of intellect, and of this there is no doubt, there was never
any danger of his becoming an intellectual: ". . . his nature was too
pragmatic to be touched by the mystical," asserts his biographer. There
was not a drop of the ascetic in Sam Gompers. The theater, music,
and the convivialities of the saloon were ever welcome. There is not
the slightest indication that Gompers sequestered a deep inner life. But
passionate, sincere, ever-ready to defend the rights of labor, he fought
for the dignity of his fellows without reserve. "Samuel Gompers
had no life apart from the American Federation of Labor. . . . Gompers
wrote few 'private' letters. . . . His correspondence dealt almost
entirely with the affairs of labor," reports Harvey. Yet when William
Allen White etches Gompers at the 1919 Steel Conference, the "Anglo-
Saxon" attribution of mystery to the "Oriental" assumes full-dress
literary license.

Yet he was more American than the Americans, as his biographer
puts it. To that author's pious and naïve bafflement, "coming of a
race of thinkers and idealists," this English son of Dutch-Jewish stock
became the leader of "a group of hard-headed and thoroughly
empirical Celts."

But to identify Gompers simply with trade unionism "pure and
simple" and anti-intellectualism, as he was wont to do himself, is to
underestimate the man and to overlook reality. It is to put a negative
evaluation on what was essentially a positive creed, the enlargement
of human dignity—the acquisition of freedom through property in
the job. It is unfortunate that his biographer denigrates Gompers
in the fashion of the 1920's and '30's. As Selig Perlman, in one of
his seminal essays in *The Theory of the Labor Movement,* points out,
the hard-won success of the American Federation of Labor was due
to the comprehension of its leaders of the "external environment" on
the one hand and the psychology of the American worker on the other.
The conservative attitude of the American toward property was accepted
as the basic premise of union activity. Labor, always suspect of functioning on the periphery of this assumption, depended for much of its
strength on at least the passive support of the middle class. That
organized labor itself became middle class in the process is less the
gentle irony of success than it is the fulfillment of an unexpressed
major premise.

Yet Gompers never resigned himself to the limitation which latter-
day critics regarded as inherent in "job conscious" unionism, a reluctance to extend the blessings of unionism to the unorganized. For he
realized the actual weakness of the Federation and of the cause of

labor in the public mind. For this reason, Gompers undertook an almost single-handed campaign to educate the American public through nonofficial magazines and, in later years, through books. His exertions to justify and win friends for the cause of labor were truly prodigious. Besides perennially lecturing and debating, he penned six books in the final years of his life and was author or co-author of sixteen of forty-one titles in the pamphlet literature of the Federation. It would appear that Gompers' special pleading, the monolithic dedication to labor rather than a more comprehensive formulation was, what we should call today, bad public relations; but it is difficult to see, in the light of his times, any real alternative. In the opinion of his biographer, Gompers

never caught the fancy of the great public. It thought of him as a cold, sinister, and perhaps even dangerous man. His interests were too narrow to make him a popular figure. He was seldom heard except in defense of labor. Roosevelt would hunt, fish, write history, express scientific views, and quarrel with philosophers; but Gompers apparently only knew labor problems. . . .

If Sam Gompers was unable to charm his audience on the personal level, and was certainly no thespian at all compared to the magnificent "Teddy," perhaps it is to his credit that he kept the cause of labor, "dull" though it may have been, in the public eye.

Gompers was even unwilling to recognize that the disparity between the ideology of labor groups abroad and that of the American Federation of Labor was a sufficient block to mutual understanding and co-operation. This despite the fact that he concluded after his European peregrinations of 1909, in *Labor in Europe and America,* that European and American labor did not speak the same language.

The Old World is not our world. Its social problems, its economic philosophy, its current political questions are not linked up with America. All the people on the globe may be on the broad highway to social justice, peace among men of all tongues, and universal brotherhood, but all the nations and governments have not yet reached the same points on the road. In this procession, America is first.

Under these circumstances, Gompers' bid for internationalism during and after World War I, much though it yielded him personal satisfaction, was doomed to defeat. His strained efforts to found a Pan-American Federation of Labor also failed signally outside of Mexico and the Caribbean countries. His frustration in the international field was but a microcosmic reflection of the rejection of Wilson's crusade by the great American middle class whose language Gompers spoke.

II

There are fundamental points of resemblance between Sidney Hillman and Samuel Gompers. But I suspect that they are the obvious ones
—the compulsion to lead, the genius for politics and diplomacy, the
insistent pragmatism, and the complete devotion to the cause of labor.
In all other respects, Hillman differed markedly from the AFL president. Gompers personified "the older" immigration, close to the middle
class crest; Hillman rested his strength on "the newer" immigration, as
yet in process.

Unlike Gompers, who was a natural trade unionist, a cigarmaker
and a cigarmaker's son, whose own trade union was modeled on the
trade organization of mid-Victorian England, Hillman was something
of an intellectual, a former member of the Jewish underground labor
movement, and a political exile from the clutches of the Tsar. Pants
cutting, to which he was apprenticed at the clothing firm of Hart,
Schaffner, and Marx, was not destined to be his metier. In the frank
opinion of a co-worker, he was a "damned poor cutter." Although Hillman ate, drank, and slept the labor movement throughout most of his
life with slight pause for reflection, in the earliest days of his youth in
Lithuania and America, he guarded his privacy (aided and abetted, it
is true, by Tsarist prison sentences). He led the life of the ascetic
recluse, drinking little, eating less, smoking cigarettes endlessly, and
reading, continually reading. The close dissections of the modern soul
in the pages of Ibsen, Tolstoy, and Dostoevsky, and the contemporary
scriptures of progress, Darwin, Marx, Mill, Spencer, and T. H. Morgan,
comprised his literary and spiritual fare. For the rebellious rabbinical
student, this must have been revelation imbibed at white heat. For Hillman was a product of Talmudic Lithuania of the villages, the son of an
improvident grain merchant, the grandson of a hapless unworldly rabbi,
oblivious to the industrial torrent engulfing the cities and the tremendous lure of "Gentile" learning. Gompers, by contrast, was born at the
heart of the industrial revolution, in the Spitalfields district of London,
conditioned to proletarianism. For Gompers the journey with his
family in 1863 from the East Side of London to the East Side of New
York was an experience involving little more than geographic reloca-
tion, a process that abused human sensibilities only incidentally. Not so
with Sidney Hillman born thirty-seven years later. Zagare, Lithuania,
had not yet come to terms with the world of steam and steel. Medieval
tradition still enshrouded the village, a world as yet unsundered by the
Moloch of industrialism. As a lone political exile in the "husky, brawling city of the big shoulders," separated by thousands of miles from kith
and kin, mastering a language which he found difficult, Hillman, even
the tough-minded Hillman, would be overtaken by nostalgia. Uncon-

sciously he would strive to recover the essential harmony of the village, to reconstruct the moral unity, the sense of personality and social responsibility of the Lithuanian townlet, streamlined to fit the fabric of an industrial society. This he was somewhat reluctant to admit to his perfervid followers many years later, though less self-conscious about the matter than is his biographer.

I have no ultimate program. . . . In time of leisure—and that time is becoming more and more scarce—I indulge in dreams. But I don't permit them to become the policy of the organization.

Yet the embarrassing dreams never altogether deserted Hillman. His wagon would always be hitched to a star.

By 1914, many Americans had become outraged at the ravages which industrialization had condoned beneath the flag of patriotism, "Americanism," and free enterprise. Hillman entered American life in step with the Progressives and the Wilson Democrats, at the high-tide of pre-World War I liberalism. Hillman, like Gompers, intuitively grasped the prevailing middle class spirit in America, but it was a more mature America than the traditional structure which Gompers encountered three and four decades earlier. Some of the newspapers, that indefinable entity known as public opinion, and liberal and charitable citizens everywhere but especially in Chicago and New York, were receptive to social innovation. Men were at least willing to acknowledge the existence of a "labor problem" and an "industrial problem."

If early participation in political revolution brought out the uncompromising, militant spirit in Hillman, all evidence seems to agree that this was not the expression of his essential character. The "spirit of sweet reasonableness" which Joseph Schaffner, his employer, detected in his earliest encounter with Hillman, was joined with "marvelous tact"; the "messianic" quality, ever present, was never truculent, never obtrusive in the former socialist. How different in temperament from the bellicose Gompers!

Matthew Josephson persistently emphasizes Hillman's moderation. Studied or congenital, acquired through a keen social awareness or instinctively imbibed with his mother's milk, or a combination of the two, the judicious mien revealed itself repeatedly and early as his outstanding trait. He was a man "in whom the arts of diplomacy and manipulation were instinctive," notes his biographer. Commented John E. Williams, the sage of Streator, Illinois, and one of the earliest arbitrators brought into the clothing industry:

The chief deputy is as yet only twenty [six] years old, and the most remarkable characteristic in one so young is his power of restraint. We expect youth to be fiery, enthusiastic, daring; but we rarely find it coupled with that poise, repose, self-mastery so necessary to great achievement of any sort. I have known him when he had a strike vote in his pocket

and when a wave of his hand would have summoned his comrades to
battle, refuse the temptation to make himself an idolized leader . . . and
choose the harder, less spectacular role of a practical constructive builder
of an organization that would get results for his people. And that to me
is the highest test of . . . leadership.

When the Amalgamated Clothing Workers union was formed by
secession from the United Garment Workers in 1914, it was a fore-
gone conclusion that Sidney Hillman, though far-removed from the site
of the convention and engaged in another occupation, would receive the
call to the presidency of the union. Not until 1933 did the Federation
recognize the Amalgamated. In the interim, under Hillman's devoted
leadership, the independent Amalgamated became one of the most
admired social institutions in the United States, the virtual showplace of
"industrial unionism," the "darling" of social workers, liberals, and all
men of good will. It could never be said of Hillman as it was said of
Gompers, "The greater world of labor he never glimpsed. . . ." The
leader of the "immigrant rubbish" would yet prove himself equal to the
American "urban frontier," to advert to Samuel Lubell's apt expression.
(The International Ladies' Garment Workers' Union with a similar
pedigree, though without any single outstanding leader, was to make
comparable strides in a "sister" industry.)

In the early years between 1910 and 1914 when Hillman's genius
for mediation revealed itself, for restoring "the amalgam that dropped
out of society," to borrow a phrase of J. H. Randall's, much of the
machinery for labor-industry relations, adopted in industry after industry in later years, was tried and tested. The "Protocol of Peace" drawn
up in settlement of the cloakmakers' strike of 1910, the "Great Revolt,"
with the architectonic assistance of that staunch advocate of "industrial
peace," Louis Brandeis, served as a model and an inspiration for the
"Hart, Schaffner, and Marx Plan" drawn up in Chicago some months
later. This was something more than arbitration "pure and simple."
Hillman called it "industrial self-government," the beginning of "the
recognition of human rights in the shops," "industrial democracy" on
trial. What did it mean to Hillman and his fellows? Said he testifying
before the Industrial Commission of 1915:

I believe that there is such a change that really it cannot be explained.
The people really felt themselves a little more like men and women. Before
there was not a feeling like that in any non-union shop. Contrary to any
statement by people who defend the open shop, I do not feel it is
possible to have the full feeling of manhood.

With the dedication and spirit of men on trial, the union officers
sweated over the regulation of endless minutes—questions of shop
standards, of quality, of piecework prices, and of workers' discipline.
Hillman believed in the vital importance of this achievement for

American society as a whole. As he expressed it later when summing up the achievements of the New Deal administration:

It is the party that has the power to create new conditions in industrial or political relations that is, in an important sense, progressive. Such a party (or labor organization) may recondition our social relationships.

Even from its earliest days, the Amalgamated was to become the prototype for the modern industrial union. The Amalgamated never was discouraged by barriers of culture and language as impediments to organization. Its newspapers were printed not only in English but in French, Italian, Yiddish, Polish, Lithuanian, and Bohemian. At the time when nativism and anti-immigration sentiment was at its height, Hillman replied to the detractors of his fellow immigrants that "Americanism is not talking about it, but working out in its own sphere of action a system that will create less unrest."

Much of the activity undertaken by the Amalgamated must be regarded as a product of the spirit of social service and social responsibility which animated that organization. Here Hillman's guiding hand constantly asserted itself. A firm believer in self help, "the liberation of the workers is a matter for the workers themselves," Hillman provided that example rather than precept would invest the union with public confidence and respect. His union was the first to realize the value of a research department to deal with employers on their own level—even to assist and instruct them at their own game. Acquaintance with the innovation of labor banking through Warren S. Stone of the Brotherhood of Locomotive Engineers, stimulated the Amalgamated to enter this field. The provision for unemployment insurance funds and the successful ventures into co-operative housing were novelties duplicated by few other unions. While the conservative craft unions of the Federation were anesthetized by the soporific prosperity of the 1920's and their own social and ideological bankruptcy under new industrial conditions, Hillman kept his eye on the future, confident of his mission on the "urban frontier."

The big chance came in 1933. In 1930, at a time when "free enterprise" had virtually thrown the towel into the ring, Hillman and his associates had already outlined a program that foreshadowed the New Deal. Bust had followed Boom, and social messianism, unknown to itself, had been carried into office by the tranquil decision of the ballot box.

Hillman's training and temperament were ideally fitted for the gigantic tasks of the years ahead. His "greatest talent as a political personality in the world of labor, or that of national affairs, resided in his special ability to bring men and groups of opposing tendencies together to work in a tolerable accord for some common end." In this role Hillman was almost unique among labor leaders—an ideal foil to the constitutionally obstinate John L. Lewis. Having observed the benevolent role of government vis-à-vis labor during World War I, as a member of the Board of Control and Labor Standards for Army Clothing, Hillman was able to anticipate the greater opportunities and responsibilities which would accrue to organized labor in an era of "statism." It was hardly chance that of the five-man Labor Advisory Board for the National Recovery Administration, two should come from the Amalgamated. In Roosevelt's kitchen cabinet, Hillman represented labor. In 1940, as assistant to William Knudsen, Hillman became a member of the National Defense Advisory Commission; soon thereafter, he became associate director general of its successor, the Office of Production Management. For the first time in American history, labor had entered into a long term partnership with government. Newly organized labor was acquiring status and dignity. The formation of the CIO, the organization of industrial unions in rubber, steel, motors, textiles, aluminum, Labor's Non-Partisan League, and the Political Action Committee of the CIO, all contributed to the activization of a new potential middle class, the extension of the American dream to what Europeans and even many Americans were beginning to regard as the "submerged classes."

The CIO's and to some extent Hillman's miscalculations in the international field, like Gompers' failures, were closely associated with the prevailing spirit of the times. The World Federation of Trade Unions organized during the second World War, when pro-Russian sentiment was dominant and the crisis of war overshadowed all other considerations, permitted the Soviet-dominated unions to play a major and potentially insidious role. Only in 1949 with the founding of the International Confederation of Free Trade Unions was the error in judgment perceived and rectified. So much the American, Hillman like Roosevelt, entertained the notion that personal sincerity and amiability would win over opposition abroad as it had at home.

It was Hillman's destiny to insinuate millions of Americans into the consciousness of the American middle class by demonstrating labor's ability to master the instrumentalities—financial, social, political, and technological—of our modern complex industrial society. First tested in the bailiwick of his own union and then injected into the mainstream of American life during the Roosevelt Revolution, so commonplace have these changes become, so "middle class," so "American" that their value is no longer open to question.

If much of the spirit of Sidney Hillman lives on in American labor, it is significant that the impress of Sam Gompers lies equally deep. With the acceptance of labor in the last two decades, with the informal coalescence of craft and industrial unionism, and with the onset of a less than benevolent administration, the real test of the new labor statesmanship is now in the offing.

Despite differences in tactics and basic goals, neither Hillman nor

Gompers misunderstood the middle class temper and drive of America. C. Wright Mills's judgment that "socially and ideologically the wage workers are more middle class than has been assumed" is but a vindication of the basic insights of labor's most acute and optimistic leaders. To be middle class in the United States has been a state of mind, a novel presumption, the birthright of all, and a challenge to technology and human inertia rather than a relationship to the instruments of production. But with middle class power and responsibility goes middle class conscience. Fortunately this axiom has not been lost on labor's leaders in the past, nor does it seem in danger of submergence in the future by labor's new leaders.

"AMID THE JINGLE OF GOLD...
I FEEL THE DEADLY SILENCE OF SOLITUDE"

——

David Levinsky

The Loneliness of Success

Business success for the Jewish entrepreneur was achieved most characteristically in the clothing and related industries which fellow Jewish immigrants revolutionized and dominated. The Rise of David Levinsky, *the classic Jewish immigrant novel written by Abraham Cahan (1860-1951), editor of the uniquely successful socialist* Jewish Daily Forward, *portrays the hollowness of economic achievement divorced from a living social context. [Abraham Cahan,* The Rise of David Levinsky, *New York, 1917, pp. 525-526, 529-530.]*

Am I happy?

There are moments when I am overwhelmed by a sense of my success and ease. I become aware that thousands of things which had formerly been forbidden fruit to me are at my command now. I distinctly recall that crushing sense of being debarred from everything, and then I feel as though the whole world were mine. One day I paused in front of an old East Side restaurant that I had often passed in my days of need and despair. The feeling of desolation and envy with which I used to peek in its windows came back to me. It gave me pangs of self-pity for my past and a thrilling sense of my present power. The prices that had once been prohibitive seemed so wretchedly low now. On another occasion I came across a Canal Street merchant of whom I used to buy goods for my push-cart. I said to myself: "There was a time when I used to implore this man for ten dollars' worth of goods, when I regarded him as all-powerful and feared him. Now he would be happy to shake hands with me."

I recalled other people whom I used to fear and before whom I used to humiliate myself because of my poverty. I thought of the time when I had already entered the cloak business, but was struggling and squirming and constantly racking my brains for some way of raising a hundred dollars; when I would cringe with a certain East Side banker and vainly beg him to extend a small note of mine, and come away in a sickening state of despair.

At this moment, as these memories were filing by me, I felt as though now there were nobody in the world who could inspire me with awe or render me a service.

And yet in all such instances I feel a peculiar yearning for the very days when the doors of that restaurant were closed to me and when the Canal Street merchant was a magnate of commerce in my estimation. Somehow, encounters of this kind leave me dejected. The gloomiest past is dearer than the brightest present. In my case there seems to be a special reason for feeling this way. My sense of triumph is coupled with a brooding sense of emptiness and insignificance, of my lack of anything like a great, deep interest.

I am lonely. Amid the pandemonium of my six hundred sewing-machines and the jingle of gold which they pour into my lap I feel the deadly silence of solitude. . . .

I often long for a heart-to-heart talk with some of the people of my birthplace. I have tried to revive my old friendships with some of them, but they are mostly poor and my prosperity stands between us in many ways.

Sometimes when I am alone in my beautiful apartments, brooding over these things and nursing my loneliness, I say to myself:

"There are cases when success is a tragedy."

There are moments when I regret my whole career, when my very success seems to be a mistake.

I think that I was born for a life of intellectual interest. I was certainly brought up for one. The day when that accident turned my mind from college to business seems to be the most unfortunate day in my life. I think that I should be much happier as a scientist or writer, perhaps. I should then be in my natural element, and if I were doomed to loneliness I should have comforts to which I am now a stranger. That's the way I feel every time I pass the abandoned old building of the City College.

The business world contains plenty of successful men who have no brains. Why, then, should I ascribe my triumph to special ability? I should probably have made a much better college professor than a cloak-manufacturer, and should probably be a happier man, too. I know people who have made much more money than I and whom I consider my inferiors in every respect.

Many of our immigrants have distinguished themselves in science, music, or art, and these I envy far more than I do a billionaire. As an example of the successes achieved by Russian Jews in America in the last quarter of a century it is often pointed out that the man who has built the greatest sky-scrapers in the country, including the Woolworth Building, is a Russian Jew who came here a penniless boy. I cannot boast such distinction, but then I have helped build up one of the great industries of the United States, and this also is something to be proud of. But I should readily change places with the Russian Jew, a former Talmud student like myself, who is the greatest physiologist in the New World, or with the Russian Jew who holds the foremost place among American writers and whose soulful compositions are sung in almost every English-speaking house in the world. I love music to madness. I yearn for the world of great singers, violinists, pianists. Several of the greatest of them are of my race and country, and I have met them, but all my acquaintance with them has brought me is a sense of being looked down upon as a money-bag striving to play the maecenas. I had a similar experience with a sculptor, also one of our immigrants, and an East Side boy who had met with sensational success in Paris and London. I had him make my bust. His demeanor toward me was all that could have been desired. We even cracked Yiddish jokes together and he hummed bits of synagogue music over his work, but I never left his studio without feeling cheap and wretched.

When I think of these things, when I am in this sort of mood, I pity myself for a victim of circumstances.

At the height of my business success I feel that if I had my life to live over again I should never think of a business career.

I don't seem to be able to get accustomed to my luxurious life. I am always more or less conscious of my good clothes, of the high quality of my office furniture, of the power I wield over the men in my pay. As I have said in another connection, I still have a lurking fear of restaurant waiters.

I can never forget the days of my misery. I cannot escape from my old self. My past and my present do not comport well. David, the poor lad swinging over a Talmud volume at the Preacher's Synagogue, seems to have more in common with my inner identity than David Levinsky, the well-known cloak-manufacturer.

"WHY...PROHIBIT A MAN FROM BACKING HIS OWN JUDGMENT?"

Daniel Bell

Crime as an American Way of Life

For successive waves of immigrants outside the mainstream of American public morality shaped by the small-town Protestant ethos, marginal business—especially gambling, liquor purveying, and the amusement industries—offered attractive if not respectable opportunities for economic success. Daniel Bell (1919-), a sociologist, portrays the intricate ties between politics, crime, business, and the immigrant communities—a different form of Big Business organization. [Daniel Bell, "Crime as an American Way of Life," Antioch Review, XIII, Summer 1953, pp. 131-154.]

In the 1890's, the Reverend Dr. Charles Parkhurst, shocked at the open police protection afforded New York's bordellos, demanded a state inquiry. In the Lexow investigation that followed, the young and dashing William Travers Jerome staged a set of public hearings that created sensation after sensation. He badgered "Clubber" Williams, First Inspector of the Police Department, to account for wealth and property far greater than could have been saved on his salary; it was earned, the Clubber explained laconically, through land speculation "in Japan." Heavy-set Captain Schmittberger, the "collector" for the "Tenderloin precincts"—Broadway's fabulous concentration of hotels, theaters, restaurants, gaming houses, and saloons—related in detail how protection money was distributed among the police force. Crooks, policemen, public officials, businessmen, all paraded across the stage, each adding his chapter to a sordid story of corruption and crime.

The upshot of these revelations was reform—the election of William L. Strong, a stalwart businessman, as mayor, and the naming of Theodore Roosevelt as police commissioner.

It did not last, of course, just as previous reform victories had not lasted. Yet the ritual drama was re-enacted. Twenty years ago the Seabury investigation in New York uncovered the tin-box brigade and the thirty-three little MacQuades. Jimmy Walker was ousted as Mayor and in came Fiorello La Guardia. Tom Dewey became district attorney, broke the industrial rackets, sent Lucky Luciano to jail, and went to the Governor's chair in Albany. Then reform was again swallowed up in the insatiable maw of corruption until Kefauver and the young and dashing Rudolph Halley threw a new beam of light into the seemingly bottomless pit.

How explain this repetitive cycle? Obviously the simple moralistic distinction between "good guys" and "bad guys," so deep at the root of the reform impulse, bears little relation to the role of organized crime in American society. What, then, does?

II

Americans have had an extraordinary talent for compromise in politics and extremism in morality. The most shameless political deals (and "steals") have been rationalized as expedient and realistically necessary. Yet in no other country have there been such spectacular attempts to curb human appetites and brand them as illicit, and nowhere else such glaring failures. From the start America was at one and the same time a frontier community where "everything goes," and the fair country of the Blue Laws. At the turn of the century the cleavage developed between the Big City and the small-town conscience. Crime as a growing business was fed by the revenues from prostitution, liquor and gambling that a wide-open urban society encouraged and which a middle-class Protestant ethos tried to suppress with a ferocity unmatched in any other civilized country. Catholic cultures rarely have imposed such restrictions, and have rarely suffered such excesses. Even in prim and proper Anglican England, prostitution is a commonplace of Piccadilly night life, and gambling one of the largest and most popular industries. In America the enforcement of public morals has been a continuing feature of our history.

Some truth may lie in Svend Ranulf's generalization that moral indignation is a peculiar fact of middle-class psychology and represents a disguised form of repressed envy. The larger truth lies perhaps in the brawling nature of American development and the social character of crime. Crime, in many ways, is a Coney Island mirror, caricaturing the morals and manners of a society. The jungle quality of the American business community, particularly at the turn of the century, was reflected in the mode of "business" practiced by the coarse gangster elements, most of them from new immigrant families, who were "getting ahead," just as Horatio Alger had urged. In the older, Protestant tradition the intense acquisitiveness, such as that of Daniel Drew, was rationalized by a compulsive moral fervor. But the formal obeisance of the ruthless businessman in the workaday world to the church-going pieties of the Sabbath was one that the gangster could not make. Moreover, for the young criminal, hunting in the asphalt jungle of the crowded city, it was not the businessman with his wily manipulation of numbers but the "man with the gun" who was the American hero. "No amount of commercial prosperity," once wrote Teddy Roosevelt, "can supply the lack of the heroic virtues." The American was "the hunter, cowboy, frontiersman, the soldier, the naval hero." And in the crowded slums, the gangster. He was a man with a gun, acquiring by personal merit what was denied to him by complex orderings of a stratified society. And the duel with the law was the morality play *par excellence:* the gangster, with whom ride our own illicit desires, and the prosecutor, representing final judgment and the force of the law.

Yet all this was acted out in a wider context. The desires satisfied in extra-legal fashion were more than a hunger for the "forbidden fruits" of conventional morality. They also involved, in the complex and ever shifting structure of group, class, and ethnic stratification, which is the warp and woof of America's "open" society, such "normal" goals as independence through a business of one's own, and such "moral" aspirations as the desire for social advancement and social prestige. For crime, in the language of the sociologists, has a "functional" role in the society, and the urban rackets—the illicit activity organized for continuing profit rather than individual illegal acts —are one of the queer ladders of social mobility in American life. Indeed, it is not too much to say that the whole question of organized crime in America cannot be understood unless one appreciates (1) the distinctive role of organized gambling as a function of a mass consumption economy; (2) the specific role of various immigrant groups as they one after another become involved in marginal business and crime; and (3) the relation of crime to the changing character of the urban political machines.

III

As a society changes, so does, in lagging fashion, its type of crime. As American society became more "organized," as the American businessman became more "civilized" and less "buccaneering," so did the American racketeer. And just as there were important changes in the structure of business enterprise, so the "institutionalized" criminal enterprise was transformed too.

In the America of the last fifty years the main drift of society has been toward the rationalization of industry, the domestication of the crude self-made captain of industry into the respectable man of manners, and the emergence of a mass-consumption economy. The most significant transformation in the field of "institutionalized" crime was the increasing relative importance of gambling as against other kinds of illegal activity. And, as a multi-billion-dollar business, gambling underwent a transition parallel to the changes in American enterprise as a whole. This parallel was exemplified in many ways: in gambling's industrial organization (e.g., the growth of a complex technology such as the national racing wire service and the minimization of risks by such techniques as lay-off betting); in its respectability, as was evidenced in the opening of smart and popular gambling casinos in resort towns and in "satellite" adjuncts to metropolitan areas; in its functional role in a mass-consumption economy (for sheer volume of money changing hands, nothing has ever surpassed this feverish activity of fifty million American adults); in the social acceptance of the gamblers in the important status world of sport and entertainment, i.e., "café society."

In seeking to "legitimize" itself, gambling had quite often actually become a force against older and more vicious forms of illegal activity. In 1946, for example, when a Chicago mobster, Pat Manno, went down to Dallas, Texas, to take over gambling in the area for the Accardo-Guzik combine, he reassured the sheriff as to his intent as follows: "Something I'm against, that's dope peddlers, pickpockets, hired killers. That's one thing I can't stomach, and that's one thing the fellows up there—the group won't stand for, things like that. They discourage it, they even go to headquarters and ask them why they don't do something about it."

Jimmy Cannon once reported that when the gambling raids started in Chicago, the "combine" protested that, in upsetting existing stable relations, the police were only opening the way for ambitious young punks and hoodlums to start trouble. Nor is there today, as there was twenty or even forty years ago, prostitution of major organized scope in the United States. Aside from the fact that manners and morals have changed, prostitution *as an industry* doesn't pay as well as gambling. Besides, its existence threatened the tacit moral acceptance and quasi-respectability that gamblers and gambling have secured in the American way of life. It was, as any operator in the field might tell you, "bad for business."

The criminal world of the last decade, its tone set by the captains of the gambling industry, is in startling contrast to the state of affairs in the two decades before. If a Kefauver report had been written then, the main "names" would have been Lepke and Gurrah, Dutch Schultz, Jack "Legs" Diamond, Lucky Luciano, and, reaching back a little further, Arnold Rothstein, the czar of the underworld. These men (with the exception of Luciano, who was involved in narcotics and prostitution) were in the main industrial racketeers. Rothstein, it is true, had a larger function: he was, as Frank Costello became later, the financier of the underworld—the pioneer big businessman of crime, who, understanding the logic of co-ordination, sought to *organize* crime as a source of regular income. His main interest in this direction was in industrial racketeering, and his entry was through labor disputes. At one time, employers in the garment trades hired Legs Diamond and his sluggers to break strikes, and the Communists, then in control of the cloakmakers union, hired one Little Orgie to protect the pickets and beat up the scabs; only later did both sides learn that Legs Diamond and Little Orgie were working for the same man, Rothstein.

Rothstein's chief successors, Lepke Buchalter and Gurrah Shapiro, were able, in the early '30's, to dominate sections of the men's and women's clothing industries, of painting, fur dressing, flour trucking, and other fields. In a highly chaotic and cut-throat industry such as clothing, the racketeer, paradoxically, played a stabilizing role by regulating competition and fixing prices. When the NRA came in and assumed this function, the businessman found that what had once been a quasi-economic service was now pure extortion, and he began to demand police action. In other types of racketeering, such as the trucking of perishable foods and water-front loading, where the racketeers entrenched themselves as middlemen—taking up, by default, a service that neither shippers nor truckers wanted to assume—a pattern of accommodation was roughly worked out and the rackets assumed a quasi-legal veneer. On the water-front, old-time racketeers perform the necessary function of loading—but at an exorbitant price, and this monopoly was recognized by both the union and the shippers, and tacitly by government.

But in the last decade and a half, industrial racketeering has not offered much in the way of opportunity. *Like American capitalism itself, crime shifted its emphasis from production to consumption.* The focus of crime became the direct exploitation of the citizen as consumer, largely through gambling. And while the protection of these huge revenues was inextricably linked to politics, the relation between gambling and "the mobs" became more complicated.

IV

Although it never showed up in the gross national product, gambling in the last decade was one of the largest industries in the United States. The Kefauver Committee estimated it as a twenty-billion-dollar business. This figure has been picked up and widely quoted, but in truth no one knows what the gambling "turnover" and "take" actually is, nor how much is bet legally (pari-mutuel, etc.) and how much illegally. In fact, the figure cited by the committee was arbitrary and arrived at quite sloppily. As one staff member said: "We had no real idea of the money spent. . . . The California crime commission said twelve billion. Virgil Peterson of Chicago estimated thirty billion. We picked twenty billion as a balance between the two."

If comprehensive data are not available, we do know, from specific instances, the magnitude of many of the operations. Some indications can be seen from these items culled at random:

—James Carroll and the M & G syndicate did a 20-million-dollar annual business in St. Louis. This was one of the two large books in the city.

—The S & G syndicate in Miami did a 26-million-dollar volume yearly; the total for all books in the Florida resort reached 40 millions.

—Slot machines were present in 69,786 establishments in 1951 (each paid $100 for a license to the Bureau of Internal Revenue); the usual average is three machines to a license, which would add up to 210,000 slot machines in operation in the United States. In legalized areas, where the betting is higher and more regular, the average gross "take" per machine is $50 a week.

—The largest policy wheel (i.e., "numbers") in Chicago's "Black Belt" reported taxable net profits for the four-year period from 1946 through 1949, after sizable deductions for "overhead," of $3,656,968. One of the large "white" wheels reported in 1947 a gross income of $2,317,000 and a net profit of $205,000. One CIO official estimated that perhaps 15 per cent of his union's lower echelon officials are involved in the numbers racket (a steward, free to roam a plant, is in a perfect situation for organizing bets).

If one considers the amount of betting on sports alone—an estimated six billion on baseball, a billion on football pools, another billion on basketball, six billion on horse racing—then Elmo Roper's judgment that "only the food, steel, auto, chemical, and machine-tool industries have a greater volume of business" does not seem too far-fetched.

While gambling has long flourished in the United States, the influx of the big mobsters into the industry—and its expansion—started in the '30's when repeal of Prohibition forced them to look about for new avenues of enterprise. Gambling, which had begun to flower under the nourishment of rising incomes, was the most lucrative field in sight. To a large extent the shift from bootlegging to gambling was a mere transfer of business operations. In the East, Frank Costello went into slot machines and the operation of a number of ritzy gambling casinos. He also became the "banker" for the Erickson "book," which "laid off" bets for other bookies. Joe Adonis, similarly, opened up a number of casinos, principally in New Jersey. Across the country, many other mobsters went into bookmaking. As other rackets diminished, and gambling, particularly horse-race betting, flourished in the '40's, a struggle erupted over the control of racing information.

Horse-racing betting requires a peculiar industrial organization. The essential component is time. A bookie can operate only if he can get information on odds up to the very last minute before the race, so that he can "hedge" or "lay off" bets. With racing going on simultaneously on many tracks throughout the country, this information has to be obtained speedily and accurately. Thus, the racing wire is the nerve ganglion of race betting.

The racing-wire news service got started in the '20's through the genius of the late Moe Annenberg, who had made a fearful reputation for himself as Hearst's circulation manager in the rough-and-tumble Chicago newspaper wars. Annenberg conceived the idea of a telegraphic news service which would gather information from tracks and shoot it immediately to scratch sheets, horse parlors, and bookie joints. In some instances, track owners gave Annenberg the rights to send news from tracks; more often, the news was simply "stolen" by crews operating inside or near the tracks. So efficient did this news distribution system become, that in 1942, when a plane knocked out a vital telegraph circuit which served an Air Force field as well as the gamblers, the Continental Press managed to get its racing wire service for gamblers resumed in fifteen minutes, while it took the Fourth Army, which was responsible for the defense of the entire West Coast, something like three hours.

Annenberg built up a nationwide racing information chain that not only distributed wire news but controlled sub-outlets as well. In 1939, harassed by the Internal Revenue Bureau on income tax, and chivvied by the Justice Department for "monopolistic" control of the wire service, the tired and aging Annenberg simply walked out of the business. He did not sell his interest, or even seek to salvage some profit; he simply gave up. Yet, like any established and thriving institution, the enterprise continued, though on a decentralized basis. James Ragen, Annenberg's operations manager, and likewise a veteran of the old Chicago circulation wars, took over the national wire service through a dummy friend and renamed it the Continental Press Service.

The salient fact is that in the operation of the Annenberg and Ragen wire service, formally illegal as many of its subsidiary operations may have been (i.e., in "stealing" news, supplying information to bookies, etc.), gangsters played no part. It was a business, illicit, true, but primarily a business. The distinction between gamblers and gangsters, as we shall see, is a relevant one.

In 1946, the Chicago mob, whose main interest was in bookmaking rather than gambling casinos, began to move in on the wire monopoly. Following repeal, the Capone lieutenants had turned, like Lepke, to labor racketeering. Murray ("The Camel") Humphries muscled in on the teamsters, the operating engineers, and the cleaning-and-dyeing, laundry, and linen-supply industries. Through a small-time punk, Willie Bioff, and union official George Browne, Capone's chief successors, Frank ("The Enforcer") Nitti and Paul Ricca, came into control of the motion-picture union and proceeded to shake down the movie industry for fabulous sums in order to "avert strikes." In 1943, when the government moved in and smashed the industrial rackets, the remaining big shots, Charley Fischetti, Jake Guzik, and Tony Accardo decided to concentrate on gambling, and in particular began a drive to take over the racing wire.

In Chicago, the Guzik-Accardo gang, controlling a sub-distributor of the racing news service, began tapping Continental's wires. In Los Angeles, the head of the local distribution agency for Continental was beaten up by hoodlums working for Mickey Cohen and Joe Sica. Out of the blue appeared a new and competitive nationwide racing information and distribution service, known as Trans-American Publishing, the money for which was advanced by the Chicago mobs and Bugsy Siegel, who, at the time, held a monopoly of the bookmaking and wire-news service in Las Vegas. Many books pulled out of Continental and bought information from the new outfit, many hedged by buying from both. At the end of a year, however, the Capone mob's wire had lost about $200,000. Ragen felt that violence would erupt and went to the Cook County district attorney and told him that his life had been threatened by his rivals. Ragen knew his competitors. In June 1946 he was killed by a blast from a shotgun.

Thereafter, the Capone mob abandoned Trans-American and got a "piece" of Continental. Through their new control of the national racing-wire monopoly, the Capone mob began to muscle in on the lucrative Miami gambling business run by the so-called S & G syndicate. For a long time S & G's monopoly over bookmaking had been so complete that when New York gambler Frank Erickson bought a three months' bookmaking concession at the expensive Roney Plaza Hotel, for $45,000, the local police, in a highly publicized raid, swooped down on the hotel; the next year the Roney Plaza was again using local talent. The Capone group, however, was tougher. They demanded an interest in Miami bookmaking, and, when refused, began organizing a syndicate of their own, persuading some bookies at the big hotels to join them. Florida Governor Warren's crime investigator appeared— a friend, it seemed, of old Chicago dog-track operator William Johnston, who had contributed $100,000 to the Governor's campaign fund —and began raiding bookie joints, but only those that were affiliated with S & G. Then S & G, which had been buying its racing news from the local distributor of Continental Press, found its service abruptly shut off. For a few days the syndicate sought to bootleg information from New Orleans, but found itself limping along. After ten days' war of attrition, the five S & G partners found themselves with a sixth partner, who, for a token "investment" of $20,000 entered a Miami business that grossed $26,000,000 in one year.

v

While Americans made gambling illegal, they did not in their hearts think of it as wicked—even the churches benefited from the bingo and lottery crazes. So they gambled—and gamblers flourished. Against this open canvas, the indignant tones of Senator Wiley and the shocked righteousness of Senator Tobey during the Kefauver investigation rang oddly. Yet it was probably this very tone of surprise that gave the activity of the Kefauver Committee its piquant quality. Here were some Senators who seemingly did not know the facts of life, as most Americans did. Here, in the person of Senator Tobey, was the old New England Puritan conscience poking around in industrial America, in a world it had made but never seen. Here was old-fashioned moral indignation, at a time when cynicism was rampant in public life.

Commendable as such moralistic fervor was, it did not make for intelligent discrimination of fact. Throughout the Kefauver hearings, for example, there ran the presumption that all gamblers were invariably gangsters. This was true of Chicago's Accardo-Guzik combine, which in the past had its fingers in many kind of rackets. It was not nearly so true of many of the large gamblers in America, most of whom had the feeling that they were satisfying a basic American urge for sport and looked upon their calling with no greater sense of guilt than did many bootleggers. After all, Sherman Billingsley did start out as a speakeasy proprietor, as did the Kreindlers of the "21" club; and today the Stork Club and the former Jack and Charlie's are the most fashionable night and dining spots in America (one prominent patron of the Stork Club: J. Edgar Hoover).

The S & G syndicate in Miami, for example (led by Harold Salvey, Jules Levitt, Charles Friedman, Sam Cohen, and Edward [Eddie Luckey] Rosenbaum), was simply a master pool of some two hundred bookies that arranged for telephone service, handled "protection," acted as bankers for those who needed ready cash on hard-hit books, and, in short, functioned somewhat analogously to the large factoring corporations in the textile field or the credit companies in the auto industry. Yet to Kefauver, these S & G men were "slippery and arrogant characters. . . . Salvey, for instance, was an old-time bookie who told us he had done nothing except engage in bookmaking or finance other bookmakers for twenty years." When, as a result of committee publicity and the newly found purity of the Miami police, the S & G syndicate went out of business, it was, as the combine's lawyer told Kefauver, because the "boys" were weary of being painted "the worst monsters in the world." "It is true," Cohen acknowledged, "that they had been law violators." But they had never done anything worse than gambling, and "to fight the world isn't worth it."

Most intriguing of all were the opinions of James J. Carroll, the St. Louis "betting commissioner," who for years had been widely quoted on the sports pages of the country as setting odds on the Kentucky Derby winter book and the baseball pennant races. Senator Wiley, speaking like the prosecutor in Camus's novel, *The Stranger,* became the voice of official morality:

SENATOR WILEY: Have you any children?

MR. CARROLL: Yes, I have a boy.

SENATOR WILEY: How old is he?

MR. CARROLL: Thirty-three.

SENATOR WILEY: Does he gamble?

MR. CARROLL: No.

SENATOR WILEY: Would you like to see him grow up and become a gambler, either professional or amateur?

MR. CARROLL: No. . . .

SENATOR WILEY: All right. Is your son interested in your business?

MR. CARROLL: No, he is a manufacturer.

SENATOR WILEY: Why do you not get him into the business?

MR. CARROLL: Well, psychologically a great many people are unsuited for gambling.

Retreating from this gambit, the Senator sought to pin Carroll down on his contributions to political campaigns:

SENATOR WILEY: Now this morning I asked you whether you contributed any money for political candidates or parties, and you said not more than $200 at any one time. I presume that does not indicate the total of your contributions in any one campaign, does it?

MR. CARROLL: Well, it might, might not, Senator. I have been an "againster" in many instances. I am a reader of *The Nation* for fifty years and they have advertisements calling for contributions for different candidates, different causes. . . . They carried an advertisement for George Norris; I contributed, I think, to that, and to the elder La Follette.

Carroll, who admitted to having been in the betting business since 1899, was the sophisticated—but not immoral!—counterpoint to moralist Wiley. Here was a man without the stigmata of the underworld or underground; he was worldly, cynical of official rhetoric, jaundiced about people's motives, he was—an "againster" who believed that "all gambling legislation originates or stems from some group or some individual seeking special interests for himself or his cause."

Asked why people gamble, Carroll distilled his experiences of fifty years with a remark that deserves a place in American social history: "I really don't know how to answer the question," he said. "I think gambling is a biological necessity for certain types. I think it is the quality that gives substance to their daydreams."

In a sense, the entire Kefauver materials, unintentionally, seem to document that remark. For what the Committee revealed time and time again was a picture of gambling as a basic institution in American life, flourishing openly and accepted widely. In many of the small towns, the gambling joint is as open as a liquor establishment. The town of Havana, in Mason County, Illinois, felt miffed when Governor Adlai Stevenson intervened against local gambling. In 1950, the town had raised $15,000 of its $50,000 budget by making friendly raids on the gambling houses every month and having the owners pay fines. "With the gambling fines cut off," grumbled Mayor Clarence Chester, "the next year is going to be tough."

Apart from the gamblers, there were the mobsters. But what Senator Kefauver and company failed to understand was that the mobsters, like the gamblers, and like the entire gangdom generally, were seeking to become quasi-respectable and establish a place for themselves in American life. For the mobsters, by and large, had immigrant roots, and crime, as the pattern showed, was a route of social ascent and place in American life.

VI

The mobsters were able, where they wished, to "muscle in" on the gambling business because the established gamblers were wholly vulnerable, not being able to call on the law for protection. The Senators, however, refusing to make any distinction between a gambler and a gangster, found it convenient to talk loosely of a nationwide conspiracy of "illegal" elements. Senator Kefauver asserted that a "nationwide crime syndicate does exist in the United States, despite the protestations of a strangely assorted company of criminals, self-serving politicians, plain blind fools, and others who may be honestly misguided, that there is no such combine." The Senate Committee report states the matter more dogmatically: "There is a nationwide crime syndicate known as the Mafia. . . . Its leaders are usually found in control of the most lucrative rackets in their cities. There are indications of a centralized direction and control of these rackets. . . . The Mafia is the cement that helps to bind the Costello-Adonis-Lansky syndicate of New York and the Accardo-Guzik-Fischetti syndicate of Chicago. . . . These groups have kept in touch with Luciano since his deportation from the country."

Unfortunately for a good story—and the existence of the Mafia would be a whale of a story—neither the Senate Crime Committee in its testimony, nor Kefauver in his book, presented any real evidence that the Mafia exists as a functioning organization. One finds police officials asserting before the Kefauver committee their *belief* in the Mafia; the Narcotics Bureau *thinks* that a worldwide dope ring allegedly run by Luciano is part of the Mafia; but the only other "evidence" presented—aside from the incredulous responses both of Senator Kefauver and Rudolph Halley when nearly all the Italian gangsters asserted that they didn't know about the Mafia—is that certain crimes bear "the earmarks of the Mafia."

The legend of the Mafia has been fostered in recent years largely by the peephole writing team of Jack Lait and Lee Mortimer. In their *Chicago Confidential,* they rattled off a series of names and titles that made the organization sound like a rival to an Amos and Andy–Kingfish society. Few serious reporters, however, give it much credence. Burton Turkus, the Brooklyn prosecutor who broke up the "Murder, Inc." ring, denies the existence of the Mafia. Nor could Senator Kefauver even make out much of a case for his picture of a national crime syndicate. He is forced to admit that "as it exists today [it] is an elusive and furtive but nonetheless tangible thing," and that "its organization and machinations are not always easy to pinpoint." His "evidence" that many gangsters congregate at certain times of the year in such places as Hot Springs, Arkansas, in itself does not prove much; people "in the trade" usually do, and as the loquacious late Willie Moretti of New Jersey said, in explaining how he had met the late Al Capone at a race track, "Listen, well-charactered people you don't need introductions to; you just meet automatically."

Why did the Senate Crime Committee plump so hard for its theory of the Mafia and a national crime syndicate? In part, they may have been misled by their own hearsay. The Senate Committee was not in the position to do original research, and its staff, both legal and investigative, was incredibly small. Senator Kefauver had begun the investigation with the attitude that with so much smoke there must be a raging fire. But smoke can also mean a smoke screen. Mob activities is a field in which busy gossip and exaggeration flourish even more readily than in a radical political sect.

There is, as well, in the American temper, a feeling that "somewhere," "somebody" is pulling all the complicated strings to which this jumbled world dances. In politics the labor image is "Wall Street," or "Big Business"; while the business stereotype was the "New Dealers." In the field of crime, the side-of-the-mouth low-down was "Costello."

The salient reason, perhaps, why the Kefauver Committee was taken in by its own myth of an omnipotent Mafia and a despotic Costello was its failure to assimilate and understand three of the more relevant sociological facts about institutionalized crime in its relation to the political life of large urban communities in America, namely: (1) the rise of the American Italian community, as part of the inevitable process of ethnic succession, to positions of importance in politics, a process that has been occurring independently but almost simultaneously in most cities with large Italian constituencies—New York, Chicago, Kansas City, Los Angeles; (2) the fact that there are individual Italians who play prominent, often leading roles today in gambling and in the mobs; and (3) the fact that Italian gamblers and mobsters often possessed "status" within the Italian community itself and a "pull" in city politics.[1] These three items are indeed related—but not so as to form a "plot."

1. Toward the end of his hearings, Senator Kefauver read a telegram from an indignant citizen of Italian descent, protesting against the impression the committee had created that organized crime in America was a distinctly Italian enterprise. The Senator took the occasion to state the obvious: that there are racketeers who are Italians does not mean that Italians are racketeers. However, it may be argued that

VII

The Italian community has achieved wealth and political influence much later and in a harder way than previous immigrant groups. Early Jewish wealth, that of the German Jews of the late nineteenth century, was made largely in banking and merchandising. To that extent, the dominant group in the Jewish community was outside of, and independent of, the urban political machines. Later Jewish wealth, among the East European immigrants, was built in the garment trades, though with some involvement with the Jewish gangster, who was typically an industrial racketeer (Arnold Rothstein, Lepke and Gurrah, etc.). Among Jewish lawyers, a small minority, such as the "Tammany lawyer" (like the protagonist of Sam Ornitz's *Haunch, Paunch and Jowl*), rose through politics and occasionally touched the fringes of crime. Most of the Jewish lawyers, by and large the communal leaders, climbed rapidly, however, in the opportunities that established and legitimate Jewish wealth provided. Irish immigrant wealth in the northern urban centers, concentrated largely in construction, trucking, and the waterfront, has, to a substantial extent, been wealth accumulated in and through political alliance, e.g., favoritism in city contracts.[2] Control of the politics of the city thus has been crucial for the continuance of Irish political wealth. This alliance of Irish immigrant wealth and politics has been reciprocal; many noted Irish political figures lent their names as important window-dressing for business corporations (Al Smith, for example, who helped form the U.S. Trucking Corporation, whose executive head for many years was William J. McCormack, the alleged "Mr. Big" of the New York waterfront), while Irish businessmen have lent their wealth to further the careers of Irish politicians. Irish mobsters have rarely achieved status in the Irish community, but have served as integral arms of the politicians, as strong-arm men on election day.

The Italians found the more obvious big city paths from rags to riches preempted. In part this was due to the character of the early Italian immigration. Most of them were unskilled and from rural stock. Jacob Riis could remark in the '90's, "the Italian comes in at the bottom and stays there." These dispossessed agricultural laborers found jobs as ditch-diggers, on the railroads as section hands, along the docks, in the service occupations, as shoemakers, barbers, garment workers, and

---

to the extent the Kefauver Committee fell for the line about crime in America being organized and controlled by the Mafia, it did foster such a misunderstanding. Perhaps this is also the place to point out that insofar as the relation of ethnic groups and ethnic problems to illicit and quasi-legal activities is piously ignored, the field is left open to the kind of vicious sensationalism practiced by Mortimer and Lait.

2. A fact that should occasion little shock if one recalls that in the nineteenth century American railroads virtually stole 190,000,000 acres of land by bribing Congressmen, and that more recently such scandals as the Teapot Dome oil grabs during the Harding administration, consummated, as the Supreme Court said, "by means of conspiracy, fraud, and bribery," reached to the very doors of the White House.

stayed there. Many were fleeced by the "padrone" system, a few achieved wealth from truck farming, wine growing, and marketing produce; but this "marginal wealth" was not the source of coherent and stable political power.

Significantly, although the number of Italians in the U.S. is about a third as high as the number of Irish, and of the 30,000,000 Catholic communicants in the United States, about half are of Irish descent and a sixth of Italian, there is not one Italian bishop among the hundred Catholic bishops in this country, or one Italian archbishop among the 21 archbishops. The Irish have a virtual monopoly. This is a factor related to the politics of the American church; but the condition also is possible because there is not significant or sufficient wealth among Italian Americans to force some parity.

The children of the immigrants, the second and third generation, became wise in the ways of the urban slums. Excluded from the political ladder—in the early '30's there were almost no Italians on the city payroll in top jobs, nor in books of the period can one find discussion of Italian political leaders—finding few open routes to wealth, some turned to illicit ways. In the children's court statistics of the 1930's, the largest group of delinquents was the Italian; nor were there any Italian communal or social agencies to cope with these problems. Yet it was, oddly enough, the quondam racketeer, seeking to become respectable, who provided one of the major supports for the drive to win a political voice for Italians in the power structure of the urban political machines.

This rise of the Italian political bloc was connected, at least in the major northern urban centers, to another important development which tended to make the traditional relation between the politician and the protected or tolerated illicit operator more close than it had been in the past. This is the fact that the urban political machines had to evolve new forms of fund-raising since the big business contributions, which once went heavily into municipal politics, now—with the shift in the locus of power—go largely into national affairs. (The ensuing corruption in national politics, as recent Congressional investigations show, is no petty matter; the scruples of businessmen do not seem much superior to those of the gamblers.) One way urban political machines raised their money resembled that of the large corporations which are no longer dependent on Wall Street: by self-financing—that is, by "taxing" the large number of municipal employees who bargain collectively with City Hall for their wage increases. So the firemen's union contributed money to O'Dwyer's campaign.

A second method was taxing the gamblers. The classic example, as *Life* reported, was Jersey City, where a top lieutenant of the Hague machine spent his full time screening applicants for unofficial bookmaking licenses. If found acceptable, the applicant was given a "location," usually the house or store of a loyal precinct worker, who kicked into the machine treasury a high proportion of the large rent exacted. The one thousand bookies and their one thousand landlords in Jersey City formed the hard core of the political machine that sweated and bled to get out the votes for Hague.

A third source for the financing of these machines was the new, and often illegally earned, Italian wealth. This is well illustrated by the career of Costello and his emergence as a political power in New York. Here the ruling motive has been the search for an entrée—for oneself and one's ethnic group—into the ruling circles of the big city.

Frank Costello made his money originally in bootlegging. After repeal, his big break came when Huey Long, desperate for ready cash to fight the old-line political machines, invited Costello to install slot machines in Louisiana. Costello did, and he flourished. Together with Dandy Phil Kastel, he also opened the Beverly Club, an elegant gambling establishment just outside New Orleans, at which have appeared some of the top entertainers in America. Subsequently, Costello invested his money in New York real estate (including 79 Wall Street, which he later sold), the Copacabana night club, and a leading brand of Scotch whisky.

Costello's political opportunity came when a money-hungry Tammany, starved by lack of patronage from Roosevelt and La Guardia, turned to him for financial support. The Italian community in New York has for years nursed a grievance against the Irish and, to a lesser extent, the Jewish political groups for monopolozing political power. It complained about the lack of judicial jobs, the small number— usually one—of Italian Congressmen, the lack of representation on the state tickets. But the Italians lacked the means to make their ambitions a reality. Although they formed a large voting bloc, there was rarely sufficient wealth to finance political clubs. Italian immigrants, largely poor peasants from Southern Italy and Sicily, lacked the mercantile experience of the Jews, and the political experience gained in the seventy-five-year history of Irish immigration.

During the Prohibition years, the Italian racketeers had made certain political contacts in order to gain protection. Costello, always the compromiser and fixer rather than the muscle-man, was the first to establish relations with Jimmy Hines, the powerful leader of the West Side in Tammany Hall. But his rival, Lucky Luciano, suspicious of the Irish, and seeking more direct power, backed and elected Al Marinelli for district leader on the Lower West Side. Marinelli in 1932 was the only Italian leader inside Tammany Hall. Later, he was joined by Dr. Paul Sarubbi, a partner of Johnny Torrio in a large, legitimate liquor concern. Certainly, Costello and Luciano represented no "unified" move by the Italians as a whole for power; within the Italian community there are as many divisions as in any other group. What is significant is that different Italians, for different reasons, and in various fashions, were achieving influence for the first time. Marinelli became county clerk of New York and a leading power in Tammany. In 1937, after being blasted by Tom Dewey, then running for district attorney, as a "political ally of thieves . . . and big-shot racketeers," Marinelli was removed from office by Governor Lehman. The subsequent conviction by Dewey of Luciano and Hines, and the election of La Guardia, left most of the Tammany clubs financially weak and foundering. This was the moment Costello made his move. In a few years, by judicious financing, he controlled a block of "Italian" leaders in the Hall—as well as some Irish on the upper West Side, and some Jewish leaders on the East Side—and was able to influence the selection of a number of Italian judges. The most notable incident, revealed by a wire tap of Costello's phone, was the "Thank you, Francisco" call in 1943 by Supreme Court nominee Thomas Aurelio, who gave Costello full credit for his nomination.

It was not only Tammany that was eager to accept campaign contributions from newly rich Italians, even though some of these *nouveaux riches* had "arrived" through bootlegging and gambling. Fiorello La Guardia, the wiliest mind that Melting Pot politics has ever produced, understood in the early '30's where much of his covert support came from. (So, too, did Vito Marcantonio, an apt pupil of the master: Marcantonio has consistently made deals with the Italian leaders of Tammany Hall—in 1943 he supported Aurelio, and refused to repudiate him even when the Democratic Party formally did.) Joe Adonis, who had built a political following during the late '20's, when he ran a popular speakeasy, aided La Guardia financially to a considerable extent in 1933. "The Democrats haven't recognized the Italians," Adonis told a friend. "There is no reason for the Italians to support anybody but La Guardia; the Jews played ball with the Democrats and haven't gotten much out of it. They know it now. They will vote for La Guardia. So will the Italians."

Adonis played his cards shrewdly. He supported La Guardia, but also a number of Democrats for local and judicial posts, and became a power in the Brooklyn area. His restaurant was frequented by Kenny Sutherland, the Coney Island Democratic leader; Irwin Steingut, the Democratic minority leader in Albany; Anthony DiGiovanni, later a Councilman; William O'Dwyer, and Jim Moran. But, in 1937, Adonis made the mistake of supporting Royal Copeland against La Guardia, and the irate Fiorello finally drove Adonis out of New York.[3]

La Guardia later turned his ire against Costello, too. Yet Costello

---

3. Adonis, and associate Willie Moretti, moved across the river to Bergen County, New Jersey, where, together with the quondam racketeer Abner "Longie" Zwillman, he became one of the political powers in the state. Gambling flourished in Bergen County for almost a decade, but after the Kefauver investigation the state was forced to act. A special inquiry in 1953 headed by Nelson Stamler, revealed that Moretti had paid $286,000 to an aide of Governor Driscoll for "protection" and that the Republican state committee had accepted a $25,000 "loan" from gambler Joseph Bozzo, an associate of Zwillman.

survived and reached the peak of his influence in 1942, when he was instrumental in electing Michael Kennedy leader of Tammany Hall. Despite the Aurelio fiasco, which first brought Costello into notoriety, he still had sufficient power in the Hall to swing votes for Hugo Rogers as Tammany leader in 1945, and had a tight grip on some districts as late as 1948. In those years many a Tammany leader came hat in hand to Costello's apartment, or sought him out on the golf links, to obtain the nomination for a judicial post.

During this period, other Italian political leaders were also coming to the fore. Generoso Pope, whose Colonial Sand and Stone Company began to prosper through political contacts, became an important political figure, especially when his purchase of the two largest Italian-language dailies (later merged into one), and of a radio station, gave him almost a monopoly of channels to Italian-speaking opinion of the city. Through Generoso Pope, and through Costello, the Italians became a major political force in New York.

That the urban machines, largely Democratic, have financed their heavy campaign costs in this fashion rather than having to turn to the "moneyed interests," explains in some part why these machines were able, in part, to support the New and Fair Deals without suffering the pressures they might have been subjected to had their source of money supply been the business groups. Although he has never publicly revealed his political convictions, it is likely that Frank Costello was a fervent admirer of Franklin D. Roosevelt and his efforts to aid the common man. The basic measures of the New Deal, which most Americans today agree were necessary for the public good, would not have been possible without the support of the "corrupt" big-city machines.

VIII

There is little question that men of Italian origin appeared in most of the leading roles in the high drama of gambling and mobs, just as twenty years ago the children of East European Jews were the most prominent figures in organized crime, and before that individuals of Irish descent were similarly prominent. To some extent statistical accident and the tendency of newspapers to emphasize the few sensational figures give a greater illusion about the domination of illicit activities by a single ethnic group than all the facts warrant. In many cities, particularly in the South and on the West Coast, the mob and gambling fraternity consisted of many other groups, and often, predominantly, native white Protestants. Yet it is clear that in the major northern urban centers there was a distinct ethnic sequence in the modes of obtaining illicit wealth, and that uniquely in the case of the recent Italian elements, the former bootleggers and gamblers provided considerable leverage for the growth of political influence as well. A substantial number of Italian judges sitting on the bench in New York today are indebted in one fashion or another to Costello; so too are many Italian district leaders—as well as some Jewish and Irish politicians. And the motive in establishing Italian political prestige in New York was generous rather than scheming for personal advantage. For Costello it was largely a case of ethnic pride. As in earlier American eras, organized illegality became a stepladder of social ascent.

To the world at large, the news and pictures of Frank Sinatra, for example, mingling with former Italian mobsters could come somewhat as a shock. Yet to Sinatra, and to many Italians, these were men who had grown up in their neighborhoods, and who were, in some instances, bywords in the community for their helpfulness and their charities. The early Italian gangsters were hoodlums—rough, unlettered, and young (Al Capone was only twenty-nine at the height of his power). Those who survived learned to adapt. By now they are men of middle age or older. They learned to dress conservatively. Their homes are in respectable suburbs. They sent their children to good schools and had sought to avoid publicity.[4] Costello even went to a psychiatrist in his efforts to overcome a painful feeling of inferiority in the world of manners.

As happens with all "new" money in American society, the rough and ready contractors, the construction people, trucking entrepreneurs, as well as racketeers, polished up their manners and sought recognition and respectability in their own ethnic as well as in the general community. The "shanty" Irish became the "lace curtain" Irish, and then moved out for wider recognition.[5] Sometimes acceptance came first in established "American" society, and this was a certificate for later recognition by the ethnic community, a process well illustrated by the belated acceptance in established Negro society of such figures as Sugar Ray Robinson and Joe Louis, as well as leading popular entertainers.

Yet, after all, the foundation of many a distinguished older American fortune was laid by sharp practices and morally reprehensible methods. The pioneers of American capitalism were not graduated from

4. Except at times by being overly neighborly, like Tony Accardo, who, at Yuletide 1949, in his elegant River Forest home, decorated a 40-foot tree on his lawn and beneath it set a wooden Santa and reindeer, while around the yard, on tracks, electrically operated skating figures zipped merrily around while a loud speaker poured out Christmas carols. The next Christmas, the Accardo lawn was darkened; Tony was on the lam from Kefauver.

5. The role of ethnic pride in corralling minority group votes is one of the oldest pieces of wisdom in American politics; but what is more remarkable is the persistence of this identification through second and third generation descendants, a fact which, as Samuel Lubell noted in his *Future of American Politics,* was one of the explanatory keys to political behavior in recent elections. Although the Irish bloc as a solid Democratic bloc is beginning to crack, particularly as middle-class status impels individuals to identify more strongly with the G.O.P., the nomination in Massachusetts of Jack Kennedy for the United States Senate created a tremendous solidarity among Irish voters and Kennedy was elected over Lodge although Eisenhower swept the state.

Harvard's School of Business Administration. The early settlers and founding fathers, as well as those who "won the west" and built up cattle, mining, and other fortunes, often did so by shady speculations and a not inconsiderable amount of violence. They ignored, circumvented, or stretched the law when it stood in the way of America's destiny, and their own—or, were themselves the law when it served their purposes. This has not prevented them and their descendants from feeling proper moral outrage when under the changed circumstances of the crowded urban environments later comers pursued equally ruthless tactics.

IX

Ironically, the social development which made possible the rise to political influence sounds, too, the knell of the Italian gangster. For it is the growing number of Italians with professional training and legitimate business success that both prompts and permits the Italian group to wield increasing political influence; and increasingly it is the professionals and businessmen who provide models for Italian youth today, models that hardly existed twenty years ago. Ironically, the headlines and exposes of "crime" of the Italian "gangsters" came years after the fact. Many of the top "crime" figures long ago had forsworn violence, and even their income, in large part, was derived from legitimate investments (real estate in the case of Costello, motor haulage and auto dealer franchises in the case of Adonis) or from such quasi-legitimate but socially respectable sources as gambling casinos. Hence society's "retribution" in the jail sentences for Costello and Adonis was little more than a trumped-up morality that disguised a social hypocrisy.

Apart from these considerations, what of the larger context of crime and the American way of life? The passing of the Fair Deal signalizes, oddly, the passing of an older pattern of illicit activities. The gambling fever of the past decade and a half was part of the flush and exuberance of rising incomes, and was characteristic largely of new upper-middle class rich having a first fling at conspicuous consumption. This upper-middle class rich, a significant new stratum in American life (not rich in the nineteenth century sense of enormous wealth, but largely middle-sized businessmen and entrepreneurs of the service and luxury trades —the "tertiary economy" in Colin Clark's phrase—who by the tax laws have achieved sizable incomes often much higher than the managers of the super-giant corporations) were the chief patrons of the munificent gambling casinos. During the war decade when travel was difficult, gambling and the lush resorts provided important outlets for this social class. Now they are settling down, learning about Europe and culture. The petty gambling, the betting and bingo which relieve the tedium of small town life, or the expectation among the urban slum dwellers of winning a sizable sum by a "lucky number" or a "lucky horse" goes on. To quote Bernard Baruch: "You can't stop people from gambling on horses. And why should you prohibit a man from backing his own judgment? It's another form of personal initiative." But the lush profits are passing from gambling, as the costs of coordination rise. And in the future it is likely that gambling, like prostitution, winning tacit acceptance as a necessary fact, will continue on a decentralized, small entrepreneur basis.

But passing, too, is a political pattern, the system of political "bosses" which in its reciprocal relation provided "protection" for and was fed revenue from crime. The collapse of the "boss" system was a product of the Roosevelt era. Twenty years ago Jim Farley's task was simple; he had to work only on some key state bosses. Now there is no longer such an animal. New Jersey Democracy was once ruled by Frank Hague; now there are five or six men each top dog, for the moment, in his part of the state or faction of the party. Within the urban centers, the old Irish-dominated political machines in New York, Boston, Newark, and Chicago have fallen apart. The decentralization of the metropolitan centers, the growth of suburbs and satellite towns, the break-up of the old ecological patterns of slum and transient belts, the rise of functional groups, the increasing middle-class character of American life, all contribute to this decline.

With the rationalization and absorption of some illicit activities into the structure of the economy, the passing of an older generation that had established a hegemony over crime, the general rise of minority groups to social position, and the break-up of the urban boss system, the pattern of crime we have discussed is passing as well. Crime, of course, remains as long as passion and the desire for gain remain. But big, organized city crime, as we have known it for the past seventy-five years, was based on more than these universal motives. It was based on certain characteristics of the American economy, American ethnic groups, and American politics. The changes in all these areas mean that it too, in the form we have known it, is at an end.

"MAN IS A WEAK ANIMAL AND A SELF-INDULGENT ONE"

Ella Wheeler Wilcox

The Restlessness of the Modern Woman

The social and economic changes of the late nineteenth century affected the lives and ideals of women more drastically than any other group. Ella Wheeler Wilcox (1855-1919), poet, essayist, and women's adviser, counseled her audience to avoid seduction by masculine ideals of economic success and to cultivate traditional roles assiduously for woman's own and the general social good. [Ella Wheeler Wilcox, "The Restlessness of the Modern Woman," Cosmopolitan, XXXI, July 1901, pp. 314-317.]

The mighty forces of mysterious space
Are one by one subdued by lordly man.
The awful lightnings, that for eons ran
Their devastating and untrammeled race,
Now bear his messages from place to place
Like carrier-doves. The winds lead on his van.
The lawless elements no longer can
Resist his strength, but yield wtih sullen grace.
His bold feet scaling heights before untrod—
Light, darkness, air and water, heat and cold,
He bids go forth and bring him power and pelf,
And yet, though ruler, king and demigod,
He walks, with his fierce passions uncontrolled,
The conqueror of all things—save himself.

Reader, how many contented women do you know—really contented?

I fear you can count them on the fingers of one hand, if you give the subject a fair and careful analysis.

I am inclined to believe the happiest women in the world are the hard-working ones. Not the overtaxed drudges, but wives and mothers, whose hands and minds are busy from morning until night with household duties, or the women who hold responsible positions requiring all their waking hours and thoughts.

Certainly the leisure class shows few specimens of contentment. The increase of wealth in our land has not brought an increase of happiness. Luxury has not been escorted into our midst by peace. The sewing-machine, the trolley, the automobile, the revolving stairway, have all been time- and effort-savers for our women, but they have not been joy-producers, if we are to judge by the appearance or the conversation of our associates.

The less women have to do, the more time they find to wonder what they want to do.

I wish every toiling woman in the land who is longing to be rich could see the satirist's picture called "The Happy Rich." It represents a man and wife seated at an elaborately appointed table, where every delicacy of the season is supplied, while fine, imposing butlers and other attendants await orders. Meantime the unhappy couple sink back in their respective chairs, without appetite and with unutterably bored expressions on their faces.

The busy housewife who has to prepare the meals for a hungry family, is to be envied in preference to the ennuied woman of wealth who has worn out pleasure and lost the road to usefulness.

It seems to me the very first ambition of a girl's life should be to seek some way to be useful to those nearest her. I believe that if this wish were to root in her mind, no matter what her station, whether high or low, rich or poor, and whether she were plain or beautiful, she could never know a dull or restless hour.

Sorrow must come to every heart. It is the storm which prepares the soil of the human nature for immortal blossoms. But restlessness and aimless, purposeless discontent are like venomous insects which destroy vegetation.

One who studies American womanhood with any care, must be alarmed at the growing restlessness of the sex.

My mountain of mail is often a volcano of seething unrest. It seems a relief to many women—women, doubtless, whom the world supposes to be happy wives and mothers—to write anonymously to one they believe to be sympathetic, of the discontent which surges in their hearts.

To turn from these letters to a social function, is to encounter the same elements in another form. Beneath jeweled corsages beat restless hearts; from under the flower-laden brims of modish hats look unhappy eyes, gazing out into the world with longing for an indefinable something—a happiness imagined but unattained.

Three women have recently written asking me to send them some magic potion in the form of advice by mail, to cure their malady of unrest. All three declared their husbands to be good men and good providers for the home, and two were the mothers of healthy and bright children. Yet, these women were unhappy. One believed she loved another man better than her husband; the other two were unable to define the cause of their restlessness. "Life somehow does not seem worth living," said one. "I drag through the days, glad when night comes and I can go to sleep. Can you tell me how to find an object, an aim, which shall give me an interest in existence?"

At a summer resort I encountered a handsome, richly attired woman with personal graces and accomplishments, the mother of a lovely child. But her face was marred by an expression of discontent. There was an element of gaiety in the hotel, composed of people whom the lady in question had not met.

"Their fun makes me unhappy," she said. "I never enjoy anything as a spectator; I must be one of the actors to be happy."

"That is unfortunate," I said, "for life holds so many occasions for all of us wherein we are given only the part of spectators."

"Life is a disappointment to most of us," she answered.

"Life is greatly, almost wholly, what we make it," I ventured.

"Perhaps," she replied. "But we cannot help our temperaments. I am naturally restless. I have a lovely home and a good husband, but married people tire of each other if too much together. I must have diversion and variety. My only enjoyment is in going away and seeing new scenes, new people. I have a horror of growing old—and I confess the future appalls me. I cannot bear quiet and monotony."

Yet this woman was possessed of every earthly blessing—health, beauty, accomplishments, home, husband and children. But she lacked the peace and happiness which must come from within.

"It is my temperament. I cannot help it," she insisted. And just as strenuously I contend that we can overcome any inheritance, and conquer every unreasonable trait, if we set about it with a philosophical determination to do so.

Another wife and mother confessed to me that her greatest happiness lay in the admiration of men. "I love to be admired and sought after," she said. "I am true to my husband, but his love has become a settled, understood affair, and I need the excitement of having men flatter me. It is the only thing that keeps life interesting." The lady differed from many others of her sex only in being more frank.

Certainly the admiration of men is a great stimulant. But a man never really admires, in his secret heart, a woman whose deportment he would object to in a wife. He may feel passion for her, but he does not admire her.

It is a very good plan for a woman who is drifting into a doubtful line of conduct with a man, to stop and ask herself, "If I were his wife, how would he like to have me treat another man as I am treating him?" Upon the answer she is able to make herself, may depend her estimate of his admiration.

While I believe the tendency of humanity is constantly upward, toward a higher plane, it is an indisputable fact that this restlessness of woman is a giant evil, and one of serious growth.

It is puzzling to attempt to trace it to its source.

When it is possible to put the cause of any unfortunate condition on man's broad shoulders, I always do so, since, having so much more gray matter in his brain than woman, he is better able to bear the blame. I have often contended that bad lovers and husbands made bad women—restless, discontented, and reckless women. Once I framed this thought in verse and called it—

A Woman's Answer

You call me an angel of love and of light,
A being of goodness and heavenly fire,
Sent out from God's kingdom to guide you aright,
In paths where your spirit may mount and aspire.
You say that I glow like a star on its course,
Like a ray from the altar, a spark from the source.

Now list to my answer—let all the world hear it;
I speak unafraid what I know to be true—
A pure, faithful love is the creative spirit
Which makes women angels! I live but in you.
We are bound soul to soul by life's holiest laws;
If I am an angel—why, you are the cause.

As my ship skims the sea, I look up from the deck.
Fair, firm at the wheel shines Love's beautiful form.
And shall I curse the bark that last night went to wreck,
By the pilot abandoned to darkness and storm?
My craft is no stancher, she too had been lost
Had the wheelman deserted, or slept at his post.

I laid down the wealth of my soul at your feet
(Some woman does this for some man every day).
No desperate creature who walks in the street
Has a wickeder heart than I might have, I say.
Had you wantonly misused the treasures you won —
As so many men with heart-riches have done.

This fire from God's altar, this holy love-flame,
That burns like sweet incense forever for you,
Might now be a wild conflagration of shame,
Had you tortured my heart, or been base or untrue.
For angels and devils are cast in one mold,
Till love guides me upward or downward, I hold.

I tell you the women who make fervent wives
And sweet, tender mothers, had Fate been less fair,
Are the women who might have abandoned their lives
To the madness that springs from and ends in despair.
As the fire on the hearth which sheds brightness around,
Neglected, may level the walls to the ground.

The world makes grave errors in judging these things.
Great good and great evil are born in one breast:
Love horns us and hoofs us, or gives us our wings,
And the best could be worst, as the worst could be best.
You must thank your own worth for what I grew to be,
For the demon lurked under the angel in me.

I quoted this to a bachelor who was unmercifully scoring women
as weak, faithless and vain, and this was his reply:—

"The poor abused wife has my sympathy. I know many a one,
and I feel it will smack of doubt to you when I say it is not the abused
wife who is the easy victim of man's flattery. It is the woman with
the too attentive, confiding, and unsuspecting husband, who will listen
to any tale the lady may invent. To repeat a very slangy expression
I heard from a young wife in referring to her husband—he was 'a
soft thing.' And that soft thing I know is one of the truest husbands
and best fellows living."

Nevertheless, I must believe such base and unworthy specimens
of my sex to be the exception. The woman who can jest about the
blindness of a loving man to her infidelities, is a monstrosity. Her sin
is less shocking than her view of it.

If woman's restlessness cannot be attributed to man's shortcomings, it must be traced back to herself. The present false standards
of wealth which have been set up in our country have a great deal
to do with this and all other glaring evils of the day. Yet why should
a woman with a comfortable home, a good husband, and sweet children, permit the demon of unrest to enter her mind and destroy
her peace, because she cannot astonish the world with splendid toilets,
and entertain her friends in a villa at Newport or buy a castle in
Europe, as some of our multimillionaires are doing?

I must confess I find men as a mass to be far more rational-minded,
more appreciative of their blessings, and more reasonable in their demands upon fate, than women.

In the present day, here in America, a man usually knows when he is well off, and a woman does not.

The majority of men who are straining every nerve to accumulate great fortunes, instead of stopping to enjoy comfortable incomes, are stimulated to this course of action by restless, ambitious, and discontented wives and daughters.

This is a statement which will call down the wrath of my own sex upon me; it is made after reading thousands of letters, and listening to thousands of confessions, from both women and men, relative to their inmost hopes, desires, dreams, and ambitions.

I know man is a weak animal and a self-indulgent one, where he demands strength and nobility from woman; I know how he stifles his own conscience, while he commands her to listen to hers; but, with this exception, I find him a less dangerous factor in our present feverish social conditions than I find women to be.

Very few women realize their enormous influence upon men—outside of the sex influence. They do not know that women make the atmosphere in the home from which men—most men—form their ideals of life and derive their ambitions.

A restless, uneasy, discontented manner of the wife he loves has sent many a man into Wall Street, filled with the ambition to conquer or die, to overcome others or be overcome. Perhaps the wife pleaded with him not to go—and used all her logic to no avail, unconscious that her unexpressed discontent was a stronger argument in favor of speculation than all her words were against it.

Madam, you who read these words, will you give yourself a little mental analysis, and try to decide whether you are adding to the great wave of feminine restlessness which sweeps through the land; and if you are, what the cause is, and what the result will be upon yourself and others?

Then if you seek a cure, look about you and try to see what is the nearest avenue of usefulness open to you. One woman writes me that she thinks of leaving her husband and children in the care of friends to go forth and lecture to mothers upon the necessity of being comrades to their children! There is a desire for usefulness run riot; the letter would have seemed humorous had it not been tragic in its utter lack of common sense.

After all, a lack of good, every-day common sense is at the bottom of all this feminine restlessness, when we come down to facts.

Uncommon sense, uncommon talents, uncommon women, we have everywhere in our wonderful land, but what we need is women with just, well-balanced minds, endowed with practical common sense, and governed by loving hearts—women who have appreciation, gratitude, and self-control added to their other womanly qualities.

—

Jill Conway

Jane Addams: An American Heroine

American middle class women of talent, like their male counterparts in the late nineteenth and early twentieth centuries, modeled their roles after the ideology of extreme individualism. As the historian Jill Conway (1934-   ) so neatly demonstrates, Jane Addams, more than any other woman of her generation, was both symbol and reality of woman's capacity for socially creative public achievement. [Jill Conway, "Jane Addams: An American Heroine," Daedalus, Spring 1964, pp. 761-779.]

Two generations of middle-class American women from 1880 to the close of the 1920's were dominated by aspirations of a nature now quite alien. They desired a public life of restless activism, and saw fulfillment for these desires only in terms of extreme individualism. It would have been inconceivable for Jane Addams or Lillian Wald to fulfill this desire for a public role through the career of a husband, just as Eleanor Roosevelt, perhaps the last legatee of this tradition, found it necessary to create a public life of her own apart from that of the President. Three problems of the period were the basis of this drive to acquire a public life. They were not exclusively feminine problems, but all were perceived with particular acuteness by educated women of the middle class.

The first was a sense of mission. Women of their day, they believed, had a special position in history and a special duty to posterity. They were the first group of women in the United States to receive education at the college and graduate level, and they had to bring all this enlightened and disciplined femininity to bear upon the improvement of their world. A sense of mission is a painful burden if undirected, and consequently the second problem of their world was an oppressive sense of unreality. They had a total belief that a trained and well-stocked mind would fit them for new roles in life. Yet they found none immediately. They needed problems to solve in order to justify these providential gifts of knowledge and leisure, and there were too few of these to satisfy their compulsive desire to be useful. The third difficulty was sociological. If pioneer societies set no bounds on human achievement by the confining pattern of the past, they also supply no models to aspire to except masculine ones. The class societies of the old world did have definite public roles for women of birth, education, and leisure, such as the life of the political salon, the literary circle, or the chatelaine of estates. In Chicago achievement for an aspiring woman lay in Mrs. Potter Palmer's world of conspicuous consumption until Jane Addams set out to define new roles for women in the hitherto masculine preserve of public life. A mobile society had no recognized activities which a lady of wealth and leisure might pursue except bigger and more grandiose versions of what all American women were expected to do.

This drive to activism and participation in a masculine world was reinforced by the dominant philosophies of the day. Knowledge and truth for Americans of these generations were not objects of contemplation but means to successful action. Experience was almost the only guide to perceptions of reality. It followed that an education which did not lead to an active life was meaningless. The value of knowledge lay in its social utility to an era that accepted the Spencerian vision of society. Education was a positive aid in raising the race and it was to be assessed by the degree to which it allowed the recipient to participate in the struggle for survival. This utilitarian notion of the education they had received added to the burden of guilt of post-Civil War American women. Every powerful force in their culture urged that they should pursue active and socially beneficial careers, yet their society provided no such outlet. Their predicament was exacerbated by the persistence of certain of the Victorian notions of femininity even though the Victorian social restraints had been removed. They believed, for instance, that women were custodians of race morality, were exempt from the baser human passions, and, because of the maternal instincts, were less prone to violence than men. Thus all Victorian notions of feminine delicacy had become concentrated in the notion of the refinement of women's moral perceptions, and it seemed that they should redeem public life from the baser masculine passions.

No woman of this generation more clearly represents the predicament and its resolution than does Jane Addams. She had a mind whose brilliance and driving power made her acutely responsive to the intellectual and cultural forces of nineteenth-century America. Her personality was characterized by an extreme drive to power which she recognized and strove to discipline from early youth. Intellect made it impossible to accept the achievement of a philistine Chicago, while her complex personality demanded exceptional performance in any task she chose. Since Chicago was the milieu in which she chose to work out her demanding predicament, her solution was one of activism of epic proportions. Yet she was by nature an intellectual, and much of her impact on her society comes from the lucidity of her published reflections on her life and its meaning.

Her remarkable personality, her exceptional intellectual endowments, and her very real achievement in public life do not, however, explain completely the kind of national response she evoked. Its actual dimensions are mythical, and she is remembered pietistically in the education of succeeding generations of American children. It is curious that only she should be remembered in this fashion when many other women of her generation equalled her in terms of any public achievement which posterity can measure. Lillian Wald in New York began settlement work at approximately the same time, and in the course of her career she was instrumental in the professionalization of nursing as a career for women and in the foundation of the Federal Children's Bureau. She was active in politics and as successful in raising money for good causes. Mary Richmond as a social worker probably outshone all her contemporaries. Women like Florence Sabin and Alice Hamilton developed careers of tireless public service in the medical profession. Florence Kelley probably displayed greater administrative genius in masterminding the campaigns of the National Consumers' League for social reform for over forty years and providing the legal mind necessary to pursue endless minutiae of evidence to swing some final campaign for social legislation. In hours traveled and speeches made in these causes, she surely exceeded Jane Addams. The same might be said of Julia Lathrop as head of the Federal Children's Bureau and of her career in Washington. Finally, as guardians of immigrant groups and systematizers of philanthropy, Grace and Edith Abbott might be said to excel her achievement. Yet none of these women of national reputation and significance played the kind of charismatic role for two generations which Jane Addams did. The impact of this charismatic personality is remarkable and can be detected from her early youth. One of her contemporaries described its impact in personal relations. "There was, despite her affectionate warmth and sympathy and understanding, something impersonal about that relation, akin to sharing in some blessing of nature, that like the sunlight, shone alike on the just and the unjust. One shared the gift gladly and gratefully, and without a personal stake in it exactly." Such an impact came from the quality of discipline about her personality. Unlike her fellow women public figures whose public lives were a natural expression of their personalities, Jane Addams, by an act of will, conformed herself to an American model of excellence. A potential expatriate, like Gertrude Stein or Henry James, she chose to return after years of fascinated pleasure in a European world. She chose Chicago and her deepest roots, rather than the attenuated loyalties of the East Coast, and she deliberately became the model of feminine excellence in the American terms which she understood so perfectly. It was no easy choice, and it was this struggle triumphantly surmounted which gave her a genuine air of secular sanctity.

For her contemporaries it seemed logical that Jane Addams, and she alone, should second the nomination of Theodore Roosevelt at the Progressive convention of 1912 on behalf of all American women. It seemed logical to them, and to Jane Addams also, for she wrote an article shortly afterwards explaining why one woman should perform this symbolic act of participation in national politics on behalf of all her sisters. As a political campaigner she was believed by the organizers of the Progressive party to be a vote-getter without equal. She toured the country from Maine to California speaking on T.R.'s behalf, and wrote tirelessly for Progressive press releases. In all sections of the country, during the campaign, speakers at rallies could have the assistance of Jane Addams Choirs singing selections from the Jane Addams song book, which sold well at a few cents a copy to raise campaign funds. Within the Progressive National Committee there is no question of her influence. She coached the Rough Rider on social issues and instructed him in feminism, and explained about moral equivalents to war, and he listened attentively. Such a position was held by Lillian Wald in the Democratic machine in New York from the time of the 1912 Wilson campaign to Al Smith's campaign in 1928, yet none of these activities seemed to involve the mystical participation of women in the United States, or to provoke a lyrical response from Democratic choirs.

Her impact on American life was not confined to politics. It was felt at all levels of intellect and emotion throughout the nation. Jane Addams wrote very well on education, on women's problems in an urban society, on the social meaning of democracy, on prostitution, on faith, on what reflection had led her to believe was the meaning of her life at Hull-House. She was probably the most gifted of her contemporaries as a popular writer, though she was not a systematic thinker like the Abbott sisters, nor did she have the incisive mind of Florence Kelley. Yet her correspondence with William James suggests that he placed immense value upon her ideas. Hers, he said, was the most gifted mind of his generation. She "inhabited reality," said the great pragmatist, and in her *being* summed up the experience of his America. John Dewey wrote gratefully of learning much from visits to Hull-House and conversation with Miss Addams. She had helped, he felt, in the elaboration of his ideas on education, and in defining a democratic society. On every issue of public life she was urged to write for the *Atlantic Monthly* by William Ellery Sedgwick, as a universally accepted popular conscience.

This kind of adulation was national. Internationally, before her involvement in the peace movement during the First World War, she was well known also, although in a circle confined to social workers and intellectuals in England and feminists in Europe. Frequent visits to Europe, proficiency in languages, and tireless attendance at conventions in part explain this kind of reputation. Yet there was more to it than that. People wished to introduce her abroad as a perpetual exhibition of what was good about America and modern American women. Aylmer Maude was anxious that she should meet Tolstoy for this reason, and her legendary journey across Russia to converse with the great Russian sage on questions of democratic morality was the product of this kind of urge on the part of her contemporaries. In this way she came to be well known in London and Paris, long before her pacifism made her famous during the First World War.

What was it about her life that it should symbolize American womanhood and the best aspirations of the American world of her time? From 1889 her winters were generally spent in Chicago in a life of administrative social work. Her genius, as she herself recognized while still cloistered in Rockford Seminary, was administrative. After the pioneer years at Hull-House, when she had captured the support of Chicago society through the all-powerful Chicago Women's Club, her days were spent in conferences with the powerful and wealthy, arranging the financing of ever increasing projects for Hull-House, acquiring more real estate, discussing investments, soliciting donations, and most efficiently of all, directing publicity. Here was the organizational genius which brought into being the ideas of her gifted associates, but inevitably this left her less and less time for close contact with the urban slum world which she had first sought. She had sought it in a curiously Victorian way which must be elucidated to explain her impact on her generation. Her childhood in a small-town rural world had been the epitome of second-generation life on the frontier. Standards had slipped a little. She called her father and stepmother Pa and Ma, and for years her grammar and spelling were a little shaky. Schooling remedied formal errors and gave her the desire to "go East, and become a cultivated person." She had plans to attend Vassar or Smith which were all firmly denied. She could form no estimate of them as educational institutions. She wanted to meet sophisticated people and encounter another world outside the comfortable barbarities of Cedarville, Illinois, and she knew dimly the formal way to get there. It never became open to her, and so, almost a generation later, traveled, educated, and independent, she created an equivalent in Hull-House. Europe had been her education in a brilliantly enlarging sense. Paris, Dresden, Rome, Florence, Assisi allowed her to form a notion of the kind of excellence she had once hoped to find "back East." But for her the life of the expatriate was impossible. Her roots were solidly in small-town Illinois. Wealth, leisure, and intellect must be disciplined to the active service of an American ideal. This service she found by an inspired combination of her European world of intellect and beauty and the Puritan ethic. She went home to found a salon in a slum. It was to be a beautiful house created by her acquired taste, which left her remote from Cedarville. It was to be inhabited by a circle of gifted and brilliant friends. But it was to be firmly rooted in an American past by being directed toward doing good. Hull-House became an intellectual center in Chicago, justified in an anti-intellectual society by its dedication to social work. Life there was beautiful, graceful, and convivial; since it was American, it was also incredibly responsible, hard-working, and idealistic. By day the residents slaved at remedying social problems—garbage collection, aid to unwed mothers, and political reform amongst immigrant groups. At night they came home to a house where everyone of intellect and repute in the United States and every important foreign traveler visited. Actresses, authors, musicians, royalty, heads of state all came to Hull-House and dined and talked. In the summer no one visited Chicago voluntarily, and the spirit went out of it all. Miss Addams had believed in the foundation of Hull-House that perceptions of reality were to be found only in the sordid reality of the urban slum world. This was how she had justified her return—she was to live and act on the "new urban frontier" of American experience. Yet in this she was the prisoner of an American mystique, and soon she began to retire thankfully in the summers to the homes of friends on the East Coast. For she began to realize that it was not the slums and the unwed mothers which represented reality for her, but a society which would permit her to write and think about them. She was an intellectual captured by the activism of American life. In Hull-House she had found a way of life which allowed some reconciliation of action and contemplation, but she paid a price. Summers in Bar Harbor allowed her to recapitulate her experience, to sum up contemporary philosophy, to survey pressing social issues, but not the literary and intellectual achievement which another society might have allowed her. A biographer is left with the distressing sense that she had the qualities of mind and spirit to transcend her society; instead she became its model.

The one European import which could not travel to her Chicago salon was a sense of humor. She and her companions were relentlessly serious about what they did, and any kind of frivolity was totally alien to their temperaments. A sense of the comic escaped them because they perceived no gap between the reality of what they achieved and the greatness of their aspirations. They believed their dedication to a life of the mind and a career of social reform was to an end totally achievable. The good society was within their grasp. Freedom for women, which they were in the process of defining, although its definition temporarily escaped them, was perfectly possible and merely waited to be discovered. Hence their high seriousness and their inability to perceive the absurd. This made them high-spirited but not witty, happy but never gay, and curiously one-dimensional. Like characters in a Dickens novel, one always knows what they are going to say.

So much for what Jane Addams did. What was she like? Obsessively devoted to her father, she remained emotionally frozen after his death in her twenty-first year. She had innocent, intense, and shatteringly emotional relationships with several women friends. Outside these she was a sad and aloof personality. Kindly, but essentially unknowable to many of her closest co-workers, she directed all of her formidable energies into her public role. It was this regal but unglamorous personality which evoked a fan mail during her lifetime similar to that of a twentieth-century film star. A day's correspondence could bring a letter from a German nun who found *The First Twenty Years at Hull-House* inspirational reading, notes from small children requiring advice on all aspects of life, and emotional thanks from bereft people whose dying relatives had been comforted by reading her ideas on human experience.

This response occurred because she exemplified in her person a philosophy of extreme individualism, which during her active public life was not confronted by insoluble problems, and to which two generations of Americans had a profound commitment. Her principal belief was in an inevitable evolutionary progress of which man's will and intellect were the motive force. This was a kind of intellectual Darwinism which involved a Puritan evolutionary ethic. Man was predestined to rise, but by means of a driving intellectual effort amongst the chosen. Work and the calling were merely thereby transposed to the evolutionary notion of man. All the problems of urban industrial America could be solved, she believed, by the combined efforts of individual intellects and wills. This belief was immensely attractive to her generation because it had the advantage of being neither conservative nor radical. It allowed her to define social problems while pointing to a comfortable solution, and to make these problems seem less anguishing since in evolutionary terms they were preconditions of a developing "good society." Her impact on her contemporaries was so great because she seemed to validate this view of society in her own career. The effort of her own will and intellect had created a new kind of role for women during her own life, and her individual efforts as a social worker had had phenomenal success which was visible to contemporaries.

Her career was edifying in another sense to a generation plagued by religious uncertainty and repelled by the materialism of the gilded age. Her concept of the settlement house and a life of service to society offered contemporaries an ideal of personal commitment to a demanding but simple discipline. In Europe or Asia this might mean vows of poverty or silence. She brought the intensity of discipline and devotion of the mendicant order to busy winters of administrative social work in Chicago and to quiet contemplative summers in Maine, supplying as she always did a specifically American version of a universal desire for a life of discipline. It was one built about comfort, utility, and success, but it was nonetheless a life of discipline.

In all areas of deep sensitivity in American culture during these years, she was a kind of apostle, preaching a gospel of comfortable adjustment to things. To a society perplexed by the violent disruption of rural life and the equally undisciplined growth of cities, she preached the acceptance of change. She had a real and creative vision of urban life based on profound disillusionment with her own small-town origins, and she wrote about cities and their growth in an edifying and comforting way. Urban life was the new decree of an evolutionary providence and was not to be decried or feared, but defined and understood. The city was an exciting and creative event in man's evolution, not a tragic falling off from an idyllic rural past. It was exciting because for the first time, in an urban world, man created his own environment. Man was therefore no longer dimly striving to understand God's creation but could control and direct a world which he had created for himself. This was a heady prospect, for in Darwinian terms control of the environment conjured up a vision of infinite and rapid progress directed toward rationally conceived ends. The urban world, moreover, was one in which the true meaning of democracy could be found. Jane Addams had an ideal vision of the Greek city-state which she transposed without any apparent feeling of incongruity to Chicago and to American urban life. Rural life was necessarily imprisoning because it placed a special value on certain kinds of strengths and skills. The modern city and technology offered man an infinite variety of occupations in which his creative instincts could be fulfilled and created leisure unknown in the backbreaking routine of the farm. Here was freedom for humanity impossible in the past. Many of her friends were doctrinaire socialists, and she knew a great deal about Marx, though it is not clear whether she read his writings. She shared his vision of a society transformed by technology, but for her the transformation was happy and harmonious. Industry set the individual free by releasing him from the extended family of his rural past. Young men were no longer dominated by past generations. They need not wait patiently to inherit land and livelihood. They could dispose of their intellect and skills as they chose in the great factories of the new society.

Women were freed by the city in even more exciting ways. They were free to support themselves and to live alone. The maiden aunt acquired dignity and independence by industrial labor. Men and women acquired anonymity and could direct their lives in relation to themselves alone. Fulfillment was to be found here by the individual.

Jane Addams saw such isolation as desirable freedom. For her it bore no hint of loneliness, nor did it suggest destruction of human relationships which might have value above those of the individual. The freeing of youth from the limitations of the past was of enormous value in evolutionary terms, for the young of the race carried all its creative impulses, and only if they were free to develop them could progress occur. This was transposing the experience of the frontier to her evolutionary view of life. The young were free to respond to a new environment where outmoded skills might be a positive hindrance.

All this optimism was not made bland by a refusal to recognize the cost in human terms of the creation of an industrial society. Her notion of pain and human suffering was very real, but it was Greek. She wished for no personal resolution of the problems it presented. It was enough that the race should rise. This was a convenient postponement of the problem of evil. It was also a satisfactory externalization of the personal difficulties which freed one's energies for the busy pursuit of social problems and allowed one to compromise about them now in terms of a belief about their resolution in the future. It was thus possible to be a ruthless individualist without ever paying the price, for one always gracefully avoided the confrontation of absolute and insoluble problems. This solution to the dilemmas of the post-Civil War era in the United States answered to a need felt as powerfully in rural Illinois as in Boston, Washington, or New York, for it made the change from the rural America of Jefferson and Lincoln to that of a great urban society possible without a major disturbance in the simple individualism of an agricultural world.

To make change acceptable was one thing; to make it edifying answered to a nation-wide reform impulse. The ghettos of immigrant labor in the growing cities were merely scars imported from another world, and Americans must not reject but strive to heal them. The healing process, however politely put, was Americanization. Immigrants at Hull-House practiced their folk arts as a kind of therapeutic release, not because they were felt to be a folk. They attended lectures in sociology and economics and American government and were encouraged to practice thrift and industry. Their language and their culture were understood and respected, but they were taught to see themselves as part of the inevitable evolutionary process which demanded adaptation above all things. This was an exceptional response in an American world which saw immigrants either as a threat to American values or as a labor force to be exploited. Its kindness and generosity cannot be too strongly stressed. Philosophically, nonetheless, it was based on an evolutionary view within which all differences could be resolved in the name of progress, and as such it was merely a broader application of an already dominant philosophy.

This philosophy was one bound to appeal to post-Civil War Americans. In a curious way, however, its appeal was integrally related to the person of the philosopher. As a reformer wishing to change and understand society, Jane Addams also wished to change and understand herself. Her career was a great success story in terms which every American understood. She had come from a small town to the city and achieved mythical success. Unlike Theodore Dreiser's heroines, she had done it in a socially acceptable fashion. As a good Sister Carrie she had stormed to the top of Mrs. Potter Palmer's Chicago and thus participated in the gilded age without becoming besmirched by it. In the process, because of her profound commitment to an intellectual life, she had paused to write and reflect about what she was doing. She wrote with the simple directness of someone who had personally confronted the problems which concerned her. Hers was not an abstract or doctrinaire position in one sense, for she wrote from experience. In a society confused and puzzled about ideas and experience, she wrote about her own confusion and puzzlement, and their resolution. A social reformer in a class society possesses an unquestioned identity, outside of which he wishes to operate to change the social order. In a world of ceaseless social mobility such is not the case. The identity of the reformer is established by the process of reform, while society as a whole rightly comes to estimate his ideas by his person as much as by his policies. Hence for Americans the personality of Lincoln is the subject of as much, or possibly more, debate than his policies, while a British historian devotes much less time to the personalities of Lord Shaftesbury or Sydney and Beatrice Webb. Jane Addams as a person became the final test for her ideas, for she embodied her own solution to the problems of contemporary society.

The society which responded to her was one perplexed by the creation of wealth and leisure, while its predominant values were those of frontier activism and the Puritan ethic. The Spencerian adaptation of Darwinian biology was accepted as explanation of the social process. It served to justify the untrammeled individualism of industrial entrepreneurs which had created the problems of urban poverty and brought about the appearance of what seemed to be real social divisions in a society whose identity lay in its acceptance of the democratic ideal. This identity was threatened in another direction by the "new" immigration of the post-Civil War era. Its size and composition resulted in the great ghettos of exploited urban labor whose existence seemed to challenge the notion of a democratic society on the one hand and to threaten the health of a society which believed it progressed by evolution on the other. In the 1890's these anxieties were intensified because it seemed that with the closing of the frontier, the actual time left for the fulfillment of the American dream might be running out. . . .

There were special problems, too, and of these none was more perplexing and disturbing to Americans than that of the role of women. It was a problem of enormous intensity. There was no national or sectional problem which was not in some aspect part of the difficulty in defining the role of women. Wealth and leisure for the urban middle class raised anguishing problems for women unused to seeking public roles, and unable because of America's predominantly frontier culture to conceive of nonactivist roles for women. A Puritan ethic made leisure for these unhappy ladies an object of restless guilt; hence the frenetic and pathetic search of urban leisured women for release from their privileged inutility. Spencer was a torment to them. Reality lay in participation as an individual unit in the struggle for survival. Fulfillment could be found only in an individualism as untrammeled as that of the industrial entrepreneur. Nothing is more universal than the cry of privileged American women of this generation that their wealth, education, and social status cut them off from *reality*. The problem of wealth in a society of democratic belief had even wider implications. For women it was *unearned* wealth and carried with it guilt and feelings of obligation to society which must be reconciled.

The national problem of identity was also a feminine one. The genteel society which was emerging in the late nineteenth century did not set much store by simple childbearing. Rather it strove to limit families. Nor did it value the practical helpmate, for hers were not the skills of the new economy. Feminine skills in the rural frontier tradition offered little in the new apartment hotels of the big cities; labor-saving devices ate endlessly into the realm in which old-style feminine efficiency could operate. Since one defines oneself in a mobile society by what one does, the question of identity was desperate and, from the accounts of those who lived through it, a searing experience. The new immigrants exacerbated feminine problems in two ways. They provided cheap domestic labor and thus increased the leisure of the merely comfortably wealthy. In another sense, they helped to dramatize the erosion of old feminine values. Because of their economic position women were drawn into the factories of urban industry, and because they were exploited they worked until there was no energy left for homes and children. Contemporaries barely sensed their tragedy and instead saw them as the new type of womanhood, the creation of the city. The close of the frontier meant the release of women from the old ideal of the self-sufficient household which had hitherto held unquestioned moral value.

The new environment of urban life also suggested congeniality for feminine endeavor. Perhaps nothing was more stimulating to this expectation than the appearance of imperialistic aspirations in the American people. The notion of the acuteness of feminine moral perceptions came into its own. In the city, women, exempt as they were from masculine aggressiveness, could band together to create a better world. Here was a real issue and a noble task, and they seized it joyfully, as any scrutiny of membership of anti-imperialist leagues will show. Attempts to redefine democracy raised the question of female suffrage in the larger context of the whole democratic mystique. Curiously, it was never argued with the violence and bitterness which accompanied the issue in Great Britain, for it was genuinely seen by all parties to the debate to be part of a much larger problem which all Americans shared in common. Women suffragists encountered the perennial problems of the Constitution and probably no campaign aroused such prolonged discussion of constitutional issues as did the long-drawn-out but remarkably amiable one to secure ratification of the Equal Rights Amendment. By the late 1890's it was not merely the problems of cultivated women of leisure which attracted attention, but the phenomenon of the working-class woman, who was by then a significant part of the labor force. The most exploited laborers in the immigrant ghettos were women and children, and in the process of redefining democracy it seemed as if the role of the state might have to be redefined to protect them. City government, said women of these generations, was "housekeeping on a large scale," and it was in civic reform that they first found an outlet for their energy and reforming zeal. Education at the college and graduate level brought women in significant numbers into national intellectual life and this fostered a new awareness of feminine problems. Harriet Monroe and Willa Cather were pioneers of their generation in the assertion that feminine insights provided new and necessary views of experience. The major fields of attraction for feminine endeavor were sociology, medicine, law, and government, for these in one fashion or another offered an explanation of the predicament of American women and provided possible avenues toward its resolution. They were all avenues toward an urban existence and led to unquestioning acceptance of the goodness of urban life. The problem of charity touched women very deeply. Protestant, Catholic, or Jew, they came from traditions in which femininity was equated with caring for the sick and aiding the poor and sheltering the child. Southern child labor in the canning factories, therefore, touched a nerve of conscience, and problems of urban poverty seemed to be especially delicate for the refined moral perceptions of literate and privileged women. In exceptional cases the logic of their belief in the special intensity of women's moral perceptions made women such as Florence Kelley and Jane Addams confront the problems of the Negroes in American society and attempt to formulate some definition of a democratic belief which would encompass them generations before the issue was faced more generally.

It was the essence of Jane Addams' greatness that she perceived, defined and reflected about every one of these issues. The limitations of her milieu are reflected in her intellectual history. It is not one of the progression of an individual intellect, but one which reflects and redefines a culture. Her reflections on contemporary problems are often a perfect image of the intellectual world of her time. She was captivated by Darwin and Spencer at a time when all her contemporaries were captivated. She abandoned them as philosophers of philanthropy when all her fellow philanthropists did after the great depression of 1893-1894. Her notion of a settlement house was conventional in terms of the social theory of her time, and her view of urban life and the role of women in it was one endlessly discussed at the University of Chicago from the time of its foundation to the outbreak of the First World War. She thought of culture, art, and education in John Dewey's terms and her acceptance of pragmatism was never questioned during a long lifetime of disconcerting questioning of the meaning of experience. Yet despite these qualifications, hers was one of the most creative and influential minds in late nineteenth- and early twentieth-century America. Her genius was twofold: first, the gift of organization which created Hull-House, combined with an instinctive search for intellectual excellence which brought to it the collection of gifted residents and visitors who helped to make it what it was—a center of endless experiment and discussion of social problems, and a place where gifted young men and women could discover and develop their gifts in relation to the newly developing urban industrial society. Second, in her literary and reflective capacity, she was the exponent of a positive social morality which served to humanize the predominant Puritan ethic. She strove to articulate the problems of her society and to suggest an ethical response to them in terms of a life of public service. Her life was a model of democratic ethics in terms of positive achievement. It was for this reason that she became a legend in her lifetime, and that her writings were received with pietistic reverence. They had something of the character of revelation for their readers, for they cast light on confusion. They made aspirations guiltily suppressed seem valid; they brought hope for the resolution of anxieties half understood, and they did so in terms of unswerving adherence to the American democratic ideal, redefined but comfortingly recognizable. With the revelation came the charismatic figure. She was the model of feminine virtue which answered to every need of American women of her day. She embodied in her person a solution to the problem of the role of women which was acceptable for both men and women, for her active public career carried with it no threat to the accepted fabric of society. It was a model of respectability. Her innovations as a moralist were concerned with the nature of charity and economic morality in a democracy dedicated to free enterprise. On other issues she re-enforced convention rather than attacking it. It was her good fortune to attempt to redefine the role of women in a democratic society without reference to sexual mores in a world which was as reticent as she herself upon the subject. For her readers, as for her, all sexual liberty was license. It was a dimension of liberty which no one was anxious to explore publicly.

In one respect only did she offend the popular consciousness, and this was in a characteristically American vein. Her commitment to pragmatism was so complete and her notion of human perfectibility so unqualified that she could not conceive of absolute problems insoluble by redefinition or negotiation. Hence her pacifism. She accepted the notion of man's innate aggressiveness, but believed that in an evolving world man should learn to direct his aggressions positively. She applied the notion of woman's finer moral perceptions to the problem of war and developed the belief that it was the natural role of educated women to lead the world in the eradication of violence. Her preoccupation with the control of violence was an aspect of her concern with the freeing of women from the inferior status of the past. A world which still resorted to violence to settle disputes would, she felt, always impose burdens on women, for they would be penalized for their inferior strength. Thus the outbreak of war in 1914 seemed to her to threaten the position of women throughout the world. She directed her amazing talents as an organizer and publicist to the peace movement and continued to do so unflinchingly after the entry of the United States into the war in 1917. Her popularity suffered enormously and as a consequence her leadership of welfare and charitable movements was questioned violently until the late twenties. No matter how strongly asserted, her pacifism was still that of the extreme individualist believer in progress. It was a matter of converting individual wills to the creed of nonviolence; she never envisioned a planned society where conflicts of interest might not arise. Characteristically, her political hero during the twenties and until her death in 1935 was Herbert Hoover. They both shared a faith in a kind of individualism which a world war and an economic crisis of catastrophic proportions could not dim.

The high fervor for the creation of a better world and a more just social order which swept the nation during the New Deal reinstated Jane Addams as the national heroine and shortly before her death she was feted in Washington on the occasion of her seventy-fifth birthday as no other woman has been in this country. The myth remains unmarred and the one deviation from popular opinion is more sympathetic to a later generation. Today no woman aspires to such a role, nor do the conditions of our world seem likely to permit such achievement. It is not that there are no crises of feminine identity or that their pain is any less acute. Rather, their solutions are found elsewhere. Public roles for women abound in many professional spheres and entry into them is clear and unambiguous. The acquisition of a professional discipline is now such a routine business that it no longer serves to define the identity of any educated woman. This has happened for two reasons. The romantic notion of the special moral character of women has disappeared, dispelled by the cool analysis of a feminine unconscious fully as given to dark urges as is its masculine counterpart. Eugene O'Neill's Anna Christie was the victim of a wicked masculine world; today she would be a statistic in a Kinsey Report. A feminine career exempt from this notion of mission must be justified in less exalted terms and no longer serves as a total explanation of what one is or seeks to achieve as a woman. Second, the philosophy of extreme individualism which led women of Jane Addams' generation to see achievement only as individual achievement has gone because two generations of Americans have confronted problems too massive for any individual solution. Jane Addams' joyful recognition of the personal isolation possible in an urban world has been replaced by the recognition that such epic loneliness may be destructive. Both the aspiration to achieve alone, then, and the certainty of success are gone. Most of the spheres in which women of Jane Addams' generation found impressive public careers are now controlled by agencies of federal and state governments guided by experts and subject to bureaucratic control in which none but the most naive would seek total personal fulfillment.

The generation which succeeded Jane Addams discovered Freud, gained the knowledge necessary to control conception, and replaced her notion of freedom for women to participate in public life with a concern for freedom from sexual restraint. In the post-Freudian world it was less possible to externalize problems of emotional adjustment and to channel psychic energy into a public role. A woman of Jane Addams' emotional difficulties born into this generation would have sought psychiatric assistance instead of founding Hull-House; she would have sought the answers to her problems in self-awareness rather than in activism; and she would have expected to find their resolution in personal relationships.

Today the problem which remains to perplex American women is the absence of an ideal which is both specifically feminine and unmistakably intellectual. Knowledge, as in Jane Addams' day, is still justified in terms of utility. For Jane Addams, achievement for a woman was clear. It was defined in terms of the militant feminism of her day, and it meant entering into any activity in public life, for that had hitherto been a masculine preserve. She was fortunate that she could turn her remarkable intellectual powers to a task which was both socially necessary and yet in many ways distinctively feminine. Hull-House, and the values which it symbolized, was feminine, activist, and magnificently public. Today it is a monument, not a necessity. The intellectual bases of the old self-confident feminism are gone, and with them the kind of life which it inspired. Intellect, utility, femininity—these are harmonized no longer by any militant faith. There is instead an emerging idea of femininity which asserts the value of early marriage, large families, and the importance of the skills of the home, but it does not define an ideal of intellectual excellence appropriate to such a role. Since discipline of the mind must still be directed toward some utilitarian end, the young woman graduate retains the expectation that her education is the preliminary to some useful activity. She no longer seeks fulfillment in a public role, for she is aware that fulfillment is to be found in marriage and the home, but she is oppressed by the need to prove the utility of her intellect. The notion of knowledge as an end in itself, a notion which can produce either a salon or the contemplative life, is foreign to the American temper outside purely academic circles. The American woman of intellect instead seeks to justify herself by achievement in professional or business life, and to achieve in these she must conform herself to a masculine ideal of excellence. A pleasure in knowledge for its own sake, so typical of European women of the same background and education, is not possible for the American woman, and hence to devote herself to her home and family is to accept a life devoid of intellectual significance. Popular culture provides many instances of acceptance of such a belief. Film heroines who are clever are formidably unfeminine, and conquest by the hero inevitably means not a realization of their gifts, but an abandonment of them for unreflecting domesticity.

The educated American woman today cannot be inspired to achievement in Jane Addams' terms, for she has no Utopian vision of feminine equality to be gained in a better society, nor would she value such a society could she believe in its possibility. She would like her intellect and femininity to place her in a harmonious relation to society, not outside it. The young woman in search of the vivid intellectual experience which took Jane Addams to Hull-House and her salon would today search for it in graduate school. This is often not because she has a vocation for a life of learning and scholarship, but because her society does not offer her any but a professional life of independent intellectual pursuits. Here her problems are simply exacerbated. American institutions of higher learning exemplify in the most spirited fashion the notions of competition which permeate American life, and despite herself the young scholar assumes the dogged belligerence of graduate life. She is further than ever from her ideal of informed and harmonious femininity, and she has been forced to adopt a public stance which seems ludicrously opposed to it. She is not a model of anything which her society values, nor does she often have the satisfaction of personal fulfillment, for she must repress many feminine desires to retain her position in a ruthlessly competitive world.

A special set of circumstances and a brilliant insight allowed Jane Addams her salon in a form which allowed her to express and embody all the best values and aspirations of her world. Her insight was a reconciliation of feminine intellect and public life. Today our need is for a similar insight, reconciling intellect and private life. What is feminine intellect about? What is achievement for an intelligent and gifted woman today? What is the feminine liberty so passionately sought by Miss Addams' generation? Is it simply freedom to adopt a masculine notion of excellence? These are our problems today, unsolved, and as yet too little thought of.

Frederick Douglass
The Future of the Colored Race

In the generation immediately following the Civil War, the future of the American Negro could be viewed with a wholeness of vision that was not to recur for nearly a century. The first major spokesman for the emancipated American Negro, Frederick Douglass (1817-1895), saw the full integration and assimilation of the Negro into American society as inevitable. [Frederick Douglass, "The Future of the Colored Race," North American Review, CXLII, May 1886, pp. 437-440.]

It is quite impossible, at this early date, to say with any decided emphasis what the future of the colored people will be. Speculations of that kind, thus far, have only reflected the mental bias and education of the many who have essayed to solve the problem.

We all know what the negro has been as a slave. In this relation we have his experience of two hundred and fifty years before us, and can easily know the character and qualities he has developed and exhibited during this long and severe ordeal. In his new relation to his environments, we see him only in the twilight of twenty years of semi-freedom; for he has scarcely been free long enough to outgrow the marks of the lash on his back and the fetters on his limbs. He stands before us, to-day, physically, a maimed and mutilated man. His mother was lashed to agony before the birth of her babe, and the bitter anguish of the mother is seen in the countenance of her offspring. Slavery has twisted his limbs, shattered his feet, deformed his body and distorted his features. He remains black, but no longer comely. Sleeping on the dirt floor of the slave cabin in infancy, cold on one side and chilled and retarded circulation on the other, it has come to pass that he has not the vertical bearing of a perfect man. His lack of symmetry, caused by no fault of his own, creates a resistance to his progress which cannot well be overestimated, and should be taken into account, when measuring his speed in the new race of life upon which he has now entered. As I have often said before, we should not measure the negro from the heights which the white race has attained, but from the depths from which he has come. You will not find Burke, Grattan, Curran, and O'Connell among the oppressed and famished poor of the famine-stricken districts of Ireland. Such men come of comfortable antecedents and sound parents.

Laying aside all prejudice in favor of or against race, looking at the negro as politically and socially related to the American people generally, and measuring the forces arrayed against him, I do not see how he can survive and flourish in this country as a distinct and separate race, nor do I see how he can be removed from the country either by annihilation or expatriation.

Sometimes I have feared that, in some wild paroxysm of rage, the white race, forgetful of the claims of humanity and the precepts of the Christian religion, will proceed to slaughter the negro in whole-sale, as some of that race have attempted to slaughter Chinamen, and as it has been done in detail in some districts of the Southern States. The grounds of this fear, however, have in some measure decreased, since the negro has largely disappeared from the arena of Southern politics, and has betaken himself to industrial pursuits and the acquisi-tion of wealth and education, though even here, if over-prosperous, he is likely to excite a dangerous antagonism; for the white people do not easily tolerate the presence among them of a race more prosperous than themselves. The negro as a poor ignorant creature does not contradict the race pride of the white race. He is more a source of amusement to that race than an object of resentment. Malignant resistance is aug-mented as he approaches the plane occupied by the white race, and yet I think that resistance will gradually yield to the pressure of wealth, education, and high character.

My strongest conviction as to the future of the negro therefore is, that he will not be expatriated nor annihilated, nor will he forever remain a separate and distinct race from the people around him, but that he will be absorbed, assimilated, and will only appear finally, as the Phoenicians now appear on the shores of the Shannon, in the features of a blended race. I cannot give at length my reasons for this conclusion, and perhaps the reader may think that the wish is father to the thought, and may in his wrath denounce my conclusion as utterly impossible. To such I would say, tarry a little, and look at the facts. Two hundred years ago there were two distinct and separate streams of human life running through this country. They stood at opposite extremes of ethnological classification: all black on the one side, all white on the other. Now, between these two extremes, an intermediate race has arisen, which is neither white nor black, neither Caucasian nor Ethiopian, and this intermediate race is constantly increasing. I know it is said that marital alliance between these races is unnatural, abhorrent, and impossible; but exclamations of this kind only shake the air. They prove nothing against a stubborn fact like that which confronts us daily and which is open to the observation of all. If this blending of the two races were impossible we should not have at least one-fourth of our colored population composed of persons of mixed blood, ranging all the way from a dark-brown color to the point where there is no visible admixture. Besides, it is obvious to common sense that there is no need of the passage of laws, or the adoption of other devices, to prevent what is in itself impossible.

Of course this result will not be reached by any hurried or forced processes. It will not arise out of any theory of the wisdom of such blending of the two races. If it comes at all, it will come without shock or noise or violence of any kind, and only in the fullness of time, and it will be so adjusted to surrounding conditions as hardly to be observed. I would not be understood as advocating intermarriage between the two races. I am not a propagandist, but a prophet. I do not say that what I say *should* come to pass, but what I think is likely to come to pass, and what is inevitable. While I would not be understood as advocating the desirability of such a result, I would not be understood as deprecating it. Races and varieties of the human family appear and disappear, but humanity remains and will remain forever. The American people will one day be truer to this idea than now, and will say with Scotia's inspired son: "A man's a man for a' that."

When that day shall come, they will not pervert and sin against the verity of language as they now do by calling a man of mixed blood, a negro; they will tell the truth. It is only prejudice against the negro which calls every one, however nearly connected with the white race, and however remotely connected with the negro race, a negro. The motive is not a desire to elevate the negro, but to humiliate and degrade those of mixed blood; not a desire to bring the negro up, but to cast the mulatto and the quadroon down by forcing him below an arbitrary and hated color line. Men of mixed blood in this country apply the name *"negro"* to themselves, not because it is a correct ethnological description, but to seem especially devoted to the black side of their parentage. Hence in some cases they are more noisily opposed to the conclusion to which I have come, than either the white or the honestly black race. The opposition to amalgamation, of which we hear so much on the part of colored people, is for the most part the merest affectation, and will never form an impassable barrier to the union of the two varieties.

—

Booker T. Washington
The Atlanta Exposition Address

The realities of late nineteenth-century America forced Negro leaders to accept the prevailing individualist ideology. The most influential Negro leader in the nation's history settled for immediate economic liberty *rather than* immediate liberty. *Booker T. Washington's (1856-1915) testament and rationale for Negro accommodation to second-class citizenship was his famous Atlanta Exposition Address of 1895. [Booker T. Washington,* Up From Slavery, New York, 1901, pp. 218-225.]

Mr. President and Gentlemen of the Board of Directors and Citizens.

One-third of the population of the South is of the Negro race. No enterprise seeking the material, civil, or moral welfare of this section can disregard this element of our population and reach the highest success. I but convey to you, Mr. President and Directors, the sentiment of the masses of my race when I say that in no way have the value and manhood of the American Negro been more fittingly and generously recognized than by the managers of this magnificent Exposition at every stage of its progress. It is a recognition that will do more to cement the friendship of the two races than any occurrence since the dawn of our freedom.

Not only this, but the opportunity here afforded will awaken among us a new era of industrial progress. Ignorant and inexperienced, it is not strange that in the first years of our new life we began at the top instead of at the bottom; that a seat in Congress or the state legislature was

more sought than real estate or industrial skill; that the political convention of stump speaking had more attractions than starting a dairy
farm or truck garden.

A ship lost at sea for many days suddenly sighted a friendly vessel.
From the mast of the unfortunate vessel was seen a signal, "Water,
water; we die of thirst!" The answer from the friendly vessel at once
came back, "Cast down your bucket where you are." A second time the
signal, "Water, water; send us water!" ran up from the distressed
vessel, and was answered, "Cast down your bucket where you are."
And a third and fourth signal for water was answered, "Cast down
your bucket where you are." The captain of the distressed vessel, at
last heeding the injunction, cast down his bucket, and it came up full
of fresh, sparkling water from the mouth of the Amazon River. To
those of my race who depend on bettering their condition in a foreign
land or who underestimate the importance of cultivating friendly relations with the Southern white man, who is their next-door neighbour,
I would say, "Cast down your bucket where you are"—cast it down in
making friends in every manly way of the people of all races by whom
we are surrounded.

Cast it down in agriculture, mechanics, in commerce, in domestic
service, and in the professions. And in this connection it is well to bear
in mind that whatever other sins the South may be called to bear,
when it comes to business, pure and simple, it is in the South that the
Negro is given a man's chance in the commercial world, and in nothing
is this Exposition more eloquent than in emphasizing this chance. Our
greatest danger is that in the great leap from slavery to freedom we
may overlook the fact that the masses of us are to live by the productions of our hands, and fail to keep in mind that we shall prosper in
proportion as we learn to dignify and glorify common labour and put
brains and skill into the common occupations of life; shall prosper in
proportion as we learn to draw the line between the superficial and
the substantial, the ornamental gewgaws of life and the useful. No race
can prosper till it learn that there is as much dignity in tilling a field
as in writing a poem. It is at the bottom of life we must begin, and
not at the top. Nor should we permit our grievances to overshadow
our opportunities.

To those of the white race who look to the incoming of those of
foreign birth and strange tongue and habits for the prosperity of the
South, were I permitted I would repeat what I say to my own race,
"Cast down your bucket where you are." Cast it down among the eight
millions of Negroes whose habits you know, whose fidelity and love
you have tested in days when to have proved treacherous meant the
ruin of your firesides. Cast down your bucket among these people who
have, without strikes and labour wars, tilled your fields, cleared your
forests, builded your railroads and cities, and brought forth treasures

from the bowels of the earth, and helped make possible this magnificent representation of the progress of the South. Casting down your bucket among my people, helping and encouraging them as you are doing on these grounds, and to education of head, hand, and heart, you will find that they will buy your surplus land, make blossom the waste places in your fields, and run your factories. While doing this, you can be sure in the future, as in the past, that you and your families will be surrounded by the most patient, faithful, law-abiding, and unresentful people that the world has seen. As we have proved our loyalty to you in the past, in nursing your children, watching by the sick-bed of your mothers and fathers, and often following them with tear-dimmed eyes to their graves, so in the future, in our humble way, we shall stand by you with a devotion that no foreigner can approach, ready to lay down our lives, if need be, in defence of yours, interlacing our industrial, commercial, civil, and religious life with yours in a way that shall make the interests of both races one. In all things that are purely social we can be as separate as the fingers, yet one as the hand in all things essential to mutual progress.

There is no defence or security for any of us except in the highest intelligence and development of all. If anywhere there are efforts tending to curtail the fullest growth of the Negro, let these efforts be turned into stimulating, encouraging, and making him the most useful and intelligent citizen. Effort or means so invested will pay a thousand per cent interest. These efforts will be twice blessed—"blessing him that gives and him that takes."

There is no escape through law of man or God from the inevitable:—

> The laws of changeless justice bind
>   Oppressor with oppressed;
> And close as sin and suffering joined
>   We march to fate abreast.

Nearly sixteen millions of hands will aid you in pulling the load upward, or they will pull against you the load downward. We shall constitute one-third and more of the ignorance and crime of the South, or one-third its intelligence and progress; we shall contribute one-third to the business and industrial prosperity of the South, or we shall prove a veritable body of death, stagnating, depressing, retarding every effort to advance the body politic.

Gentlemen of the Exposition, as we present to you our humble effort at an exhibition of our progress, you must not expect overmuch. Starting thirty years ago with ownership here and there in a few quilts and pumpkins and chickens (gathered from miscellaneous sources), remember the path that has led from these to the inventions and productions of agricultural implements, buggies, steam-engines, newspapers, books, statuary, carving, paintings, the management of drug-stores and banks, has not been trodden without contact with thorns and thistles. While we take pride in what we exhibit as a result of our independent efforts, we do not for a moment forget that our part in this exhibition would fall far short of your expectations but for the constant help that has come to our educational life, not only from the Southern states, but especially from Northern philanthropists, who have made their gifts a constant stream of blessing and encouragement.

The wisest among my race understand that the agitation of ques-tions of social equality is the extremest folly, and that progress in the enjoyment of all the privileges that will come to us must be the result of severe and constant struggle rather than of artificial forcing. No race that has anything to contribute to the markets of the world is long in any degree ostracized. It is important and right that all privileges of the law be ours, but it is vastly more important that we be prepared for the exercises of these privileges. The opportunity to earn a dollar in a factory just now is worth infinitely more than the opportunity to spend a dollar in an opera-house.

In conclusion, may I repeat that nothing in thirty years has given us more hope and encouragement, and drawn us so near to you of the white race, as this opportunity offered by the Exposition; and here bending, as it were, over the altar that represents the results of the struggles of your race and mine, both starting practically empty-handed three decades ago, I pledge that in your effort to work out the great and intricate problem which God has laid at the doors of the South, you shall have at all times the patient, sympathetic help of my race; only let this be constantly in mind, that, while from representations in these buildings of the product of field, of forest, of mine, of fac-tory, letters, and art, much good will come, yet far above and beyond material benefits will be that higher good, that, let us pray God, will come, in a blotting out of sectional differences and racial animosities and suspicions, in a determination to administer absolute justice, in a willing obedience among all classes to the mandates of law. This, then, coupled with our material prosperity, will bring into our beloved South a new heaven and a new earth.

"EDUCATION MUST NOT SIMPLY TEACH WORK — IT MUST TEACH LIFE"

W. E. B. DuBois
The Talented Tenth

To many Negroes it was clear that the acceptance of economic goals could not satisfy Negro aspirations for genuine independence. William E. B. DuBois (1868-1963), beginning with his book The Souls of Black Folk, *roundly condemned the compromise of Negro manhood and called for the development of Negro leaders rather than an exclusive concern with the creation of Negro yeomen, small traders, and artisans.* [W. E. B. DuBois, The Souls of Black Folk, *Chicago, 1903, pp. 41-45, 50-59.*]

Easily the most striking thing in the history of the American Negro since 1876 is the ascendancy of Mr. Booker T. Washington. It began at the time when war memories and ideals were rapidly passing; a day of astonishing commercial development was dawning; a sense of doubt and hesitation overtook the freedmen's sons,—then it was that his leading began. Mr. Washington came, with a single definite programme, at the psychological moment when the nation was a little ashamed of having bestowed so much sentiment on Negroes, and was concentrating its energies on Dollars. His programme of industrial education, conciliation of the South, and submission and silence as to civil and political rights, was not wholly original; the Free Negroes from 1830 up to war-time had striven to build industrial schools, and the American Missionary Association had from the first taught various trades; and Price and others had sought a way of honorable alliance with the best of the Southerners. But Mr. Washington first indissolubly linked these things; he put enthusiasm, unlimited energy, and perfect faith into this programme, and changed it from a by-path into a veritable Way of Life. And the tale of the methods by which he did this is a fascinating study of human life.

It startled the nation to hear a Negro advocating such a programme after many decades of bitter complaint; it startled and won the applause of the South, it interested and won the admiration of the North; and after a confused murmur of protest, it silenced if it did not convert the Negroes themselves.

To gain the sympathy and cooperation of the various elements comprising the white South was Mr. Washington's first task; and this, at the time Tuskegee was founded, seemed for a black man, well-nigh impossible. And yet ten years later it was done in the word spoken at Atlanta: "In all things purely social we can be as separate as the five fingers, and yet one as the hand in all things essential to mutual progress." This "Atlanta Compromise" is by all odds the most notable thing in Mr. Washington's career. The South interpreted it in different ways: the radicals received it as a complete surrender of the demand for civil and political equality; the conservatives, as a generously conceived working basis for mutual understanding. So both approved it, and to-day its author is certainly the most distinguished Southerner since Jefferson Davis, and the one with the largest personal following.

Next to this achievement comes Mr. Washington's work in gaining place and consideration in the North. Others less shrewd and tactful had formerly essayed to sit on these two stools and had fallen between them; but as Mr. Washington knew the heart of the South from birth and training, so by singular insight he intuitively grasped the spirit of the age which was dominating the North. And so thoroughly did he learn the speech and thought of triumphant commercialism, and the ideals of material prosperity, that the picture of a lone black boy poring over a French grammar amid the weeds and dirt of a neglected home soon seemed to him the acme of absurdities. One wonders what Socrates and St. Francis of Assisi would say to this.

And yet this very singleness of vision and thorough oneness with his age is a mark of the successful man. It is as though Nature must needs make men narrow in order to give them force. So Mr. Washington's cult has gained unquestioning followers, his work has wonderfully prospered, his friends are legion, and his enemies are confounded. To-day he stands as the one recognized spokesman of his ten million fellows, and one of the most notable figures in a nation of seventy millions. One hesitates, therefore, to criticise a life which, beginning with so little, has done so much. And yet the time is come when one may speak in all sincerity and utter courtesy of the mistakes and shortcomings of Mr. Washington's career, as well as of his triumphs, without being thought captious or envious, and without forgetting that it is easier to do ill than well in the world.

The criticism that has hitherto met Mr. Washington has not always been of this broad character. In the South especially has he had to walk warily to avoid the harshest judgments,—and naturally so, for he is dealing with the one subject of deepest sensitiveness to that section. Twice—once when at the Chicago celebration of the Spanish-American War he alluded to the color-prejudice that is "eating away the vitals of the South," and once when he dined with President Roosevelt—has the resulting Southern criticism been violent enough to threaten seriously his popularity. In the North the feeling has several times forced itself into words, that Mr. Washington's counsels of submission overlooked certain elements of true manhood, and that his education programme was unnecessarily narrow. Usually, however, such criticism has not found open expression, although, too, the spiritual sons of the Abolitionists have not been prepared to acknowledge that the schools founded before Tuskegee, by men of broad ideals and self-sacrificing spirit, were wholly failures or worthy of ridicule. While then, criticism has not failed to follow Mr. Washington, yet the prevailing public opinion of the land has been but too willing to deliver the solution of a wearisome problem into his hands, and say, "If that is all you and your race ask, take it."

Among his own people, however, Mr. Washington has encountered the strongest and most lasting opposition, amounting at times to bitterness, and even to-day continuing strong and insistent even though largely silenced in outward expression by the public opinion of the nation. Some of this opposition is, of course, mere envy; the disappointment of displaced demagogues and the spite of narrow minds. But aside from this, there is among educated and thoughtful colored men in all parts of the land a feeling of deep regret, sorrow, and apprehension at the wide currency and ascendancy which some of Mr. Washington's theories have gained. These same men admire his sincerity of purpose, and are willing to forgive much to honest endeavor which is doing something worth the doing. They cooperate with Mr. Washington as far as they conscientiously can; and, indeed, it is no ordinary tribute to this man's tact and power that, steering as he must between so many diverse interests and opinions, he so largely retains the respect of all. . . .

Mr. Washington represents in Negro thought the old attitude of adjustment and submission; but adjustment at such a peculiar time as to make his programme unique. This is an age of unusual economic development, and Mr. Washington's programme naturally takes an economic cast, becoming a gospel of Work and Money to such an extent as apparently almost completely to overshadow the higher aims of life. Moreover, this is an age when the more advanced races are coming in closer contact with the less developed races, and the race-feeling is therefore intensified; and Mr. Washington's programme practically accepts the alleged inferiority of the Negro races. Again, in our own land, the reaction from the sentiment of war time has given impetus to race-prejudice against Negroes, and Mr. Washington withdraws many of the high demands of Negroes as men and American citizens. In other periods of intensified prejudice all the Negro's tendency to self-assertion has been called forth; at this period a policy of submission is advocated. In the history of nearly all other races and peoples the doctrine preached at such crises has been that manly self-respect is worth more than lands and houses, and that a people who voluntarily surrender such respect, or cease striving for it, are not worth civilizing.

In answer to this, it has been claimed that the Negro can survive only through submission. Mr. Washington distinctly asks that black people give up, at least for the present, three things,—

First, political power,

Second, insistence on civil rights,

Third, higher education of Negro youth,—

and concentrate all their energies on industrial education, the accumulation of wealth, and the conciliation of the South. This policy has been courageously and insistently advocated for over fifteen years, and has been triumphant for perhaps ten years. As a result of this tender of the palm-branch, what has been the return? In these years there have occurred:

1. The disfranchisement of the Negro.

2. The legal creation of a distinct status of civil inferiority for the Negro.

3. The steady withdrawal of aid from institutions for the higher training of the Negro.

These movements are not, to be sure, direct results of Mr. Washington's teachings; but his propaganda has, without a shadow of doubt, helped their speedier accomplishment. The question then comes: Is it possible, and probable, that nine millions of men can make effective progress in economic lines if they are deprived of political rights, made a servile caste, and allowed only the most meagre chance for developing their exceptional men? If history and reason give any distinct answer to these questions, it is an emphatic NO. And Mr. Washington thus faces the triple paradox of his career:

1. He is striving nobly to make Negro artisans business men and property-owners; but it is utterly impossible under modern competitive methods, for workingmen and property-owners to defend their rights and exist without the right of suffrage.

2. He insists on thrift and self-respect, but at the same time counsels a silent submission to civic inferiority such as is bound to sap the manhood of any race in the long run.

3. He advocates common-school and industrial training, and depreciates institutions of higher learning; but neither the Negro common-schools, nor Tuskegee itself could remain open a day were it not for teachers trained in Negro colleges, or trained by their graduates. . . .

Today even the attitude of the Southern whites toward the black is not, as so many assume, in all cases the same; the ignorant Southerner hates the Negro, the workingmen fear his competition, the money-makers wish to use him as a laborer, some of the educated see a menace in his upward development, while others—usually the sons of the masters—wish to help him to rise. National opinion has enabled this last class to maintain the Negro common schools, and to protect the Negro partially in property, life, and limb. Through the pressure of the money-makers, the Negro is in danger of being reduced to semi-slavery, especially in the country districts; the workingmen, and those of the educated who fear the Negro, have united to disfranchise him, and some have urged his deportation; while the passions of the ignorant are easily aroused to lynch and abuse any black man. To praise this intricate whirl of thought and prejudice is nonsense; to inveigh indiscriminately against "the South" is unjust; but to use the same breath in praising Governor Aycock, exposing Senator Morgan, arguing with Mr. Thomas Nelson Page, and denouncing Senator Ben Tillman, is not only sane, but the imperative duty of thinking black men.

It would be unjust to Mr. Washington not to acknowledge that in several instances he has opposed movements in the South which were unjust to the Negro; he sent memorials to the Louisiana and Alabama constitutional conventions, he has spoken against lynching, and in other ways has openly or silently set his influence against sinister schemes and unfortunate happenings. Notwithstanding this, it is equally true to assert that on the whole the distinct impression left by Mr. Washington's propaganda is, first, that the South is justified in its present attitude toward the Negro because of the Negro's degrada-tion; secondly, that the prime cause of the Negro's failure to rise more quickly is his wrong education in the past; and, thirdly, that his future rise depends primarily on his own efforts. Each of these propositions is a dangerous half-truth. The supplementary truths must never be lost sight of: first, slavery and race-prejudice are potent if not sufficient causes of the Negro's position; second, industrial and common-school training were necessarily slow in planting because they had to await the black teachers trained by higher institutions,—it being extremely doubtful if any essentially different development was pos-sible, and certainly a Tuskegee was unthinkable before 1880; and, third, while it is a great truth to say that the Negro must strive and strive mightily to help himself, it is equally true that unless his striving be not simply seconded, but rather aroused and encouraged, by the initiative of the richer and wiser environing group, he cannot hope for great success.

In his failure to realize and impress this last point, Mr. Washington is especially to be criticised. His doctrine has tended to make the whites, North and South, shift the burden of the Negro problem to the Negro's shoulders and stand aside as critical and rather pessimistic spectators; when in fact the burden belongs to the nation, and the hands of none of us are clean if we bend not our energies to righting these great wrongs. . . .

The black men of America have a duty to perform, a duty stern and delicate,—a forward movement to oppose a part of the work of their greatest leader. So far as Mr. Washington preaches Thrift, Patience, and Industrial Training for the masses, we must hold up his hands and strive with him, rejoicing in his honors and glorying in the strength of this Joshua called of God and of man to lead the headless host. But so far as Mr. Washington apologizes for injustices, North or South, does not rightly value the privilege and duty of voting, belittles the emasculating effects of caste distinctions, and opposes the higher training and ambition of our brighter minds,—so far as he, the South, or the Nation, does this,—we must unceasingly and firmly oppose them. By every civilized and peaceful method we must strive for the right which the world accords to men, clinging unwaveringly to those great words which the sons of the Fathers would fain forget: "We hold these truths to be self-evident: That all men are created equal; that they are endowed by their Creator with certain unalienable rights; that among these are life, liberty, and the pursuit of happiness."

Michael Harrington

If You're Black, Stay Back

In the 1960's the consequences of the historic exclusion of the Negro from the mainstream of American life were depicted in a popular study of the culture of poverty by Michael Harrington (1928-   ). The Negro, argued Harrington, lives in a world of double poverty, where social exclusion buttresses economic racism in a vicious round that cannot be broken by the achievement of simple legal equality. [Michael Harrington, The Other America: Poverty in the United States, *New York, 1962, pp. 71-81.]*

If all the discriminatory laws in the United States were immediately repealed, race would still remain as one of the most pressing moral and political problems in the nation. Negroes and other minorities are not simply the victims of a series of iniquitous statutes. The American economy, the American society, the American unconscious are all racist. If all the laws were framed to provide equal opportunity, a majority of the Negroes would not be able to take full advantage of the change. There would still be a vast, silent, and automatic system directed against men and women of color.

To belong to a racial minority is to be poor, but poor in a special way. The fear, the lack of self-confidence, the haunting, these have been described. But they, in turn, are the expressions of the most institutionalized poverty in the United States, the most vicious of the vicious circles. In a sense, the Negro is classically the "other" American, degraded and frustrated at every turn and not just because of laws.

There are sympathetic and concerned people who do not understand how deeply America has integrated racism into its structure. Given time, they argue, the Negroes will rise in the society like the Irish, the Jews, the Italians, and all the rest. But this notion misses two decisive facts:

that the Negro is colored, and no other group in the United States has ever faced such a problem, and that the Negro of today is an internal migrant who will face racism wherever he goes, who cannot leave his oppression behind as if it were a czar or a potato famine. To be equal, the Negro requires something much more profound than a way "into" the society; he needs a transformation of some of the basic institutions of the society.

The Negro is poor because he is black; that is obvious enough. But, perhaps more importantly, the Negro is black because he is poor. The laws against color can be removed, but that will leave the poverty that is the historic and institutionalized consequence of color. As long as this is the case, being born a Negro will continue to be the most profound disability that the United States imposes upon a citizen.

Perhaps the quickest way to point up the racism of the American economy is to recall a strange case of jubilation.

Late in 1960 the Department of Labor issued a study, "The Economic Situation of Negroes in the United States." It noted that in 1939, nonwhite workers earned, on the average, 41 per cent as much as whites, and that by 1958 their wages had climbed to 58 per cent of that of whites. Not a little elation greeted this announcement. Some of the editorialists cited these statistics as indicating that slow and steady progress was being made. (At this rate, the Negro would reach parity with the white some time well after the year 2000.)

To begin with, the figures were somewhat more optimistic than the reality. Part of the Negro gain reflected the shift of rural Negroes to cities and Southern Negroes to the North. In both cases, the people involved increased their incomes by going into a more prosperous section of the country. But within each area their relative position remained the same: at the bottom. Then, the statistics take a depression year (1939) as a base for comparison, and contrast it to a year of recession (1958). This tended to exaggerate the advance because Negroes in 1939 were particularly victimized.

Another important aspect of the problem was obscured by the sweeping comparisons most editorialists made between the 1939 and 1958 figures. Even the Department of Labor statistics themselves indicate that the major gain was made during World War II (the increase from 1939 to 1947 was from 41.4 per cent to 54.3 of the white wage). In the postwar period the rate of advance slowed to a walk. Moreover, most of the optimism was based upon figures for Negro men. When the women are included, and when one takes a median family income from the Current Population Reports, Negroes rose from 51 per cent of white family income in 1947 to 57 per cent in 1952—and then declined back to the 1947 level by 1959.

But even without these qualifications, the fact is stark enough: the United States found cause for celebration in the announcement that Negro workers had reached 58 per cent of the wage level of their white co-workers. This situation is deeply imbedded in the very structure of American society.

Negroes in the United States are concentrated in the worst, dirtiest, lowest-paying jobs. A third continue to live in the rural South, most of them merely subsisting within a culture of poverty and a society of open terror. A third live in Southern cities and a third in Northern cities, and these have bettered their lot compared to the sharecroppers. But they are still the last hired and the first fired, and they are particularly vulnerable to recessions.

Thus, according to the Department of Labor in 1960, 4 per cent of Negro employees were "professional, technical and kindred workers" (compared to 11.3 per cent for the whites); 2.7 per cent were "managers, officials and proprietors" (the white figure is 14.6 per cent). In short, at the top of the economic structure there were 6.7 per cent of the Negroes—and 25.9 per cent of the whites. And this, in itself, represented considerable *gains* over the past two decades.

Going down the occupational scale, Negroes are primarily grouped in the bottom jobs. In 1960, 20 per cent of the whites had high-skill industrial jobs, while the Negro share of this classification was 9 per cent. Semiskilled mass production workers and laborers constituted around 48 per cent of the Negro male population (and 25.3 per cent of the white males). Negro women are the victims of a double discrimination. According to a New York State study, Negro female income as a percentage of white actually declined between 1949 and 1954 (and, in 1960, over a third of Negro women were still employed as domestics).

In part, this miserable structure of the Negro work force is an inheritance of the past. It reflects what happens to a people who have been systematically oppressed and denied access to skill and opportunity. If this completely defined the problem, there would be a basis for optimism. One could assume that the Negro would leave behind the mess of pottage bequeathed him by white America and move into a better future. But that is not the case. For the present position of the Negro in the economy has been institutionalized. Unless something basic is done, it will reproduce itself for years to come.

Take, as an example, the problem of automation. This has caused "structural" unemployment through the American work force, that is, the permanent destruction of jobs rather than cyclical layoffs. When this happens, the blow falls disproportionately upon the Negro. As the last significant group to enter the factory, the Negroes have low seniority (if they are lucky enough to be in union occupations), and they are laid off first. As one of the least skilled groups in the work force, they will have the hardest time getting another job. The "older" Negro (over forty) may well be condemned to job instability for the rest of his life.

All of this is immediate and automatic. It is done without the intervention of a single racist, yet it is a profound part of racism in the United States.

However, more is involved than the inevitable working of an impersonal system. The Negro lives in the other America of poverty for many reasons, and one of them is conscious racism reinforcing institutional patterns of the economy. In 1960, according to the report of Herbert Hill, Labor Secretary of the National Association for the Advancement of Colored People, Negroes made up only 1.69 per cent of the total number of apprentices in the economy. The exact figure offered by Hill has been disputed; the shocking fact which he describes is agreed upon by everyone. This means that Negroes are denied access precisely to those jobs that are not low-paying and vulnerable to recession.

The main cause of this problem is the attitude of management, which fundamentally determines hiring policy. But in the case of apprenticeship programs, the labor movement and the Federal and state agencies involved also bear part of the responsibility. In the AFL-CIO, it is the politically conservative unions from the building trades who are the real stumbling block; the mass-production unions of the CIO have some bad areas, but on the whole they pioneered in bringing Negroes into the plants and integrating local organizations.

With the companies, one of the real difficulties in dealing with this structure of racism is that it is invisible. Here is a huge social fact, yet no one will accept responsibility for it. When questioned as to why there are no Negroes in sales, or in the office, the personnel man will say that he himself has nothing against Negroes. The problem, he will claim, is with subordinates who would revolt if Negroes were brought into their department, and with superiors who impose the policy. This response is standard up and down the line. The subordinates and the superiors make the same assertion.

Indeed, one of the difficulties in fighting against racist practices in the American economy is the popularity of a liberal rhetoric. Practically no one, outside of convinced white supremacists in the South, will admit to discriminatory policies. So it is that the Northern Negro has, in one sense, a more personally frustrating situation than his Southern brother. In Dixie, Jim Crow is personified, an actual living person who speaks in the accents of open racism. In the rest of the country, everybody is against discrimination for the record, and Jim Crow is a vast impersonal system that keeps the Negro down.

In the past few years, some Negro groups have been using the boycott to force companies to abandon racist hiring practices. This may well be an extraordinarily momentous development, for it is a step out of the other America, and equality will come only when the Negro is no longer poor.

But, as one goes up the occupational ladder, the resistance to hiring

Negroes becomes more intense. The office, for example, is a bastion of racism in American society. To some of the people involved, white-collar work is regarded as more personal, and even social, than factory work. So the integration of work appears like the integration of the neighborhood or the home. And a wall of prejudice is erected to keep the Negroes out of advancement.

Perhaps the most shocking statistic in all this is the one that describes what happens when a Negro does acquire skill and training. North, East, South, and West the pattern is the same: the more education a Negro has, the more economic discrimination he faces. Herman Miller, one of the best-known authorities on income statistics, has computed that the white Southern college graduate receives 1.85 times the compensation of his Negro counterpart, and in the North the white edge is 1.59.

What is involved in these figures is a factor that sharply distinguishes racial minorities from the old immigrant groups. When the Irish, the Jews, or the Italians produced a doctor, it was possible for him to begin to develop a practice that would bring him into the great society. There was prejudice, but he was increasingly judged on his skill. As time went on, the professionals from the immigrant groups adapted themselves to the language and dress of the rest of America. They ceased to be visible, and there was a wide scope for their talents.

This is not true of the Negro. The doctor or the lawyer will find it extremely difficult to set up practice in a white neighborhood. By far and large, they will be confined to the ghetto, and since their fellow Negroes are poor they will not receive so much money as their white colleagues. The Negro academic often finds himself trapped in a segregated educational system in which Negro colleges are short on salaries, equipment, libraries, and so on. Their very professional advancement is truncated because of it.

For the mass in the racial ghetto the situation is even more extreme. As a result of the segregation of neighborhoods, it is possible for a city like New York to have a public policy in favor of integration, and yet to maintain a system of effective segregation. In the mid-fifties, for example, the New York public-school system took a look at itself, dividing schools into Group X, with a high concentration of Negroes or Puerto Ricans, and Group Y where Negroes and Puerto Ricans were less than 10 per cent of the student body. They found that the X schools were older and less adequate, had more probationary and substitute teachers, more classes for retarded pupils, and fewer for bright children. This situation had developed within a framework of a public, legal commitment to integrated education. (Some steps have been taken to remedy the problem, but they are only a beginning.)

In the other America each group suffers from a psychological depression as well as from simple material want. And given the long history and the tremendous institutionalized power of racism, this is particularly and terribly true of the Negro.

Some commentators have argued that Negroes have a lower level of aspiration, of ambition, than whites. In this theory, the Jim Crow economy produces a mood of resignation and acceptance. But in a study of the New York State Commission Against Discrimination an even more serious situation was described: one in which Negro children had more aspiration than whites from the same income level, but less opportunity to fulfill their ambition.

In this study, Aaron Antonovsky and Melvin Lerner described the result as a "pathological condition . . . in our society." The Negro child, coming from a family in which the father has a miserable job, is forced to reject the life of his parents, and to put forth new goals for himself. In the case of the immigrant young some generations ago, this experience of breaking with the Old Country tradition and identifying with the great society of America was a decisive moment in moving upward. But the Negro does not find society as open as the immigrant did. He has the hope and the desire, but not the possibility. The consequence is heartbreaking frustration.

Indeed, Antonovsky suggests that the image of Jackie Robinson or Ralph Bunche is a threat to the young Negro. These heroes are exceptional and talented men. Yet, in a time of ferment among Negroes, they tend to become norms and models for the young people. Once again, there is a tragic gap between the ideal and the possible. A sense of disillusion, of failure, is added to the indignity of poverty.

A more speculative description of the Negro psychology has been written by Norman Mailer. For Mailer, the concept of "coolness" is a defense reaction against a hostile world. Threatened by the Man, denied access to the society, the Negro, in Mailer's image, stays loose; he anticipates disillusion; he turns cynicism into a style.

But perhaps the final degradation the Negro must face is the image the white man has of him. White America keeps the Negro down. It forces him into a slum; it keeps him in the dirtiest and lowest-paying jobs. Having imposed this indignity, the white man theorizes about it. He does not see it as the tragic work of his own hands, as a social product. Rather, the racial ghetto reflects the "natural" character of the Negro: lazy, shiftless, irresponsible, and so on. So prejudice becomes self-justifying. It creates miserable conditions and then cites them as a rationale for inaction and complacency.

One could continue describing the psychological and spiritual consequences of discrimination almost endlessly. Yet, whatever the accurate theory may be, it is beyond dispute that one of the main components of poverty for the Negro is a maiming of personality. This is true generally for the poor; it is doubly and triply true for the race poor.

How can the Negroes escape their prison in the other America?

To begin with, this wall of prejudice will be breached only when it is understood that the problem of race is not just a matter of legal and political equality. It is important that the right to the vote be won in the South, that discriminatory legislation be struck down, and so on. But that is only the beginning. The real emancipation of the Negro waits upon a massive assault upon the entire culture of poverty in American society: upon slums, inferior education, inadequate medical care, and all the rest. These things are as much a part of being a Negro as the color of a man's skin.

Housing is perhaps the most crucial element in racial poverty. As long as Negroes and other minorities are segregated into neighborhoods, the impact of all civil-rights legislation is softened. It is possible to have a public policy for integrated schooling, but if the school districts are themselves a product of residential discrimination, the schools will continue to be Jim Crow. But, here again, America at the beginning of the sixties does not seem prepared to devote the resources to the problem that are required if it is to be solved. And because of this, the terrible indignity of the ghetto will continue.

On the job, the Negro is the prime victim of the unwillingness of the society to face the crisis brought about by automation. It is, of course, the Negro "type" of job that is being destroyed. The crisis is hitting precisely in those areas where gains in integrated work were made in the past two decades, in the semiskilled jobs of mass-production industries. The Government, as noted before, is not making adequate provisions for planning and retraining and all the rest. And given the racist character of the American economy, this is a particularly severe blow against the Negro. It amounts to rebuilding the wall of prejudice, to destroying advances which have already been made.

In a sense, this technological crisis offers America a unique opportunity. The old system is being transformed. If the nation were to attack the problem of structural unemployment, it could at the same time make great strides toward racial equality. For any serious program aimed at providing displaced workers with skill and opportunity will automatically help the Negro as a Negro, so long as it does not contain racist features. A new and integrated structure could be built; the crisis could be a starting point for enormous progress.

But in recent years Negroes were more and more asked to accept their position in society, to sacrifice their own needs to the common good. Once again, the poorest were asked to pay the way of the better off. This took the form of various sincere people calling upon the Negro movement not to "obstruct" various welfare programs by insisting that they be integrated. In other words, the Negroes were being asked to help to build a welfare state that would discriminate against them in a double sense, that would not really benefit them because they are so poor as to be beyond the reach of the new benefits, and that would continue and reinforce the racist pattern of all American society.

It is crucial that the nation understand that there can be no progress toward destroying the other America at the price of Negro rights. This is not simply a matter of morality and ethics, important as those factors are. It is also a brute sociological fact. The poor, as I have documented in describing other parts of the culture of poverty, are generally speaking those people who are beneath the welfare state. A quarter of them are Negro. Any program aimed at really aiding the dispossessed cannot exclude the Negroes without excluding millions of others who desperately need help. A housing program with discrimination against the black man is at the same time discriminatory against the white man, for it will perpetuate the segregation of poverty and it will keep the poor generally on the margin of the society. The only kind of housing program that could break through the social isolation of the poor and that could render these millions visible and return them to our society is an integrated program. And as long as the slums remain (or even as they are replaced by "poor farm" housing projects tucked away in some corner of the city), the culture of poverty will remain.

Clearly, the Negroes cannot achieve their emancipation on their own. They are, quite literally, a minority in the society, and they do not possess the political power to win the vast and comprehensive changes in public policy that are necessary if there is to be real equality. Here, once again, the fate of the lowest, the most dispossessed, depends on what the better off, and particularly the labor movement, will do.

If, as is quite possible, America refuses to deal with the social evils that persist in the sixties, it will at the same time have turned its back on the racial minorities. There will be speeches on equality; there will be gains as the nation moves toward a constitutional definition of itself as egalitarian. The Negro will watch all this from a world of double poverty. He will continue to know himself as a member of a race-class condemned by heredity to be poor. There will be occasional celebrations—perhaps the next one will be called in twenty years or so when it is announced that Negroes have reached 70 per cent of the white wage level. But that other America which is the ghetto will still stand.

There is a bitter picket-line chant that one sometimes hears when a store is being boycotted in the North:

> If you're white, you're right,
> If you're black, stay back.

It is an accurate sociological statement of the plight of the Negro in American society.

"STOP BUYING EXPENSIVE CARS, FINE CLOTHES, AND SHOES BEFORE BEING ABLE TO LIVE IN A FINE HOME"

E. U. Essien-Udom

The Black Muslim Gospel

The rules of thrift and industry exemplified in the Protestant ethic ironically find their most ardent contemporary converts and disciples among Negroes who have rejected Protestant Christianity. Elijah Poole, known as Elijah Muhammad (1897-   ), has enunciated for his Black Muslim followers rules of good conduct and success that are clearly reminiscent of an earlier age. The maxims have gained the Black Muslims the praise, if not the support, of many Negroes totally unsympathetic with racism, whether Negro or white. [E. U. Essien-Udom, Black Nationalism: A Search for an Identity in America, *Chicago, 1962, pp. 27-29.*]

Although it would be hard to determine how much of Muhammad's effort is deliberate and how much is unconscious, the impression is given that he is trying to create a Negro ethos and hence a self-consciously unified Negro community. Examining his exoteric teachings reinforces this impression.

Because it symbolizes the oppression of the Negro, the white culture's political and religious basis is rejected: the Muslims do not vote in local or national elections; they resist induction into the United States military services; and they categorically reject Christianity as the "graveyard" of the Negro people. The Negro subculture is as well rejected as "uncivilized," and as impeding their material, cultural, and moral advancement.

In order to create, to fashion a unified community, Muhammad first directs his attack against those forces which have so disastrously atomized and weakened Negro society. He seeks to provide the Negro with a spiritual and moral context within which shaken pride and confidence may be restored and unused or abused energies directed toward an all-encompassing goal: to heal the wound of the Negro's dual membership in American society. Specifically, Muhammad denounces the matriarchal character of Negro society; the relative lack of masculine parental authority which makes the enforcement of discipline within the family difficult; the traditional lack of savings- and capital-accumulation habits; and the folk belief that "white is right," which leads to a dependence upon the initiative of the white man. Personal indolence and laziness are sternly deprecated. Habits of hard work and thrift are extolled.

The Muslims disapprove of the expression of undisciplined, spontaneous impulses. The pursuit of a "righteous" life as prescribed by the "Laws of Islam" and by Muhammad's directives is seen as the major purpose of existence. These laws and directives prohibit the following: extra-marital sexual relations, the use of alcohol, tobacco, and narcotics, indulging in gambling, dancing, movie-going, dating, sports, long vacations from work, sleeping more than is necessary to health, quarreling between husband and wife, lying, stealing, discourtesy (especially toward women), and insubordination to civil authority, except on the ground of religious obligation. Maintaining personal habits of cleanliness and keeping fastidious homes are moral duties. The eating of pork, cornbread, collard greens, and other foods traditional among southern Negroes is strictly proscribed. No one is permitted to straighten his hair. Women may not dye their hair or conspicuously use cosmetics. Intemperate singing, shouting, laughing loudly are forbidden. Violation of any of these or other rules is punished immediately by suspensions from the movement for periods ranging from thirty days to a maximum of seven years, depending on the gravity of the offense. The most important sanctions which appear to regulate the behavior of Muslims are loss of membership in the movement and the chastisement from Allah.

Muhammad's effort to inculcate a sense of self-esteem in the Muslims by encouraging them to practice and assimilate habits that we associate with the middle class is obvious in his teachings. The quest for respectability within and without the Negro community is a primary goal. Their enthusiastic desire to be independent of white control is demonstrated partly by their willingness to overstretch their resources in order to maintain private elementary and high schools in Chicago and Detroit. The effort to strengthen the Muslims' sense of pride is apparent in Muhammad's emphasis on the "glorious" past of the Black Nation: the special relationship between the Muslims and Allah and their connection with "Arabian-Egyptian" civilization.

It should be stressed, however, that Islam is not offered to Negroes merely as a divisive symbol. To the believers it is a living faith and a positive way of life, enabling them, in unacknowledged ways, to follow with devotion moral values reminiscent of the New England Puritans and to aspire to a style of life usually associated with the middle class. The Muslims, being the elect of God, are obligated to pursue a righteous life which would justify their special status in His sight. The pursuit of wealth is good only in so far as it enhances the common good—the elevation of the Nation of Islam and, in general, the masses of American Negroes. The Muslims are determined to rise on the social scale by their own efforts. Imbued with a common purpose, the Muslims appear to drown their fears, frustrations, anxieties, and doubts in the hope of attaining a national home and in the promise and assurance of redemption *now* in the "New World of Islam," purged of the suffering and corruption of the world about them. Such is the sense of "tragic optimism" which has characterized the organized effort of the Negro nationalists to assert their identity and to discover their human worth and dignity in American society.

Theodore Roosevelt to No Shirt
The Indian Dilemma

No group was as ill-suited to the ideology of individualism and success as the American Indian. This letter from Theodore Roosevelt (1858-1919) to an Indian leader clearly delineates the cultural impasse between American governmental policy and the imperatives of Indian group survival—an impasse which President Roosevelt was temperamentally unsuited to resolve, no less understand. [Elting E. Morison, ed., The Letters of Theodore Roosevelt, *Cambridge, 1951, IV, 1185-1188.]*

Washington, May 8, 1905

My Friend: I received from the hands of the Commissioner of Indian Affairs, the book that was sent to me through you, showing photographic scenes in the country inhabited by the Umatilla tribe. The Commissioner also delivered to me your letter, in which you tell me of some of the things that are troubling you.

It is true, as you say, that the earth is occupied by the white people and the red people; that, if the red people would prosper, they must follow the mode of life which has made the white people so strong; and that it is only right that the white people should show the red people what to do and how to live right. It is for that reason, because I wish to be as much a father to the red people as to the white, that I have placed in charge of the Indian Office a Commissioner in whom I have confidence, knowing him to be a strong friend of the red people and anxious to help them in every way.

But I am sorry to learn that when you sent the Commissioner word that you wished to come to Washington and he sent you a message not to come then but to send your complaints in writing, you followed your own will, like a headstrong child, instead of doing what the Commissioner advised. That is not the way to get along nicely in your new mode of life, and is not a good example to set to your people. You see, also, what the result was: you traveled three thousand miles across the country, at considerable expense, to see me, and then had to go back without seeing me. If you had done what the Commissioner wished you to do, you would have avoided all this. I hope that you and your people will lay this lesson to heart for the future.

Now, as to the things which are troubling you: I think a good many of these are due more to misunderstanding than to anything else. When a part of your reservation was ceded by you to the Government, this land was offered for sale to white settlers, and the Government was to take out of the money received for the lands enough to repay itself for the cost of laying out the plans and conducting the sales. It takes time to sell land, and the law allows the settlers a good while to complete their purchases; but there is a fair balance now accumulated in the Treasury to the credit of your people, and I will talk with my advisers and see whether it will not be well to give you another per capita payment pretty soon. But I think you are mistaken about any promise to you of $25 every year to every Indian. Nobody would have had a right to promise you this. What the Government people probably told you was that they would try to fix it that way; but of course no one could foresee how fast the lands were going to sell, or how much money was coming in for them, or when.

You must have misunderstood, also, what the Government told you when you were in Washington a few years ago. No one could have told you that you were "to live your way for about 25 years," and that "after that 25 years is up we will make a new treaty." I dare say that what you have in your mind was some statement about your patents. When you took your allotments, the patents issued for them were trust patents, the trust continuing for 25 years. That is, the Government keeps its hand on your land for 25 years and does not let anyone tax it or lay any judgment upon it, and at the same time does not let you sell or mortgage it. This is done, as you know, for your protection, and in order to give you 25 years in which to prepare yourselves for the day when the Government will lift its hand off your land and let you do with it what you please, just as the white man does with his land. In some cases, possibly, the Government may think it best to continue keeping its hand on the Indians' land for a while longer; but it does not wish to do this generally, because if they are always treated like children the Indians will never learn to take care of themselves; and it is my hope that the Umatillas will try to learn wise ways of living, so that, when the 25 years of their trust patents expire, they will be able to stand on their feet and support themselves without looking to the Government for everything.

This brings me to another point in your letter, where you give your reason for wishing your leases to be so arranged that you will have two payments every year instead of one. You say: "I have to have money to make my living . . . and of course I want my money whenever I need it." I suppose you realize that you will get only the same amount of money, whether you get it in one payment or two. In other words, if a white lessee is going to give you $100 a year for the use of a piece of land, he will either give you the whole $100 in one payment or only $50 if he makes two payments. Now, if your lessee pays you $100 all at one time, it is not necessary that you should spend it all at one time; you can just as well spend $50 of it and keep the other $50 for six months, if that is what you wish to do. If he pays you only $50 at one time, the other $50 remains in his pocket till the next payment: surely, it ought to be just as safe in your pocket as in his. Besides, the lesson in saving would be of great value to you. No matter how much the Government or the white people do for the Indian, he will always remain poor if he foolishly spends his money just as fast as he gets it. The white man grows rich by learning to spend only part of his money and lay the other part aside until it is absolutely necessary to use it. Then he finds that he can be just as happy and do without a great many things which formerly he supposed he absolutely must have.

I am very sorry that the leasing arrangements generally seem so unsatisfactory to you, but you must remember that the Indians, rather than the Government, are to blame for that. The chief reason why the arrangements are so confused now is that the Indians went ahead for a time and made informal contracts without the Government's approval, and got their affairs into a very bad tangle. It will take some time to straighten this out, and meanwhile you will have to be patient. But, when everything is set right, there are certain things the Government intends to do. For one thing, it does not wish any Indian to lease his whole allotment if he is strong and able to work, unless he is engaged in some occupation by which he is earning a living for himself and his family; but he must reserve at least 40 acres for his own use and cultivation. Children, women, and old men, who cannot take care of any of their own land, will be allowed to lease. Indians, however, who wish to lease their lands only for the purpose of shirking work, will not be permitted to do so. I wish you to tell this to your people very plainly, and say to them that the President intends to support the Commissioner in every way in insisting that able-bodied Indians shall earn their living, just as able-bodied white men do.

You quote the Superintendent as saying, in regard to the lands of dead Indians:

"I will lease out them land to some white mens myself, and I will do with that money just what I feel like."

The Superintendent is not authorized to lease the lands of deceased Indians; such lands can be leased only by the heirs of the deceased allottees. I can hardly believe, therefore, that the Superintendent made such a statement, knowing that he would not be allowed to carry it out. I should prefer to believe that you misunderstood him; but the Commissioner will have that matter inquired into. The land of any Indian who dies passes to his heirs, and may be leased only by them, or for them if they are incapable of doing business for themselves. The difficulty always is, to know who the heirs are. Here is where the courts come in. When an Indian takes an allotment he becomes a citizen, and then he passes under the laws of the State of Oregon in all these matters of inheritance. As far as possible, it is my desire that the Superintendent shall find out, and report to the Indian Office, who the heirs are; but sometimes this cannot be done, and usually because of the mixed up marriage relations which the Indians themselves voluntarily continue. Under the Oregon law, for instance, a man may have only one wife at a time, and she must be married to him for life or until legally divorced. If a husband and wife live thus decently together and have children it is perfectly easy to know who are the heirs; but if they separate and go off and find other mates, and live with them without marriage, and have children by them, this confuses the whole matter so that it is often impossible to say who will inherit under the law. Whenever, for this cause or any other there is doubt about an heirship, it is necessary to carry the matter into court and have it decided as white people do in such cases. This is tedious and expensive, and should be avoided whenever it can be without diminishing the protection to the Indians' property; but the whole object of court proceedings is to have disputes so settled that they cannot be torn open again by anybody.

Finally, I note that you say that certain Indians fenced 400 or 500 acres of land each for pastures, and then rented the land to white cattlemen, and that some white men went to work and made a big pasture, 500 acres or more, and paid much money to the Indians.

Under the Act providing for allotments to Umatilla Indians and the reduction of their reservation, a sufficient quantity of land was set aside for the use of the Indians in common as grazing lands. The Indian Office has held that no Indians on the reservation had the right to fence the unallotted land for grazing purposes, thereby taking in the available springs and water suitable for the stock. In October, 1904, the special Indian Agent who was then in charge of the Umatilla Agency was instructed to call the attention of offenders to this provision of the Umatilla Act, and to point out to them that they were doing the other Indians of the reservation an injustice, in addition to violating the law. It was suggested that he call them together in council and request them to remove the fences complained of, and that, if they failed or refused to remove the fences, he should remove them from the springs and elsewhere on the unallotted lands so as to give the use of the same in common to all the Indians. The Indian Office has no knowledge that any of these lands, or other lands held in common by the Indians, have been leased to white men for pasturage, or that white men have cattle upon the reservation.

Now, my friend, I hope that you will lay what I have said to heart. Try to set your people a good example of upright and industrious life, patience under difficulties, and respect for the authority of the officers I have appointed to care for your affairs. If you try as hard to help them as you do to find something in their conduct to censure, you will be surprised to discover how much real satisfaction life holds in store for you.

Wishing you and your people every good gift, and with a desire to give you all the aid I can to become worthy citizens of the United States, I am, *Your friend*

V

The Axioms
of Exclusion

In early twentieth-century America, the unprecedented complexities of a pluralistic society encouraged and sustained exclusionist postures and practices which soon became ends in themselves. But the commitment to social homogeneity among the economic elite, as well as by those further down the line, was not made without misgivings. Indeed, it was admitted that the process often resulted in "excessive compatibility . . . 'single track minds' and excessively crystallized attitudes and in the destruction of personal responsibility."

═══

Chester I. Barnard

The Economy of Incentives

*The assumption that social homogeneity was essential to economic
organization was tantamount to conviction among most business leaders
in the first half of the twentieth century. Chester I. Barnard (1886-
1961), president of the New Jersey Bell Telephone Company and the
Rockefeller Foundation, gave classic utterance to the social formula
which guided Big Business personnel policies.* [Chester I. Barnard,
The Functions of the Executive, *Cambridge, 1938, pp. 139-148.*]

It has already been demonstrated that an essential element of organizations is the willingness of persons to contribute their individual
efforts to the cooperative system. The power of cooperation, which is
often spectacularly great when contrasted with that even of large
numbers of individuals unorganized, is nevertheless dependent upon
the willingness of individuals to cooperate and to contribute their
efforts to the cooperative system. The contributions of personal efforts
which constitute the energies of organizations are yielded by individuals because of incentives. The egotistical motives of self-preservation
and of self-satisfaction are dominating forces; on the whole, organizations can exist only when consistent with the satisfaction of these
motives, unless, alternatively, they can change these motives. The
individual is always the basic strategic factor in organization. Regardless of his history or his obligations he must be induced to cooperate,
or there can be no cooperation.

It needs no further introduction to suggest that the subject of incentives is fundamental in formal organizations and in conscious efforts
to organize. Inadequate incentives mean dissolution, or changes of
organization purpose, or failure of cooperation. Hence, in all sorts of

organizations the affording of adequate incentives becomes the most definitely emphasized task in their existence. It is probably in this aspect of executive work that failure is most pronounced, though the causes may be due either to inadequate understanding or to the breakdown of the effectiveness of organization.

The net satisfactions which induce a man to contribute his efforts to an organization result from the positive advantages as against the disadvantages which are entailed. It follows that a net advantage may be increased or a negative advantage made positive either by increasing the number or the strength of the positive inducements or by reducing the number or the strength of the disadvantages. It often occurs that the positive advantages are few and meager, but the burdens involved are also negligible, so that there is a strong net advantage. Many "social" organizations are able to exist under such a state of affairs. Conversely, when the burdens involved are numerous or heavy, the offsetting positive advantages must be either numerous or powerful.

Hence, from the viewpoint of the organization requiring or seeking contributions from individuals, the problem of effective incentives may be either one of finding positive incentives or of reducing or eliminating negative incentives or burdens. For example, employment may be made attractive either by reducing the work required—say, by shortening hours or supplying tools or power, that is, by making conditions of employment less onerous—or by increasing positive inducement, such as wages.

In practice, although there are many cases where it is clear which side of the "equation" is being adjusted, on the whole specific practices and conditions affect both sides simultaneously or it is impossible to determine which they affect. Most specific factors in so-called working conditions may be viewed either as making employment positively attractive or as making work less onerous. We shall, therefore, make no attempt to treat specific inducements as increasing advantages or as decreasing disadvantages; but this underlying aspect is to be kept in mind.

More important than this is the distinction between the objective and the subjective aspects of incentives. Certain common positive incentives, such as material goods and in some senses money, clearly have an objective existence; and this is true also of negative incentives like working hours, conditions of work. Given a man of a certain state of mind, of certain attitudes, or governed by certain motives, he can be induced to contribute to an organization by a given combination of these objective incentives, positive or negative. It often is the case, however, that the organization is unable to offer objective incentives that will serve as an inducement to that state of mind, or to those attitudes, or to one governed by those motives. The only alternative then available is to change the state of mind, or attitudes, or motives, so that the available objective incentives can become effective.

An organization can secure the efforts necessary to its existence, then, either by the objective inducements it provides or by changing states of mind. It seems to me improbable that any organization can exist as a practical matter which does not employ both methods in combination. In some organizations the emphasis is on the offering of objective incentives—this is true of most industrial organizations. In others the preponderance is on the state of mind—this is true of most patriotic and religious organizations.

We shall call the processes of offering objective incentives "the method of incentives"; and the processes of changing subjective attitudes "the method of persuasion." Using these new terms, let us repeat what we have said: In commercial organizations the professed emphasis is apparently almost wholly on the side of the method of incentives. In religious and political organizations the professed emphasis is apparently almost wholly on the side of persuasion. But in fact, especially if account be taken of the different kinds of contributions required from different individuals, both methods are used in all types of organizations. Moreover, the centrifugal forces of individualism and the competition between organizations for individual contributions result in both methods being ineffective, with few exceptions, for more than short periods or a few years.

The Method of Incentives

We shall first discuss the method of incentives. It will facilitate our consideration of the subject if at the outset we distinguish two classes of incentives; first, those that are specific and can be specifically offered to an individual; and second, those that are general, not personal, that cannot be specifically offered. We shall call the first class specific inducements, the second general incentives.

The specific inducements that may be offered are of several classes, for example: (a) material inducements; (b) personal non-material opportunities; (c) desirable physical conditions; (d) ideal benefactions. General incentives afforded are, for example: (e) associational attractiveness; (f) adaptation of conditions to habitual methods and attitudes; (g) the opportunity of enlarged participation; (h) the condition of communion. Each of these classes of incentives is known under various names, and the list does not purport to be complete, since our purpose now is illustrative. But to accomplish this purpose it is necessary briefly to discuss the incentives named.

(a) Material inducements are money, things, or physical conditions that are offered to the individual as inducements to accepting employment, compensation for service, reward for contribution. Under a money economy and the highly specialized production of material goods, the range and profusion of material inducements are very great. The complexity of schedules of money compensation, the difficulty of securing the monetary means of compensation, and the power of exchange which money gives in organized markets, have served to exaggerate the importance of money in particular and material inducements in general as incentives to personal contributions to organized effort. It goes without elaboration that where a large part of the time of an individual is devoted to one organization, the physiological necessities—food, shelter, clothing—require that material inducements should be present in most cases; but these requirements are so limited that they are satisfied with small quantities. The unaided power of material incentives, when the minimum necessities are satisfied, in my opinion is exceedingly limited as to most men, depending almost entirely for its development upon persuasion. Notwithstanding the great emphasis upon material incentives in modern times and especially in current affairs, there is no doubt in my mind that, unaided by other motives, they constitute weak incentives beyond the level of the bare physiological necessities.

To many this view will not be readily acceptable. The emphasis upon material rewards has been a natural result of the success of technological developments—relative to other incentives it is the material things which have been progressively easier to produce, and therefore to offer. Hence there has been a forced cultivation of the love of material things among those above the level of subsistence. Since existing incentives seem always inadequate to the degree of cooperation and of social integration theoretically possible and ideally desirable, the success of the sciences and the arts of material production would have been partly ineffective, and in turn would have been partly impossible, without inculcating the desire of the material. The most significant result of this situation has been the expansion of population, most of which has been necessarily at the bare subsistence level, at which level material inducements are, on the whole, powerful incentives. This has perpetuated the illusion that beyond this subsistence level material incentives are also the most effective.

A concurrent result has been the creation of sentiments in individuals that they ought to want material things. The inculcation of "proper" ambitions in youth have greatly stressed material possessions as an evidence of good citizenship, social adequacy, etc. Hence, when underlying and governing motives have not been satisfied, there has been strong influence to rationalize the default as one of material compensation, and not to be conscious of the controlling motives or at least not to admit them.

Yet it seems to me to be a matter of common experience that material rewards are ineffective beyond the subsistence level except to a very limited proportion of men; that most men neither work harder for more material things, nor can be induced thereby to devote more than a fraction of their possible contribution to organized effort. It is likewise a matter of both present experience and past history that many of the most effective and powerful organizations are built up on incentives in which the materialistic elements, above bare subsistence, are either relatively lacking or absolutely absent. Military organizations have been relatively lacking in material incentives. The greater part of the work of political organizations is without material incentive. Religious organizations are characterized on the whole by material sacrifice. It seems to me to be definitely a general fact that even in purely commercial organizations material incentives are so weak as to be almost negligible except when reinforced by other incentives, and then only because of wholesale general persuasion in the form of salesmanship and advertising.

It will be noted that the reference has been to material incentives rather than to money. What has been said requires some, but not great, qualification with reference to money as an incentive—solely for the reason that money in our economy may be used as the indirect means of satisfying non-materialistic motives—philanthropic, artistic, intellectual, and religious motives for example—and because money income becomes an index of social status, personal development, etc.

(b) Inducements of a personal, non-materialistic character are of great importance to secure cooperative effort above the minimum material rewards essential to subsistence. The opportunities for distinction, prestige, personal power, and the attainment of dominating position are much more important than material rewards in the development of all sorts of organizations, including commercial organizations. In various ways this fact applies to many types of human beings, including those of limited ability and children. Even in strictly commercial organizations, where it is least supposed to be true, money without distinction, prestige, position, is so utterly ineffective that it is rare that greater income can be made to serve even temporarily as an inducement if accompanied by suppression of prestige. At least for short periods inferior material rewards are often accepted if assurance of distinction is present; and usually the presumption is that material rewards ought to follow or arise from or even are made necessary by the attainment of distinction and prestige. There is unlimited experience to show that among many men, and especially among women, the real value of differences of money rewards lies in the recognition or distinction assumed to be conferred thereby, or to be procured therewith—one of the reasons why differentials either in money income or in material possessions are a source of jealousy and disruption if not accompanied by other factors of distinction.

(c) Desirable physical conditions of work are often important conscious, and more often important unconscious, inducements to cooperation.

(d) Ideal benefactions as inducements to cooperation are among the most powerful and the most neglected. By ideal benefaction I mean the capacity of organizations to satisfy personal ideals usually relating to non-material, future, or altruistic relations. They include pride of workmanship, sense of adequacy, altruistic service for family or others, loyalty to organization in patriotism, etc., aesthetic and religious feeling. They also include the opportunities for the satisfaction of the motives of hate and revenge, often the controlling factor in adherence to and intensity of effort in some organizations.

All of these inducements—material rewards, personal non-material opportunities, desirable physical conditions, and ideal benefactions—may be and frequently are definitely offered as inducements to contribute to organizations. But there are other conditions which cannot usually be definitely offered, and which are known or recognized by their absence in particular cases. Of these I consider associational attractiveness as exceedingly, and often critically, important.

(e) By associational attractiveness I mean social compatibility. It is in many cases obvious that racial hostility, class antagonism, and national enmities absolutely prevent cooperation, in others decrease its effectiveness, and in still others make it impossible to secure cooperation except by great strengthening of other incentives. But it seems clear that the question of personal compatibility or incompatibility is much more far-reaching in limiting cooperative effort than is recognized, because an intimate knowledge of particular organizations is usually necessary to understand its precise character. When such an intimate knowledge exists, personal compatibility or incompatibility is so thoroughly sensed, and the related problems are so difficult to deal with, that only in special or critical cases is conscious attention given to them. But they can be neglected only at peril of disruption. Men often will not work at all, and will rarely work well, under other incentives if the social situation from their point of view is unsatisfactory. Thus often men of inferior education cannot work well with those of superior education, and vice versa. Differences not merely of race, nation, religion, but of customs, morals, social status, education, ambition, are frequently controlling. Hence, a powerful incentive to the effort of almost all men is favorable associational conditions from their viewpoint.

Personal aversions based upon racial, national, color, and class differences often seem distinctly pernicious; but on the whole they are, in the immediate sense, I believe, based upon a sound feeling of organization necessities. For when there is incompatibility or even merely lack of compatibility, both formal communication and especially communication through informal organization become difficult and sometimes impossible.

(f) Another incentive of the general type is that of customary working conditions and conformity to habitual practices and attitudes. This is made obvious by the universal practice, in all kinds of organization, of rejecting recruits trained in different methods or possessing "foreign" attitudes. It is taken for granted that men will not or cannot do well by strange methods or possessing "foreign" attitudes. It is taken for granted that men will not or cannot do well by strange methods or under strange conditions. What is not so obvious is that men will frequently not attempt to cooperate if they recognize that such methods or conditions are to be accepted.

(g) Another indirect incentive that we may regard as of general and often of controlling importance is the opportunity for the feeling of enlarged participation in the course of events. It affects all classes of men under some conditions. It is sometimes, though not necessarily, related to love of personal distinction and prestige. Its realization is the feeling of importance of result of effort because of the importance of the cooperative effort as a whole. Thus, other things being equal, many men prefer association with large organizations, organizations which they regard as useful, or organizations they regard as effective, as against those they consider small, useless, ineffective.

(h) The most intangible and subtle of incentives is that which I have called the condition of communion. It is related to social compatibilty, but is essentially different. It is the feeling of personal comfort in social relations that is sometimes called solidarity, social integration, the gregarious instinct, or social security (in the original, not in its present debased economic, sense). It is the opportunity for comradeship, for mutual support in personal attitudes. The need for communion is a basis of informal organization that is essential to the operation of every formal organization. It is likewise the basis for informal organization within but hostile to formal organization.

—

Melville Dalton

Ancestry and Conformity

The relations between ethnic identity and success, whether real or imagined, are spelled out in this detailed description and analysis by Melville Dalton (1907-   ), a social researcher who has uniquely blended theory with fact. Milo is a factory in Magnesia, a city in a heavily industrialized region in mid-America known as Mobile Acres. [Melville Dalton, Men Who Manage, New York, 1959, pp. 182-184, 268-270.]

In Mobile Acres, as elsewhere, there were feelings of varying intensity about differences in national origin. Talk of this was of course more open and crude on lower levels than on the higher, but some feeling was common on all levels. Those in the groups least acceptable to the majority naturally missed nothing of the animus against them. Especially, low-level minority staff employees made the common lament of minority groups, "You've got to be twice as smart to get half as far." Obstructors were identified by the repeated charge that there are too many Johnny Bulls and Kraut-eaters around here." At the work level one might find brunette Scottish, Welsh, Irish, Scandinavian, and German extractees referring to those (sometimes blond) of Italian, Polish, Slovak, and Lithuanian descent as "dagoes," "hunkies," and "wops." Thus both majority and minority members identified each other more, or as much, by personal knowledge sharpened by rivalry than by physical traits.

We have already referred to name changing. Workers and first-line foremen of Slavic origin were especially sensitive about their polysyllabic names and the related problem of spelling and pronunciation that brought ridicule on them. Several minority families developed permanent rifts over name changing by the children.

Resentment over failure to rise sometimes led minority persons openly to charge discrimination. Paul Sarto, a first-line foreman of Italian descent, despaired of becoming a general foreman and resented the fact that two German-born associates had reached that level. His resentment exploded during one of the weekly cost meetings held in his department after regular quitting time. Some thirty minutes into these meetings, he typically arose, announced he was going home, and left. On one occasion his chief, Ames, objected. Sarto answered:

I've told you what I had to say and I've listened to you guys beat around the bush for half an hour after quitting time. I've got nothing to stick around here for. I'm not going any higher. I've got the wrong complexion to get any place. I'm going to stay right where I am regardless of how much I do. I don't want any hard feelings about it, but facts are facts. See you tomorrow.

The meaning of other cases was similar.

The alleged exclusive selection by ethnic stock was checked by studying the national origins, surnames, and birthplaces of the managers. This was done in part by personal knowledge, by checking with intimates to uncover name changes and get the family name, by use of personnel records, by free interviewing with doubtful persons, etc.

We see that Sarto was both wrong and right—2 Italians did make the grade of general foreman, but 16 German ethnics did also. The important thing for the minorities though, is that the Anglo-Saxons constituted at least half of each group of managers, that the German ethnics were next in number, and the two together made up all the superintendents. And the Anglo-German combination increased directly from bottom to top. In percentage the Anglo-Saxons were lower and the Germans higher in the staffs than elsewhere. Together they made up 83 per cent of that body, their lowest combined proportions in any group but the first-line foremen.

Differences in the various levels leave little doubt that one's ethnic make-up was a factor in his success. But the differences take on still greater meaning when, as the Milo Catholics did, we look at Magnesia's ethnic pattern. Using a new city directory and making surnames the gauge of national origin, a random sample showed the Anglo-Saxons to make up only 26 per cent, and the Germans 12 per cent, of Magnesia's population. And though only a minority of Milo's dominant ethnics were foreign born, the census data showed that this reservoir in Magnesia was also limited: those born in Germany and the British Isles together constituting less than 15 per cent of the city's population. Thus ethnics composing probably less than 38 per cent of the community filled 85 per cent of Milo's advisory and directive forces.

The storm today for and against the individual's conformity to the larger society and to his career organizations bears on our study. We can indicate the connection under (1) conformity as a means, and (2) conditions promoting conformity.

Conformity as a Means

The individual is a product of groups. In his development from infancy, he conforms to major demands of his group, or seems to when he cannot. If he fails he is punished. Over the years he is shaped by conformity to ever mounting expectations. As a responsible adult he continues to be punished for nonconformity. In the role of say, production worker, he observes output standards, or is excluded as a "rate-buster," an ostracism few can tolerate. As a staff functionary, he must either curb his "free-wheeling" impulses or reduce his career hopes. G. H. Mead makes the point that much human behavior is built up internally and covertly before it reaches overt expression, which it often does not. This is exploratory conformity which, when the individual learns that his fermenting actions will be unacceptable, enables him obligingly to seem to conform. Obviously weariness with the battle, a limitation of every nervous system and habit structure, also forces a measure of conformity.

Thus we need not be confirmed cynics to admit that much conformity is purposeful—though some of it may be an end in itself. We profess to be individualists but find it wise to observe proprieties for the sake of reward. This is an ancient practice. To preserve order and ease of control in the sphere of government, for example, individualistic monarchs from Antiochus IV through Augustus and Lorenzo the Magnificent have clothed their force by seeming conformity to democratic processes. Maturing societies increasingly demand more conformity and control of feelings as a mark of "good-breeding." Other pressures for another kind of conformity are tritely obvious when such societies are also, as with ours, assuming a larger and more dangerous role in world affairs.

The spread of bureaucratic structures requires increasing conformity. This pressure reaches its highest form where corps of specialists are developed to uncover deviations and maintain records of merit and demerit. Here executives with festering egos demand superficial obeisance, if not a clear "yes." As all covertly battle for the enlarged package of honors and rewards that come at each higher level, seeming conformity is saintly and overt individualism is madness.

Conditions Promoting Conformity

In the larger society conformity has become a medium of exchange. Life demands that we be aware of neighbors with whom we are unlikely ever to be intimate because of the rapid events and superficial experiences in which we are all caught up. We know our mobile neighbors are different, but the distractions of our *"ersatz* diversion and synthetic excitement" keep us from knowing how different. In our touch-and-go life we necessarily base many of our actions on flimsy impression. Denied full knowledge, our inconstant relations only spur us to wear a better disguise before those who are stranger than strangers. For even where relations have a pseudo-permanence, we find that many of those with whom we must live are intentionally elusive. Bound to them by an interest, and having to take positions toward things we cannot keep up with, we cooperate to support the front we share. We have no choice but to don a protective coloration as we dip and sample here and there.

In earlier days, before transportation and communication devices shrank our physical world and enlarged our social universe, our organizations were different and our individualism more exposed. Today there are no means of pinning the personality down to one organization. Shifting and tangential society and organizations are increasingly based on front and prefigured defenses. The social façade covers name-changing, religion-changing, and the hiding of one's past, which gears . . . with the necessity in large organizations that status-givers reward in part on the basis of surmises about candidates.* Capability is measured more by fugitive impressions than by testing, because the essential survival abilities are often overlooked as aspirants prepare relevant impressions to fit the irrelevant criteria they must meet.

To deal with the world, the organization must present an inviting exterior and a promise of superior execution. Swamped in doubts, the leader must have assurance of internal loyalty when he acts. Conformity is one assurance he rewards. As T. H. Huxley noted in a famous letter to Herbert Spencer on the question of whether the remains of unconventional George Eliot should rest in Westminster Abbey, "Those who elect to be free in thought and deed must not hanker after the rewards . . . which the world offers to those who put up with its fetters."

In today's vast systems of rationality the individual conforms as he evades their schemes of detection. Some members find room for personal

---

* To my suggestion that he refine his personnel forms for recruitment of staff people, a West Coast executive declared that he had "no time to check on people, and besides they don't put down the facts. I don't mind people lying about their past —we all lie [looking at me challengingly]. I just want them to be able to do what they say they can."

choice and ingenuity as they strain and thrill in meeting appearances. Others conform to avoid conflict and to maintain the demanded tranquillity and uniformity which de Tocqueville saw as the passion of people and government alike in all democratic countries. Such conformity is especially characteristic of American middle class groups today. But many individual managers and workers do "fight the organization" and there are "individual dynamics" as we saw in the anonymous communications, deliberate misinterpretation of rules for personal, protective, and constructive reasons; the unofficial use of materials and services to reward differential contributions, to cement essential relations; the adaptation of labor contracts; and the "agreements between gentlemen," which allow each "to assume that the other is acting honorably even if he is morally certain that he is not."

The typical firm is thus a shifting set of contained disruptions, powered and guided by differentially skilled and committed persons. Its unofficial aspects bulk large but are shrouded in a bureaucratic cloak. To satisfy our eternal urge toward consistency we may call this conformity hypocritical, but we must not hypocritically refuse to recognize its protective function for what it is and denounce as hypocrites those executives who do. Conformity in this sense has a function similar to the built-in but unconscious false appearances among other animals, which biologists call "protective mimicry." The individual in the large organization or mobile society, like the uncalculating animals, is also a defenseless creature who calculatingly practices deception for safety's sake against the invisible threats around him.* Since only isolated fanatics spurn such protective coloration, most of those who attack the practice do so to camouflage their own interests.

---

* These threats are too widely known and believed to be entirely fanciful, and they have long had a function in systems of authority and responsibility. Over four centuries ago a diplomat-historian confidentially advised a practice that is more possible now than then: "When one in authority desires to chastise or revenge himself on an inferior, let him not act hastily, but await time and occasion. For if only he go warily, an opportunity will surely come when, without displaying rancour or passion, he may satisfy his desire either wholly or in part." Francesco Guicciardini, *Ricordi,* S. F. Vanni, New York, 1949, p. 21.

"AND THEN THERE ARE THE
UNOFFICIAL SPECIFICATIONS..."

Vance Packard

Some Types that Seldom Survive

Barriers of sex, education, religion, race, and ethnic background have continued to narrow the pool of talent from which American business leaders are being drawn. Vance Packard (1914-   ), in a popular book from which this selection is taken, spreads a wide net and reveals how pervasive and well established is the tendency toward conformity in the higher echelons of business. [Vance Packard, The Pyramid Climbers, New York, 1962, pp. 29-40.]

> One major automobile corporation instructs its college interviewers to determine if the applicant "looks like us."—Lawrence Bloomgarden, Institute of Human Relations

The screening of candidates permitted to enter the competition on the pyramids of business power is considerably more intensive than the screening of gladiators for the arenas of ancient Rome. Our modern competitor must have a sound body, cool nerves, passable teeth, and a psyche that can survive the tapping of all manner of little rubber hammers. There are the official specifications for position (these may fill several pages). And then there are the unofficial specifications which may never be acknowledged or even realized. Such unwritten knockout factors often prevent a candidate from making even the so-called first list of serious prospects.

Some years ago an admiring book, *America's Fifty Foremost Business Leaders,* edited by B. C. Forbes, made this remarkable statement: "Neither birth nor education, neither nationality nor religion, neither heredity nor environment are passports or obstacles to the highest success in this land of democracy." Only "worth," he said, counts.

This happy bit of mythology has rarely fitted the situation that prevails in large business organizations as a whole and it has little relevance in the sixties. One accident of birth alone virtually eliminates from serious consideration half the human race residing within the U.S.—the elimination that occurs when an applicant for a management post is asked to check the appropriate box containing the letter M or F. A check in the F box is usually a knockout factor.

I am uneasily aware that . . . I have used the pronoun *he* exclusively in referring to "the executive." Feminine readers might think me guilty of a male conceit. The word he, like the word man, can of course blanket both sexes in general usage. In the case of writing about the modern executive, however, I am being reasonably precise in using *he* in its specific gender sense. Although nearly four out of ten jobholders in the U.S.A. now are female, women rarely attain the executive suites of substantial corporations except in secretarial capacities. They are perhaps the most discriminated-against of all minority groups in industry. A Harvard doctoral dissertation by David Carson on executive-training programs for supermarket chains contains this sentence: "The selection process for the executive training program at (name of chain) was specifically designed for men only, and 'Manpower Inventory' in this company—and in the others included in this study— meant Male only."

In the early fifties the Harvard Business School's division of research sent a research team into ninety-five business organizations to study executive opportunities for women. Its report said: "Very few women were found to be holding top executive jobs in the sense of corporate officers or senior executives. A number of women in a variety of fields, however, were found in positions of 'second in command.'" Several executives indicated that this was the highest level a woman could hope to attain in the near future. The prevailing sentiment was expressed by the head of a Chicago management-consulting firm in these terms: "The highest position that women are going to reach in the foreseeable future in any large numbers is that of assistant to a top executive. This will be primarily an expansion of the secretarial function!"

The shutout of women is gradually easing. Women who reach the higher levels of sizable organizations, however, still tend to represent special situations or achieve their success within special fields more open to women than most. Many of the women heading corporations are the widows of former owners. A few others attained their eminence without family connections but started with the company when it was small. The best opportunities for women to rise to at least the department-head level appear to be in personnel, research, accounting, advertising, publishing, and design. General Foods had a woman as vice-president in early 1962; so did McGraw-Hill and a number of major advertising agencies.

Women are presently considered more acceptable in "inside" jobs than "outside" jobs, where they would have to deal with outside businessmen. It is often considered risky to startle this outsider by assigning a woman to deal with him.

One of the best areas of opportunity for women is in department stores, possibly because they sell primarily to women. A vice-president of a large department-store chain advises: "We had a vice-president in charge of advertising for several years who was a woman at seventy-five thousand a year and she could have stayed. We have a dozen women in the thirty-to-thirty-five-thousand-dollar class." Women also occasionally hold important positions in banks. One analysis of ninety-four banks in Michigan revealed that women were officers in three of them.

Male executives have developed a number of explanations and rationalizations to account for the prevailing barrier against women. The women are accused both of making too much of the job and of not being sufficiently dedicated to it. One merchandiser who has had considerable experience in dealing with women as executives said: "Their only defect comes down to an inability to wear epaulets lightly. When they succeed in avoiding this weakness—which perhaps developed out of their struggles to win recognition—our company has no difficulty in keeping young men working under their direction." (That, of course, was a male talking.) If they are unmarried, the possibility that they will marry and leave represents the kind of major uncontrollable factor that worries many corporate managers. Whether they marry or not, they are less likely than men to strive for the usual reasons of economic anxiety—"my wife's country-club bill, a house in Scarsdale, two sons in college, and a daughter who expects a five-thousand-dollar wedding in June," as one middle-aged executive described his economic anxieties to me.

One barrier blocking many women from real advancement in the typical corporation is the fact that in large cities executives are often expected to lunch at an approved local executive club. Many of these will either not permit a woman on the premises or allow them to enter only by a side door. Cleveland Amory reports that New York's

Hemisphere Club became the first important executive luncheon club to recognize by its admission policy that executives can be F as well as M.

A second convenient and widespread way of screening out unlikely candidates among would-be executives is to throw out all applicants who write None where the candidate is asked to list his college degree or degrees. This will still eliminate nearly nine out of ten U.S. males.

A college diploma is becoming an almost universal requirement for admission to the management group. Many companies tell clerical and production-line workers that there is room at the top for the best of them. But in recent years only one top manager in ten has come from such a background, and the number will decrease.

In projecting what management will be like in the 1980s, Harold J. Leavitt, professor of industrial administration and psychology at Carnegie Tech, notes: "Apprenticeship as a basis for training managers will be used less and less, since movement up through the line will become increasingly unlikely. Top management training will be taken over increasingly by the universities."

The study of executive training for supermarkets cited earlier has this to say about the role of education: "In general the supermarket trade is changing its approach toward the selection of junior executives from haphazard choice of experienced men from the rank and file to the rational selection of novices who show promise of developing into competent executives. Some companies tend to overlook company employees in their enthusiasm to exploit other sources, such as colleges." It quoted one executive as offering this explanation: "It's so easy for any young person to attend college today that I wonder about the intelligence and the ambition of those who don't." (This might be considered debatable, despite increased enrollments, in view of the fact that college costs have been rising faster than family income and the fact that two thirds of the brightest young people in the land —those with IQs of higher than 117—have not had the benefit of a college diploma.)

The most startling explanation for the insistence on a diploma was offered by an executive taking part in a round table on executive potential sponsored by the McKinsey Foundation for Management Research. He said: "We desperately need a means of screening. Education is one quick means of preliminary screening without having to think too much about it."

About two thirds of today's present top managers are college graduates and another 10 per cent have spent some time in college. It should be remembered, however, that such men exemplify the opportunities for management training that existed a quarter-century ago. Today the proportion of beginners in management training who have college degrees is closer to 90 per cent.

In 1957 the American Management Association made an analysis of the careers of 335 company presidents to find what clues their careers suggested for ambitious young men now. Conclusion Number 1, according to one account, was: "Go to college. Princeton if you can make it. But in any case get a sheepskin." An official of the AMA told me: "The guy who has just a high school education is not much in evidence (in executive circles) any more. Most of the guys who come to our meetings and seminars are college graduates." He felt there had been a clear change in this respect in the past decade. William A. Hertan, president of Executive Manpower Corporation (headquarters New York City), points out that there is now so much stress on the college degree that one candidate in twelve seeking an executive post falsifies his record to give himself a degree.

Entrance requirements aside, the evidence that a man must have a college education to succeed as an executive in many fields of business is somewhat less than overwhelming. In a check I made of some of the spectacular stories of fortune-building through entrepreneurial success in recent years, most of the men had never been near a college. A University of Wyoming sociologist, Dr. Edwin G. Flittie, spent a month observing executives at the headquarters of a major utility company in the West. Afterward he commented:

In some companies advancement beyond a certain point is contingent upon college training. In carefully observing management employees during the interviews I have concluded that those at the level of middle management or above who have had no college training possess as much poise, sophistication and social adeptness as those who possess a college background. Further, the verbal abilities of these people in terms of fluency and proper usage of English are at least equal to those of most of the college-trained people. Certain of these men were almost apologetic in talking to me (a college professor) for their lack of college training. It is my opinion that most of these men are at least as well qualified to perform their jobs as their college-trained associates. I would include several of these "noncollege" managers as among the most outstanding people with whom I had contact.

Certain industries are much more flexible than others about requiring a college diploma. Until recently the railroad industry did not disqualify good prospects because they had no college degrees. Merchandisers have been the least insistent of all about the diploma. They go by results. The man who doesn't produce, and quickly, is out—regardless of his academic pedigree.

U.S. companies are not alone in having upgraded educational requirements for their managers. In the Soviet Union and in France there is a general insistence that management candidates have the equivalent of a college education. Professor David Granick of the University of Wisconsin found that all plant directors on the Leningrad Regional

Economic Council were college graduates, as were most of the rest of the council's staff. Russian managers seem to run heavily to engineers. On the other hand, in West Germany, which has been undergoing a sensational business growth, relatively little stress is placed on educational background, according to Professor Granick in his recent report, *The European Business Executive.*

The most formidable educational requirements I've personally encountered operate in Japan. To enter the management of a major company there a man must not only have a college degree but he must also land his job within the first year after graduation. Otherwise he must try a smaller company. Furthermore, nearly three quarters of the men accepted by major companies are graduates of a specific university—the University of Tokyo.

A third general category of people who are often screened out in wholesale lots at an early stage of the selection are the non-WASPs. The non-WASPs who survive the preliminary screening usually must have a lot more going for them in the way of qualifications than WASP candidates in order to be accepted and to make much headway up the sides of the typical modern business pyramid.

A WASP—as originally defined by sociologist Digby Baltzell—is a White Anglo-Saxon Protestant. WASPs have traditionally been the in-group of the U.S. business world. They have been the gate-keepers to management of most large industries and financial institutions, notwithstanding the cheery assertion in *America's Fifty Foremost Business Leaders* that "neither nationality nor religion, neither heredity nor environment" have been obstacles to great success. To a large extent, the WASPs still are the in-group, although some moves have recently been made toward less flatly rejecting non-WASPs.

An early rationale for confining executive selection to a homogeneous group was developed in the late thirties by telephone executive Chester I. Barnard in his still widely read *The Functions of the Executive* (now in its fourteenth printing). Barnard listed as incentives to get executives to work more smoothly together the possibility of "communion" and "social compatibility" and "comfort in social relations." From such concepts he leaped into the idea that often "men cannot be promoted or selected, or even must be relieved because . . . they 'do not fit,' even where there is no question of formal competence. This question of 'fitness' involves such matters as education, experience, age, sex, personal distinctions, prestige, race, nationality, faith, politics, sectional antecedents; and such very specific personal traits as manners, speech, personal appearance, etc." That was quite a mouthful, and some believe that whatever his intention, the statements have had a profound influence in serving to encourage the WASPs in their conviction that fellow WASPs make the best colleagues for the executive suite.

One non-WASP who usually has difficulty getting a nod from the gatekeepers of larger enterprises is the Jew. Approximately 8 per cent of the college-trained population of the United States is Jewish. Against this, consider the fact that Jews constitute less than one half of 1 per cent of the total executive personnel in leading American industrial companies.

This startling statistic can scarcely be due to any lack of interest or aptitude on the part of Jewish college graduates. The world's most famous—and perhaps most difficult—graduate school for business administration is at Harvard University. One graduate in seven who emerges from this school is Jewish. You get quite a different ratio, however, when you look at the middle-aged managers U.S. industry sends to Harvard each year to take part in the school's Advanced Management Program. These are men who are usually being groomed for important positions. Harvard has no control over the selection of the men who are sent. They are chosen by the participating companies. One person who has watched this program at close range for some years estimates that the proportion of Jewish managers sent to participate has been about one in two hundred!

An official of the American Jewish Committee who tries to keep abreast of employment practices affecting executives has made a study of the management of many major companies. He reports: "We went over a directory containing the names of two thousand management people at U.S. Steel very thoroughly with knowledgeable people. Even making allowance for questionable cases, we could find only nine or ten Jewish managers there at that time."

A study of the management roster of a paper-making company turned up only one Jewish executive out of 1500, and he was in research. A detailed study of the 1028 top officials of Philadelphia's six leading banks revealed that only six were Jewish.

One curious fact is that several of the corporate giants that were pioneered by Jews or got much of their growth under Jewish leadership have gradually fallen into patterns pretty much like those of industry as a whole. The proportion of Jews among the younger executives at Sears, Roebuck and Radio Corporation of America is pretty much like that found in other giant companies. Those present—as in most of the industrial giants—are likely to be mainly clustered in advisory or creative "inside" staff jobs as in research. They are steered away from the main "line" of authority posts and from positions calling for a good deal of "outside contact." In short, the discriminatory pattern for Jewish executives is much what it is for that other minority group, women executives.

Some fields of industry and finance are much more exclusionary than others in regard to Jews. The industries that seem least receptive to the idea that Jews can be executives are automobile manufacturing, commercial banking, insurance, public utilities, and such heavy industries as steel, coal, and oil. An official of the AJC has stated that at the top levels of virtually all of the nation's hundred largest industrial corporations—particularly those operating in the steel, automotive, chemical, petroleum, and electrical-equipment fields—all levels of management positions remain closed to Jews. A similar situation is found in the fifty largest American financial institutions.

Perhaps as a result of this apparent lack of opportunity on the giant pyramids, especially the more conservative ones, Jews have tended to concentrate in fields that have been fairly recently pioneered, such as mass communications and mass entertainment, or fields that require an unusual amount of risk-taking venturesomeness, such as merchandising and investment banking.

In the past year or so, some slight increase in open-mindedness about Jews has been noted in a number of the large industrial companies. And in a few, signs of a new liberalism have developed which officials of the American Jewish Committee consider most hopeful. American Motors (which has been headed by George Romney, a Mormon) has been showing a liberal viewpoint toward Jewish managers that is startling in an industry that has long had a closed mind on the subject. The leadership at International Business Machines has advanced a Jew to vice-presidency (research and development) and is taking other steps to shake up old, frozen attitudes. At Reynolds Aluminum the director of research is Jewish.

Studies are under way at four universities—Harvard, Cornell, Michigan, and California—to try to get a better understanding of the prejudices at work in the selection and development of managers. (The AJC expects that these studies will help considerably in bringing about a change of attitudes.) The Harvard investigators, under Dr. Lewis B. Ward, have been following the careers of twenty-five Jewish and twenty-five gentile graduates as they progress in forty different companies.

Dr. Ward comments that one significant contrast seems apparent between the companies that do not hire Jewish people for management and those that do: the companies with no Jews seem to have more organization-man types and "put considerably more store in adjustment and modesty and lack of troublesomeness. The companies hiring Jewish boys, on the other hand, are much more tolerant of positive qualities that might be troublesome, such as intelligence, aggressiveness, and so on. I get the feeling that what they are telling us is that 'we are willing to try to get along with someone that will not fit into the job easily in order to get a gain in creativity, motivation, and intelligence.' " He also noted the paradox that some of the managements which seem most democratic with regard to hiring minorities appear to be among the more arbitrary in their treatment of subordinates. There is less emphasis upon keeping subordinates informed and soliciting their opinions before making decisions.

The preference for WASPs in most of the major executive suites also affects Catholic candidates—particularly those of Italian or Slavic background—though less drastically. A good example of the difference was reported by Seymour Freedgood when he studied a hundred-odd auto executives living in the Bloomfield Hills area outside Detroit. He reported of these executives: "In one case out of ten he is a Roman Catholic of Irish or Italian ancestry. None of the hundred top auto executives is a Jew, and no Jewish families live in Bloomfield Hills proper."

Sociologist Melville Dalton, in his study of informal factors influencing the careers of 226 people on one corporate pyramid, concluded that being Catholic was a real handicap.

An interesting pattern of Protestant-Catholic division can be seen in the insurance companies in Manhattan. They tend to be either predominantly Protestant or predominantly Catholic. This separation is so drastic that the Catholic-dominated companies are clustered in parts of the financial district different from the Protestant-dominated companies. For example, John Street is predominantly Protestant, Maiden Lane predominantly Catholic. William Street is split down the middle on the basis of religious dominance.

The fields in which Catholics appear to be most heavily represented are the railroads and public utilities. Social historian Moses Rischin surmises that the one big reason Catholics are strong in the railroads is that in the early days of the railroads Irish laborers played a major role in their building. In those days it was easier to move up into management from a laboring position. Less stress was placed on proof of education. Dr. Rischin attributes the prominence of Catholics in the public-utilities field to the Irish role in municipal politics in the years when utilities were being established. "The political, administrative and organizational gifts of the Irish proved especially congenial in these fields," he adds.

A final large group that is eliminated by the WASP formula, of course, is the millions of people whose skin happens to be something other than pinkish-beige. The absence of dark-skinned people in the management ranks of major corporations is virtually absolute.

Some of the graduate schools of business administration have had Negro students, but the impression is that virtually all have gone into business for themselves or into Negro-run businesses. Some banks have started hiring Negroes for clerical jobs. In 1961 the first Negro appeared on the floor of the New York Stock Exchange in a role other than that of runner or clerk. He was a customer's man, a difficult and responsible role. Early in 1962 Pepsi-Cola named a Negro, Harvey C. Russell, to a newly created vice-presidency. He has been directing the company's activities in reaching the Negro and Spanish market. As this is written, the New York State Commission Against Discrimination has launched a campaign to create a climate in which it will be possible for Negroes to have a chance to become executives in business and industry. But that's about all that can be said for now.

All of these categorical grounds for screening out candidates because of sex, education, religion, race, and ethnic background greatly narrow the field of executive possibilities. These limiting factors also help account for the close and restricted climate in which the candidates who *are* chosen will have to function.

═══

William H. Whyte, Jr.

How to Cheat on Personality Tests

*The imperatives of organization have been bred into a bevy of tests
tailored to ferret out the nonconformists. Although the professional
testers, committed to objectivity, would deny that their personality tests
are the voice of the Organization, William H. Whyte, Jr., (1917-
) attempts to demonstrate that the tests do not test anything but
potential loyalty.* [*William H. Whyte, Jr.*, The Organization Man,
New York, 1956, pp. 180-181, 405-410.]

COMPOSITE PERSONALITY TEST

Self-Report Questions
1) Have you enjoyed reading books as much as having company in?
2) Are you sometimes afraid of failure?
3) Do you sometimes feel self-conscious?
4) Does it annoy you to be interrupted in the middle of your work?
5) Do you prefer serious motion pictures about famous historical
personalities to musical comedies?

Indicate whether you agree, disagree, or are uncertain:
6) I am going to Hell.
7) I often get pink spots all over.
8) The sex act is repulsive.
9) I like strong-minded women.

10) Strange voices speak to me.

11) My father is a tyrant.

Hypothetical Question—Dominance Type

12) You have been waiting patiently for a salesperson to wait on you. Just when she's finished with another customer, a woman walks up abruptly and demands to be waited upon before you. What would you do?

a) Do nothing

b) Push the woman to one side

c) Give her a piece of your mind

d) Comment about her behavior to the salesperson

Opinion Questions: Degree of Conservatism

Indicate whether you agree or disagree with the following questions:

13) Prostitution should be state supervised.

14) Modern art should not be allowed in churches.

15) It is worse for a woman to have extramarital relations than for a man.

16) Foreigners are dirtier than Americans.

17) "The Star-Spangled Banner" is difficult to sing properly.

Word Association Questions

Underline the word you think goes best with the word in capitals:

18) UMBRELLA (rain, prepared, cumbersome, appeasement)

19) RED (hot, color, stain, blood)

20) GRASS (green, mow, lawn, court)

21) NIGHT (dark, sleep, moon, morbid)

22) NAKED (nude, body, art, evil)

23) AUTUMN (fall, leaves, season, sad)

Hypothetical Situations—Judgment Type

24) What would you do if you saw a woman holding a baby at the window of a burning house:

a) Call the fire department

b) Rush into the house

c) Fetch a ladder

d) Try and catch the baby

25) Which do you think is the best answer for the executive to make in the following situation:

Worker: "Why did Jones get the promotion and I didn't?"

Executive:

a) "You deserved it but Jones has seniority."

b) "You've got to work harder."

c) "Jones's uncle owns the plant."

d) "Let's figure out how you can improve."

Opinion Questions: Policy Type

    26) A worker's home life is not the concern of the company.

        Agree.............   Disagree...........

    27) Good supervisors are born, not made.

        Agree.............   Disagree...........

    28) It should be company policy to encourage off-hours participation by employees in company-sponsored social gatherings, clubs, and teams.

        Agree.............   Disagree...........

Opinion Questions: Value Type

    29) When you look at a great skyscraper, do you think of:

    a) our tremendous industrial growth

    b) the simplicity and beauty of the structural design

    30) Who helped mankind most?

    a) Shakespeare

    b) Sir Isaac Newton

The important thing to recognize is that you don't win a good score: you avoid a bad one. What a bad score would be depends upon the particular profile the company in question intends to measure you against, and this varies according to companies and according to the type of work. Your score is usually rendered in terms of your percentile rating —that is, how you answer questions in relation to how other people have answered them. Sometimes it is perfectly all right for you to score in the 80th or 90th percentile: if you are being tested, for example, to see if you would make a good chemist, a score indicating that you are likely to be more reflective than ninety out of a hundred adults might not harm you and might even do you some good.

By and large, however, your safety lies in getting a score somewhere between the 40th and 60th percentiles, which is to say, you should try to answer as if you were like everybody else is supposed to be. This is not always too easy to figure out, of course, and this is one of the reasons why I will go into some detail in the following paragraphs on the principal types of questions. When in doubt, however, there are two general rules you can follow: (1) When asked for word associations or comments about the world, give the most conventional, run-of-the-mill, pedestrian answer possible. (2) To settle on the most beneficial answer to any question, repeat to yourself:

    a) I loved my father and my mother, but my father a little bit more.

    b) I like things pretty well the way they are.

    c) I never worry much about anything.

    d) I don't care for books or music much.

    e) I love my wife and children.

    f) I don't let them get in the way of company work.

Now to specifics. The first five questions in the composite test are examples of the ordinary, garden variety of self-report questions.[1] Generally speaking, they are designed to reveal your degree of introversion or extroversion, your stability, and such. While it is true that in these "inventory" types of tests there is not a right or wrong answer to any *one* question, cumulatively you can get yourself into a lot of trouble if you are not wary. "Have you enjoyed reading books as much as having company in?" "Do you sometimes feel self-conscious?"—You can easily see what is being asked for here.

Stay in character. The trick is to mediate yourself a score as near the norm as possible without departing too far from your own true self. It won't necessarily hurt you, for example, to say that you have enjoyed reading books as much as having company in. It will hurt you, however, to answer every such question in that vein if you are, in fact, the kind that does enjoy books and a measure of solitude. Strive for the happy mean; on one hand, recognize that a display of too much introversion, a desire for reflection, or sensitivity is to be avoided. On the other hand, don't overcompensate. If you try too hard to deny these qualities in yourself, you'll end so far on the other end of the scale as to be rated excessively insensitive or extroverted. If you are somewhat introverted, then, don't strive to get yourself in the 70th or 80th percentile for extroversion, but merely try to get up into the 40th percentile.

Since you will probably be taking not one, but a battery of tests, you must be consistent. The tester will be comparing your extroversion

1. Leading tests of this type include:

The Personality Inventory by Robert G. Bernreuter. Published by The Stanford University Press, Stanford, California. Copyright 1935 by The Board of Trustees of Leland Stanford Junior University. All rights reserved.

125 questions; measures several different things at once; scoring keys available for neurotic tendency; self-sufficiency; introversion-extroversion; dominance-submission; self-confidence; sociability.

Thurstone Temperament Schedule by L. L. Thurstone. Copyright 1949 by L. L. Thurstone. Published by Science Research Associates, Chicago. Ill. 140 questions. Measures, at once, seven areas of temperament; to wit, degree to which one is active, vigorous, impulsive, dominant, stable, sociable, reflective. "The primary aim of the Thurstone Temperament Schedule . . . is to evaluate an individual in terms of his relatively permanent temperament traits. One of the values of the schedule is that it helps provide an objective pattern, or profile, of personal traits which you can use to predict probable success or failure in a particular situation."

Minnesota T-S-E Inventory by M. Catherine Evans and T. R. McConnell. Copyright 1942 by Science Research Associates, Chicago, Ill.

150 questions. Measures three types of introversion-extroversion—thinking, social, and emotional.

The Personal Audit by Clifford R. Adams and William M. Lepley, Psycho-Educational Clinic, Pennsylvania State College. Published by Science Research Associates, Chicago, Ill. Copyright 1945 by Clifford R. Adams. All rights reserved.

450 questions. Nine parts, of 50 questions each. Each part measures "a relatively independent component of personality." Extremes of each trait listed thus: seriousness-impulsiveness; firmness-indecision; tranquillity-irritability; frankness-evasion; stability-instability; tolerance-intolerance; steadiness-emotionality; persistence fluctuation; contentment-worry.

score on one test with, say, your sociability score on another, and if these don't correlate the way the tables say they should, suspicion will be aroused. Even when you are taking only one test, consistency is important. Many contain built-in L ("lie") scores, and woe betide you if you answer some questions as if you were a life of the party type and others as if you were an excellent follower. Another pitfall to avoid is giving yourself the benefit of the doubt on all questions in which one answer is clearly preferable to another, viz.: "Do you frequently day-dream?" In some tests ways have been worked out to penalize you for this. (By the same token, occasionally you are given credit for excessive frankness. But you'd better not count on it.)

Be emphatic to the values of the test maker. Question five asks:

"Do you prefer serious motion pictures about famous historical personalities to musical comedies?" If you answer this question honestly you are quite likely to get a good score for the wrong reasons. If you vote for the musical comedies, you are given a credit for extroversion. It might be, of course, that you are a very thoughtful person who dislikes the kind of pretentious, self-consciously arty "prestige" pictures which Hollywood does badly, and rather enjoy the musical comedies which it does well. The point illustrated here is that, before answering such questions, you must ask yourself which of the alternatives the test maker, not yourself, would regard as the more artistic.

Choose your neurosis. When you come across questions that are like the ones from 6 to 11—"I often get pink spots all over"—be very much on your guard. Such questions were originally a by-product of efforts to screen mentally disturbed people; they measure degrees of neurotic tendency and were meant mainly for use in mental institutions and psychiatric clinics.[2] The Organization has no business at all to throw these questions at you, but its curiosity is powerful and some companies have been adopting these tests as standard. Should you find yourself being asked about spiders, Oedipus complexes, and such, you must, even more than in the previous type of test, remain consistent and as much in character as possible—these tests almost always have lie scores built into them. A few mild neuroses conceded here and there won't give you too bad a score, and in conceding neuroses you should know that more often than not you have the best margin for error if you err on the side of being "hypermanic"—that is, too energetic and active.

Don't be too dominant. Question 12, which asks you what you would

2. Outstanding example is the *Minnesota Multiphasic Personality Inventory,* Revised Edition, by Starke R. Hathaway and J. Charnley McKinley. Published by The Psychological Corporation, N. Y. 495 questions. This yields scores on hypochondriasis, depression, hysteria, psychopathic deviation, masculinity and femininity, paranoia, psychoasthenia, schizophrenia, hypomania. It also yields a score on the subject's "test-taking attitude," with a score for his degree of "defensiveness-frankness." If the subject consistently gives himself the benefit of the doubt, or vice versa, the scoring reveals the fact. This is not a test for the amateur to trifle with.

do if somebody barged in ahead of you in a store, is fairly typical of the kind of questions designed to find out how passive or dominant you may be. As always, the middle course is best. Resist the temptation to show yourself as trying to control each situation. You might think companies would prefer that characteristic to passivity, but they often regard it as a sign that you wouldn't be a permissive kind of leader. To err slightly on the side of acquiescence will rarely give you a bad score.

Incline to conservatism. Questions 13 through 17, which ask you to comment on a variety of propositions, yield a measure of how conservative or radical your views are.[3] To go to either extreme earns you a bad score, but in most situations you should resolve any doubts you have on a particular question by deciding in favor of the accepted.

Similarly with word associations. In questions 18 through 23, each word in capitals is followed by four words, ranging from the conventional to the somewhat unusual. The trouble here is that if you are not a totally conventional person you may be somewhat puzzled as to what the conventional response is. Here is one tip: before examining any one question closely and reading it from left to right, read vertically through the whole list of questions and you may well see a definite pattern. In making up tests, testers are thinking of ease in scoring, and on some test forms the most conventional responses will be found in one column, the next most conventional in the next, and so on. All you have to do then is go down the list and pick, alternately, the most conventional, and the second most conventional. Instead of a high score for emotionalism, which you might easily get were you to proceed on your own, you earn a stability score that will indicate "normal ways of thinking."

Don't split hairs. When you come to hypothetical situations designed to test your judgment, you have come to the toughest of all questions.[4] In this kind there are correct answers, and the testers make no bones about it. Restricted as the choice is, however, determining which are the correct ones is extremely difficult, and the more intelligent you

3. An example of this kind of testing is the *Conservatism-Radicalism Opinionaire* by Theodore F. Lentz and Colleagues of The Attitude Research Laboratory. Published by Character Research Association, Washington University, St. Louis, Mo., Dept. of Education. Copyright 1935. 60 statements are given; the subject indicates whether he tends to agree or disagree. His score is obtained by checking the number of times he sides with the conservative statement side *vs.* the radical one.

4. Two tests of this type are:

Tests of Practical Judgment by Alfred J. Cardall, N.B.A., Ed.D. Published by Science Research Associates, Inc., Chicago, Ill. Copyright 1942, 1950 by Science Research Associates, Inc. All rights reserved. 48 Forced-choice questions "designed to measure the element of practical judgment as it operates in everyday business and social situations." How were the "best" answers chosen? "Rigorous statistical analysis was supplemented by consensus of authority. . . ."

Practical Social Judgment by Thomas N. Jenkins, Ph.D. Copyright 1947. All rights reserved. Executive Analysis Corporation, N. Y. 52 questions about hypothetical situations; subject must choose the "best" and the "poorest" of given answers.

are the more difficult. One tester, indeed, states that the measurement of practical judgment is "unique and statistically independent of such factors as intelligence, and academic and social background." He has a point. Consider the question about the woman and the baby at the window of the burning house. It is impossible to decide which is the best course of action unless you know how big the fire is, whether she is on the first floor or the second, whether there is a ladder handy, how near by the fire department is, plus a number of other considerations.

On this type of question, let me confess that I can be of very little help to the reader. I have made a very thorough study of these tests, have administered them to many people of unquestioned judgment, and invariably the results have been baffling. But there does seem to be one moral: don't think too much. The searching mind is severely handicapped by such forced choices and may easily miss what is meant to be the obviously right answer. Suppress this quality in yourself by answering these questions as quickly as you possibly can, with practically no pause for reflection.

The judgment questions from 25 through 28 are much easier to answer.[5] The right answers here are, simply, those which represent sound personnel policy, and this is not hard to figure out. Again, don't quibble. It is true enough that it is virtually impossible to tell the worker why he didn't get promoted unless you know whether he was a good worker, or a poor one, or whether Jones's uncle did in fact own the plant (in which case, candor could be eminently sensible). The mealy-mouthed answer d)—"Let's figure out how you can improve"—is the "right" answer. Similarly with questions about the worker's home life. It isn't the concern of the company, but it is modern personnel dogma that it should be, and therefore "agree" is the right answer. So with the questions about whether good supervisors are born or made. To say that a good supervisor is born deprecates the whole apparatus of modern organization training, and that kind of attitude won't get you anywhere.

Know your company. Questions 29 and 30 are characteristic of the kind of test that attempts to measure the relative emphasis you attach to certain values—such as aesthetic, economic, religious, social.[6] The profile of you it produces is matched against the profile that the com-

---

5. An example of this kind of test is *How Supervise?* by Quentin W. File, edited by H. H. Remmers. Published by The Psychological Corporation, N. Y. Copyright 1948, by Purdue Research Foundation, Lafayette, Indiana. 100 questions on management policy and attitudes.

6. *A Study of Values*, Revised Edition, by Gordon W. Allport, Philip E. Vernan, and Gardner Lindzey. Copyright 1951, by Gordon W. Allport, Philip E. Vernan, and Gardner Lindzey. Copyright 1931 by Gordon W. Allport and Philip E. Vernan. Published by Houghton, Mifflin Co.

45 forced-choice questions. Answers are scored to give a measure of the relative prominence of six motives in a person: theoretical, economic, aesthetic, social, political, and religious. A profile is charted to show how he varies from the norm on each of the six.

pany thinks is desirable. To be considered as a potential executive, you will probably do best when you emphasize economic motivation the most; aesthetic and religious, the least. In question 29, accordingly, you should say the skyscraper makes you think of industrial growth. Theoretical motivation is also a good thing; if you were trying out for the research department, for example, you might wish to say that you think Sir Isaac Newton helped mankind more than Shakespeare and thereby increase your rating for theoretical learning. Were you trying out for a public relations job, however, you might wish to vote for Shakespeare, for a somewhat higher aesthetic score would not be amiss in this case.

There are many more kinds of tests and there is no telling what surprises the testers will come up with in the future. But the principles will probably change little, and by obeying a few simple precepts and getting yourself in the right frame of mind, you have the wherewithal to adapt to any new testing situation. In all of us there is a streak of normalcy.

VI

The Dilemmas
of Maturity

The individualist ethic and the organization ethic each generated distinctive and representative types of success, but both seemed obsolete. At mid-twentieth century it had become apparent that a new "autonomous" type was emerging, able to grapple with human and technological complexities that neither the organization ethic nor the individualist ethic had anticipated.

Joseph A. Schumpeter

The Obsolescence of the Entrepreneurial Function

The advanced bureaucratic society has in many aspects of its organiza-
tion approached the military. Joseph Schumpeter (1883-1950), the
economist, has argued that we may be approaching a stage when the
classic entrepreneur, who has played the strategic role in the economy,
will become an anachronism and business itself will no longer attract
the highly talented and energetic. [Joseph A. Schumpeter, Capitalism,
Socialism and Democracy, *3rd ed., New York, 1950, pp. 131-134.]*

In our discussion of the theory of vanishing investment opportunity, a reservation was made in favor of the possibility that the economic wants of humanity might some day be so completely satisfied that little motive would be left to push productive effort still further ahead. Such a state of satiety is no doubt very far off even if we keep within the present scheme of wants; and if we take account of the fact that, as higher standards of life are attained, these wants automatically expand and new wants emerge or are created, satiety becomes a flying goal, particularly if we include leisure among consumers' goods. However, let us glance at that possibility, assuming, still more unrealistically, that methods of production have reached a state of perfection which does not admit of further improvement.

A more or less stationary state would ensue. Capitalism, being essentially an evolutionary process, would become atrophic. There would be nothing left for entrepreneurs to do. They would find themselves in much the same situation as generals would in a society perfectly sure of permanent peace. Profits and along with profits the rate of interest would converge toward zero. The bourgeois strata that live on profits and interest would tend to disappear. The management of industry and trade would become a matter of current administration, and the personnel would unavoidably acquire the characteristics of a bureaucracy. Socialism of a very sober type would almost automatically come into being. Human energy would turn away from business. Other than economic pursuits would attract the brains and provide the adventure.

For the calculable future this vision is of no importance. But all the greater importance attaches to the fact that many of the effects on the structure of society and on the organization of the productive process that we might expect from an approximately complete satisfaction of wants or from absolute technological perfection can also be expected from a development that is clearly observable already. Progress itself may be mechanized as well as the management of a stationary economy, and this mechanization of progress may affect entrepreneurship and capitalist society nearly as much as the cessation of economic progress would. In order to see this it is only necessary to restate, first, what the entrepreneurial function consists in and, secondly, what it means for bourgeois society and the survival of the capitalist order.

We have seen that the function of entrepreneurs is to reform or revolutionize the pattern of production by exploiting an invention or, more generally, an untried technological possibility for producing a new commodity or producing an old one in a new way, by opening up a new source of supply of materials or a new outlet for products, by reorganizing an industry and so on. Railroad construction in its earlier stages, electrical power production before the First World War, steam and steel, the motorcar, colonial ventures afford spectacular instances of a large genus which comprises innumerable humbler ones —down to such things as making a success of a particular kind of sausage or toothbrush. This kind of activity is primarily responsible for the recurrent "prosperities" that revolutionize the economic organism and the recurrent "recessions" that are due to the disequilibrating impact of the new products or methods. To undertake such new things is difficult and constitutes a distinct economic function, first, because they lie outside of the routine tasks which everybody understands and, secondly, because the environment resists in many ways that vary, according to social conditions, from simple refusal either to finance or to buy a new thing, to physical attack on the man who tries to produce it. To act with confidence beyond the range of familiar beacons and to overcome that resistance requires aptitudes that are present in only a small fraction of the population and that define the entrepreneurial type as well as the entrepreneurial function. This function does not essentially consist in either inventing anything or otherwise creating the conditions which the enterprise exploits. It consists in getting things done.

This social function is already losing importance and is bound to lose it at an accelerating rate in the future even if the economic process itself of which entrepreneurship was the prime mover went on unabated. For, on the one hand, it is much easier now than it has been in the past to do things that lie outside familiar routine—innovation itself is being reduced to routine. Technological progress is increasingly becoming the business of teams of trained specialists who turn out what is required and make it work in predictable ways. The romance of earlier commercial adventure is rapidly wearing away, because so many more things can be strictly calculated that had of old to be visualized in a flash of genius.

On the other hand, personality and will power must count for less in environments which have become accustomed to economic change— best instanced by an incessant stream of new consumers' and producers' goods—and which, instead of resisting, accept it as a matter of course. The resistance which comes from interests threatened by an innovation in the productive process is not likely to die out as long as the capitalist order persists. It is, for instance, the great obstacle on the road toward mass production of cheap housing which presupposes radical mechanization and wholesale elimination of inefficient methods of work on the plot. But every other kind of resistance—the resistance, in particular, of consumers and producers to a new kind of thing because it is new —has well-nigh vanished already.

Thus, economic progress tends to become depersonalized and automatized. Bureau and committee work tends to replace individual action. Once more, reference to the military analogy will help to bring out the essential point.

Of old, roughly up to and including the Napoleonic Wars, generalship meant leadership and success meant the personal success of the man in command who earned corresponding "profits" in terms of social prestige. The technique of warfare and the structure of armies being what they were, the individual decision and driving power of the leading man—even his actual presence on a showy horse—were essential elements in the strategical and tactical situations. Napoleon's presence was, and had to be, actually felt on his battlefields. This is no longer so. Rationalized and specialized office work will eventually blot out personality, the calculable result, the "vision." The leading man no longer has the opportunity to fling himself into the fray. He is becoming just another office worker—and one who is not always difficult to replace.

Or take another military analogy. Warfare in the Middle Ages was a very personal affair. The armored knights practiced an art that required lifelong training and every one of them counted individually by virtue of personal skill and prowess. It is easy to understand why this craft should have become the basis of a social class in the fullest and richest sense of that term. But social and technological change undermined and eventually destroyed both the function and the position of that class. Warfare itself did not cease on that account. It simply became more and more mechanized—eventually so much so that success in what is now a mere profession no longer carries that connotation of individual achievement which would raise not only the man but also his group into a durable position of social leadership.

Now a similar social process—in the last analysis the same social process—undermines the role and, along with the role, the social position of the capitalist entrepreneur. His role, though less glamorous than that of medieval warlords, great or small, also is or was just another form of individual leadership acting by virtue of personal force and personal responsibility for success. His position, like that of warrior classes, is threatened as soon as this function in the social process loses its importance, and no less if this is due to the cessation of the social needs it served than if those needs are being served by other, more impersonal, methods.

But this affects the position of the entire bourgeois stratum. Although entrepreneurs are not necessarily or even typically elements of that stratum from the outset, they nevertheless enter it in case of success. Thus, though entrepreneurs do not *per se* form a social class, the bourgeois class absorbs them and their families and connections, thereby recruiting and revitalizing itself currently while at the same time the families that sever their active relation to "business" drop out of it after a generation or two. Between, there is the bulk of what we refer to as industrialists, merchants, financiers, and bankers; they are in the intermediate stage between entrepreneurial venture and mere current administration of an inherited domain. The returns on which the class lives are produced by, and the social position of the class rests on, the success of this more or less active sector—which of course may, as it does in this country, form over 90 per cent of the bourgeois stratum —and of the individuals who are in the act of rising into that class. Economically and sociologically, directly and indirectly, the bourgeoisie therefore depends on the entrepreneur and, as a class, lives and will die with him, though a more or less prolonged transitional stage—eventually a stage in which it may feel equally unable to die and to live—is quite likely to occur, as in fact it did occur in the case of the feudal civilization.

To sum up this part of our argument: if capitalist evolution— "progress"—either ceases or becomes completely automatic, the economic basis of the industrial bourgeoisie will be reduced eventually to wages such as are paid for current administrative work excepting remnants of quasi-rents and monopoloid gains that may be expected to linger on for some time. Since capitalist enterprise, by its very achievements, tends to automatize progress, we conclude that it tends to make itself superfluous—to break to pieces under the pressure of its own success. The perfectly bureaucratized giant industrial unit not only ousts the small or medium-sized firm and "expropriates" its owners, but in the end it also ousts the entrepreneur and expropriates the bourgeoisie as a class which in the process stands to lose not only its income but also what is infinitely more important, its function. The true pacemakers of socialism were not the intellectuals or agitators who preached it but the Vanderbilts, Carnegies, and Rockefellers. This result may not in every respect be to the taste of Marxian socialists, still less to the taste of socialists of a more popular (Marx would have said, vulgar) description. But so far as prognosis goes, it does not differ from theirs.

"ANOTHER ACT OF CREATION IS NECESSARY"

Fritz Redlich

The Business Leader as a "Daimonic" Figure

The ruggedly individualistic entrepreneur of the nineteenth century clearly appears to be a declining species. But Fritz Redlich (1892-   ) argues contrary to Schumpeter that the entrepreneur, in a guise attuned to the complex realities of our new society, is not only needed but essential. Only the profound failure of imagination by business leaders themselves is obstructing the emergence of the new-style entrepreneur. [Fritz Redlich, "The Business Leader as a 'Daimonic' Figure, II," The American Journal of Economics and Sociology, XII, April 1953, pp. 289-299.]

Much more self-destructive . . . than weakness of businessmen has been their very efficiency and success, and in this connection the daimonic dominates the field and has full sway. Schumpeter, in his book *Capitalism, Socialism and Democracy,* has pointed to the fact and in most respects this author agrees with his analysis. But he wishes to put a different emphasis on various phenomena, necessary in this context, since Schumpeter looks at capitalism, while this author studies its standard bearer.

First of all, the tremendous success of certain businessmen due to creative achievements has led to an accumulation of power first in their hands and subsequently in that of business as such. This accumulation of power in turn forced those detrimentally affected thereby to grasp for power too, in order to withstand the pressure and to hold ground. Loyalty to the established system became for many people burdensome, because short-term advantages to be derived therefrom appeared out of proportion to the pressure.

Very rarely in history is it possible to see so clearly the beginning of a chain of events as in this case. At the time when big business was brought into existence and in consequence of this creative achievement that power accumulation took place of which we are speaking, the prevailing philosophy of government held by the majority of politicians and by the people at large was that of laissez-faire: the less government the better. Only in reaction to the increasing power of business leaders, underprivileged strata in America, such as were farmers at that time and labor, forced first the states and later the national government to assume protective functions. This implied government assuming more power than ever before in our history.

In the second instance, farmers and labor built up powerful organizations of their own. "Businessmen's activities," as Taylor rightly stressed, "have led to a collection of aggressive special interests, power groups (corporations, labor unions, farm organizations) the relations among which so nearly approach a state of war as to keep us unsafely close to a forced choice between the extremely coercive state or chaos."

When one agrees that this chain of events is in the last analysis due to creative achievements of business leaders which *ipso facto* resulted in power, we face the clearest possible case of daimonic self-destruction, for in this warlike situation the businessman has already now lost relatively more power than farm groups or labor have gained. At least so it appears at this moment; and the downfall of the investment banker as the dominating force in our national economy is a case in point.

This situation is all the more dangerous for the business leader since he is not a leader by "charisma," as Sombart used to express it. That is to say, he is as a rule not a born leader of men; and simple foremen and trade union officials usually possess that quality to a much larger extent. A recent American writer has stated with respect to the innovating businessman that the latter is "a leader only in the sense that he has followers whom he does not want," which is a clever formulation of an obvious fact.

T. N. Whitehead in a masterful . . . presentation of the subject has described the business leader not as leading human beings, but as organizing them. The business leader, as he explains, is not a member of the group which embraces his employees, working by their side and sharing their daily lives. This implies that the group is not oriented primarily toward the business executive and his close co-operators (the entrepreneur of theory), but toward some informal leader of its own choosing. Or to put it differently, the business leader is in danger of directing a "formed society" from the outside. The latter may develop a defense mechanism and sentiments of antagonism.

The business leader, as a rule, is the member of a social stratum other than that to which his employees belong. He is guided by the idea of economic progress, while his employees think in terms of their needs. Since his control has no relation to their lives, the business leader endangers the integration of the group with which he works. So far Whitehead.

Schumpeter, finally, has pointed out that there is no trace of mystic glamor about the business leader, which is what counts in the rule of men. Business leadership, as he correctly stressed, does not lead to leadership of nations, since "the ledger and the cost calculation absorb and confine" and do not develop those characteristics which the national leader requires. In America their traditional contempt for government until recently kept business leaders from seeking high and exacting public office. It is only necessary to compare the number of businessmen who became United States presidents with the number of soldiers who did so and their respective shares in the total population to see the point.

In the last analysis the accumulation of power did more harm than good to business. An aggravating element was the fact that control over the means of production which gave power was to a large extent absentee control (for example, the control by the investment banker). Moreover, it was and is the power of men who have only a comparatively small personal stake in the social structure concerned (the gigantic enterprises) from which they derive that power. The situation in turn easily leads to irresponsibility, which prevails in American business for historical and ideological reasons anyway. It is the scourge of American entrepreneurship.

To complete the picture, what has often been discussed must be repeated; namely, that concentration of power changed the structure of competition so as to make it what Professor Easterbrook has called "the competition of power aggregations."

Two examples may suffice: Competition between stock insurance companies and mutuals was fought out in Massachusetts before the Legislature and pivoted around the question of whether or not the mutuals should be permitted to write non-assessable policies. And the second: There was in 1910 an aggressive new national bank in Salt Lake City which tried to build up business at the expense of its older competitors by underbidding their rates for certain services. All the banks were members of the Salt Lake City Clearing House, whose controlling majority finally determined on fixing those rates in order to stop that sort of competition which, in fact, was traditional price competition of the "classical" type. When the aggressor refused to abide by that regulation, the clearing house was dissolved and a new clearing house was founded forthwith. Its constitution contained the rule in question and when the young bank refused to sign this new constitution with the obnoxious clause, it lost its clearing privileges. This in turn meant considerable extra costs besides inconvenience and destroyed the new bank's competitive standing.

The author does not want to be misunderstood: he does not believe in the possibility or desirability of a restoration of "perfect" competition. He agrees with Schumpeter that monopolistic competition has real advantages for economic development.

But from the particular angle of this investigation he must stress the consequences of the disappearance of competition of the classical type: the specific stimulus which it had provided ceased to work. It is that stimulus which contributed so much to the success of the capitalistic business leader, a success which in turn led to that power accumulation which now proves to be a danger to the businessman's future. Thus a process of daimonic self-destruction began which can be characterized as classical. The phases are: competition, stimulation, exertion, achievement, success, large scale enterprise.

At this point the daimonic comes into play:

LARGE SCALE ENTERPRISE

cut-throat competition		accumulation of power	
abandoning competition	competition of power aggregates	building of hostile power aggregates	
ceasing stimulus		relative loss of power	government control

A second trend toward daimonic self-destruction has been pointed out by Schumpeter too. He has correctly stressed that Gustav von Schmoller, the great Berlin economist, was aware of it as early as the first decade of this century. Schmoller expected that the development of large-scale enterprise which can easily be considered the businessman's greatest organizational achievement, would lead to a bureaucratization which would make large-scale enterprise amenable to be taken over by government administrators. There is undoubtedly a strong trend in this direction.

More than twenty-five years ago, when a student at the University of Berlin, this author learned that the difference between business and government administration was flexibility versus rigidity. The former found expression in the balance sheet, the latter in the budget. If this was an analysis true for the time, the adoption of budgeting by business enterprises possesses historical significance as marking the point at which large-scale business and government administration began to converge. In America Jacob Schiff claimed the merit of having introduced budgeting into railroad practice in the Nineteen Hundreds.

So much is certain, that administrative flexibility which distinguished small and medium scale enterprise from government agencies was unavoidably lost with the development of those gigantic concerns to which we owe the present stream of goods and services.

Those large scale business concerns must be managed on the basis of rules and regulations just as are government agencies. They work under the same organizational disadvantages which are reflected in what the public is prone to call "red tape." There is the same rigidity, the same "layering," the same difficulty for younger and lesser, though brilliant, employees to be seen, to have access to the man at the top, and to rise. Finally, to nepotism in the corporation corresponds patronage in the government agency.

There are, of course, still many highly dynamic industries which could not be efficiently managed by government administrators, but many enterprises, especially in the field of utilities, undoubtedly can. One could almost claim that in some fields the best ally of the businessman, especially of the irresponsible businessman, is today the irresponsible, if not corrupt, politician. The politician if incompetent as an officeholder and at the same time unwilling to abandon the age-old game of patronage and dubious self-aggrandizement is probably the worse of two evils.

The creative achievement of building large-scale enterprises has undermined the businessman's position for still another reason. If one calls "entrepreneur" the man or the men who alone or in common establish the purpose and the spirit of an enterprise, determine its major policies, and thus become responsible for its fate, one can readily see that in the modern large scale concern entrepreneurial functions are fulfilled in co-operation by top executives and numerous employees way down the line.

They are thus fulfilled partly by real employees, not by quasi-employees, such as presidents and vice-presidents of corporations. The latter, unless they are men of genius, are just as small cogs in the machine, as are the men down the line who help to make up the team. The only difference may be that, located as they are at the top of the engine, they can be noticed. The chief executive co-ordinates, but the intrinsic value of those whom he co-ordinates will to a large extent determine his achievements.

To return to the earlier train of thought, the assumption and execution of entrepreneurial functions in the large scale enterprise today go hand in hand with an employee psychology, that is to say, with the psychology of a man who does the job, often in a superb way, but who is not responsible for the final outcome and who can be fired any day. His work can be disavowed and so can his intentions, for while he prepares decisions and puts them into effect, he does not actually make them. Motives back of actual decisions may be entirely different from those that prompted the auxiliary employee-entrepreneur in preparing them originally. They may be, for example, due to financial or personal considerations and to the concern being a member of a holding-company controlled group of enterprises. Nevertheless the auxiliary employee-entrepreneur is indispensable for the functioning both of the individual enterprise and the system of free enterprise as such. But his ambiguous social role which is reflected in his way of thinking is not favorable to the survival of that system and consequently to that of its standard bearer, the independent or quasi-independent business leader.

James Jackson Storrow, by 1910 the leader of the Boston investment banking house, Lee, Higginson, and Company, stated on one occasion that he never was able to get one hundred per cent from an employee unless he opened a profit and loss account with the man as a manager. However, for the thousands of those auxiliary employee-entrepreneurs who are today carrying the load of modern large-scale enterprises, there is no profit and loss account, and there can be none. It would not even be possible to determine how much each of them contributed to the earnings of the concern. Profit sharing plans or the distribution of stock among employees which many businessmen consider the solution of the problem are of no avail for they are not vital. Recognition, prestige, and security would remunerate those men, many of whom are professionals of the first order, but all too often these are not forthcoming.

When one recognizes the importance of the auxiliary employee-entrepreneur for the functioning of an economic system based on large-scale enterprise one can readily see the danger thereto and to its standard bearer. The business leader by his creative achievements has built organizations which are too big to be run without the assistance of innumerable employees. But his cooperators, the auxiliary employee-entrepreneurs, are not vitally interested in the organizations that are run by businessmen. If the enterprise in which they work were organized as a government enterprise (assuming clean and efficient government), they would hold the same position as before, carry it just as before, be perhaps a little worse paid, but a little more secure than before, and would do the job with the same psychological inhibitions as before.

To sum up, the businessman's creative achievement of building large-scale industry, large-scale transportation enterprises, large-scale public utilities has brought into being conditions under which many of the carriers of the load in those enterprises are no longer vitally interested in their functioning as *free* (capitalistic) enterprises, that is to say, organizations handled by business leaders.

So far the analysis has paralleled Schumpeter's; at this point, however, we part company. One of the reasons why Schumpeter expects an ultimate breakdown of capitalism is the disappearance of innovation as a decisive function of business leaders. Innovation, according to Schumpeter, has become easier and easier, and finally a matter of organized routine. It has become amenable to team work and so the creative entrepreneur, highly remunerated for his achievements, who provided the capitalist class with ever new recruits, is disappearing. Through his achievements, so Schumpeter thinks, the creative entrepreneur has made himself superfluous.

With all due respect for Schumpeter, I think there are several flaws in his analysis. While the factual statements regarding team work and specialized activities in the field of innovation are undoubtedly correct, I do not think that far reaching innovation is becoming easier or will become so, that is to say, I do not see the daimonic in action just here. It is true that consumers' resistance to innovation has been broken down to a large extent and that it is comparatively easy to introduce minor innovations. But as for revolutionary innovations (and these are the ones which Schumpeter has in mind) it will be just as difficult as before, so the author believes, to introduce them into the practice. To be sure, resistance thereto will be located at different centers and the motives behind that resistance are becoming different from what they were in the past. In the future resistance to revolutionary innovations will be located with the most powerful corporations, trade organizations, and labor unions, and there will be extraordinary resistance to innovation *within* gigantic enterprises when it means writing off scores or hundreds of millions of capital. The creative entrepreneur of the future, presumably a corporation official, will have to overcome first of all formidable resistance in his own enterprise, and he will probably have to be a diplomat rather than a salesman or advertiser.

It must be permitted at this point to draw an imaginary picture, although one strictly controlled by economic knowledge: There is no field at present which challenges inventors and creative entrepreneurs as does that of housing. Consequently, let us assume the problem were solved and a safe and sanitary four-room unit could be provided at a total cost of $3500. That would mean a revolution of American community life. It would bring about one similar to that wrought by the mechanization of the cotton industry, railroads, electricity, or automobile. The stage would be set for another upswing of the Kondratjeff-wave. On the other hand, when one knows the tie between real estate values and communal finance; or that between local politics, real estate interests, good old families, banks, slums; or the interplay between contractors, politicians, and labor unions, one can fancy what would happen. I doubt if any creative entrepreneur of the past ever faced a task more formidable than that of the man who would set to work to introduce the $3500 home.

Moreover the masses are again ready to offer as stiff a resistance to innovation as they did in the more remote past. But while the masses in the past resisted innovation in their capacity as craftsmen fearing injury to their trades or as consumers, now they are on the point of resisting because innovation means insecurity, as they have recognized intuitively. Overcoming this resistance is even less easy than overcoming consumers' resistance in bygone days, or that of powerless craftsmen who were left to face disaster. It cannot be overcome by dangling glittering new goods before the prospects' eyes. Marginal utility not only determines the evaluation by consumers of units of a store of a specific good, but also that of units of a store of all goods available at a period. The urge for new things is decreasing in such a material civilization as ours which overabounds in the variety of goods and services on the market. The need for the creative entrepreneur as such seems to this author to be as strong as ever. The characteristics of the type will undoubtedly change.

To sum up, success in innovation, which to a certain extent has made innovation easier, is not in this author's opinion one of the factors contributing to daimonic self-destruction.

Even if one disagrees with Schumpeter on the question of whether the success of the innovating business leader has led to daimonic self-destruction by making innovation teachable routine, the existence of daimonic self-destructiveness of business leaders should now be clear beyond a doubt. In the end daimonic destructiveness and daimonic self-destructiveness have merged to form a tragic concatenation. Of course the modern business leader is the descendant of medieval merchants who were part and parcel of Western civilization. But when in the eighteenth and nineteenth centuries the creative, the innovating, business leader appeared in comparatively large numbers he began by his very achievement to undermine the European civilization and he helped to bring it to the brink of that collapse where it now stands. Schumpeter touched upon the problem when he discussed the destruction of those strata which had protected the business leader in the era of early and in the first decades of high capitalism. But one must go much further. The author thinks that he cannot make the point clearer than by using Toynbee's words:

The introduction of any new dynamic forces or creative movements into the life of a society ought to be accompanied by a reconstruction of the whole existing set of institutions if a healthy harmony is to be preserved.

Otherwise it is followed by disintegration, due to

disharmony between the institutions of which a society is composed . . . [and the] new social forces . . . which the existing set of institutions was not originally designed to carry.

This is exactly what has happened to Western Civilization when the creative business leader began revolutionizing it. There was no reconstruction, there was just daimonic destruction to make room for building a productive apparatus such as the world has never before seen. The revolutionary forces represented by the creative business leader could not be absorbed because of the speed alone with which the creative-destructive process took place. Whitehead in a masterful way has described that process substantially as follows:

In a modern society a part of the purposeful activities are, as before, performed as social living, while another has been singled out for a different form of social organization. These latter activities have been withdrawn from the main stream of social living and are highly organized from the standpoint of technical efficiency. This fraction of purposeful activities is known as business. For the purpose of technical efficiency business organization is controlled without regard for the social lives of those involved. So long as business formed a relatively small part of the total activities, this situation was most dangerous to social integration. But since at the present time a very large part of all activities has come under the control of business and the business leader, society is becoming seriously and increasingly disorganized and the businessman's functions come near to disintegrating the society for whose economic future he is providing. Every achievement of the creative entrepreneur has been accompanied by a corresponding impoverishment of social living. Business and businessmen have risen, and at the same time reduced the importance of older institutions as integrators of society without shouldering the function themselves.

Or to put it differently, in the process of daimonic destructiveness the business leader is destroying the civilization to which he belongs and thereby the soil in which he roots. Thus in the last act of the tragedy daimonic destructiveness has turned daimonic self-destructiveness and this is what was meant when the author spoke earlier of a concatenation of daimonic destructiveness and daimonic self-destructiveness.

Here it is necessary, however, to distinguish between European and American conditions. So far, America has been and is part and parcel of Western civilization, but it may be on the point of parting company from it. The amorphousness of American society, the absence of a proletariat as Europe has it and of a proletariat in the sense of Toynbee, and finally various other social phenomena may be indicative of that trend which, if it exists at all, must be in a very early stage. If, as seems possible, the next few hundred years should experience the emergence of a genuine American civilization (*Kulturkreis*) affiliated to the Western, modern business may well appear as one of its basic institutions and the creative business leader may, *sub specie aeternitatis*, have been among those who laid the cornerstone of the new civilization. To a large extent that will depend on the wisdom of the American businessmen as a class, to repeat: wisdom and not technical skill, but one cannot see very much of that.

TO SUM UP: in the opinion of the author by a daimonic process of destruction and self-destruction the *ruggedly individualistic and socially irresponsible* businessman of the nineteenth century has doomed himself, not because of his weakness or wickedness, but *because of his creative achievements* for our material civilization. *Because* of his achievements he is becoming an archaic type. What is now needed is a creative achievement of first magnitude, but one of a character entirely different from the business leaders' creative achievements of the past: the type "businessman" must be reshaped so as to fit into a coming economic order (style) which will be as different from that prevailing in the nineteenth century as it should be, so at least we hope, different from that of communism. But in order to make room for that achievement the leading businessmen must reorient their thinking. They had better forget Adam Smith, John Stuart Mill, invisible hand, and natural law, and look at the world without out-of-date theorizing. They need that humility of which Donald K. David speaks. What the businessman has experienced in the last decades is the nemesis of creativity. Another act of creation is necessary if he is to have a new lease of life, that is to say, if he wants to be permitted to contribute what he actually has to offer.

"WE HAVE CREATED...A TOTALITARIAN ORGANIZATION IN INDUSTRY"

―――

Boris Emmet and John E. Jeuck

New Patterns of Organization

Big Business, increasingly a captive of its administrative mechanism, has been aware of the irony of its individualist ideology in the face of its own practices. Solutions have been hard to find, but the attempt to promote initiative through decentralization and thus to counter totalitarian tendencies suggests real concern in circles where such concern might be least anticipated. [*Boris Emmet and John E. Jeuck,* Catalogues and Counters: A History of Sears, Roebuck and Company, *Chicago, 1950, pp. 371-373.*]

The development of Sears' administrative system was guided largely by a policy expressed in the early thirties by President Wood:

While systems are important, our main reliance must always be put on men rather than on systems. If we devise too elaborate a system of checks and balances, it will only be a matter of time before the self-reliance and initiative of our managers will be destroyed and our organization will be gradually converted into a huge bureaucracy.

The essence of that statement was summed up in Wood's frequent reiteration, "If you have the right man and he is properly trained, all your problems will take care of themselves." This emphasis on men as against systems is basically what the company executives have in mind in their constant references to "decentralization," expressed in the latest organization structure of Sears.

In a letter dated October 14, 1948, Wood outlined to his officers what he termed "official policy of the Company, to be translated into action all through the Company in all layers of authority":

We complain about government in business, we stress the advantages of the free enterprise system, we complain about the totalitarian state, but in our industrial organizations, in our striving for efficiency we have created more or less of a totalitarian organization in industry, particularly in large industry. The problem of retaining our efficiency and discipline in these large organizations and yet allowing our people to express themselves, to exercise initiative and to have some voice in the affairs of the organization is the greatest problem for large industrial organizations to solve.

That problem of "letting people express themselves and exercise initiative," while at the same time retaining "efficiency and discipline," has been approached by Sears in a manner which seems distinctively Wood's. The emphasis on individual initiative could not become so exaggerated as to imperil the very heart of a business as big as Sears—good administration.

There must be kept in mind two basic factors which make the company's type of organization practicable. First is the fact that the store managers need to perform no buying function—central purchasing guarantees the procurement of goods, their delivery to the stores, a satisfactory gross margin, and an established merchandise pattern for each type of store. In addition, central purchasing creates the general sales-promotion plans, including store planning and methods of display. Second in importance is the fact that the company's principal administrative, operating, and control procedures have been formalized and are therefore an integral part of company policy from which no local deviations are permitted.

The Sears principle of decentralized retail administration is now the cornerstone of organization policy, responsible to a great extent for the company's retail success, as well as for some difficulties which occur now and then, such as local overpricing of goods, poor service, out-of-stock conditions, and excessive and unbalanced inventories. But company officers believe strongly that the advantages of decentralization far outweigh its disadvantages.

Under the Sears system of decentralized management, the local retail unit has sufficient autonomy to provide for itself and its employees most of the advantages of an independent operation. The local manager has authority and responsibility to make all or nearly all important day-to-day decisions. He is limited by the general framework of company policies, but within that framework he has adequate leeway for handling on the spot practically all questions which arise. Because of his own intimate knowledge of the immediate situation and of the people involved, his decisions can carry a far larger measure of effectiveness than would be possible if the decision-making authority were reserved to a functionary in a central office.

Sears has been careful to strengthen and preserve the integrity of the line organization because it feels that only on the basis of a strong, independent line can autonomous local management ever be a reality. In Sears the staff has therefore deliberately been kept small, and there is a clear understanding that its functions are advisory and not authoritative. Those who have gravitated into staff work have had to develop a high order of skill in operating on this basis to accomplish their responsibilities. In other words, in the Sears organization the staff operates to *strengthen* the line, not to undermine it.

Basic to the principle of decentralized management is a tendency to rely on individual initiative and confidence in the capacity and judgment of the people in the organization. This is clear, of course, so far as store managers and other key executives are concerned, but it is also substantially true of people at all levels in the organization, particularly in the retail stores.

Superficially, it might appear that the roots of the company's present policy and philosophy lie far back in its history, for Sears apparently developed, during its first twenty-five or thirty years, on a loose, informal basis where there was ample leeway for individual growth and for the display of individual judgment and initiative. Most business organizations pass through a similar stage of vigor and informality during their earlier years; but this earlier stage is often followed by a gradual solidifying of the structure, a tightening of controls, and a growth of administrative hierarchies and of staff bureaucracies.

This process of maturing was already far advanced in Sears by the middle 1920's. But Wood, on his accession to power, did two things which restored the vigor and youth of the company. He launched the retail program and thereby, in a very real sense, created a new organization engaged in a new enterprise. Of equal immediate importance but greater long-range significance, he developed a type of administrative structure and provided a caliber of executive leadership calculated to preserve and strengthen the dynamic characteristics usually associated with young organizations, so that those characteristics might not be lost as the rejuvenated organization itself began to move into its own period of maturity.

The success of that effort may perhaps be evident in the extent to which Sears, particularly in its parent and retail branches, is still characterized, after a quarter of a century, by the vigor, flexibility, drive, and enthusiasm of a young organization. It is significant that the only branch of the company for which this statement is not wholly true is mail order, which had already reached maturity when General Wood came on the scene.

A higher order of administrative skill is required to manage effectively an informal, loosely knit organization such as Sears than to manage one of the more conventional pattern. It was Sears' good fortune to find in Wood a man who had that order of skill to an unusual degree and who was able to communicate that skill to his close associates and key executives with whom he surrounded himself. If Sears, Roebuck can be considered an example of the dictum that an "organization is the lengthened shadow of a man," it were wise to keep in mind the weakness of most such organizations—that the shadow seldom long survives the man. This fate is unlikely in the case of Sears because of the extent to which Wood has been able to develop, among his officers and executive staff, a comparable degree of skill for administering the type of organization which Sears has become. . . .

Francis X. Sutton

The Motivations and Rewards of the Business Executive

The motivations and rewards of the business executive, as compared with those of the independent entrepreneur, have rarely been explored candidly and systematically. Francis X. Sutton (1917-   ), the sociologist, outlines the real and professed incentives of the business executive as well as the inhibitions to their candid avowal as part of the American business creed. [Francis X. Sutton, Seymour E. Harris, Carl Kaysen, and James Tobin, The American Business Creed, *Cambridge, 1956, pp. 99-107.]*

The motivations of an individual in any role are characteristically manifold and complex. Motivations may include intrinsic satisfaction in the tasks expected, instrumental advantages of varied sorts (money income is one type), the "self-satisfaction" of behaving "decently," and many other factors. A balanced and systematic picture of the motivational forces characteristic in a role is by no means easy. This is one of the core problems of social science, and at present there are certainly no more than rough beginnings of a satisfactory systematic approach. In view of the difficulty of the problem, it is not surprising that the business creed fails to provide a systematic treatment of the motivations of the business executive, although it contains considerable reference to the importance of incentives, of the profit motive, of feelings of responsibility.

An examination of the creed's discussion of the motivations of the businessman can conveniently begin with the classical strand of business ideology, although its analysis is not very conspicuous in the present-day creed. The "classical" strand of business ideology is historically rooted in the broad philosophical tradition known as utilitarianism, to which the dominant Anglo-American tradition in economics is closely related. It shares with more academic economic thought a central concern with certain special empirical features of our Western society. These are the data of market transactions and pecuniary calculations. Commodity prices, wage rates, interest, and profits are analyzed with an eye to understanding their quantitative variation; and this analysis requires some theoretical assumptions relating to motivation. The assumptions suggested by the term "economic man" have been a fruitful source of analytical results. In professional economics this apparatus has been subjected to the restraints of parsimony and elegance and kept to certain minimal assumptions about preference schedules. But the tradition leads, especially in ideology, to stronger presumptions about motivations.

Concerning the occupational role of an individual, economics has asked only, "What price must be paid to secure the participation of the individual?" It follows that the economist need analyze motivations only insofar as they have direct bearing on the wage, salary, or profit that must be paid to secure the individual's participation. Within this narrow context, the economist is justified in treating people as if their only positive interest in their jobs were in the rewards. Other motivations are excluded from economic analysis because they are irrelevant, not because their existence or their importance is denied.

The restricted interest of the economist is not logically bound up with any particular set of views on occupational motivations. In fact, it has become so through the common tendency to assume that an abstract idea mirrors a concrete situation; in this process certain elements of the original idea are given more specific and elaborate meaning than they possessed originally. Ideologies in particular are peculiarly susceptible to this "misplaced concreteness" and the business ideology is no exception. Here the abstract assumption of the economist is extended to an empirical proposition as to which motivations are most important. In the classical view, the motivation of workers is intimately and exclusively related to wages; "work" is conceived to be a deprivation or burden with the wage reward as pecuniary compensation for the "disutility" of work. (The classical view is undoubtedly influenced by a tradition of rather sharp distinction between "work" and "leisure"; with the presumption that one "enjoys" leisure but "works" only to provide means for other enjoyments.) The motivations of the independent entrepreneur and of the business executive have been less clearly interpreted along these lines. But there has certainly been a tendency to treat performance in these roles as involving only "disutility," with the pecuniary return in profits or salaries as compensation for the tedium, worry, and effort endured. It is obvious that such views are at best abstract or one-sided. Intuitively, and hence unsystematically, those acquainted with our society know better than to regard the view as comprehensive of all strategic factors.

In the sphere of the business executive, the classical tradition in both economics and business ideology has spoken in terms of a "profit motive." As Professor Parsons has shown in a well-known essay, to speak of a "profit motive" is misleading, since the term "motive" suggests a part of the given, natural equipment of individuals, regardless of their participation in particular social institutions. It is certainly evident that the businessman's motivation to make a profit is not a simple acquisitiveness in this sense; profits are made only in the contexts of business enterprises, in other words in a particular kind of social organization, and the "profit motive" thus must refer to motivations understandable only within an institutional context. All of this becomes very clear and explicit in the managerial strands of the business ideology, as we shall see, but it has often been obscured in the classical tradition. Where the institutional framwork of business is not explicitly noted, the fact that motivations are dependent on that framework can hardly receive proper recognition. Thus, the motivation of the businessman to make a profit very readily appears as simple "selfishness" or "lust for money." Here again the conceptual scheme used for dealing with economic problems focuses attention on certain abstract categories; these are then confused with concrete reality and are given an exclusive or at least a prominent position.

In the classical view, then, a businessman is interested in the financial state of his business primarily because it determines his income. Any source of satisfaction in the role other than money income is ignored. Our NAM vice-president once admitted that there are some people who work because they somehow enjoy it, but in good classical fashion he regarded this as more or less accidental and atypical. In an interesting argument, Klein interprets the "profit motive" in terms of the uses of the personal income so attained:

Search history as we may, and we can find but two motives which ever have stimulated man to economic activity beyond the most meager requirements of subsistence. Those two motives are (1) the desire for personal advancement and (2) fear . . . The desire for self-aggrandizement may be evidenced by the purchase of the finest yacht afloat. It may also be expressed in the much less obtrusive personal satisfaction which comes from doing well for one's family and appearing well before one's neighbors. Fear is fear . . .

Personal advancement is whatever raises the individual in his own estimation. Such increased self-esteem may come with clothes and jewelry. It may come from the ability to contribute largely to charities. It need not be, and usually is not, unworthy. The personal desires most Americans strive to satisfy are decent and honorable.

This discussion is specifically tied to a justification of profits. The motivations to profit-making are the two listed; once "fear" is allayed "personal advancement" becomes important and here, curiously, the only specified modes are in the form of expenditures. Such things as the prestige of running a large organization are neglected.

Views like Klein's, which interpret profits and the money compensation of businessmen primarily from the point of view of consumption behavior, are not widespread. The notion that businessmen go into business primarily to make money in order to increase their personal consumption has been widely resisted in this country. American businessmen express surprise at their European colleagues who seem indeed to go into business in the hope of accumulating sufficient means to get out of it as soon as possible. To W. J. Cameron, those who retire when they have "made enough" are "deserters." Mr. Queeny criticizes high salaries in good Puritan fashion; they may encourage extravagant living at the expense of devotion to work and duty. Such statements confirm a general impression that American businessmen do not really work for money alone; for an adult male American, having a job is so much the expected pattern that there is little place for the wealthier man of leisure. The feeling that a man should go on working even though his wealth would permit him to retire at an early age is certainly not restricted to a few unreconstructed Puritans in our society but is very widely accepted.

The strong intrinsic motivations of business roles are so manifest on the American scene that it is not surprising that they gain some expression in business ideology. Discussions of executives' salaries and their relation to corporate profits bring these motivations to the fore. The conspicuous fact that most of the executives in large enterprises are compensated by salaries and bonuses set at the discretion of others (usually the Board of Directors) makes apparent a gap between profits and rewards. Yet in the classical view the profits are supposedly the outcome of and incentive for executives' efforts. The common solution is to treat profits as "markers" or indices of achievement and thus as symbols. Queeny has suggested that other symbols such as "scrambled eggs on visors" might be used. But he argues that, for top management at least, profits are a "natural marker, since they are directly related to the expressions of approval or disapproval of the ultimate judges— the consumers."

How is the spectacularly high remuneration of some executives treated in the ideology? In most societies one finds a reasonably good correspondence between income and prestige, but in America there are extraordinary exceptions to the rule. For instance, eight executives in General Motors each receive compensation more than three times that of the President of the United States. A Justice of the Supreme Court, whose job has been shown in repeated surveys to possess higher prestige than any other in the country, receives $25,000 a year. Yet in 1950, both E. I. duPont de Nemours and General Motors were paying eight not-so-old men salaries and bonuses to the tune of $300,000 each. Top-ranking executives generally receive far more than top-ranking professionals, although the professions tend to outrank business executive roles in prestige. However, there is reason to believe that within the business world itself the correlation between income and prestige holds good.

The theme most commonly found in the ideology is that high compensations are necessary to induce the best talent, which is assumed to be scarce, to take on the responsibilities of high executive positions. Thomas McElroy, president of Procter and Gamble, sees in the present income tax structure a serious barrier to offering the requisite inducements. An identification of "responsibility" and "disutility" seems to be assumed; there is no suggestion that the prestige and nonpecuniary advantages of a high position might compensate for additional "worry" even if the salary were actually less. The well-known pressures on people in business hierarchies to be ambitious and to accept the challenge of new responsibilities are also neglected in this view. A man who dislikes heavy responsibility is unlikely to say so when he refuses a promotion; he will rationalize his decision in terms of income and say, for instance, that he cannot afford to move.

Beardsley Ruml has devoted himself with characteristic independence and originality to these problems. He refuses to argue that very high incomes are wholesome for those able to get them, or that they are wholesome for the community or nation. That they occur he takes to be a consequence of competitive bidding for scarce talents. The assumed motivation only appears when he traces out the consequences of a law limiting compensation. The consequence would be "to deprive the generation of a substantial and irreplaceable portion of the productiveness of its highest genius," since "high talent can work part time, and that is exactly what would happen if the rate of pay per month, per year, or per lifetime were to be limited by law." Thus, while he asserts that high executives should never get high incomes merely for "applied time," he seems to conclude that capable executives will adjust their working time to pecuniary compensation. Here we have a striking classical remnant put forward by a sophisticated exponent of managerial views.

Ruml remarks further that high compensation should never be a mere "reward for honor earned," and there is very little attention anywhere in the ideology to the correlation between prestige and income.

It is difficult to rationalize this correlation in an egalitarian tradition, thus it is not surprising that the ideology does not give realistic weight to high income as evidence that a man and his organization are important and successful. However, the belief that practicality is the key attribute of the business executive and his role one in which "results count" introduces a helpful ambiguity. The president of Procter and Gamble speaks of executives' salaries as a "compensation for achievement" and, incidentally, offers the remarkably teleological argument that money is the "acceptable" form of compensation since it is the only form giving individuals freedom to choose those material things of greatest importance to them. High compensation for executives is thus suggested to be not merely a nonrational symbolic recognition of their high status but a reward for high accomplishment.

Concerning the nonpecuniary motivations of business executives a heterogeneous array of factors are discussed in the business ideology. The classical view focuses attention on pecuniary rewards and provides a narrow but clear analysis of motivations. Once the classical is abandoned, a variety of possibilities opens up. The managerial view, as was noted in Chapter 3, stresses the various responsibilities of business. These discussions hover between description and exhortation; but the picture which emerges is of a corporation manager motivated by these feelings of responsibility, rather than a manager who is responsible merely because this is the most profitable way to behave. Thus, in the managerial strand of the ideology, the modern entrepreneur tends to stand in contrast to the classical entrepreneur for whom moral responsibilities are treated simply as conditions restricting and defining the range of means he may use in his rational pursuit of profit.

This extreme, moralistic view of the motivations of businessmen has long been represented in the unsystematic effusions of the service ideology. It is alleged to have increasing application as business has matured and large, stable enterprises have emerged. The old wickedness of ruthless self-aggrandizement is said to be declining. Motivational analyses involve a different sort of intrinsic concern with the day-to-day management of a business enterprise than the instrumental analysis of the classical view. The appeal of the risks and competitive struggle of business are an important part of Queeny's argument about the place of profits in motivation. He compares business gains to poker winnings and argues that the game, not only the wins and losses, has intrinsic importance in both. The comparison of business with a game—not mere "gambling" but a game with "elements of luck, skill, risk and calculation of chances" as he says—is a common metaphor in American usage and may indeed point to a peculiarity of American Society.

It should be noted that the model for this comparison is certainly that of the independent entrepreneur or the top levels in corporate hierarchies. The picture of the "intrinsic" motivations and rewards of executives whose positions are far removed from that of the classical entrepreneur is much less developed in the ideology. The fact that top executives have climbed long to reach their present eminence may be cited to show that "management has served its apprenticeship," but the obvious conclusion that hopes and expectations are intimately bound to promotions is not drawn. In government, preferment through the favor of others is recognized and labeled as "politics"; but the fact that a junior executive in business is completely dependent on the good will of a few of his superiors for promotion is not recognized in the ideology. The model of the modern corporation with an elaborated executive hierarchy presents a number of awkward problems for ideology, and these deserve a little attention.

The relation of participation in an organization to the total pattern of an individual's motivations is always a complex matter. In our society individuals are admitted a considerable latitude of self-interest in their own careers, while at the same time there are demands for loyalty to the various organizations in which they work. This is, of course, true not only in the business world but also in politics, the universities, and probably even the churches. But the business executive is faced with a special problem. The implications of the stress on teamwork and organizational loyalty which we have encountered are, in this context, limitations on the admissible range of self-concern for executives. Extreme self-abnegation, say, as in a religious order or the Communist Party, is not demanded; Ruml speaks of subjection to business organization as tolerable for executives only if they have the ability to get jobs elsewhere and the courage to do so. Still, the pressures on the executive are considerable as compared to, say, the loyalty demanded by a university from one of its professors. Executives, particularly at the higher levels, do shift from organization to organization; but in the nature of their functions they lack the core of independence which specialized technical competence, and external evidence thereof, gives to the career of a professor. While attached to a particular organization they cannot continue their "own work" in anything like the same sense. Executives are expected to be ambitious and independent (and, in this sense, self-interested), while at the same time they are subjectd to a rather severe organizational discipline.

Complexities of this sort do not readily make for clear ideological symbols; if the businessman is pictured as "loving adventure," the independent entrepreneur makes a much more convenient image. The motivations of the corporate executive get scant treatment in ideology; when they are discussed, individual self-interest is played down and merged with the interests of the organization. The possibility of conflict between self-interest and loyalty is thus ignored. An executive is ambitious for the organization in which he works.

The boasts of business firms about their successes feed the vicarious ambitions of their executives. In its house organ The Houghton Company tells how it has "again led the industry," and "intends to stay in the front ranks." Mr. Queeny has given a strong statement of the importance of power and position as a goal of businessmen. The ambition of a typical successful businessman is never satisfied. "If he is producing six things and employs 1,000 people, his ambition is to exceed a competitor twice his size. . . . Every businessman has an ideal; he wants a large and successful business, bigger and more profitable than that of his competitors." This picture is fairly close to that of the independent entrepreneur, but there is a protective distinction between the businessman and his organization. It is not simply personal aggrandizement which is an issue, but the growth of an organization. Within this organization Queeny's businessman is little motivated by the enjoyment of power. He wants a loyal, harmonious, hard-working organization with contented employees in a well-designed and efficient plant. This organization is not simply a "lengthened shadow" of himself which will fade at his death but a continuing organism, "well balanced . . . with young talent coming along."

In this sort of emphasis on the organizational context it is, then, possible to give some expression to the satisfactions of power and control. Among the rewards of high executive position such satisfactions are certainly always represented; but their ideological expression is not easy, particularly in the democratic atmosphere of American society. The ideology offers little in the way of analysis of the relation of the "greatness" of a firm to the personal satisfactions of a particular executive. This is another thorny problem. That executives derive satisfaction from being a part of a great firm can hardly be doubted, but the delicate problems involved in judging the strength of such satisfactions and the contexts of its importance hardly suit the straightforward simplicities of ideology.

One final point deserves brief notice. Chester Barnard has given emphasis to a fact which seems to be widely attested by experience not only in large businesses but in very small ones as well. It is the fact that the fear of failure seems to be a far stronger spur than the hope of profit. The realistic importance of this side of a business executive's motivation can hardly be doubted, but it is completely neglected in the ideology. It is in a sense the "maintenance" aspect of role performance; not failing may be tremendously important but in itself it "doesn't get you anywhere." As such, it makes poor material for ideology.

"A SOCIETY ... OF ARTERIOSCLEROTIC ORGANIZATIONS CANNOT RENEW ITSELF"

—

John W. Gardner

Organizing for Renewal

The catastrophe inherent in rigid organization has led John W. Gardner (1912-), president of the Carnegie Corporation, to explore solutions for organizational renewal. A department of continuous renewal, for every corporation, which would view the whole organization as a system in need of continuing innovation is only the most strategic in a series of proposals that Gardner offers for the promotion of initiative in a society where few individuals or small organizations can continue to exist independently. [*John W. Gardner,* Self-Renewal: The Individual and the Innovative Society, *New York, 1964, pp. 75-85.*]

◉

Systematic Innovation

The same flexibility and adaptiveness that we seek for the society as a whole are essential for the organizations within the society. A society made up of arteriosclerotic organizations cannot renew itself.

In the millions of words that have been written about the art of managing large-scale organizations the patient reader will find much wisdom concerning the forces that make organizations rigidify and decay. Writers on the art of management have in mind many organizational aims other than those which concern us here, but their writings contain many clues to the secret of renewal and innovation.

Perhaps the most distinctive thing about innovation today is that we are beginning to pursue it systematically. The large corporation does not set up a research laboratory to solve a specific problem but to engage in continuous innovation. That is good renewal doctrine. But such laboratories usually limit their innovative efforts to products and processes. What may be most in need of innovation is the corporation itself. Perhaps what every corporation (and every other organization) needs is a department of continuous renewal that would view the whole organization as a system in need of continuing innovation.

The same incomplete approach to innovation may be seen in our universities. Much innovation goes on at any first-rate university—but it is almost never conscious innovation in the structure or practices of the university itself. University people love to innovate away from home.

Experienced managers know that some organizations can be renewed through new leadership and new ideas. Others need a more massive infusion of new blood or far-reaching organizational changes. Still others can only be renewed by taking them apart and putting them together again. And some cannot be renewed at all.

Some management problems are of particular interest to students of renewal. Consider, for example, personnel problems. Nothing is more vital to the renewal of an organization (or society) than the system by which able people are nurtured and moved into positions where they can make their contribution. In an organization this implies effective recruitment and a concern for the growth of the individual that extends from the earliest training stages through the later phases of executive development. For a society it implies the correction of social and economic conditions that blight and smother talent in childhood; a deeply rooted tradition—going far beyond formal schooling—of the full development of individual potentialities; and the existence of social mobility such that talent from any segment of the population may move freely into significant roles in the society.

In an organization, a well-designed system of personnel rotation will yield high dividends not only in the growth of the individual but in organizational fluidity. Free movement of personnel throughout the organization reduces barriers to internal communication, diminishes hostility between divisions, and ensures a freer flow of information and ideas. It contributes on the one hand to versatility of the individual and on the other to fluidity of the organization.

In the same way, both society and the individual profit by the free movement of people from one organization to another, and from one segment of society to another. Our own society gives the impression of complete fluidity, but this is partially deceptive. There is relatively little movement, for example, between government, industry, and the academic world—despite some spectacular line-crossers. And mobility between organizations is being diminished by pension plans in which benefits are contingent upon the individual remaining with the same organization.

Another topic in management that will be of special interest to the student of renewal is communication. Management specialists have learned much about the kinds of communication channels necessary to keep a large organization functioning well. They have learned, for example, that effective channels of internal communication can prevent the erection of impenetrable walls between parts of the organization, and by so doing may do much to diminish the number of narrow, over-specialized employees. All of this serves the cause of renewal.

In some instances a reduction in communications may be useful. There are circumstances in which creativity and flexibility are greatly inhibited by excessive demands for co-ordination, administrative re-view, and endorsement from collateral branches of the organization. Experimental ventures may quickly lose all freshness and imaginative-ness if subjected to the withering heat of criticism from more conven-tional parts of the organization.

Considerations of this sort have led many an industrial corporation to provide some measure of insulation between its research division and the rest of the organization. The Air Force achieved the same effect when it set up RAND and similar research facilities as independent organizations, thus freeing the research activity from the context of forces at work in the larger organizations.

Filtered Experience

As organizations (and societies) become larger and more complex, the men at the top (whether managers or analysts) depend less and less on firsthand experience, more and more on heavily "processed" data. Before reaching them, the raw data—what actually goes on "out there" —have been sampled, screened, condensed, compiled, coded, expressed in statistical form, spun into generalizations, and crystallized into recommendations.

It is a characteristic of the information processing system that it systematically filters out certain kinds of data so that these never reach the men who depend on the system. The information that is omitted (or seriously distorted) is information that is not readily expressed in words or numbers, or cannot be rationally condensed into lists, cate-gories, formulas, or compact generalizations by procedures now available to us.

No one can run a modern organization who is not extraordinarily gifted in handling the end products of a modern information processing system. So we find at the top of our large organizations (and at the top of our government) more and more men who are exceedingly gifted in manipulating verbal and mathematical symbols. And they all under-stand one another. It is not that they see reality in the same way. It is that through long training they have come to see reality through the same distorting glasses. There is nothing more heart-warming than the intellectual harmony of two analysts whose training has accustomed them to accept as reality the same systematic distortions thereof.

But what does the information processing system filter out? It filters out all sensory impressions not readily expressed in words and numbers. It filters out emotion, feeling, sentiment, mood, and almost all of the irrational nuances of human situations. It filters out those intuitive judgments that are just below the level of consciousness.

So the picture of reality that sifts to the top of our great organizations and our society is sometimes a dangerous mis-match with the real world. We suffer the consequences when we run head on into situations that cannot be understood *except* in terms of those elements that have been filtered out. The planners base their plans on the prediction that the people will react in one way, and they react violently in quite another way.

That is why every top executive and every analyst sitting at the center of a communications network should periodically emerge from his world of abstractions and take a long unflinching look at unprocessed reality. Every general should spend some time at the front lines; every research administrator should spend some time in the laboratory doing research of his own; every sales manager should take his sample case out periodically and call on customers; every politician should get out and ring doorbells.

We should not make the mistake of underrating our information processing systems. They are extraordinarily helpful. But they are incomplete.

Massiveness and Immobility

There is a problem in organizing for renewal that has never been adequately dealt with in the literature of management, though all experts are aware of it: how to combat the almost inevitable movement of an organization toward elaborateness, rigidity, and massiveness and away from simplicity, flexibility, and manageable size. Military history illustrates the problem in an illuminating way. Since ancient times, some military forces have relied on speed, mobility, flexibility, imagination, and daring, and others have relied on sheer power, numbers, solidity, and heavy equipment. Prosperous societies have rarely been able to resist the temptation to substitute the latter for the former. And as armed forces grew larger, as their organization grew more complex, as fortifications grew more massive, they became in some respects just that much more vulnerable to an enemy that had mastered speed, mobility, and flexibility of striking power. Over the centuries military thinkers have understood this very well (though ministries of war have rarely lived by it) and have sought through technological innovation to have their cake and eat it too—to have both power and speed, both massiveness and flexibility. But, though technology can overcome much, it cannot easily overcome the vast cumbersomeness of organization that characterizes the armed forces of a major power. That is one reason why one can find in the past two decades innumerable instances in which a small, poorly equipped but flexible and daring guerrilla force has played hob with the massive and magnificently equipped forces of a major power. Only recently have our own armed forces learned how to cope with that sort of opposition.

The problem is not confined to the military; it applies to any and all organizations. If an organization has to choose between massive strength and flexibility, it almost invariably chooses massive strength. It feels impelled to equip itself for every conceivable contingency, even at the cost of an elaborateness that limits adaptability. It finds it easy to grow more complex, difficult to grow simpler; easy to grow cumbersome, almost impossible to become disencumbered.

It is not a problem of sheer size. Most experts now recognize that the large organization need not succumb to the unwieldiness and bureaucratic rigidity that we associate with bigness. They believe that if we keep these dangers in mind and design organizations in such a way as to avoid them, we can enjoy the advantages that characterize many (by no means all!) small organizations—simplicity, easy internal communication, flexibility, and adaptiveness—and at the same time benefit by the undoubted advantages of bigness—resources in depth, economies of scale, a relatively high degree of internal diversity, and the capacity to meet a great range of eventualities.

But there is not only something in organization that tends toward massiveness, elaborateness, solidity, and entrenched power, there is something that glorifies forms and formalities, the superficial and external. Consider education. We think we believe in it passionately, and perhaps we do. Yet we accept all kinds of shoddy education that is no more than going through the motions. We pretend that so many courses, so many credits, so many hours in a classroom, so many books read add up to an education. The same is true of research, on which we spend billions of dollars annually. We seem immensely satisfied with the outer husk of the enterprise—the number of dollars spent, the size of laboratories, the number of people involved, the fine projects outlined, the number of publications. Why do we grasp so desperately at externals? Partly because we are more superficial than we would like to admit. Perhaps partly because we are too lazy or too preoccupied to go to the heart of the problem. But also because it is easier to organize the external aspects of things. The mercurial spirit of great teaching and great scholarship cannot be organized, rationalized, delegated, or processed. The formalities and externals can.

New Organizational Forms

Our most melancholy thoughts about organization almost always concern the classic large-scale industrial or governmental bureaucracy—a thing of divisions, branches, bureaus, and departments, through which flow rivers of memoranda. In terms of status, it is a pyramid, and only a few at the top have the faintest idea what the whole organization is about. This is the organization the novels are written about. This is what is pictured in the organization charts. This is the setting in which the legendary office boy rises steadily to the top.

It really does exist. But taken alone it is an extraordinarily inaccurate picture of modern organization. There are at work in the world today forces that play havoc with the ordered arrangements of the industrial or governmental bureaucracy.

Consider, for example, the rise of the professions, one of the most striking developments in modern social organization. The conflict between the professions and the bureaucracies is deeply rooted in the nature of professional functioning. The loyalty of the professional man is to his profession and not to the organization that may house him at any given moment. Compare the chemist or electronics engineer in a local plant with the nonprofessional executives in the same plant. The men the chemists thinks of as his colleagues are not those who occupy neighboring offices, but his fellow professionals wherever they may be throughout the country, even throughout the world. Because of his fraternal ties with widely dispersed contemporaries, he himself is highly mobile. But even if he stays in one place his loyalty to the local organization is rarely of the same quality as that of the true organization man. He never quite believes in it.

The rise of the professions means that modern large-scale organization has been heavily infiltrated by men who have an entirely different concept of what organization is about and an entirely different image of their own relationship to it. This can have far-reaching consequences in the way the organization is run, as anyone familiar with the administration of universities and hospitals can testify.

Foes of modern large-scale organization will find it pleasant to reflect on this lack of rapport between the professions and the classic bureaucracy. But they must not imagine that the professions are wholly dependable allies. The professions themselves have rather considerable potentialities for rigidifying the society.

Another development that has profoundly altered the nature of the classic bureaucracy is the extraordinary rise of servicing organizations. The large modern organization is invaded every hour of the day and night by armies of people performing one or another sort of service. Just as the crocodile has a bird that picks its teeth and parasites in its digestive tract, so the modern large-scale organization is picked over and used as a supporting environment by an incredible variety of outsiders. Lawyers, auditors, management consultants, architects, decorators, insurance men, bankers, public relations men, advertising men, plant security people, janitorial services, landscape architects, and an endless list of others move in to contribute their highly specialized bits to the complex functioning of the whole—and then move out again. They are a vital part of the human environment and the functioning of the machinery, yet they never appear on the organization chart, and their only relationship to the organization is of a contractual nature.

The remarkable range of such professional and technical services that are available, plus the flexibility of the contractual relationship, gives the modern organization a wide range of choice in shaping its own future. Within limits, top management can put its finger on almost any function within the organization and decree that henceforth that function will be performed by an outside organization on contract. For the organization that wishes to maintain the maneuverability so essential to renewal, this offers priceless opportunities.

Particularly interesting are those instances in which the very nature of the large organization makes it necessary to reach outside for assistance. Much of the effectiveness of the management consultant, for example, is traceable to his "outsideness." Much that he does could— in theory—be done by specialists within the organization, but he has the advantage of operating outside the stultifying forces which hem them in. He can take a fresh view. He can speak out. And he *may* be listened to.

Furthermore, since professionals often do not enjoy life in the large organization and do enjoy the environment of a professional team, the servicing organization is usually able to retain a higher grade of specialist than its clients could normally recruit or hold.

Still another development that does not fit the conventional concept of organization is the emergence of associations or federations with strictly limited objectives. A number of doctors band together for the purpose of sharing certain central services—office facilities, laboratory equipment and staff, physical maintenance, and the like. A number of independent taxicab owners band together to obtain common garage facilities, accounting services, and insurance. A number of small colleges form an association to pool their money-raising efforts.

The possible significance of such arrangements is very great. It is becoming increasingly doubtful that a large number of small, unaffiliated operators can survive in a world of gargantuan organizations. Thus it becomes critically important to explore any possible arrangements by which the individual or small organization can enjoy some of the benefits of large-scale organization without any substantial loss of autonomy.

One could go on at some length enumerating the varied organizational forms that lend a kaleidoscope quality to our national life. The exuberant variety is increased by our national habit of forming voluntary associations to accomplish almost every conceivable shared purpose. Some of these—unions, political parties, professional associations, interest groups—are very powerful indeed. A number of writers have stressed the importance of such associations in the functioning of our kind of free society.

VII

The 1960's

In the second half of the twentieth century, a plurality of success patterns prevailed, including some new ones. The Gospel, if less intense than in the past, was still pervasive. Yet for the first time leisure as well as work, avocation no less than vocation, was becoming a widespread concern. The Biblical injunction to labor by the sweat of one's brow appeared applicable to only a dwindling majority. Increasingly, Americans were appraising the meaning of work and success itself in qualitative terms and with unprecedented candor and vigor.

——

Clarence B. Randall
Young Men

The responsibility for the recruitment, development, and promotion of executive talent devolves upon the businessman. Clarence Randall (1891-   ), the Andrew Carnegie of the organizational elite, avows in the following selection that Big Business must strive to select young men who are adaptable, rather than those who are tailor-made for organization. It must create conditions that will dissuade the courageous and brilliant from leaving to join more flexible smaller companies. [Clarence B. Randall, A Creed for Free Enterprise, Boston, *1952, pp. 121-137.]*

Consideration of the problems of the colleges and universities takes one directly to that most absorbing subject of all, the selection and training of young men for responsibility in industry. The businessman who overlooks this important part of his job not only dooms his company to mediocrity in the next generation, but robs himself of one of the deepest satisfactions in life. There is no greater thrill than to choose or promote a young man because he seems to have unusual promise, and then to find this judgment overwhelmingly justified by the experience of the passing years. The men we have picked or advanced provide a much surer index to our own ability than the plants we have built. Most of us spend our own business lives playing on a team we didn't select, and to be thought well of by our successors requires that we do not pass on to them a heritage of personnel blunders.

Selection is too narrow a word to use in the first instance when thinking of building for leadership. Recognition would be better, recognition and nurturing of unusual ability already existing within the organization. Inside any company in each generation some of the ablest men are never selected: they just get a job anonymously in the old-fashioned way and emerge on merit. The smart boss watches for them and does something about it as soon as they emerge. Some may have formal education, but many will not, and it is still the glory of our country that that doesn't matter. It is staying uneducated that dooms the man, not the starting that way. No man can help it if he has to leave school to support his parents, but he very much can help it if he wants an education thereafter. The thirst for knowledge need never be denied in modern America, and the man who carries his night courses through to completion while doing his full job in the shop in the day has a sense of values and a courage that merit the most thoughtful scrutiny by the boss who is looking for leadership in his organization.

There are never enough such. But as the years pass more and more young men and women from even the lowest income families are able to achieve a formal education, and so the businessman looking for future leadership turns to the various institutions of higher learning. Here the word "select" is used advisedly, for every effort must be made to obtain the best if the company is to excel its competition in the next generation. Aggressive and intelligent recruitment becomes a necessity. It now has a major part in the hot pace of competition. Those companies who rely merely upon recognition of ability among those who apply for jobs will occasionally find a top flight man, but on the average they will be choosing from among those of lesser ability, for among the applicants will be a higher ratio of those who were passed over as mediocre by the active recruiters. A comprehensive plan must resemble the seeded tournament in tennis: the dark horse who wins now and then keeps the play exciting, but there must be seeded players if quality is to be maintained.

How to pick the right group of college seniors for seeding into a company, and what to do with them after they are selected, are fascinating and altogether baffling problems, about which there are as many different viewpoints as there are individual executives who are concerned. I happen to hold strong opinions, but they are strictly personal, and some of my closest friends think I am wrong in many particulars. This variety of approach, however, as among companies even in the same industry is wholesome, and is once more typical of the strength of free enterprise.

To begin with, I am not too happy with the intense zeal of some of the college placement officers who are apt to fall into the habit of mind of scoring their own performance and that of their institution on the basis of the number of seniors whom they place with the so-called good companies. Like the justice of the peace who performs hasty marriages, they sometimes start a train of circumstances that brings unhappiness later. One of their sins, in my opinion, for example, is the coaching they give the boy on the day before he is interviewed by the company representative. Like a horse being groomed for the show ring they want him to appear well for their own sakes or that of the college. So they tell the senior to be crisp and decisive in his answers, and to give the appearance of knowing his own mind. But how can a boy be wisely crisp and decisive when he is torn by inner doubts and fears? How can a youngster who has never tried to sell anything know that he wants to enter a sales department? Or can he be sure that just because he had a good mark in physics he will do well in production? For myself, I am always wary of the senior who knows his own mind, since I am quite sure that indecision and uncertainty are normal at that time in one's life. The recruiters whom I have trained, therefore, never ask the senior what it is he wants to do, but devote themselves to trying to discover what sort of boy it is they are talking to. And the decisions as to where those selected are to be placed in the company are postponed as long as possible in the training period, to permit the boy to learn all he can about what actually goes on in the company, and the staff to learn all they can about the boy. Complete mutual understanding is a better basis for the future than snap judgment on both sides in March of senior year.

Another fundamental in my creed is that we never select a man for what he knows. It is his capacity to learn that excites me, and particularly his capacity to learn that which he knows nothing about. If he is to be a leader he will spend most of his mature life doing things for which he is not specially trained, and to be effective he must have the intellectual courage and facility to have a go at any problem, no matter how strange. A metallurgist who is afraid of a balance sheet because he had no accounting in college will never rise above the level of technician. Proven competence in some field, plus intense intellectual curiosity and audacity are the essential qualities, it seems to me. The trick is how to detect them in a twenty-minute interview.

Scholastic marks are important. It is of course true that many a man with poor grades comes to great success in later life, usually because his maturing process was slow, but as a matter of cold calculation there will be fewer such among the C's than among the B's, and fewer there than among the A's. Once the intellectual capacity is established, the interviewer can turn to the other desired qualities, but to choose a dull mind because the boy is pleasant is not being fair to the future.

The list of the other qualities must start with character. There is no substitute for character—the awareness of moral problems, and the courage to do the right thing under all conditions of life. The brilliant but dishonest mind and heart may bring disaster to the company in later years, and no young man is worthy who lacks rugged integrity.

Then comes an instinct for human relations. Here is where the intellectual must be watched carefully, for if he is too intent on the processes of the mind to be aware of what people think of him, he will not understand team play in industry.

And then comes the capacity for self-expression. Many a brilliant mind has burned itself out in industry because the man could not communicate to those of lesser intellectual power the advanced ideas which he had conceived. Writing and speaking English clearly and concisely are indispensable as working tools in modern business.

This is not intended as a complete list of qualities that may attract an interviewer, but rather to point up the opinion that I hold that there is no single scholasic discipline or training that is the best preparation for the steel industry, or any other business. Such qualities are to be found among the seniors of every school, and among students of science or students of the liberal arts. It is the qualities that we seek, and not specific knowledge acquired by the student in a particular field of concentration. And if we base our decisions on the qualities, wherever they may be found, we will surely at the same time give our companies a wide variety of educational backgrounds.

Personally, I like a full year of company training for the seeded player before he is assigned to a job, a sort of postgraduate course in the particular affairs of the one institution. This should be as broad as possible, for once he is in a groove it will be many years before the young man can look around again. That year is his own golden opportunity to equip himself with a breadth of background which may thereafter lie fallow until he approaches middle age. He should see not only things but people, and all of the key officials should study him as he studies them. If possible, he should work with his hands and not be merely an observer, but that is very hard to accomplish as he moves from department to department, since he cannot remain long enough to receive the necessary training. At any rate, he should live in the plant community, and be urged to seek every opportunity of forming friendships with employee families. If the trainees form a group, they should be encouraged to take their meals together in order that the bull session may be continuous. The cross-currents of comment that flow back and forth between the technically trained and those from the liberal arts are very humbling and very salutary on both sides, and as mutual respect develops comradeships are formed that mean a great deal in future years.

Actual placement at the end of the training year is seldom difficult. The first to be weeded out are those occasional ones who find neither the industry nor the company to their liking, and much later heartache will be avoided if such are encouraged to leave without the slightest feeling of moral obligation for the year of training. Those who remain are the keen ones who sense that this is precisely the company they want to work for, and who now are so well informed about the whole organization that they want to try out for a particular job. The indecision of senior year has given way to confidence born of knowledge and experience.

Occasionally, there is the black sheep who casts discredit on his generation and breeds cynicism in the heart of his boss—the boy who signs on with his tongue in his cheek, never intending to stay permanently, but planning deliberately to steal two or three more years of training and then sell his services in the market of those employers who are too lazy to provide training. The dishonesty lies in the fact that he permits himself to be overpaid during the early years, and leaves before he has pulled his weight.

Once the boy is placed the real battle begins, and it is one that tries the soul of the most understanding executive. Seeded players are temperamental, whether on the tennis courts or in industry, and to bring the unusual young man safely through the restiveness of his first five years is a ticklish task in human engineering. To begin with, his immediate superior will probably not be helpful. If he is not a college man himself, he may resent college men. If he happens to have one of the slower minds, he resents the facile speech and mental quickness of the boy who led his class. Having come up the hard way himself, he withholds information and assigns the newcomer repetitive tasks that fill him with dismal boredom. And the understanding boss must bite his fingernails through all this, for if he so much as inquires about the youngster he gives the kiss of death to his advancement on merit. It must always be clear that the boy is not teacher's pet, and he must have no promotion that has not been won in competition with all comers, or where his ability has not been fully recognized by all concerned. Only the boy himself can lick the problem, and he does it by infinite patience, an honest smile, and faith in his own future.

About a third of them can't take it, however, and jump during the first five years. They become morbidly convinced that they have been forgotten, that they are getting nowhere, and that the road ahead is too long for them to endure. In college they found fresh intellectual challenge as they began each new course, and to perform the same task each day for even six months in industry establishes a boredom in their lives which soon exhausts their scant supply of patience. So they walk out, and the man who came up the hard way smiles knowingly at the worthlessness of the youngster of today.

Almost invariably they jump to small companies, proud of the fifty-dollar-a-month increase which the new employer is glad to give them because it has saved him the trouble of recruiting, and buoyed up with hope that soon they will have genuine responsibility. And usually that happens. It is ordinarily true that in the early years young men advance more rapidly both in compensation and in authority in small companies than in so-called big business. Larger organizations with well-developed personnel programs protect themselves in depth with talent so far as possible, and not only have substitutes in the line of succession, but substitutes for the substitutes. The ultimate target is the thing, however, and that is something which is very difficult to explain to a young man about to be married to whom an immediate pay increase is the most important thing in life. Vaguely he thinks that at forty he will be eagerly sought after and that he will then go back to a fine job in a large institution, but it seldom works out that way. Large companies go outside for talent only as a last resort and because someone failed in their personnel planning, for they must reward those who didn't jump. And nothing makes an older man more heartsick than to watch through the years the career of a boy who jumped, and find him eventually stymied in a job too small for him, just because economic circumstances doomed his company to stagnation. And to talk to him before he leaves about the greater security to be found in a large organization is wasted effort that he sits through with reluctance, for what is to happen to him at sixty-five has less gravitational pull with him than the moon has on a millpond.

But over the years—and this process in one form or another has been going on for a long time—these jumpers, the seeded players who leave the large companies to sign on with the small, have had a marked influence on our economy. No one who has sat as I have on boards of business and civic organizations made up of men drawn from every section of the country and all industries can have failed to observe with some chagrin that the brilliant creative minds and the courageous natural leaders seem to be found more often in the smaller companies than in the large. I am afraid that this is a process of natural selection. Too many men who dare, jump, and eventually a man who didn't have the courage to leave becomes president of the large institution by seniority, simply because he was there. So the problem of the large companies is to find a way to bring the seeded players, the would-be jumpers, the men of spark and audacity through the restive period into the tranquility of recognized opportunity.

This requires subtlety and an ever-watchful eye on the part of the top management. One useful technique is what I like to call horizontal promotion, by which the promising man, whether a seeded player or one who came up the hard way, is not kept too long on one job or in one sequence. He will do much to train himself for future responsibility if given the chance, but unusual ability, like a fine machine, must be tuned up by use. The larger the company the greater degree of specialization, and if that process is not resisted it will give the company of the future a magnificent group of technicians with no one qualified to direct them. The breadth of judgment required of a seasoned executive at middle life is a function of experience, but the man of promise can acquire that experience only if his boss consciously makes it possible.

Similarly the experience in civic responsibility which these future leaders must have if the free enterprise system is to be perpetuated can be made possible only by conscious stimulation and intelligent recognition on the part of the senior executives. No longer may they gibe at the patriotic youngster who wants to serve in the National Guard: "What's the matter, haven't you got enough to do around here?" On the contrary, they must suggest the names of likely juniors to civic organizations who are recruiting workers, and go out of their way to compliment those who volunteer for such assignments. Likewise they must watch for signs of the articulate quality, and encourage the youngsters to try their wings at speaking about their own fields of interest to church groups, luncheon clubs, etc. Above all, they themselves must set a worthy example in all these things.

There is one habit which we older men have in dealing with employment which I deplore, but I must confess that in holding my opinions I find myself in a most exclusive minority. Actually, the attitude of which I complain is a piece of unreasoned folklore that is commonly accepted and practiced because, in my view, it is not thought through. These are the usual circumstances. In even those companies that for years have been outstanding in their personnel planning and administration there come emergencies. Perhaps the number two in sequence resigns, and the senior suffers a coronary, all in the same month, leaving a key spot without coverage, and creating a situation so desperate that the management has no alternative but to go outside for a replacement. There isn't time to bring in a junior by lateral transfer and give him the necessary training, for immediate experience is demanded at a mature level. Invariably under those conditions the management casts covetous eyes on the number two in the same sequence in the organization of a strong competitor, and the question arises of whether the consent of that company should be secured before the man is approached. The accepted code is that such consent must always be obtained, and that the matter should be dropped if the other company demurs.

Personally I do not consider myself bound by that code, nor do I ask others to respect it in dealing with me, for it seems to me that the practice plainly violates the freedom of individual action which we are seeking so earnestly to preserve. Who am I to decide for one of my subordinates a matter which vitally touches his whole life? He is entitled to make his own decisions as to whether the opportunity offered by the other company is greater than that of his present prospect, and it is not in keeping with our concept of the worth of the individual in a democracy to bargain about him like a piece of merchandise without his knowledge. If he leaves our company, and I am unhappy, it would indicate that we have underpaid him, or withheld from him an insight into the future to which he was entitled. So I hire the competitor's man if I want to, and make no preliminary telephone call.

And there is then one final phobia that I have about young men in which again I am sadly in the minority, though again I like to think that the conventional attitude receives wide acceptance because the individual executives do not pause to think it through. It has to do with industrial deferment from military service. Beginning in my war back in 1917, and coming strongly into favor in the last war, as well as in the successive crises since 1945, has been the concept that the chemist, the metallurgist, the engineer, and the other technically trained students must not bear arms. They constitute a special reserve of brains which the nation must not jeopardize. They are to stay in the factories and devise new weapons while the liberal arts boys do the dying. Yet from among those same impractical students of the humanities and the social sciences might come the future Churchills, the men of ideals and character, who would hold aloft the torch of leadership in their country for either war or peace. So I cannot think it is just to have a planned economy in death. The grim burden should be shared by all alike.

But I must close . . . as I began . . . by paying my respect once more to the youth in American industry today, and expressing my warm affection for them. They are magnificent, and the question is not whether they will fail us, but rather whether we will fail them.

San Francisco Examiner

Peter Chew, Publisher-Tycoon

The "rags-to-riches" American epic continues to register scores of true-life success stories on the periphery of the organizational world. Yet the rise of San Francisco's Peter Chew, Chinese-American in an America which only recently has began to accept the Oriental as an equal, is still sufficiently unusual. ["Profiles in Progress: Peter Chew, Publisher Tycoon, Landed in U.S. 25 Years Ago with One Dollar," San Francisco Examiner, *August 9, 1964.]*

Peter Chew is an outstanding representative of San Francisco's Chinese-American community.

Just about everything he touches turns to gold.

Twenty-five years ago, he came to America with only the shirt on his back and three dollars of Hong Kong money (the equivalent of one dollar U.S.).

Today, at 49, he is board chairman of the Young China Publishing Company and operates vast real estate holdings (apartments, stores, office buildings, commercial properties and the Maurice, Gaylord and Franciscan Hotels) as head of Peter Chew Investments, 680 Geary Street.

Peter Chew's story is the Horatio Alger fulfillment of the American dream, the kind of story millions like to read about, but which happens only to a chosen few.

In recent years, in City real estate and business circles, he was known as a "mystery man" because of modesty concerning his meteoric rise. He is often seen in small Chinese short-order coffee shops enjoying an 85-cent lunch with as much relish as he dines in the finest restaurants of The City. But Peter Chew has been a hot "news personality" since his recent visit to Hong Kong and Taiwan where he contributed $100,000 to the Hua Hsin nursery for orphans.

He is presently considering the establishment of a Chinese-American welfare foundation in San Francisco.

"Is there a secret system for success in business?"

Chew was recently asked this question by a special correspondent of Hong Kong's Cosmorama Pictorial.

"Honest and hard work are the basic ingredients for success," Chew told him.

"Plus a kindly smile from Lady Luck," he added, and his memory was probably reaching back more than 25 years, to a small village in Hoi Ping county of Canton province where he began his first journey to a challenge.

His family was poor—a typical family of the Good Earth which has been the backbone of the Chinese people throughout the centuries. They had little formal education but were rich in a tradition of moral and ethical honesty and perseverance.

"I remember going to big, bustling Canton, the provincial capital," he said, "and, like thousands of other struggling souls, I did many menial jobs, the kind which can leave one bitter because of the struggle for survival."

But his mother's teachings and feeling for humanity gave Chew a perceptive insight which made the bitter experiences of this critical period an education in life.

In Canton, he learned about automobiles and became a mechanic and a driver. Then, in 1939, the war clouds of Asia touched Canton as Japanese armies marched through China. It was the time for Peter Chew to realize his dream of coming to America, but he was forced to come long before he was financially ready.

So he landed in San Francisco with three Hong Kong dollars.

He again started out in menial jobs and gradually built up a laundry business. Then, when war broke out, he put his mechanical experience to use and worked in a shipyard.

All this time he studied real estate at nights and modestly invested his hard-earned money. He also maintained—sometimes at great personal sacrifice—an excellent credit rating.

"Once your credit is established, all your investments in business can benefit greatly," said Chew. "Sound credit is the lifeblood of the businessman."

Peter Chew's closest friend is his financial advisor, Donald C. Silverthorne, president and board chairman of the San Francisco National Bank. (Chew calls Silverthorne, "Papa," and the banker calls his friend, "Son.")

Though Peter Chew seems "all business," he is emphatic in saying that more people, particularly more businessmen, should participate in some way in politics.

"No one can escape being involved in the results of politics," he said, "for political power in the United States stems from the will of the people."

Peter Chew is a student of political activities and is on a first-name basis with many political figures. Through these associations, he is in close touch with social changes, many of which affect the Chinese people.

This is partly the reason why he became interested in such a social-cultural enterprise as the Young China Daily. As board chairman of its publishing company, he plans to turn the San Francisco daily into a nationwide Chinese-American newspaper.

Young China Daily news bureaus are planned for New York, Boston, Washington and other major cities, and circulation will be actively sought in those areas.

He feels the days of a Chinese written paper are gone and has already inaugurated a daily English language insert—an innovation which quickly boosted circulation from 7,000 to 8,000 daily.

Chew views The Young China as a spokesman and means of communication in Chinese-American relations and feels the eastern surge of the newspaper will increase circulation to 15,000.

Thankful for the opportunity which America has given him, Peter Chew believes the exchange of ideas between Chinese and Americans is one of the greatest goals for anyone.

He says, frankly, that money making for this project now is not important but that the investment in human ideals is much greater and more challenging than real estate.

The once-poor village lad has now been in the United States 25 years. He is wealthy and an American citizen. His heart and mind are now American, but he has never forgotten the mother land.

He himself is a disciple of Buddhism, and his respect for his mother is practiced in the finest Chinese tradition, according to his relatives and friends.

In the Chew home, Chinese and American are spoken. Peter Chew's wife, Rose, and their four children were born in America. The two older children, Richard, 15, and Patricia, 14, are in Hong Kong taking extensive studies in Chinese culture and languages and learning the lessons of life to prepare them for the business world.

Donald and Teresa, both 12, attend Marina Junior High School.

Chew hopes that his latest venture as head of The Young China will introduce Americans to Chinese culture and be a useful means of communication between Americans and Chinese.

——

David Riesman
The Uncommitted
Generation

*In an age of organization, no one has been more subject to batteries
of interviews and tests than the college student. Consistently he has
scored as a conformist. David Riesman deplores the seeming loss of
a sense of vocation, the divorce of family from occupational goals, the
conviction that work in large organizations is unrewarding, and the
notion that individuals are powerless to influence those organizations.
Indeed, Riesman sees the colleges as increasingly providing a setting
for innovation and renewal in the society. [This selection represents a
combination of three articles by David Riesman: "The Uncommitted
Generation: 'Junior Organization Men' in America," Encounter, XV,
November 1960, pp. 25-30; "The College Student in an Age of
Organization," Chicago Review, XII, Autumn 1958, pp. 64-68; and
"Where Is the College Generation Headed?" Atlantic, CCVII, April
1961, pp. 44-45.]*

In a recent lecture, addressing myself primarily to students, already a
highly self-conscious group, I was reluctant simply to list once more
the labels the older generation has already pinned on them: apathy, conformity, security-mindedness, "coolness," "beatness," and so on. Such
labels do have a certain truth, and I shall try to delineate what it is; but
they also conceal about as much as they reveal. They conceal the fact
that the college generations of the 1920's and 1930's, now nostalgically
admired, were on the whole far less responsive, serious, and decent than

students in comparable institutions today. They conceal the fact that the apparently negative qualities of apathy and conformity must be seen as an aspect of the high intelligence and sensitivity of this generation of students, who know more than their elders did and who have, justly, more to be afraid of.

In my lecture, I was able to count on a discussion period in which I might partially clarify the misunderstandings so loaded a theme was bound to generate, and in which the students could (and did) talk back. Furthermore, I could respond to some alumni who attacked the "softness" and lack of political and civic responsibility of the students, first by reminding them of how ancient and inevitable was the theme of parents' complaints against the "softening" of the children whom they had themselves indulged, and second by emphasizing the difficulties sensitive and concerned young people face today precisely because the manifest hardships with which earlier Americans coped have been, for millions, eliminated, while new challenges, appropriate to an age of abundance, still remain to be confronted.

My principal theme, however, was not to defend students against the common ethnocentrism of their elders but to help explain them to themselves, and to show how some of the students' attitudes towards the world, as shaped in school and college, are not so much a reaction to that world as it is, but a "reaction-formation" in the psychoanalytic sense: that is, a defense which has become unrealistically overgeneralized. College students today often act as if they believed that work in large organizations and, beyond that, work in general, could not be basically or humanly satisfying (or at times even honest), but was primarily a way to earn a living, to find a place in the social order, and to meet nice or not-so-nice people. This is a conclusion which, I shall suggest, is partly projected upon the occupational scene as the result of their experience with the curriculum in college and university —and as the result of experience also with college and university as organizations which are viewed as bureaucratic, monolithic, and unchangeable, at least by many students.

I do not think it is the primary task of education to prepare students for their later occupational roles, or indeed any narrowly specialized roles, nor to teach them to enjoy work regardless of its quality and meaning. Rather, the relationship of education to later life should be a dialectical and critical one. If, however, one result of going to college is to become alienated from work *per se* and defeatist about the possibility of altering one's relation to it, then it seems to me one ought to re-examine academic institutions themselves and see whether anything in them or in one's own attitudes or both might be changed.

Some time ago [Spring, 1955] several hundred interviews were done (at the behest of *Time* magazine) with seniors at twenty colleges throughout the country, most of them colleges of some or of great distinction. The seniors were supposed to be reasonably representative, but what this was taken to mean and how it was applied at various colleges and universities varied greatly. A good many student leaders were chosen, a good many bright people, but hardly any women got in (a questionnaire circulated by *Mademoiselle* gave me somewhat comparable data concerning college women). When I first examined the interviews, and now again when I have once more gone over them, I have been struck by what appears to be a not quite conscious ambivalence towards work in large organizations. On the other hand, the majority are planning to enter large organizations in pursuit of their careers: big corporations, big governments, big law offices, and so on. Only a few seek independence in their work, either in terms of old-fashioned ideals of entrepreneurship or in terms of the desire to become a foreign correspondent, to enter politics, or to follow some other individualistic or exotic calling. (Moreover, hardly anyone expresses resentment against his prospective Army service on the ground that the Army is a large organization: there is no eagerness for service, but rather resignation to it as one of the givens of life.)

And yet, when these young people are asked about their lives outside of work, a very different picture emerges. There, bigness and scale are definitely *not* valued. Only a tiny fraction want to head for the metropolis, even if their careers might make such a location convenient. They want the suburbs—not later, after some bachelor start has been made in the big city, but now, on graduation. The great majority either are already married or plan to get married soon (even if there is no special one in mind at the moment); they plan to start having children at once, and to begin building a community-centered life in the suburbs. They envisage a two-car but usually not a two-career family, in which the prospective wife will be active in the Parent-Teachers' Association, with subsidiary assistance from the husband, and in which both spouses will concern themselves with a manageable bit of real estate— a suburban neighborhood in which they can at once be active and hope to make a difference. It does not occur to them that they might be gifted and energetic enough to make a difference even in a big city. Rather, they want to be able to work through a face-to-face group—the post-collegiate fraternity of the small suburbs. Correspondingly, the very emphasis on family life which is one of the striking and in so many ways attractive qualities of young people today is an implicit rejection of large organization. The suburban family with its garden, its barbecue, its lack of privacy in the open-plan house, is itself a manifesto of decentralization—even though it makes use of centralized services such as TV, clinics, chain stores, and *House Beautiful*. The wish to build a nest, even if a somewhat transient one, is a striking feature of the interviews, in contrast with the wish to build a fortune or a career which might have dominated some comparable interviews a generation earlier.

This pattern—the acceptance of large organizations combined with tacit and uncrystallized resistance to them—appears not only in the respondents' emphasis on the family but also in what they say about their plans and attitudes towards their future work. I get a sense from the material, and from other comparable data, of a certain withdrawal of emotional adherence from work. To be sure, it has become fashionable to speak of one's work or other activities in deprecatory terms and to adopt a pose of relative indifference to the larger goals of an organization. In an era of political, economic, and cultural salesmanship, such deprecation is a way of guarding against being exploited for ends outside one's self. It is as if one had constantly to conduct psychological warfare against an outside enemy. But, as in any such process, students become to some extent the victims of their own defenses. They come to believe that work cannot really be worth doing for its own sake, whether or not it is done on behalf of a large impersonal organization—a fear of overcommitment to one's work even while one is at the workplace. In the course of getting rid of earlier collegiate or rah-rah enthusiasm, these young people have come to feel that work is not worth even their part-time devotion, and perhaps that nothing, except the family, deserves their wholehearted allegiance.

We see the same attitudes, of course, among the junior echelons now engaged in work. One hears them talk of their benevolent company as "a mink-lined rat-trap," or speak of "the rat-race," or refer to fights over principles as "ruckuses" or "blow-ups"—if somebody cares, he is said to "blow his top." In a number of business novels, of which *The Man in the Grey Flannel Suit* is representative, it is taken for granted that a sensible fellow, and indeed an honest one, will prefer suburban domesticity and a quiet niche to ulcerous competition for large business stakes, despite the view from the top and the interesting climb.

Attitudes such as these are, of course, an aspect of a general cultural shift, not confined to students and not confined to those who seek employment in large organizations; similar attitudes turn up in some measure even among those who, studiously avoiding such organizations, look for a professional career in which they hope to be their own masters. Scholars, for example, are not immune to distaste for their work, nor are architects or physicians. But while I don't intend to imply that a life without any boredom is conceivable, except for a very stupid person, still I think we are witnessing a silent revolution against work on the part even of those relatively privileged groups who have been free to choose their work and to exercise some freedom in the doing of it. This reflects, in part, the fact that much work is meaningless *per se,* save as a source of income, prestige, and sociability; but it also indicates, as I have already implied, that people too readily accept their work as it comes, without hope of making it more meaningful.

William H. Whyte, Jr., summarizes some of these tendencies in his writings (notably in *The Organization Man*) and points out that some large corporations, worried about the decline in "work-mindedness," are seeking to substitute an ideology of corporate loyalty, a "social ethic," for the inexorable attachment to work which was requisite in the building of an industrial society. Indeed, he shows how the corporation, in order to compete with the family, takes over much of the aura of domesticity, as if to say: "We may be a large organization to outsiders, but within we are, if not a happy family, at least a happy suburb, neighborly, protective, close, and clean." Such spokesmanship underplays the potential excitement of the work itself—and I believe that much work in large organizations can be intensely exciting—and overplays the fringe benefits.

What I want to stress is the fact that not all large organizations are alike, despite the sorts of institutional similarities investigated by sociologists; and of course that not all positions in them are alike. Many, although their top executives clamor for creativity and independence of mind, largely manage to process these qualities out of "their" people in the lower ranks. Others stockpile talent and expect it to keep as gold keeps at Fort Knox. Still others make products or provide services which are either anti-social or useless. But here and there one finds companies which face real and not contrived problems and apply to them an intelligence which is often remarkably disinterested and, in the best sense of the term, "academic." Young people in search of challenge and development would do well to seek out such relatively productive climates rather than to assume offhand (as is true of so many brand-name products) that they are all alike except for the advertising and the label. And this search is necessary precisely because many of the motives which impelled work in the older generations have fortunately become attenuated—motives such as money for its own sake, power, and fame—goals, that is, whose emptiness became evident with their attainment. Our industrial and commercial plant no longer "needs" such compulsive attachments to work which are based not on any genuine creative impulse but on the drying up of other alternatives.

There is a further issue concerning work in large organizations where again differentiation is required. I refer to the conception that work in organizations requires surrender of independence of judgment, if not of integrity. When I was in college, there was a prevalent feeling among the more sensitive that this was true only of business and commercial organizations, not of governmental or philanthropic ones, and young men debated whether they would enter Wall Street and make money or enter government or teaching and be saved. This dichotomy has in large measure vanished, although traces of it do survive among the less cynical. For instance, I have known many graduate students in social psychology who believe that if they teach they can be honest, but that if they work in market research they will serve manipulation and corruption, and will have no power over their own work. Such judgments oversimplify the ethical dilemmas of any calling, and are in addition snobbish: one can find "hucksterism" (often hypocritically veiled) among academic people in search of reputations, grants, and promotions, as well as among market researchers and other businessmen. Indeed, I am inclined to think that at present many observant young people don't need to be persuaded of this; many are actually overpersuaded to the point of believing that *every* occupation is a racket, and that at best some of the racketeers are less pious about it than others. And this, I suspect, is one of the reasons they tend to withdraw emotional allegiance from their work: with the impression that they have no control over it anyway, that all is in the hands of the mysterious men upstairs who run the show. If there is greater wisdom in the belief that all occupations, like all forms of power, are corrupting in some degree, there is also greater resignation, greater passivity and fatalism.

Where are such attitudes learned and confirmed? Even at some of the leading colleges, the more intellectual colleges—the colleges which produce literary magazines—the relation of students to the curriculum has a certain alienated quality, in the sense that the students do not believe they have any control over their own education.

Let me give a few examples. In the last few years I have visited a number of colleges of high quality—colleges which turn out eminent professional men, scholars, and scientists; and I have made it my business to talk with students informally, to read their student newspapers and, where possible, student council reports. At a number of these institutions, the livelier students complain of the educational fare they are getting, of the very little contact the curriculum makes with the problems that are meaningful to them. Sometimes they feel that opportunities for a civilized and intellectual life on campus are wanting—for example, that there are few inviting places to study or to talk, that social pressures in dormitories force any intellectual life out of the group setting, that student publications are either dominated by the school administration or devoted to "campus news" and trivia, that the bookstore is inadequate, or that the library is geared to research needs, rather than to attract undergraduate browsers. They often feel they have no access to the faculty for other than merely routine matters. Sometimes students complain about the prerequisites of a department, which serve its monopolistic aims or protect its mediocre teachers from boycott, rather than serve any defensible pedagogic aims.

Yet when I ask such students what they have done about these things, they are surprised at the very thought that they could do anything. They think I am joking when I suggest that, if things came to the worst, they could picket! They think I am wholly unrealistic when I say that many on the faculty might welcome student initiative in revising the curriculum, or that it might be possible to raise modest sums of money among alumni or others to bring visiting lecturers, poets, *et al.* to the campus, or to furnish commodious rooms for interest-group meetings. When I tell them that the Harvard House plan came about in considerable measure because of the report of a student council committee in 1926, which caught the attention of the philanthropist Edward Harkness, they shrug—that must have been a golden era, they say; nothing like that could happen now. Of course, as long as they think that, they will conduct themselves accordingly.

What is perplexing in this outlook is that the students appear to be so very realistic about the organization they are living in. They harbor no illusions about the faculty, the administration, the trustees. Yet they act as if the structure these men have created or inherited were part of the universe. It seems hardly ever to occur to students that a faculty is not a unit, but a set of factions, often in precarious balance, and that student activity might conceivably help tip the balance. And in spite of all that they know intellectually (and as children of vulnerable parents) about their power over their teachers, they don't put this power to use to improve the quality of their education.

At a low-level college it may be that the students have too much power. My colleague Everett C. Hughes has investigated institutions supposedly devoted to higher education where students make it impossible for the professor to demand anything of them beyond routine and comfortable performance; for instance, if they are asked to read a book they consider too difficult, they will turn in blank pages on an examination concerning it. Professors even at good and serious colleges have to preserve their own autonomy like any other professional group, and I am not recommending that they conduct "customer research" and guide themselves by a popularity poll. But I don't think it follows from this that they must remain innocent of educational sociology and psychology, unaware of the harm they do, or indifferent to the indifference they help breed.

In fact, it is the very quality of some of these professors and of the institutions at which they teach that helps to create in a paradoxical way feelings of passivity and helplessness among their students. Not only have students become better in the better colleges in recent decades, but professors have become ever so much more erudite and competent. One seldom finds any longer at a first-rate university the platform ham actors or dreary pedants who were all too common even when I was an undergraduate. The most difficult and avant-garde books—often those considered not long ago subversive or ribald—are on the freshman reading list at many institutions, and while the market for text-books is better than ever because education is everywhere such a boom industry, there are also many text-books which take account of new knowledge and are reasonably sophisticated. "Sophisticated" is in fact the word for much current higher education: the professor is one-up on the student and the student knows it. This is one of the cases where general social advance brings unanticipated negative consequences in its wake. Vis-à-vis such professors, students feel even less able than heretofore to influence their fate as students, and so they tend to leave matters in the hands of the constituted authorities, preserving (like GI's in the Army) only their privilege of griping.

Why is it that students, often so precocious about many things—about each other, about sex, about their families, and occasionally even about national and world affairs—are so comparatively inattentive to what concerns them so closely as does their curriculum?

For one thing, it seems to me that students don't want to believe that their activities might make a difference, because, in a way, they profit from their lack of commitment to what they are doing. I don't mean that they are not industrious students—they often are, much more so today, as I have said, than prior to World War II. They go through the required motions of working, but they seldom get really involved with the content of their courses. It is here that the better, more conscientious students sabotage their own education and restrict production: true enough, they turn out the credits and the grades, but they do not believe that it really matters in any fundamental sense what they think and feel.

When I have discussed this with students, they have often told me that it doesn't pay to be too interested in anything, because then one is tempted to spend too much time on it, at the expense of that optimal distribution of effort which will produce the best grades—and after all they do have to get into medical school, keep their scholarship, and "please the old man." Now I am convinced that grades contaminate education—they are a kind of currency which, like money, gets in the way of students discovering their intellectual interests—but here, too, the students in their realism are being somewhat unrealistic. They assume, for one thing, that it is hopeless to try to alter the curriculum so that it might penalize them less for serious interest in one topic at the expense of others, or so that there might be more emphasis on reading and discussion, and more opportunity for independent thinking. And here, also, the students have a distorted image of what will actually make an impression on their teachers either now or later. On this point I have some evidence to back me up.

After I had tried in vain for some time to persuade graduate students at Chicago that they could be more independent in their course and thesis work without any heroism, any martyrdom, there was a thesis done by a student which documented my arguments. The student went around to the departments and asked them which students in recent years they had recommended for jobs or advanced training or fellowships, and which they had not. Then he interviewed some of these students in various categories of faculty blessing or disapproval, looked at their grades, and so on. He concluded that those students frequently fared best who were not too obedient, who did not get an undiluted, uncomplicated straight-A record. (The straight-A students, in fact, sometimes slipped away without anyone's noticing.) Rather, the students who were often most successful were a bit rebellious, a bit off-beat, though not entirely "goof-offs"; these were the students apt to appeal to a faculty member who had not entirely repressed a rebelliousness of his own that had led him to be a teacher in the first place—a faculty member who was looking for signs of life, even if they gave him a bit of trouble at times. To be sure, such a student had to do well in something to earn this response, but he was often better off to have written a brilliant paper or two than to have divided his time, like an investment banker his money, among a variety of subjects. Those students who were the most self-consciously opportunistic and realistic in allocating their time and emotion were in fact sacrificing themselves unprofitably, suffering not only now during the studies which they regarded as an ante-room to life, but later on as well.

Now, not all departments at Chicago were alike in this matter; some gave more play to defiance and deviation than others. Moreover, this study encompassed only the social science departments. No doubt, departments and institutions differ very much in this respect. But that is just the point I want to emphasize: by concluding prematurely that all organizations are alike, that all demand the same kinds of conformity, students not only surrender the chance to experience an atmosphere that is freer and more conducive to their own development but perpetuate a myth that then controls their passage through jobs in later life. If the University of Chicago or even one's department itself can't be changed from below, how can one expect to change General Motors, or *Look* magazine, or the big hospitals of San Francisco? And if that is so, then why not settle for the fringe benefits, for a position of moderate respectability and adequate if not dazzling salary?

At work here is a characteristic social pattern in which individuals, hesitant to reveal feelings they have scarcely voiced to themselves, are misled about what in effect could be done if they expressed themselves, thereby discovering others who might share their views. (Sociologists refer to this process as "pluralistic ignorance.") Leadership, of course, whether in politics or in other affairs, often serves to help a group change its apparent mood to conform to its actual or potential but repressed views—but leadership also may, and frequently does, serve to continue enforcing the repression. Even in a large organization, radical and what were previously regarded as "impossible" changes come about almost instantaneously, once people discover that views they had previously regarded as unacceptable or idiosyncratic are in fact widely shared.

What happened in Hungary during the rebellion was apparently this on a large scale. People suddenly discovered that they were surrounded, not by potential informers, but by allies who had all along shared their hidden misgivings about the imposed Communist regime. Often, no more than a look was necessary to communicate this; often, a leader with the courage of his convictions unlocked the secret reservations that even Party members had harbored—and here the students and intellectuals were of the greatest importance. Once this discovery was made, and a union formed of those who had been gulled about what "public opinion" was, it was very difficult to erase the lesson and to reimpose conformity, not of outward behavior, but conformity of inward misconceptions and feelings of isolation and even guilt.

I confess that at times during the Hungarian and Polish insurrections, when I read the declarations of the Polish newspaper *Po Prostu* or of the Budapest Petofi Club, I felt a certain envy, realizing that the fight for freedom and for realism was in some paradoxical way easier where people were grossly and outrageously oppressed, in comparison with our situation where oppression is benevolent at best and usually bearable at worst. Our large organizations endanger and deceive their members, not by indecency and terror, but precisely by amiability and good will. (Of course, there are exceptions, but I am speaking in very general terms.) Students at the good colleges can't feel that it is worth making a fuss—let alone, of course, starting a revolution—to reduce the number of courses in which the lecturer merely repeats the outside reading, or otherwise to have themselves treated as no longer in high school. Their rebellion takes the very muted and even unconscious forms I have been describing, in which dissatisfaction shows up in withdrawal of allegiance to one's outfit, one's task, and eventually one's self.

Yet there are, as the example of Hungary shows, situations in life which are beyond our control. There is nothing to be said for the posture of those pious but naive Americans who believe that by virtue of noble declarations the tides of evil will be rolled back and righteousness triumph. Nothing is so simple-minded as the businessman who feels that if only he were let loose in Washington, everything would be straightened out. Such a man doesn't even recognize the extent to which his own business is supported by investment decisions made by large organizations, whether so-called private or public—the extent to which our prosperity rests on capital budgets controlled by a very few individuals.

The students know better, of course; they know that there are many decisions out of their conceivable control, decisions upon which their lives and fortunes truly depend. But what I am contending is that this truth, this insight, is over-generalized, and that, being believed, it becomes more and more "true." Not only do we fail to spot those instances in which intervention might change things quite substantially, but we fail to develop the competence and the confidence in ourselves that are necessary to any large endeavor. In that sense, despite our precociousness, we fail to grow up; we remain the children of organization, not the masters of it.

For Americans, there is something paradoxical about this development. Americans in the past have not been overimpressed by mechanical achievements. Workers in a steel mill are not awed by the giant rollers, and we take for granted that we are not awed by any large physical construction of our hands and brains. Contrary to the prevalent impression abroad that we are slaves to our machines, we are actually uninvolved with them, and we surely do not feel dominated by them. But it seems to be different with the organizational machines. These are as much the product of our thinking and our imagination as any technological feat; yet, as Erich Fromm has said, we worship like idolators the product we have created—an image not of stone but of other images.

It is a commonplace observation that in organizational life we use arguments to convince others which we think will appeal to them, even though they don't convince us. We try to persuade people to behave justly to Negroes because discrimination makes the United States look bad in the Cold War—as if that were why we ourselves behaved decently. Or we persuade businessmen to give money to colleges for all sorts of public-relations reasons, playing on their fear of radicalism or federal control or whatnot, whereas we ourselves devote our lives to education for quite different reasons. You will see that all arguments of this nature have two qualities: they patronize the other person and they perpetuate pluralistic ignorance. It can be contended that there may be occasions when we must appeal to others as they are, not as we could like them to be—when there isn't time for idealism. But, in our realism, we often make mistakes about what others will actually respond to, and we sacrifice the integrity and clarity of our argument to our false image of what will go over. The result: we conclude that one can't be honest while working for an organization, that one can be honest only when one is at home with one's family in the suburbs.

There is another result as well, namely, that we often end up in doubt as to what we ourselves think. We come to believe what we say to others and thus become "more sincere" in the subjective sense, but at the price of becoming still more confused as to what is actually so: we are the first victims of our own propaganda. No wonder we end up without emotional ties to what we do, for it is no longer we who do it, but some limited part of ourselves, playing a role. Not recognizing that we have done this to ourselves, we attribute to organizations the power and the primacy we have lost. And then, as I have said, we strike back, not directly, but by a kind of emotional attrition, in which we lend to our work willingness without enthusiasm, conscientiousness without creativity.

I am sure that many college students who are not only serious but dedicated know this as well as I do. Such students have managed to make college serve their purposes, and have in this way gained some rational confidence that they will be able to do the same in the organizations they will enter later—whether these are universities, business concerns, or the many voluntary organizations through which we Americans carry out much of our communal work. What I have principally sought to do in these remarks is to encourage greater and more differentiated realism than many young people already possess—a realism which does not take for granted the social structures which seem so impressive, but looks for the points of leverage where one's own effort, joined to that of others similarly freed from mythology, might make a difference. In many situations, there is more leeway than students think, and college is a good place to find this out.

Let me again make it quite clear that I understand the positive functions of what sometimes appears as mere apathy or passivity among students; for passivity toward revivalist manias and crusades is a sensible reaction, a sign of maturity. Moreover, as I noted at the outset, students are not at all apathetic about many fundamental things, among them personal relations, family life, and in many cases the arts. But even these attachments may be in danger. If one is apathetic about one's work, with all that such an attitude implies for one's relation to social and personal creation, it is hard to prevent this apathy from spreading to other areas. Freud thought that children's curiosity, repressed in the realm of sex, became as a result crippled quite generally—that is, the malignancy of repression tended to spread. This danger we have all but overcome. But the comparable spread of apathy and disenchantment from work to family life—indeed, even to sex—seems to me an analogous development. My concern is that young people today, by playing it cool and fearing to be thought squares, may create a style of life, not only in work but in every dimension of existence, which is less full, less committed, less complex, and less meaningful than mid-century opportunities allow.

Three years later, I have naturally asked myself to what extent the foregoing remarks still strike me as true. I had in 1955 and 1957 paid very brief visits to several of the Southern Negro colleges that have since been in the forefront of sit-in demonstrations; at that time they seemed to me, as to some of their own faculty members, acquiescent and cautious, preparing students to enter the army uncomplainingly, the "Black Bourgeoisie" unthinkingly. Of course, the students were aware of the struggles over integration, but for them the issues remained somewhat abstract, particularly as many of them had chosen the shelter of a segregated college, as in their prospective occupations—teaching, the ministry, Negro business—many would choose the still segregated occupations.

As so often, appearances were deceptive; some of these students carried out the first sit-ins and refused to become daunted or disorganized when either their own pressured administration or reactive whites sought to end the picketing and protests; a brave few, in active civil disobedience, have chosen jail rather than bail. Relatively immune to the economic boycotts that can hamstring their parents, and free, too, of the traditional Negro leadership in their communities, they have discovered their organizational powers and talents. This has been bracing and highly educative.

Meanwhile, among white students in the North, sympathetic picketing of the chain stores was rapidly organized, and many campuses had their first taste of political life in twenty years. The young people I have been describing are markedly tolerant; in the 1955 interviews, hardly any exhibited bigotry (at the Southern universities many said that once the old folks are gone, the race problem will die with them). Moreover, tolerance appears to them a virtue that is civic and personal, tied into one's own immediate human reactions and relations; to be tolerant to classmates, one does not have to fight city hall, though one may sometimes have to fight alumni guardians of the more collegiate fraternities.

Furthermore, the simplicity of the race issue, the near lack of rational or civilized defense of segregation and discrimination, allows Northern students to extrapolate public activity on the basis of private decency, without feeling themselves to be involved in "politics" or in ideology. True, the planned picketing has involved these highly individualistic students in more organization and decision-making than appeals to most of them; the term "politician" is as much one of contempt on the better campuses as it is generally in American life. Even so, many students have discovered, though less dramatically than the Southern Negro students, that they are capable of action in areas outside the usual complaints about library hours, dormitory food, and parking, and that even such seemingly large outfits as Woolworth's are not invulnerable.

So, too, there have recently been some energetic student actions in the

area of curriculum. In the spring of 1958, students at the University of
Wisconsin submitted a petition to the administration requesting more
challenge and stimulation in their courses and in their educational program generally. During the same period, undergraduates at Chicago
mobilized to defend the general education program against attempts
to subordinate it to the requirements of the graduate departments. A
group of students at Wesleyan last year arranged a series of discussions
on education, geared to the problems and opportunities faced by a
liberal arts college; apparently the students helped influence curricular
change. While, in some instances, students could graduate before realizing that what they did had any impact, others learned from their experiences that institutions are man-made and subject to change.

It is understandably seldom that such sporadic and ad hoc actions
have been carried over into political controversies on the national scene.
There have been occasional protests against compulsory ROTC, based
as much on the unintellectual waste of time of the programs as on any
explicit antimilitarist views. The student political party (Slate) at
Berkeley was a factor in last year's protest against the Un-American
Activities Committee hearings in San Francisco—a brave protest, since
many students fear it will go on their records in an FBI dossier. And,
increasingly, the issues of peace and disarmament have found a student
audience. Students are picketing weekly on Boston Common under the
auspices of the Committee for a Sane Nuclear Policy and are encounter-
ing, as they did to only a minor degree in picketing the chain stores,
violent and jeering attacks as Reds or yellow appeasers. Challenge at
Michigan and Yale, Concern at Ohio Wesleyan, Tocsin at Harvard
are among the groups that have sprung up to discuss peace and other
political questions. Only a very small minority are involved—but then
only a small minority were involved in the supposedly activist 1930s.
Probably some of these organizations will last only for the college
lifetimes of a handful of committed students.

Indeed, the very fact that academic values have triumphed on many
campuses puts heavy competition in the way of all extracurricular activity, including politics. I recall one student who recently felt he had
to choose between active participation in organizing a student chapter
of SANE and writing a senior distinction thesis; he believed that if he
did not do the latter, he would not get into graduate school (not an
unrealistic fear) and would jeopardize his whole career (in my judgment, a less realistic fear). Perhaps more important, the professors
have taught, especially the better students, that all questions are complex,
all ideologies suspect, and all larger passions fanatical; the fear of being
naive prevents many young people from feeling confidence in any action
or reaction. (Some of these same adults then criticize the students for
apathy!) Questions of foreign policy and disarmament *are* complex—
in a way that the race question is not—and students have in the past

feared to take a position that expert or "classified" knowledge might explode. Once they begin, however, these same academic values lead them to a seriousness illustrated by the Tocsin students, who have organized seminars on technical problems of disarmament and, as the phrase goes, "done their homework" in Kahn, Kissinger, King-Hall, the *Bulletin of the Atomic Scientists,* and so on.

The long-buried idealism of many gifted and sensitive students has come out most strongly, however, in their response to President Kennedy's proposal of a Peace Corps. It is exciting to watch a group of them examining in detail what American students might contribute to secondary education in Nigeria and what qualities of judgment, self-reliance, pertinacity, and technique such students would need to be of real help. I have seen students who seemed, even in their own eyes, cool customers, ready to ride the organizational escalator, discover in themselves unexpected resources of dedication when beckoned by a chance to serve in an underdeveloped country. To be sure, such service appears to many students as quite unpolitical, outside the polemical orbit of American domestic struggles; and one could argue that there are escapist elements in this choice, this interpretation. But one has to start somewhere, and when one is emerging from privatism, the first movements are apt to be tentative.

We must still ask whether there will be any carry-over from these campus stirrings into the attitudes that college graduates take toward their work: will they continue to regard it as mere "bread," needful for existence, but not a locus either for defining the self or changing the world? If one is apathetic about one's work, it is hard to prevent this apathy from spreading to other areas, even to those on which one had originally thought to build one's life: domesticity, the arts, and personal relations. But, conversely, the vitality and sense for relevant accomplishment that students may gain in college should spread to their academic work and thence to their lifework. For, in the more selective colleges at present, as I have already indicated, there is very little left of the collegiate or teen-ager high jinks of the former *jeunesse dorée;* it is in the high schools now that these ersatz values reign. Thus, college is already, not always happily, an aspect of adult life, not simply a playful preparation, and experience there is no longer compartmentalized as a childish thing.

—

Eugene Burdick

From Gold Rush to Sun Rush

California, at the end of the American rainbow, has long stood as a distant El Dorado. But in the past generation this state, more than any other, has become central to the American vision of success. Eugene Burdick (1918-   ) has sketched and analyzed California's meteoric progress from sombrero land to first state in the nation in little more than a century. [Eugene Burdick, "From Gold Rush to Sun Rush," New York Times Magazine, *April 14, 1963, pp. 36 ff.*]

California is proudly flexing its sun-tanned muscles these days over the fact that, sometime in the last few months, it surpassed New York as the most populous state in the Union. The individual statistic who tipped the historic balance past the 17,300,000 mark may have been a newborn baby, or a young physicist from M.I.T. winging his way across Lake Tahoe. More likely, it was someone in a station wagon crowded with children and weary parents.

Even today, after a century of prodigious growth, California's chief source of population increase is "outsiders" who migrate to the state. The newcomers have more children than the average American family, and they come in greatest numbers by the old overland routes.

Why do they come? What do they seek? What are they like? Are they in flight from something dreaded or in search of something desired? Are they mostly men or mostly women? Are they the rejects of older communities, or the more aggressive and more brainy of Americans? No one knows the full answers, but enough information has emerged for social scientists, computing machines, and interviews to fasten down some of the reasons why the state grows by 1,600 persons a day (New York grows by 600 a day) and will have 5,000,000 more citizens than New York by 1975.

One summer day when a "Santa Ana" wind swept tons of desert dust aloft to combine with the smog to give Los Angeles a brown, hazy atmosphere, I visited Muscle Beach at Santa Monica. Sitting on a bench, peering through the warm, brown, swirling air, were a dozen senior citizens watching a group of young men and women go through the tortures which produce heavily muscled and almost ridiculously perfect physiques. A week later, I saw almost the same thing in San Francisco except that the oldsters had to peer through the iodine-smelling fog to see the weights lifted by the muscular young men.

I concluded that California was made up of the dessicated very ancient and the narcissistic very young. I was profoundly wrong. So are most of the "single factor" theories of California's growth.

Indeed, one generally overlooked fact is that for every immigrant who stays in California, between three and four drift away. This means that since 1900 something like 50,000,000 Americans have come, taken a look—and left. In fairness, it should be pointed out that the immigration pattern in most of the growth states is probably much the same. The American is a wanderer and he does not usually settle for the first thing he sees.

Those who cried, "California, here I come!" and meant it have come in waves which seem radically different in motivation. But as Neil Morgan, author of the book *Westward Tilt,* has demonstrated, people who pick up and leave have some characteristics in common. They tend to be more adventuresome, more affluent (travel is expensive), more inventive, more mobile than the average. They are, a priori, readier to take a chance and more given to risky ventures—whether the ventures be religious, economic, political, or social.

The first wave was that of the forty-niners. They were younger than other Americans, and, in fact, they were often not Americans. The disappointed young men of Europe's revolutions of 1848 found California's gold a natural attraction. Also, if they stayed behind they might lose their necks. Simultaneously, the most adventuresome and restless young men of the Midwest and East responded to the cry of "Gold!"

The result was a sudden mushrooming of men who came to get rich and brought physical endurance, avarice, cosmopolitanism, and tolerance. Their great lack was women. Only recently, after more than a century, has California achieved a slight surplus of females—a situation which most of the United States has enjoyed for generations.

The men of the gold rush came for wealth, adventure, and, as their letters show, simple desire to "git up and go." When the California gold petered out, many of them sailed away on the slim clipper ships to Australia, the opium trade, and points west.

The second wave came because of a technological feat: the completion of the transcontinental railroad. To build the railroad thousands of Chinese were imported. No one inquired as to their motives. In many cases, they were ordered by their families or "contracted out" by local Chinese politicians. They labored out their time and then either went back to China or settled in the cities. The Chinese are essentially city people, and there is almost no city in California which does not have a few, although the biggest group is, of course in San Francisco.

Once people could ride the rails to California, there was a change in migrants. One group came to get well. The railroad companies plastered Eastern cities with throwaways and quarter-cards extolling the warm sun and the pure air of the place. Its climate was guaranteed to cure all respiratory afflictions, rheumatism, the common cold, vapors, asthma, and what-have-you. Some of the suburbs of Los Angeles, such as Pasadena, resembled nothing so much as town-sized sanitariums. The letters written back by the invalids indicated an almost fanatical enthusiasm for the therapeutic qualities of California's climate.

A much larger group, however, were the younger married couples who wanted to strike out on their own, or young bachelors seeking to escape the confines of Midwestern or Eastern towns. They were urged along by rumors of fantastic fortunes to be made, and by the fact that the railroad fare, at times, dipped to $1.

One of them wrote, "Five years at most was to be given to rifling California of her treasures, and then that country was to be thrown aside like a used-up newspaper . . ." Few of the new arrivals had any notion of becoming "Californians." Nor did they wish to be day laborers or work for a wage. They meant to make a fortune and spend it in the East.

There were those who were disappointed and who took the long ride back (not at $1). But just enough speculators became rich in real estate and railroads to finance great mansions around San Francisco and Los Angeles. The bright image of quick wealth tarnished very, very slowly. Growing numbers of the migrants began to put down tentative roots, usually in the cities, and the notion of being a Californian became something less than ludicrous.

Then the basis for the third wave was found, and once again it was underground: oil. Just after the turn of the century, the combination of the orange, cheap land, sunshine, and oil turned California mad. From 1900 to 1910, the population increased by 60 per cent—three times faster than the rest of the country.

Now the people who came were still young, but they brought skills necessary to develop industry and some executive ability. They were still better educated than the average American and although they were, on the whole, somewhat uncertain about how long they would stay, they were willing to tax themselves heavily to start a powerful educational system.

The new immigrants were as rapacious as those who had come before, but it was also clear that a new sense of permanence was starting to manifest itself. Many of the newcomers expected to get rich, but there was a growing realization that it might take some time—and also that California might not be a bad place to spend a fortune once it was in hand. There was a growing number of immigrants who, for the first time, came not to loot the place, but with the idea of living as they had lived "back East," only with better wages and more sunshine.

Few came to be farmers of conventional crops. That role was left to the ethnic minorities, such as the Japanese and the Filipinos and, later, the Mexicans. The Anglo-Saxon newcomers flocked to the cities and the small sun-kissed towns. A few well-heeled newcomers did turn to the development of such exotic crops as the lemon, grapefruit, and avocado and were aided by the development of the refrigerated freight car.

After World War I, two new technical objects changed California's image and gave a new character to the fourth wave of immigrants. The objects were the motion-picture camera and the automobile.

Hollywood converted California into a myth which spread over the entire world. Now the state was rich with the promise of beautiful women, high-priced movie stars, the hint of a Rabelaisian life which had not been known since the Deer Park of Versailles.

In hard fact, the riches of Hollywood were available to very few, but I remember, as a boy in Los Angeles, three mothers from our home town in Iowa who arrived within a year of one another, each clutching the hand of a girl who looked very much like Shirley Temple—and was there for precisely that reason. When I was in high school, girls appeared who wore full movie make-up to school and were always late because they had spent the early morning in the long pathetic lines outside the studios waiting to be "tapped" as extras. No one thought it strange.

The automobile, coupled with the creation of an excellent system of highways, probably was more of a lure than Hollywood. It is clear that California has always attracted restless people, and when the immigrant had made the long journey to California this restlessness did not end. Californians change residence two or three times as often as other Americans, and a favorite recreation was, and is, a long drive in an automobile.

By the late twenties, California, which had from the start seemed the logical place to go for those who wanted to get rich, had also acquired a bubblelike quality: the shimmering thing called glamour. The dream image inflated itself in miraculous ways and with bewildering results. Much of it, like the Hollywood spell, was pure will-o'-the-wisp, giving off false and dazzling flashes. Other developments, such as the oil wells, the fishing industry, the availability of the beautiful mountains and beaches, the neat, prim charm of the sun-baked villages of the south, the excellence of the schools, the fertility of the land, the forests of the north were solid economic and social muscle.

The realities of California began to become apparent. It was during the twenties boom that, for the first time, something like a normal cross section of America began to migrate to the state. Carpenters, plumbers, electricians, school teachers, physicians, and intellectuals began to see the state as a place where one could live the good life and get a tan simultaneously.

Those who came were still far from typical. They still leaned toward the young, they were better educated, they wandered more, they took bigger economic risks. There were still more men than women in the prosperity wave. They came more from the Midwest than from the Eastern seaboard.

Then an odd thing happened. The Anglo-Saxons, who in the Midwest are the backbone of the small farming communities, in California went straight into the anonymity of the big cities. The result is that the great north-south valleys of California are dotted with towns of extremely mixed nationality and background and one finds Roman Catholics in large proportions in rural areas—a phenomenon that occurs nowhere else in the United States.

The Great Depression had a deceptive impact on Californian migration. The impression is that the dusty, wind-ruined derelicts of the Midwest flooded the state. But, Steinbeck notwithstanding, the new immigrants were not the desperately poor. The desperately poor cannot travel; they freeze into a posture of immobility.

The Dust Bowl refugees who came into California during the thirties were the most solvent, the most aggressive, the most daring survivors of the economic and natural catastrophe they had suffered. The Okies, like those before them, were moving from strength. They fled a disaster, but they had the courage to go where opportunity was great. They had lost an economic battle, but were still fighting.

I have interviewed students on campuses, like Berkeley, Stanford, Mills, U.C.L.A., and Cal Tech, and found a solid core who look me in the eye when they respond to the question, "Where did your parents come from?" and say, "They were Okies." They say it even if their parents were not literally from Oklahoma, for they know that a generic answer is expected. Their parents are now managers of the big mechanized farms, or owners of smaller, neatly run farms, or owners of substantial businesses. They are seldom workers paid by the hour.

The fifth and last wave is harder to label. It is still in that state of suspension which the surfers call "feathering"—it has not yet broken into parts that can be analyzed. We are still in it, and there are more than a few who have a feeling that we may be drowned by it. Let us call it "the wave of World War II and its backwashes."

Abruptly in 1941 the motive for coming to California changed. People no longer came as seekers—they were ordered as Pfc.'s and Seamen 1st. The long, empty, brown foothills of California suddenly sprouted with training camps. San Diego and Treasure Island swarmed with sailors who had no conscious desire to visit California. Airmen and marines and doggies milled in the "liberty towns" of the state and professed to hate it—and I believe them.

But after the war, their memories of California underwent a strange reversal. One-third-of-a-million servicemen elected to take their discharges in California and stay. Hundreds of thousands of others took a quick visit home and then returned to settle down.

There are whole communities of tract houses where the breadwinners share one characteristic: they met California under orders. Not one came of his own free will. But they loved what they saw and they stayed. It is that simple.

Another vast slice of people came to California during World War II for the single reason that it was "where the jobs are." Shipbuilding in San Francisco and a vast aircraft industry around Los Angeles and San Diego were the chief inducements. Again, the immigrants were largely males, but there were also a substantial number of wives and single girls. More came from Texas than any other state.

This wave had no illusions about getting rich in California, and most of them saw their westward migration as temporary. But, like the servicemen, great numbers of them stayed on.

When the war ended, the armament plants rapidly collapsed, but they left a pattern of industry which was solidly based. The Kaiser steel mill in Fontana continued to produce steel; automobiles poured out of what had been tank factories; television and hi-fi plants absorbed countless technicians; the housing boom kept thousands on payrolls, and the spectacular highway schemes of the state kept the bulldozer operators busy.

After the war, the migration to California continued unabated. But now its character had changed radically. Much of the money for research and development work for both private busines and Government was being spent in California. Such work calls for brains, training, and curiosity more than for brawn. A new breed picked up and headed for California. This was the highly trained person, often with a Ph.D., who wanted to combine his intellectual interests with a pleasant place in the sun.

Getting rich figured little in the life view of this group. They flocked to the universities and laboratories for work and to the new suburbs for living. This group is much more sport-minded than any of the preceding groups, and surfing, tennis, golf, and sailing have replaced the saloon as an outlet for excess energy.

The California economy was still skewed impossibly out of balance by any rational standard. It was saved by the cold war. The new weird warfare called for experts in electronics and physics—and for experimenters. California had such people in abundance. Without missing a step, they swung into the mysteries of BMEWS, the Rand Corporation, the Polaris, the Sidewinder—all the exotica of modern warfare. Today California gets more defense contracts than any other single state— and the second-runner is not even close.

Agriculture also underwent a curious transformation after World War II. Today, California is the largest agricultural producer in America, but the work is done by vast, efficient, mechanized corporations. Most of the farm workers actually live in towns or cities, and work as skilled technicians on the sweeping new systems which exploit the land as if they were working in a factory. They have no sense of being rooted in the land.

During this period the Negro also discovered California. Negroes flocked to the Bay Area and Los Angeles by the hundreds of thousands and, although they have enjoyed nothing like equality in employment, the improvement over their former lot is obviously one of the attractions.

Another is the long tradition of tolerance which has existed in the state. Neil Morgan reports his astonishment at visiting Crystal Springs Country Club, outside San Francisco, and finding that a majority of the golfers were Negroes. No one else found the situation surprising. This is not to argue that the Negro influx has been without incident or unpleasantness, but, given the numbers who came in a brief time, there has been remarkably little conflict.

The Negroes also came seeking what the new intellectuals and almost all of the previous "waves" had sought—a superior education for their children. California's school system is rated close to the top by any criterion, and it has probably been one of the state's greatest "secret" attractions since the eighteen-nineties.

What is the situation today? First, it is clear that, although no one expects a new wave, California is still growing about three times as fast as the rest of the United States. Most of that growth comes from migrants who come seeking a steady job, the sun, a superior education. The California myth has been trimmed down, and the chief attraction is no longer the *mystique* of the oranges, gold, and Hollywood.

Contrary to the popular belief, California is not predominantly a refuge for the old and the retired. Its immigrants are still more young than old, and the tendency is increasing. The economic opportunities and the absence of intolerance have also given the state more than its share of Orientals, in particular, and of the foreign-born in general.

The new Californian, regardless of origin or age or sex, is more hedonistic than the American average. He spends more on liquor, recreation, leisure, and travel.

Lost in the massive surge of the waves have been small and disturbing eddies which are only now emerging. It is, for example, beyond dispute that the "Western tilt" has slid many neurotics into California. San Francisco has the highest suicide, alcoholism, and accident-prone rates in the United States. (Its accident rate is a startling five times greater than that of the next city, Cincinnati. No one knows why.) The other big cities of California are not far behind in suicide and alcoholism. And, with its tradition of tolerance, California has attracted a higher ratio of homosexuals than the rest of the United States, although they tend to congregate in the two large cities and a few seaside resort towns.

California also has a persistent fascination for the cultist, extremist, and lover of the esoteric. Its "health food" stores are a major industry. There is at least one Hindu cult which has its largest congregation in Los Angeles, and there are hundreds of religious and social cults which have their only congregations in California. In the Mojave Desert one can still see the burnt and sand-blown artifacts of utopian communities. Political extremes, of both right and left, find their largest followings in the state.

But, by and large, most Californians, whether immigrants or native-born, are happy with their lot. The more thoughtful of them are aware that they have attracted extremes of all sorts who present a difficult problem of assimilation. They are also aware of gigantic future problems of finance, taxation, and development. But the present is so sunny, euphoric, and pleasant that it seems subversive to worry about the future. In this sense, California has very, very few subversives.

"THE ACADEMIC ENTREPRENEUR...
A MAN OF AFFAIRS AS WELL AS LEARNING"

Christopher Rand

Academic Entrepreneurs

In the post-World War II years, the emergence on large university campuses of the professor-director as an entrepreneur of learning, technology, and social change may suggest that the new type of twentieth-century entrepreneur is already fully fashioned. In this selection, Christopher Rand (1912-   ) depicts the transformed world of Cambridge, Massachusetts—the hub of a new universe with counterparts throughout the country. [Christopher Rand, Cambridge U.S.A., New York, 1964, pp. 3-8, 125-128.]

Some months ago, when I went back to Cambridge to live . . . , I found the place greatly changed. New defense plants had shot up in the town itself and in its environs, attracted largely by the presence at the Massachusetts Institute of Technology of scientists working on problems closely related to the national security. There were more Indians, Africans, and other non-indigenous types in town than there had been in 1949, and I was told that the Cambridge professors, for their part, were spending more time in foreign lands, for they had broadened the scope of their interests and were exerting more influence on the world as a whole. As the weeks passed, I learned that the social sciences as well as the sciences were booming, owing to a combination of new money and new technology that had given them a new hold on life and a new approach to it. Before long, I concluded that I had found a renaissance in Cambridge.

Like any renaissance, the one in Cambridge has its patrons, but these are patrons very different from the Medici; they are the faceless United States government and the great impersonal foundations, on whose funds all the changes I have been so struck by are dependent. Again, like any renaissance, the one in Cambridge is deeply concerned with widening the boundaries of knowledge through exploration, which in the present context means research, as opposed to teaching—and group research preeminently. Its savants, being engaged on complex projects that cut across the old academic disciplines, usually work in teams. These teams sometimes operate in defense plants—designing warning nets or missiles, say—and sometimes in new institutions called "centers," which have sprouted from the universities themselves. Either way, the savants lead an existence in which they are only loosely tied to the institutions that formally employ them. Nearly always, a team is administered by a new type of leader—the academic entrepreneur, who is a man of affairs as well as learning, who knows how to raise money and put an organization together, and who is able to get results in the outside world. Because their aim is to perfect new weapons or to solve our foreign problems or to doctor to our social ills, the teams do their work in a mood of urgency, and as a result their renaissance is pushing knowledge ahead furiously. Some parts of the academic life are much altered by this, but not all. For instance, the position of arts and letters in Cambridge and its world is almost exactly what it was.

I should explain what I mean by Cambridge and its world. Only the center of that world lies in Cambridge proper; namely, the grounds of Harvard and M.I.T., lying a mile apart on the north bank of the Charles River, which flows eastward into Boston Harbor. Then, just north of Cambridge, there is Tufts University, and a few miles west there is Brandeis University. Fourteen years ago, I remember, when I used to walk out that way sometimes on a Sunday, Brandeis consisted of little more than a grotesque old turreted castle on a hill. Now the castle has been joined by a great many rectangular buildings made of brick, glass, and concrete, which appear rather jammed together on their rise of ground but are chic and modern-looking—very much a part of the new era. Just west of Brandeis lies Route 128, which is also very much a part of the new era.

Route 128 hardly existed during my former sojourn in Cambridge, which occupied the school year 1948-49. That year has nothing to do with this report, except to serve as a baseline for it. In 1948-49, the Korean War had not been thought of (at least not by us Americans), nor had Sputnik or the Russian nuclear threat or various other alarms that have since been spurring us on. Peace was viewed as the normal condition, and civilian production, dammed up since Pearl Harbor, was ready to burst forth. In time, all this came to have a bearing on the development of Route 128, but at first the route was no more than a simple expression of highway theory; it was a "ring road," designed to keep long-distance traffic out of Boston. It describes a semicircle around the heart of the city, at a radius of some ten to fifteen miles, with its two ends resting on or near the shores of Massachusetts Bay. (To make a full circle around Boston, a road would have to be amphibious.) Thanks to Route 128, a motorist can travel from the Maine border, say, to the Connecticut border, or from New Hampshire to Cape Cod, without losing time or adding to the congestion of the city. The plan for the road was much criticized at the start. Just after the war, Massachusetts was in a slump, taxes were high, and the textile mills were fleeing southward, so Route 128, inevitably, was damned as an extravagance of the politicians. Yet it was built, and it has been humming ever since.

Around the time the road was finished, something had begun happening to Boston that was also happening to other American cities—business firms of certain types were leaving the core for the outskirts. One reason was that these firms had waited two decades to build new plants and could now do so. Another was that downtown traffic was getting to be too much for both their trucks and their employees to cope with. And a third was that objects within the plants were coming more and more to be moved horizontally, by fork lifts and similar vehicles, rather than vertically, by elevators. This change created a demand for wide-spreading structures to replace high-rising ones, and hence for considerable ground space. According to experts in the Boston office of Cabot, Cabot & Forbes, the real-estate firm that has masterminded the exodus to the outskirts, these three pressures were felt most heavily at the outset by companies that operated warehouses, such as the New England distributors of goods produced on a national scale. In 1948, Cabot, Cabot & Forbes lured several such firms, including the local branches of General Electric, Squibb, and Parke, Davis, to the "suburbs." Actually, the move made by these first companies was a timid one—to East Cambridge, just across the Charles from downtown Boston. Three or four years later, though, Cabot, Cabot & Forbes settled a few firms in *West* Cambridge, halfway to Route 128, and soon it was putting others on Route 128 itself. Light manufacturing companies and mere business offices had now joined the parade, and Cabot, Cabot & Forbes had begun settling them in industrial parks. Such parks, which constitute another new feature of our century, are business areas laid out in open country and governed much like residential tracts, the tenants agreeing to build on only so much of their land, to plant the rest attractively, and otherwise to observe the amenities. In the early fifties, Cabot, Cabot & Forbes and a few other real-estate firms were busy establishing such parks along Route 128 and erecting in them anomalous oblong one-story buildings of a type that could be rented, as a multiple unit or separately, to a mixed bag of clients. And thus they prepared the way for the so-called r.-and-d. firms—the initials stand for "research and development"—and did it so successfully that before long such firms were arriving almost daily along the route.

The Cambridge scientific community had been active industrially in the Second World War, developing radar and other such devices. Then had come a lull—though the electronics business stayed alive, in consequence of the demand for television sets and deep freezes. Finally toward the end of the fifties, there was the space-and-missile boom, and that precipitated activity on an unprecedented scale. Under the guidance of scientists and engineers from the local universities, small plants in the Cambridge area began to specialize in making "sophisticated" items—a specialty that proved invaluable in the manufacture of electronic components for space vehicles. A number of so-called wonder firms have "spun off" from M.I.T.—the items they produce having been designed either in the Institute's laboratories or in lofts in the Cambridge industrial warrens nearby. Many a shoestring firm, starting out in these warrens with little other than M.I.T. brains, has shown sufficient promise to pick up financing—perhaps old Boston money from State Street—and move to better surroundings, and since the late fifties such surroundings have meant, primarily, Route 128, where the firm will have an adaptable new building, direct access to highways, lots of parking space, and a pleasant landscape for its scientists to contemplate. Also, it will gain prestige. The arrival of an electronics firm on Route 128—so one hears in Cambridge—produces much the same result as the transfer of a department store to Fifth Avenue; its sales and its stock value at once go up.

Today, Route 128 is simply "the Road" to its habitués, and "the Space Highway" or "the Golden Semicircle" to the business press. It is a modern superhighway, with many lanes, no stop lights, frequent overpasses, where it is crossed by radial roads fanning out from Boston, and a country landscape on either side, which the passing motorist may vaguely perceive to be broken here and there by long, low, characterless buildings that flaunt unenlightening names like Itek, Tracerlab Keleket, Tech Weld, Sylvania, and Raytheon. . . .

The ethics of making arms is a matter on which the consensus— of Harvard, of M.I.T., of Cambridge as a whole—is important these days. The arms business on Route 128, and Cambridge's involvement in it, has been criticized here on many grounds—that there is graft and laxity in the letting of government contracts, that the new money is distorting academic values, that Cambridge talents are being wasted in "technological leaf-raking" on Route 128, and so on. But the worst sin, by academic standards, is that Cambridge scholars are engaged in the munitions trade—an activity that a mere quarter of a century ago, on the eve of the Second World War, was regarded as heinous by our intellectuals almost to a man. In those days, Schneider-Creusot and Sir Basil Zaharoff were the great devils; now the devil is more apt to be the Pentagon, for the image of America's coming under the domination of military men and militarism is a real one to many thoughtful people here. They would like to struggle against this domination, yet they see themselves, or their institutions, implicated in it—they see their community compromised right and left by military patronage. Some academics bow to the new situation; some continue to fight it stubbornly, a leading battler being David Riesman, now a professor of social sciences at Harvard. Various Cambridge scientists have also attended the Pugwash Conferences, aimed at relaxing the Cold War, in the past few years. And student peace movements are encouraged here by Riesman and others. Last year, I attended a peace conference at Boston University where several Cambridge professors held forth and where one *non*-Cambridge professor pointed in M.I.T.'s direction and complained about the amount of federal money that the Institute is accepting. These gestures may not alter the situation, but they do express a restlessness in the academic psyche.

Such restlessness is plentiful now, much of it engendered by Cambridge's new power in the world. A young Harvard scholar was discussing it all with me the other day. "Look how acquisitive the universities here are," he said. "Look how they collect things. Harvard's library is the third-largest in America, and its Chinese-Japanese library is the largest outside the Far East. But still they keep on growing. Look at the university presses and the journals and the paper that comes out of this community—the fantastic ribbon of paper between here and other institutions, spreading influence. Look at all the learned societies, with their annual meetings here and there. Look at the tug of war between administration and teaching now. All this growth in Cambridge means more administration. How big is Harvard's bureaucracy now? How big is its maintenance staff? Does anybody know? I wonder."

Much is being said now—in this and other veins—against the new activities. But none of what is being said is apt to change things, for the new élite, with all its peculiarities, is well established. It can be seen as a new caste, not unlike the Brahmin caste of India. Metaphorically, the Brahmins are supposed to form the head of the Indian community, while the Kshatriyas, or warrior caste, form its body, the workers form its legs, and so on. In the old tradition, the Brahmins and the Kshatriyas have been complementary, unable to get along without each other. The Kshatriyas, men of action, have made good rulers, but only if they have had Brahmins to instruct them. And so it is today with the Johnsons and McNamaras, not to mention the Khrushchevs; without their Brahmins they are helpless. To be sure, the old Indian Brahmins have often been bad people—parasitic, hypocritical, intellectually negative, and so on. But this hasn't harmed them greatly; they have run India for thousands of years, and not even the centuries of Buddhist dominance could get them out. Our own new élite may have its faults, but so far it seems really less deplorable than the old Brahmins were; some would call our élite automatically better because it is recruited by competition, not by birth. In this it is like—to change our model—the Chinese mandarinate, another durable group, which was always replenished through scholarly examinations. It attracted opportunists more often than altruists, but still it endured. Our own new élite is already showing signs of opportunism in its younger echelons, and it may get worse. But even this will hardly fell it, for we *need* the scholars. We can't defend our country without them, we can't run our economy without them, we can't even attempt a foreign policy without them. Next to technological force, technological aid is our main binder for the Free World now, and it can't conceivably be applied without technologists.

John Kenneth Galbraith

Labor, Leisure and the New Class

The decline of toil for toil's sake in an affluent society has engaged the attention of leading publicists and social planners, and none more so than the economist John Kenneth Galbraith (1908-   ). In the selection below, Galbraith suggests that high productivity and the development of a rapidly expanding New Class make it possible for society to recast its traditional economic goals into educational ones. By maximizing the human rather than the economic returns from work, a leisure class without historic precedent appears to be in the making. [John Kenneth Galbraith, The Affluent Society, *Boston, 1958, pp. 334-348.]*

In a society of high and increasing affluence there are three plausible tendencies as regards toil. As the production of goods comes to seem less urgent, and as individuals are less urgently in need of income for the purchase of goods, they will work fewer hours or days in the week. Or they will work less hard. Or, as a final possibility, it may be that fewer people will work all the time.

In the last century a drastic decline has occurred in the work week. In 1850 it is estimated to have averaged just under seventy hours, the equivalent of seven ten-hour days a week or roughly six at from six in the morning to six at night. A hundred years later the average was 40.0 hours or five eight-hour days.

This decline reflects a tacit but unmistakable acceptance of the declining marginal urgency of goods. There is no other explanation. However, such is the hold of production on our minds that this explanation is rarely offered. The importance and rewards of leisure are urged, almost never the unimportance of goods. Or, since production per hour has been increasing as the work week has declined, it is said that we are able to reduce the work because more is produced in less time. No mention is made of the fact that even more would be produced in more time. Or, finally, the decline is related to the feeling that steps must be taken to share the available work as productivity per worker rises. This also implies that the marginal urgency of production is low or negligible, but again the point remains unmade.

A reduction in the work week is an exceedingly plausible reaction to declining marginal urgency of product. Over the span of man's history, although a phenomenal amount of education, persuasion, indoctrination, and incantation have been devoted to the effort, ordinary people have never been quite persuaded that toil is as agreeable as its alternatives. Thus to take increased well-being partly in the form of more goods and partly in the form of more leisure is unquestionably rational. In addition, the institution of overtime enables the worker to go far to adjust work and income to his own taste and requirements. It breaks with the barbarous uniformity of the weekly wage with its assumption that all families have the same tastes, needs, and requirements. Few things enlarge the liberty of the individual more substantially than to grant him a measure of control over the amount of his income.

Unfortunately in the conventional wisdom the reduction in hours has emerged as the only legitimate response to increasing affluence. This is at least partly because the issue has never been faced in terms of the increasing unimportance of goods. Accordingly, though we have attributed value to leisure, a ban still lies on other courses which seem to be more directly in conflict with established attitudes on productive efficiency. In a society rationally concerned with its own happiness these alternatives have a strong claim to consideration.

II

The first of these is that work can be made easier and more pleasant.

The present-day industrial establishment is a great distance removed from that of the last century or even of twenty-five years ago. This improvement has been the result of a variety of forces—government standards and factory inspection; general technological and architectural advance; the fact that productivity could be often increased by substituting machine power for heavy or repetitive manual labor; the need to compete for a labor force; and union intervention to improve working conditions in addition to wages and hours.

However, except where the improvement contributed to increased productivity, the effort to make work more pleasant has had to support a large burden of proof. It was permissible to seek the elimination of hazardous, unsanitary, unhealthful, or otherwise objectionable conditions of work. The speed-up might be resisted—to a point. But the test was not what was agreeable but what was unhealthful or, at a minimum, excessively fatiguing. The trend toward increased leisure is not reprehensible, but we resist vigorously the notion that a man should work less hard while on the job. Here older attitudes are involved. We are gravely suspicious of any tendency to expend less than the maximum effort, for this has long been a prime economic virtue.

In strict logic there is as much to be said for making work pleasant and agreeable as for shortening hours. On the whole it is probably as important for a wage earner to have pleasant working conditions as a pleasant home. To a degree, he can escape the latter but not the former—though no doubt the line between an agreeable tempo and what is flagrant featherbedding is difficult to draw. Moreover, it is a commonplace of the industrial scene that the dreariest and most burdensome tasks, requiring as they do a minimum of thought and skill, frequently have the largest number of takers. The solution to this problem lies, as we shall see presently, in drying up the supply of crude manpower at the bottom of the ladder. Nonetheless the basic point remains: the case for more leisure is not stronger on purely *prima facie* grounds than the case for making labor-time itself more agreeable. The test, it is worth repeating, is not the effect on productivity. It is not seriously argued that the shorter work week increases productivity—that men produce more in fewer hours than they would in more. Rather it is whether fewer hours are always to be preferred to more but more pleasant ones.

III

The third of the obvious possibilities with increasing affluence is for fewer people to work. This tendency has also been operating for many years although in a remarkably diverse form. Since 1890, when one boy in four and one girl in ten between the ages of ten and fifteen were gainfully employed, large numbers of juveniles have been retired from the labor force and their number is now negligible. At the same time a number of women have been added. In 1890, 19.5 per cent of the female population ten years and over was in the labor force and by 1953 this proportion had risen to 29.7 per cent. However, this change reflects in considerable measure the shift of tasks—food preparation, clothing manufacture, even child-rearing—out of the home. Women who previously performed them have gone along to other work. The woman who takes charge of a day nursery has joined the labor force, as have the women whose children she cares for.

For seventy-five years the proportion of the male population in the labor force has been constant at around 75 per cent of those over ten years of age. There are a smaller percentage of the very young and of those over sixty-five, but this has been offset by the increase in population in the ages between twenty and sixty-five where the proportion of workers to the total is very high.

With diminishing marginal urgency of goods it is logical that the first to be spared should be old and young. We have yet, however, to view this tendency consistently and comprehensively. We are able to dispense with the labor of those who have reached retiring age because the goods they add are a low order of urgency, whereas a poor society must extract the last ounce of labor effort from all. But we have ordinarily subjected those who retire to a drastic reduction in income and living standards. Obviously, if the retirement can be afforded because the product is no longer urgent, a satisfactory—meaning for most purposes the customary—living standard can be accorded to the retired employee for the same reason. Similarly we have excluded youngsters from the labor market, partly on the ground that labor at too early an age is unduly painful and injurious to health, and partly to make way for educational opportunity. But while we have felt it possible to dispense with the goods that the youngsters produce, we have yet to provide them, at least in full and satisfactory measure, with the education that their exemption from labor was designed to make possible. If we are affluent enough to dispense with the product of juvenile labor, it again follows that we are affluent enough to provide the education that takes its place.

In addition to releasing the old and young, it may be that we need not use all of the labor force at all times. . . . If the marginal urgency of goods is low, then so is the urgency of employing the last man or the last million men in the labor force. By allowing ourselves such slack, in turn, we reduce the standards of economic performance to a level more nearly consonant with the controls available for its management. And in so widening the band of what is deemed tolerable performance lies our best hope of minimizing the threat of inflation with its further and persistent threat to social balance.

Such a step requires much more adequate provision than now for those who are temporarily unemployed. We have seen, however, that such measures are possible and, indeed, have a vital stabilizing effect. And again such compensation accords with the logic of the situation. If our need for production is of such a low order of urgency that we can afford some unemployment in the interest of stability—a proposition, incidentally, of impeccably conservative antecedents—then we can afford to give those who are unemployed the goods that enable them to sustain their accustomed standard of living. If we don't need what the unemployed do not make, we can obviously afford them what they customarily eat and wear.

IV

However, the greatest prospect that we face—indeed what must now be counted one of the central economic goals of our society—is to eliminate toil as a required economic institution. This is not a utopian vision. We are already well on the way. Only an extraordinarily elaborate exercise in social camouflage has kept us from seeing what has been happening.

Nearly all societies at nearly all times have had a leisure class—a class of persons who were exempt from toil. In modern times and especially in the United States the leisure class, at least in any identifiable phenomenon, has disappeared. To be idle is no longer considered rewarding or even entirely respectable.

But we have barely noticed that the leisure class has been replaced by another and much larger class to which work has none of the older connotation of pain, fatigue, or other mental or physical discomfort. We have failed to appreciate the emergence of this New Class, as it may be simply called, largely as the result of one of the oldest and most effective obfuscations in the field of social science. This is the effort to assert that all work—physical, mental, artistic, or managerial —is essentially the same.

This effort to proclaim the grand homogeneity of work has commanded, for different reasons, the support of remarkably numerous and diverse groups. To economists it has seemed a harmless and, indeed, an indispensable simplification. It has enabled them to deal homogeneously with all of the different kinds of productive effort and to elaborate a general theory of wages applying to all who receive an income for services. Doubts have arisen from time to time, but they have been suppressed or considered to concern special cases. The identity of all classes of labor is one thing on which capitalist and communist doctrine wholly agree. The president of the corporation is pleased to think that his handsomely appointed office is the scene of the same kind of toil as the assembly line and that only the greater demands in talent and intensity justify his wage differential. The Communist officeholder cannot afford to have it supposed that his labor differs in any significant respect from that of the comrade at the lathe or on the collective farm with whom he is ideologically one. In both societies it serves the democratic conscience of the more favored groups to identify themselves with those who do hard physical labor. A lurking sense of guilt over a more pleasant, agreeable, and remunerative life can often be assuaged by the observation "I am a worker too" or, more audaciously, by the statement that "mental labor is far more taxing than physical labor." Since the man who does physical labor is intellectually disqualified from comparing his toil with that of the brainworker, the proposition is uniquely unassailable.

In fact the differences in what labor means to different people could not be greater. For some, and probably a majority, it remains a stint to be performed. It may be preferable, especially in the context of social attitudes toward production, to doing nothing. Nevertheless it is fatiguing or monotonous or, at a minimum, a source of no particular pleasure. The reward rests not in the task but in the pay.

For others work, as it continues to be called, is an entirely different matter. It is taken for granted that it will be enjoyable. If it is not, this is a source of deep dissatisfaction or frustration. No one regards it as remarkable that the advertising man, tycoon, poet, or professor who suddenly finds his work unrewarding should seek the counsel of a psychiatrist. One insults the business executive or the scientist by sug- gesting that his principal motivation in life is the pay he receives. Pay is not unimportant. Among other things it is a prime index of prestige. Prestige—the respect, regard, and esteem of others—is in turn one of the more important sources of satisfaction associated with this kind of work. But, in general, those who do this kind of work expect to contribute their best regardless of compensation. They would be dis- turbed by any suggestion to the contrary.

Such is the labor of the New Class. No aristocrat ever contemplated the loss of feudal privileges with more sorrow than a member of this class would regard his descent into ordinary labor where the reward was only the pay. In the years following World War II a certain num- ber of grade school teachers left their posts for substantially higher paid factory work. The action made headlines because it represented an unprecedented desertion of an occupation which was assumed to confer the dignity of the New Class. The college professor, who is more securely a member of the New Class than the schoolteacher, would never contemplate such a change even as an exercise in eccentricity and no matter how inadequate he might consider his income.

In keeping with all past class behavior, the New Class seeks ener- getically to perpetuate itself. Offspring are not expected to plan their lives in order to make a large amount of money. (Those who go into business are something of an exception at least partly because income, in business, is uniquely an index of prestige.) But from their earliest years the children are carefully indoctrinated in the importance of find- ing an occupation from which they will derive satisfaction—one which will involve not toil but enjoyment. One of the principal sources of sorrow and frustration in the New Class is the son who fails to make the grade—who drops down into some tedious and unrewarding occu- pation. The individual who meets with this misfortune—the son of the surgeon who becomes a garage hand—is regarded by the community with pity not unmixed with horror. But the New Class has considerable protective powers. The son of the surgeon rarely does become a garage hand. However inadequate, he can usually manage to survive, perhaps somewhat exiguously, on the edge of his caste. And even if, as a salesman or an investment counselor, he finds little pleasure in his work, he will be expected to assert the contrary in order to affirm his membership in the New Class.

v

The New Class is not exclusive. While virtually no one leaves it, thousands join it every year. Overwhelmingly the qualification is education. Any individual whose adolescent situation is such that sufficient time and money is invested in his preparation, and who has at least the talents to carry him through the formal academic routine, can be a member. There is a hierarchy within the class. The son of the factory worker who becomes an electrical engineer is on the lower edge; his son who does graduate work and becomes a university physicist moves to the higher echelons; but opportunity for education is, in either case, the open sesame.

There can be little question that in the last hundred years, and even in the last few decades, the New Class has increased enormously in size. In early nineteenth century England or the United States, excluding the leisure class and considering the New Class as a group that lived on what it has carefully called earned income, it consisted only of a handful of educators and clerics, with, in addition, a trifling number of writers, journalists, and artists. In the United States of the eighteen-fifties it could not have numbered more than a few thousand individuals. Now the number whose primary identification is with their job, rather than the income it returns, is undoubtedly in the millions.

Some of the attractiveness of membership in the New Class, to be sure, derives from a vicarious feeling of superiority—another manifestation of class attitudes. However, membership in the class unquestionably has other and more important rewards. Exemption from manual toil; escape from boredom and confining and severe routine; the chance to spend one's life in clean and physically comfortable surroundings; and some opportunity for applying one's thoughts to the day's work, are regarded as unimportant only by those who take them completely for granted. For these reasons it has been possible to expand the New Class greatly without visibly reducing its attractiveness.

This being so, there is every reason to conclude that the further and rapid expansion of this class should be a major, and perhaps next to peaceful survival itself, *the* major social goal of the society. Since education is the operative factor in expanding the class, investment in education, assessed qualitatively as well as quantitatively, becomes very close to being the basic index of social progress. It enables people to realize a dominant aspiration. It is an internally consistent course of development.

Recent experience has shown that the demand for individuals in the occupations generally identified with the New Class increases much more proportionately with increased income and well-being. Were the expansion of the New Class a deliberate objective of the society this, with its emphasis on education and its ultimate effect on intellectual, literary, cultural, and artistic demands, would greatly broaden the opportunities for membership. At the same time the shrinking in the number of those who engage in work *qua* work is something to be regarded not alone with equanimity but with positive approval. For one of the inevitable outlets for the intellectual energies and inventiveness of the New Class will be in finding substitutes for routine and repetitive manual labor. To the extent that such labor is made scarce and more expensive, this tendency will, of course, be accelerated. To minimize the number of people doing such work is the counterpart of the goal of expanding the New Class.

It is a measure of how little we need worry about the danger from reducing the number of people engaged in work *qua* work that, as matters now stand, our concern is not that we will have too few available for toil but too many. We worry lest such technical advances as automation, an already realized dividend of the expansion of the New Class, will proceed so rapidly as to leave a surplus of those who still work. This, indeed, could be the greater danger.

VI

I venture to suggest that the unprofessional reader will find rather reasonable and rational the ideas here offered. Why should men struggle to maximize income when the price is many dull and dark hours of labor? Why especially should they do so as goods become more plentiful and less urgent? Why should they not seek instead to maximize the rewards of all the hours of their days? And since this is the plain and obvious aspiration of a great and growing number of the most perceptive people, why should it not be the central goal of the society? And now to complete the case, we have a design for progress. It is education or, more broadly, investment in human as distinct from material capital.

But in the more sophisticated levels of the conventional wisdom, including, regrettably, some professional economists, any such goal will seem exceedingly undesirable. The production of material goods, urgent or otherwise, is the accepted measure of our progress. Investment in material capital is our basic engine of progress. Both this product and the means for increasing it are measurable and tangible. What is measurable is better. To talk of transferring increasing numbers of people from lives spent mostly in classical toil to lives which, for the most part, are spent pleasantly has less quantitative precision. Since investment in individuals, unlike investment in a blast furnace, provides a product that can be neither seen nor valued, it is inferior. And here the conventional wisdom unleashes its epithet of last resort. Since these achievements are not easily measured, as a goal they are "fuzzy." This is widely deemed to be a fatal condemnation. The precise, to be sure, is usually the old and familiar. Because it is old and familiar it has been defined and measured. Thus does insistence on precision become another of the tautological devices by which the conventional wisdom protects itself. Nor should one doubt its power.

Yet anyone who finds this analysis and these proposals sensible should not be entirely discouraged. We are here in one of the contexts where circumstance has marched far beyond the conventional wisdom. We have seen how general are the efforts to join the New Class and how rapid is its expansion. We are not here establishing a new economic and social goal but identifying one that is already widely if not tacitly accepted. In this situation the conventional wisdom cannot resist indefinitely. The economist of impeccable credentials in the conventional wisdom, who believes that there is no goal in life of comparable urgency with the maximization of total and individual real income, would never think of applying such a standard to himself. In his own life he is an exponent of all the aspirations of the New Class. He educates and indoctrinates his children with but one thing in mind. It is not that they should maximize their income. This is abhorrent. He wants above all that they will have an occupation that is interesting and rewarding. On this he hopes, indeed, that they will take their learned parent as their model.

VIII

The Gospel Revisited

*To "Spiritualize the most Earthly Business in the World by a
Chemistry that shall fetch Heavenly Thoughts out of it," as
Cotton Mather advised, does not seem as relevant in a world
pointing to outer space as it did in a world pointing to heaven.
Yet even as a utilitarian religious tradition finds a new idiom of
accommodation, "The Vain Presumption of Living and Thriving
in the World; which does too often possess and poison the Children of this World," as Cotton Mather also put it, is perhaps more
grimly entertained in our own time than it has been for over two
centuries.*

—

Bruce Barton

The Man Nobody Knows

The close association between business and religion has persisted into the twentieth century alongside the secularized Gospel of Success. Celebrated by Russell Conwell in Acres of Diamonds, *in the 1920's it acquired in Bruce Barton (1886-   ), the advertising agency executive, a disciple of Jesus portrayed as the model Madison Avenue executive and founder of modern business.* [Bruce Barton, The Man Nobody Knows, A Discovery of the Real Jesus, *New York, 1925, pp. 8-13, 18-20, 29-31.*]

Theology has spoiled the thrill of his life by assuming that he knew everything from the beginning—that his three years of public work were a kind of dress rehearsal, with no real problems or crises. What interest would there be in such a life? What inspiration? You who read these pages have your own creed concerning him; I have mine. Let us forget all creed for the time being, and take the story just as the simple narratives give it—a poor boy, growing up in a peasant family, working in a carpenter shop; gradually feeling his powers expanding, beginning to have an influence over his neighbors, recruiting a few followers, suffering disappointments and reverses, finally death. Yet building so solidly and well that death was only the beginning of his influence! Stripped of all dogma this is the grandest achievement story of all! In the pages of this little book let us treat it as such. If, in so doing, we are criticized for overemphasizing the human side of his character we shall have the satisfaction of knowing that our overemphasis tends a little to offset the very great overemphasis which has been exerted on the other side. Books and books and books have been written about him as the Son of God; surely we have a reverent right to remember that his favorite title for himself was the Son of Man.

Nazareth, where he grew up, was a little town in an outlying province. In the fashionable circles of Jerusalem it was quite the thing to make fun of Nazareth—its crudities of custom and speech, its simplicity of manner. "Can any good thing come out of Nazareth?" they asked derisively when the report spread that a new prophet had arisen in that country town. The question was regarded as a complete rebuttal of his pretensions.

The Galileans were quite conscious of the city folks' contempt, but they bore it lightly. Life was a cheerful and easy-going affair with them. The sun shone almost every day; the land was fruitful; to make a living was nothing much to worry about. There was plenty of time to visit. Families went on picnics in Nazareth, as elsewhere in the world; young people walked together in the moonlight and fell in love in the spring. Boys laughed boisterously at their games and got into trouble with their pranks. And Jesus, the boy who worked in the carpenter shop, was a leader among them.

Later on we shall refer again to those boyhood experiences, noting how they contributed to the vigorous physique which carried him triumphantly through his work. We are quite unmindful of chronology in writing this little book. We are not bound by the familiar outline which begins with the song of the angels at Bethlehem and ends with the weeping of the women at the cross. We shall thread our way back and forth through the rich variety of his life, picking up this incident and that bit of conversation, this dramatic contact and that audacious decision, and bringing them together as best to illustrate our purpose. For that purpose is not to write a biography but to paint a portrait. So in this first chapter we pass quickly over thirty years of his life, noting only that somehow, somewhere there occurred in those years the eternal miracle—the awakening of the inner consciousness of power.

The eternal miracle! In New York one day a luncheon was tendered by a gathering of distinguished gentlemen to David Lloyd George. There were perhaps two hundred at the tables. The food was good and the speeches were impressive. But what stirred one's imagination was a study of the men at the speakers' table. There they were—some of the most influential citizens of the present-day world; and *who* were they? At one end an international financier—the son of a poor country parson. Beside him a great newspaper proprietor—he came from a tiny town in Maine and landed in New York with less than a hundred dollars. A little farther along the president of a world-wide press association—a copy boy in a country newspaper office. And, in the center, the boy who grew up in the poverty of an obscure Welsh village, and became the commanding statesman of the British Empire in the greatest crisis of history.

When and how and where did the eternal miracle occur in the lives of those men? At what hour, in the morning, in the afternoon, in the long quiet evenings, did the audacious thought enter the mind of each of them that he was larger than the limits of a country town, that his life might be bigger than his father's? When did the thought come to Jesus? Was it one morning when he stood at the carpenter's bench, the sun streaming in across the hills? Was it late in the night, after the family had retired, and he had slipped out to walk and wonder under the stars? Nobody knows. All we can be sure of is this—that the consciousness of his divinity must have come to him in a time of solitude, of awe in the presence of Nature. The western hemisphere has been fertile in material progress, but the great religions have all come out of the East. The deserts are a symbol of the infinite: the vast spaces that divide men from the stars fill the human soul with wonder. Somewhere, at some unforgettable hour, the daring filled his heart. He knew that he was bigger than Nazareth.

Success is always exciting; we never grow tired of asking what and how. What, then, were the principal elements in his power over men? How was it that the boy from a country village became the greatest leader?

First of all he had the voice and manner of the leader—the personal magnetism which begets loyalty and commands respect. The beginnings of it were present in him even as a boy. John felt them. On the day when John looked up from the river where he was baptizing converts and saw Jesus standing on the bank, he drew back in protest. "I have need to be baptized of thee," he exclaimed, "and comest thou to me?" The lesser man recognized the greater instinctively. We speak of personal magnetism as though there were something mysterious about it—a magic quality bestowed on one in a thousand and denied to all the rest. This is not true. The essential element in personal magnetism is a consuming sincerity—an overwhelming faith in the importance of the work one has to do. Emerson said, "What you *are* thunders so loud I can't hear what you say." And Mirabeau, watching the face of the young Robespierre, exclaimed, "That man will go far; he believes every word he says."

Most of us go through the world mentally divided against ourselves. We wonder whether we are in the right jobs, whether we are making the right investments, whether, after all, anything is as important as it seems to be. Our enemies are those of our own being and creation. Instinctively we wait for a commanding voice, for one who shall say authoritatively, "I have the truth. This way lies happiness and salvation." There was in Jesus supremely that quality of conviction.

The Bible presents an interesting collection of contrasts in this matter of executive ability. Samson had almost all the attributes of leadership. He was physically powerful and handsome; he had the great courage to which men always respond. No man was ever given a finer opportunity to free his countrymen from the oppressors and build up a great place of power for himself. Yet Samson failed miserably. He could do wonders singlehanded, but he could not organize. Moses started out under the same handicap. He tried to be everything and do everything; and was almost on the verge of failure. It was his father-in-law, Jethro, who saved him from calamity. Said that shrewd old man: "The thing that thou doest is not good. Thou wilt surely wear away, both thou and this people that is with thee, for this thing is too heavy for thee, for thou are not able to perform it thyself alone."

Moses took the advice and associated with himself a partner, Aaron, who was strong where he was weak. They supplemented each other and together achieved what neither of them could have done alone.

John, the Baptist, had the same lack. He could denounce but he could not construct. He drew crowds who were willing to repent at his command, but he had no program for them after their repentance. They waited for him to organize them for some sort of effective service, and he was no organizer. So his followers drifted away and his movement gradually collapsed. The same thing might have happened to the work of Jesus. He started with much less reputation than John and a much smaller group of followers. He had only twelve, and they were untrained simple men, with elementary weaknesses and passions. Yet because of the fire of his personal conviction, because of his marvelous instinct for discovering their latent powers, and because of his unwavering faith and patience, he molded them into an organization which carried on victoriously. Within a very few years after his death, it was reported in a far-off corner of the Roman Empire that "these who have turned the world upside down have come hither also." A few decades later the proud Emperor himself bowed his head to the teachings of this Nazareth carpenter, transmitted through common men.

Donald B. Meyer

The Confidence Man

Psychology blended with religion in pursuit of success in the world of organization has found its most popular exponent in Norman Vincent Peale, author of The Power of Positive Thinking. *Donald B. Meyer (1923-   ), the intellectual historian, grimly examines the poverty of aspiration that such counsels reflect.* [*Donald B. Meyer, "The Confidence Man,"* New Republic, *July 11, 1955, pp. 8-10.*]

"The greatest discovery of my generation is that human beings can alter their lives by altering their attitudes of mind." This is not Norman Vincent Peale in his own voice, but William James, called up to speak by Peale. I stand, says Peale, with James and with Emerson and Thoreau, all of whom knew that the self is its own project for itself. I offer you daily rules, Peale says, for your creation of yourself—like Franklin (13 rules) and Jefferson (10 rules). One might think it of some interest that Franklin's rules were rules Franklin gave himself; Jefferson's likewise. Nor did Emerson and Thoreau offer their experience as manuals of exact guidance for others. Insofar as they offered "guidance," they meant it radically: you are yourself.

But in any case, Peale claims quite simply to be in the mainstream of the American tradition of self-improvement, and who will deny it? Emerson and Thoreau aside, in lectures IV and V of *The Varieties of Religious Experience* James, a generous soul, tells the intellectuals they cannot afford to snub or satirize the mind-cure cult of the day. It works.

Peale tells you how to get the Higher Power to work for you. The Protestant in America has usually been in search of an ideal self, he has always stressed positive thoughts, and he has talked perpetually of power. Each new stage of things is a new assertion of it. In Peale, the word clangs from first to last, like brass, maddeningly. Wonderful are its fruits. "It is a power that can blast out all defeat and lift a person above all difficult situations." Every obstacle will yield, under all circumstances and in any conditions. Yield, White Whale. Come, all knowledge and all beauty and all virtue. With the Higher Power within you, your world will be as you wish it. . . .

At the heart of things, behind all Peale's talk of energy and vitality and confidence and power, the question curls: power and confidence for what?

Peale's readers are offered power for meeting the trials of a world which is already there, already shaped, not to be changed, already accepted by them as the fit and proper scene for their proof of themselves. This is very much the world of business, specifically, of small business, of sales and advertising, and of the lower executive bureaucracy. Here dwell Peale's typical patients: the would-be independent enterpriser, trying to live on his own guts and inspiration, still full of laissez-faire expectation but caught and exposed in the controlled markets of the modern economic system; the sales manager, endlessly responsible for new and newer gimmicks, drained endlessly by the demand put upon him that he not be himself but sell himself; the helplessly mobile junior executive gnawed upon by his dreams of status, roots withering by his changes in residence.

Some of these people—and their wives—suffer from status panic. But still more seem to suffer, more seriously, from status apathy. It is not so much that they have failed the trials, as that they do not seem to enjoy the fruits they have earned. Since they accept the managed world of business implicitly, however, as a realm of salvation, their apathy does not mean liberation to a possible new self and salvation independent of the system, but instead guilt and those feelings of inferiority to which Peale addresses himself. Plainly, many of them would enjoy being freed from the course of judgment under which they stand, but Peale, like a front-line psychiatrist, applies quick therapy and sends them back into battle. And battle it is; Peale, in sublime betrayal of the aggression within his philosophy of peace, talks of "shooting" prayers at people.

Certainly this is to violate the classic form of mind-cure, justification by faith. In its classic form, as James describes it, "it is but giving your little private convulsive self a rest, and finding that a greater Self is there." But there is nothing in this of Peale. He assumes that you want the greater Self already defined by the system and, the perfectly frank practitioner, scorning the classic answer of dissolving convulsion and frustration by dissolving the wish frustrated, explains that the Higher Power of positive thinking will mean for you something perfectly definite and predictable, which it ought to mean: higher status and more money. He does not, as James observed of Luther and Wesley, tell you that you are saved now if you would believe you are saved.

He tells you that you will be saved, since your belief will mean status and money. Recently presiding over the dinner for presentation of the annual Horatio Alger awards, Peale could hardly be more specific.

But it is not really so important whether a frustrated Horatio Alger still lurks in the breasts of the substantial number of Americans who find Peale good, as whether these are not people for whom status-and-money success is proving more and more sterile. Some oblique light is cast on the matter by another of the striking undertones in Peale's tracts. The modern business world means the world of consumption, and the world of consumption is the world of the city. Peale's readers could be described as those who, in the city, are not yet of it, have not yet, so deep is the past, found there a home. What Americans indeed have yet found their home there? Not those of the middle-class, evangelical Anglo-Saxon Protestant stock in whose essentially spiritualistic idiom Peale speaks. No American writer of the breed has yet spoken of it as home—except when it is Paris, or, now, Rome; none are soon likely to. Peale himself recommends the countryside, the lake shore, the stillness of the hills. In Manhattan, he is the small-town Midwesterner romantic over Nature. Never does the adept of positive thinking—to note only innocent things—wander through a museum, queue at a concert hall, talk about a movie, stroll a street, meet with friends in the city. Never, that is, does he seek personal resources in culture. The city for him is noise and the status panic.

On this front, unlike the other, Peale recommends escape—the 10-minute prayer, the 10-minute nap, the 10-mile drive into the country. The result is further to enforce one of the central qualities of the life of his readers—its abstraction, its devastating isolation. They must live in the city, but there is nothing there with which they can mix and join themselves. The victory in the victorious living of which Peale forever speaks—again in battle terms—remains what it has so often been in the tradition of self-salvation, a state of negative being, a victory over something, and not the creation and elaboration of a definite cultural life. Now, instead of victory over the frontier, over alcohol, over sex, over competitors, over the city, it is victory over the new inner temptations of apathy, self-doubt, and secret secession from the trials of the status system.

This is one of the ironies of the times. As Keynes and a dozen others have observed, the growth of industrial society has entailed a spiritual revolution in Protestant countries, as the focus of economic attention moves from the ascetic enterpriser to the willing consumer. Peale's readers show that this profound shift in signals from the old logic of judgment, whereby discipline meant salvation, still means serious inner disruption. Here are people who are willing to consume. They are in fact the best consumers and the best supporters of mass culture, because as they consume they are not satisfying private and independent appetites for comfort or for the expansion of a definite way of life. They are buying symbols, and nothing is easier to change and differentiate than the symbolic commodity. Everything becomes obsolescent—your clothes, your car, your furniture, your books, your conversation, and, of course, if you fail to symbolize yourself, you yourself. Consequently, despite willingness to consume, consumption nourisheth not. For the man of self-help, the symbolic coherence of this world of consumption never has been satisfactory, and its coherence has been decreasing.

Partly, this is due to the nature of symbolic commodities in any democratic industrial society: they are minute, fleeting, and irrational variations upon a standard product, and the self which identifies with them begins to feel restricted to a narrow margin itself, and to feel itself fleeting, founded on irrationality, and therefore precarious. But this affects everyone, and the incoherence is sensed more acutely by the basic Protestant community in particular. It has built the system, and it believes the system should prove what it was originally supposed to prove. Yet, all too conspicuously, consumption in widening circles of American society cannot be taken to testify to inner character; too often it testifies quite frankly to corruption. The Cadillac, for instance, has taken on ambiguity as a symbolic commodity, despite all efforts of its ad-men. The symbolic system has become infested by luck, by gambling, by impersonal power shifts and power groups, and by bureaucratization. Increasingly, it becomes its own justification, it creates and dominates the self, and the believer in the Higher Power feels confusion.

Peale wants to go back and re-impose the logic of discipline-as-salvation within the system, ignoring the problem of the fruits altogether. He tries to restore inner-direction to a people lapsing into aimlessness. It is with a peculiar worried intensity that Peale from time to time points out to his readers that, of course, if you are going to be what you wish to be, you must have a wish; you cannot picturize yourself succeeding if you have no picture of success. "Spiritual and emotional planlessness is a definite reason for the failure of many people. . . ." "Your expectation must have a clearly defined objective. Lots of people . . . have no clear-cut, precisely defined purpose."

This answer will increase the suffocation and abstraction Peale's readers feel. Things are not as they were in Horatio Alger's day. Success by the judgment of modern bureaucratic business obviously demands less and less of a true original self, demands more and more a self that is disciplined to obey signals which have nothing to do with a true and original and independent self. Partly "other-direction," partly "outer-direction," these demands become frank, intimidating, and suffocating as formalized, for instance, in the by now standard manuals for scien-

tific personality measurement, personality training, and personnel selection. The system is made God, once again, only now a more jealous,
rigid, exacting God, judging and electing, and Peale's therapy works
simply to take some of the intimidation out of the logic by getting
people to incorporate it within themselves. This is not a very pleasant
solution; Peale's world is not in fact a very pleasant one; it is grim
and merciless. But although his answer will not mean greater selves,
yet, if the disease under treatment is apathy, it is better than nothing.

There is every prospect that Peale represents a formula set for
indefinite extension in our society. His claim that do-it-yourself, psycho-
religious, self-manipulation is now an "exact science" is one of the
necessary absurdities of his role. But psychiatry, psychology, psycho-
therapy are destined for indefinite further popular use as sciences—and
not merely as pseudo-sciences—available for more and more "practical
application" everywhere, for the "adjustment" of life. The perfection
of psychological self-manipulation rather than the physical control of
nature and society has always nerved a major party of American idealism,
and it is probably more important to recognize Peale as in the mainstream than immediately to criticize him from the perspective of some
timeless realism. It is true, as James said, in a text which—like a
thousand Bible texts—Peale blandly ignores, that "we are all . . .
helpless failures in the last resort." But for any culturally compelling
embodiment of, say, the pertinent Christian realism of Reinhold Nie-
buhr, preachments against confidence are hardly to the point. The kind
of penitent failure required for the Niebuhrian illumination requires
the pretentious aspiration which fails. The first-generation Niebuhrians
were men of political pretensions, Socialists, many of them, and their
humility roots in their experience of aspiration. But to take from
classic Christian realism the attitude simply of the intellectual observer,
able often with stunning acuteness to identify and reject forms of false
freedom, of false confidence, of other-direction, and of regressive
orthodoxy clustering around him, is not enough. In itself this is a fit
and fine calling—the prophet as purifier. The purifier's role is complete,
however, and means freedom from the self, only once it can assume
or create something to be purified, true projects of the self.

But what sort of pretensions and projects are available? Not politics.
Certainly, Peale's readers are not going to listen to politics; they never
were political utopians or social idealists in the first place, and there
is no reason to complain that they should have been, or ought to be
now. There is no politics to offer against what afflicts them anyway.
Yet, politics is not the only and necessary alternative. Bureaucratization,
mass consumption, and a general automation of society are inducing
apathy. But bureaucratization and mass consumption can also make it
possible to withdraw the self from judgment by the system. The demands of the system can be met with less energy and less attention.

The system can be neutralized, deprived of its sanction as a realm of salvation, demoted and segregated within the self as a purely functional sphere, confined against interfering with the self in its attention to a thousand-and-one positive thoughts it could otherwise have.

At some point, Peale's critics—especially his religious critics—will have to compete with him in trying to restore a sense of goals. They are not confronted with people seeking that supreme solace required for the ultimate failures we "all" experience "in the last resort." These are people who know nothing of the last resort, since they have no projects in which to mix themselves and exhaust themselves in saving failure. Their apathy is their unspoken cry for such opportunities. This is especially so for the women whom Peale reaches; men will be prodded back to the trials of the system as always, no doubt; but the problem for their wives is more considerable. It is mere timeless, not timely, wisdom just to repeat over and over that life is tragedy as well as victory, that God is not ours to appropriate for our uses and profits, that Power is not the marrow of salvation. At some point, confidence and positive thoughts will have to be preached against Peale. Perhaps the Niebuhrians and the liberals today are too full of guilt over their own past sins of utopian political pretensions to preach them. But Peale's readers are not suffering from that. There will be plenty of time to worry about stirring up the Devil, about unleashing Ahabs, about chastening Prometheus. It is often said, after all, that the sorry thing about Melville's Confidence Man was the paltriness of the confidence he preached. He did not really try to fool you into thinking you could do much, or be much, or live much. He did not make you aware of greater heights any more than of greater abysses. Just possibly, that, and not his confidence, was his diabolic quality. Hell is the soul unexpended. Peale, preaching a confidence afraid to cut loose from the judgments of the status-and-money world, afraid to cut loose from a world where you are forever "guided" by rules, by roles, by rote, by science, will never incite his followers to the intensity and risks some of them at least might easily desire. But he will not lose his followers except to those who point first to intensity and risk, which must precede the discovery of limitation.

—

Donald B. Meyer

Billy Graham, Successful Debunker of Success

The religious revival of the mid-twentieth century may involve religiosity rather than religion, and psychology rather than theology. Yet the grey-flanneled exponent of fundamentalism, Billy Graham, has evoked almost universal attention, if not assent, with the sheer relevance of his knowing critique of the modern world. Donald B. Meyer brilliantly shows us why. [Donald B. Meyer, "Billy Graham, Successful Debunker of Success," New Republic, August 22, 1955, pp. 8-10.]

. . . Unlike his leading competitors in the popular religious revival, Graham does not preach that the storm does not exist (if only you believe it does not exist). He does not preach reassurance and self-help. He conforms to the mood of the post-liberal disillusionment, and indeed, in the range of his attack upon false idols, ranks with the most vigorous of the realists. The American standard of living, for instance: Graham hurls himself at "the beautiful full-color magazine advertisements . . . the shining new cars . . . the gleaming rows of electric refrigerators and automatic washing machines . . . the fat chickens cooking in brand-new copper-bottomed pots." This is remarkable. Not many men have won popularity in these days while denying the sanctity of "this fully electrified, fully automatic, chrome-plated economy of ours." Also, along with material progress, he attacks faith in political freedom, in education, in Nature, in Conscience, in Will—all articles in the faith of classic American liberal individualism. He does not mean that these are bad things in themselves; but he means that they are not saving things, that they will not suffice us in our needs any longer, and that we are damned who still put our faith in them. In this, he hardly stands alone.

But Graham, at this common point of prophetic disillusionment, turns in the direction which makes the post-liberals uneasy. He turns to the Bible; he holds it up before us, he slams it down, he thrillingly intones, "Here is the answer." He proposes what looks like fundamentalist piety, and this provokes the unpleasant apprehension of a new ground-swell of pre-liberal religious and social obscurantism.

If apprehension is justified, it is at least worthwhile to recognize that the grounds for it are a little more complicated, whether or not less unpleasant, than any old-fashioned liberal suspicions of Bible piety might indicate.

There is one aspect of the life of fundamentalist piety which is crucial: it is a life of certitude. It is the life of perfection. There are no doubts, no real choices to be made, no expanses of experience where right and wrong, the nourishing and the corrupting, the healing and the killing, cannot instantly be distinguished. As Graham says, "We are never to do anything of which we are not perfectly clear and certain." As he says, the Bible *has all* the answers; it fills in the missing pieces, it bridges the harrowing gaps. Graham understands perfectly how far it is necessary to go in order to offer such final security. Thus, he plays up, he does not play down, the Devil. The Devil is "a creature of vastly superior intelligence, a mighty and gifted spirit of infinite resource-fulness." Why does he insist upon this? Because he knows that his audiences cannot and do not want to wrestle with the problems which oppress them; by emphasizing the Devil's power, he can conclude: "You cannot argue with him for he is the greatest debator of all time." Remembering that the Devil is the Tempter, we see that Graham's audiences are not expected to know the arguments against the temptations of which they are the victims. Graham himself, pretty certainly, does not. But he does know the depth of the need. Not in Progress, not in Prosperity, not in Politics, not in Education, not in Nature, not in Conscience, not in Will, not even in your own feelings, do you place your reliance. Then where? In the Bible, which tells you to repent so that you can be saved, repent so that you do not damn yourself by trying to save yourself. It is not new confidence which is desired, nor refreshment of the Will. "I once asked an army officer which he would rather have on the field of battle—courage or obedience. He flashed right back, 'Obedience.' God would rather have your obedience than anything else."

Graham, in other words, is not, as Billy Sunday was, a mere representative of the Bible Belt leading another massive unilateral folk aggression upon modernism. Fundamentalism could not be preached today by a mere folk champion, like Sunday or William Jennings Bryan, or like Sinclair Lewis' Elmer Gantry. It is of some weight that Graham dwells very little upon the sins which fascinated the folk of the twenties, those sins of the pagan and urban East: sex, liquor, modern science, and sophisticated culture. The barbs of a Mencken or a Lewis would be thought off-target today. Far from promoting another culture-battle, Graham is leading a retreat back into the fortress of the faith, among people whom the modern world outside has burdened with expectations they have not fulfilled. Only a particular sort of preacher could do this, and Graham is that particular sort: he is glamorous. Billy Sunday was not, nor was Bryan, nor was Elmer Gantry. But Graham is glamorous. Beautifully groomed, beautifully assured, brilliant in profile, beautifully tonic, Graham comes to his audiences, a man who on the plain evidence of his personal presence is equipped to meet all the requirements of the American cult of happy, healthy living, popularity, and self-assurance. If he is to tell his audiences what they need to hear, this is essential, for he tells them that the cult is not worth pursuing.

Once an ideal, now an obsession, . . . once a mild exhibitionism, now an anxious narcissism, the cult of happy living has come to weigh heavily upon a huge proportion of Americans, upon an increasing number, pathetically. Its requirements—high color, high lines, high assurance, high mobility, sex safe but successful, cheerful and untiring consumption of goods—are in the flattest, blankest, most unsparing fashion, beyond satisfaction by most people. Most of all by the non-metropolitan folk, not absolutely surrounded by the style, dress, talk, consumption, and pace which allow even those not young, not vibrant, not beautiful or handsome, not mobile in status and manners, to endure the happiness cult in the cities. This is the audience Graham taps, people who thirty years ago were not yet deeply affected by the standards of prosperous happiness, but who, between then and now, have been exposed to the virus, whose folk culture has been overlaid by mass culture. They have been infected, and now they are ready for someone to neutralize, to de-value, to discount the cult of personality for them. World disorder is simply the occasion for facing this deeper disorder. Graham can do it. Because of what he is, because he himself is a vibrant full-color personality, he can give good conscience to those afraid to discount and dismiss the cult directly for themselves. "Repent," he cries; the glamorous figure in the spotlight, master of his superstage, fixes you with his cry, and it is the one thing you can do which he tells you to do—"repent." The sin for which you repent is the sin of having fallen victim to the impossible vision of salvation portrayed in the beautiful, full-color magazine advertisements, where life is always slim and gleaming. You are not slim and gleaming, and Graham—because he is —can give you the nerve no longer to want to be. He can tell you to seek your salvation elsewhere.

You will seek it as and where he tells you—in the Bible—if you have never really given up the pre-liberal Bible in the first place, but have only neglected it in your submission to the pervasive infiltrating cult, have become a Baptist uneasy in your Buick of a Sunday. It is easier for Graham systematically to dismiss the false idols of liberalism than for the post-liberal tragedists, because he is free to tap the still undissipated reservoirs of the pre-liberal Bible tradition, never much affected by the liberal enlightenment. Never having been liberal in their culture before, his audiences will not be troubled by Graham now. Nor will they be troubled by the fact that Graham's answer to their needs stands counter to the tradition of self-help, individual will, and competitive salvation which Norman Vincent Peale attempts to rekindle among others today. Peale, interestingly, often refers to his success with people who had long been indifferent to the church, while a huge proportion of those whom Graham "converts" are already church-members. Peale throws his converts back into the battle, Graham pulls them out of it. For it is a mistake to assume that Americans have unanimously risked their souls in the world of competition and self-help, a mistake to forget how massive have been the evangelical movements to achieve a fixed perfection, immune to the flux of Progress.

Now the post-liberal tragedists conclude, as the climax of their illumination, that there is no escape from life in fluxless certitude; they prefer courage over obedience on the battlefield. They protest especially when Graham implies that return to the Bible will meet the threat of the H-bomb as well as of unhappiness, of Communism as well as of conscience, although this has little to do with his appeal. But before Graham be dismissed, it might well be asked if his success indicates a widespread desertion and escape into the rigid sleep of perfectionism, or whether perhaps it does not suggest the first phase of a process wherein many members of our society will make their struggle in good faith. Read your Bible daily, Graham says; it has the answers. Well, the Bible is very strong literature. Generations of an older America fed on it as the staple of their intellectual and spiritual lives, and by and large it always worked on the side of individual courage, not the less so for failing in conformity to liberal creeds. It is not necessarily something so primitive, so obscurantist, or so joyless that takes place when the ordinary man or woman takes up the Bible seeking answers. When it is taken up today, the very act is already in itself a self-creative motion, for it means that an act of detachment of the self from its false idols and false consciousness has already occurred, that an act of self-recognition, distinguishing the self from the valuelessness around it, giving it a radically private reality, is already in process.

And is this not the very model of the Reform for which all hands are calling? Personality is to be extricated from the loyalties which disintegrate it. If Graham's flock does really turn to the Bible, seeking now some absolute closure against invasion from the emptiness around them, they may be expected later to re-awaken from sleep, as again believers in themselves. What a new piety might demand in the future, is not to be predicted. But it ought to be comprehended with more sympathy than it has been given in the past. When a good half of the analytic energy of intellectuals in the past ten years has been spent —in psychology, in political theory, in the novels of adolescence, in social history and economics, in work on the mass media—trying to grasp all that life which Enlightenment, rationalism, and liberalism ignored, it is mere dogmatism to re-instate the old instincts of sophistication against Graham's flock.

. . . "The Christian should stand out like a sparkling diamond against a rough background. He should be more wholesome than anyone else. He should be poised, cultured, gracious, but firm in the things that he does and does not do. He should laugh and be radiant, but he should refuse to allow the world to pull him down to its level." This is advice neither for the liberal nor for the tragic life, but it is certainly advice restoring nerve to a basic quality in popular American culture in the past, a hardness of the private self against the pressure of abstraction in the world. Longing for hardness themselves, sophisticates . . . might possibly find their own hardness through sympathy for it.

Selected Bibliography

E. Digby Baltzell, *The Protestant Establishment: Aristocracy and Caste in America,* New York, 1964.

Earl F. Cheit, ed., *The Business Establishment,* New York, 1964.

Thomas C. Cochran, *The American Business System,* Cambridge, 1957.

Arthur H. Cole, *Business Enterprise in Its Social Setting,* Cambridge, 1959.

Melville Dalton, *Men Who Manage,* New York, 1959.

Sigmund Diamond, *The Reputation of the American Businessman,* Cambridge, 1955.

J. K. Galbraith, *The Affluent Society,* Boston, 1958.

John W. Gardner, *Self-Renewal: The Individual and the Innovative Society,* New York, 1964.

Ray Ginger, *Age of Excess,* New York, 1965.

Robert W. Green, ed., *Protestantism and Capitalism: The Weber Thesis and Its Critics,* Boston, 1959.

Oscar and Mary Handlin, *The Dimensions of Liberty,* Cambridge, 1961.

Suzanne Keller, *Beyond the Ruling Class,* New York, 1963.

Seymour M. Lipset and Leo Lowenthal, ed., *Culture and Social Character: The Work of David Riesman Reviewed,* New York, 1961.

Kenneth Lynn, *The Dream of Success: A Study of the Modern American Literary Imagination,* Boston, 1955.

Edward S. Mason, ed., *The Corporation in Modern Society,* Cambridge, 1960.

Donald Meyer, "The Dissolution of Calvinism," in Arthur M. Schlesinger, Jr., and Morton White, ed., *Paths of American Thought,* Boston, 1963.

William Miller, ed., *Men in Business,* New York, 1962.

Mabel Newcomer, *The Big Business Executive,* New York, 1955.

Vance Packard, *The Pyramid Climbers,* New York, 1962.

David Potter, *People of Plenty: Economic Abundance and the American Character,* Chicago, 1954.

David Riesman, *The Lonely Crowd,* New Haven, 1950.

Kurt Samuelsson, *Religion and Economic Action,* New York, 1961.

Francis X. Sutton, et. al., *The American Business Creed,* Cambridge, 1956.

R. H. Tawney, *Religion and the Rise of Capitalism,* New York, 1926.

John Tebbel, *From Rags to Riches: Horatio Alger, Jr., and the American Dream,* New York, 1963.

Stephan Thernstrom, *Poverty and Progress: Social Mobility in a Nineteenth-Century City,* Cambridge, 1964.

W. Lloyd Warner and James Abegglen, *Occupational Mobility in American Business and Industry, 1928-1952,* Minneapolis, 1955.

Max Weber, *The Protestant Ethic and the Spirit of Capitalism,* New York, 1930.

William H. Whyte, Jr., *The Organization Man,* New York, 1956.

Irvin G. Wyllie, *The Self-Made Man in America: The Myth of Rags to Riches,* New Brunswick, 1954.